Harry Potter for Nerds II

ESSAYS FOR FANS, ACADEMICS, AND LIT GEEKS

Edited by Kathryn N. McDaniel and Travis Prinzi

D1715233

Unlocking Press
Oklahoma City, Oklahoma

Unlocking Press
328 NW 26th Street
Oklahoma City, Oklahoma 73103
www.unlockingpress.com

Book Layout ©2015 BookDesignTemplates.com

Harry Potter for Nerds II/ Kathryn N. McDaniel and Travis Prinzi, ed. —1st ed.
ISBN 978-0-9908821-1-4

Table of Contents

For anyone who's ever handed a Harry Potter book to someone else and said, "Read this." (Aunt Marti, I'm looking at you.)

Also for Dave and my very own Trio:
Hal, Josie, and Griffin.

And

For Sophia and Jack,

Always

INTRODUCTION

Harry Potter for Nerds II: Muggle Magic

Kathryn N. McDaniel

There's something that bothers me about the first *Harry Potter* movie. Really, I loved it. It brought my favorite characters and scenes to life. Hogwarts castle, the Gryffindor common room, Quidditch: They all looked just as I'd imagined, and there's genius in that. But there was one thing, that one, really important thing the filmmakers got wrong. It's a nerdy kind of thing to notice, but maybe (since you're reading this book, and perhaps a Harry Potter Nerd yourself) you noticed it, too. And it has everything to do with being "a nerd."

At the climax of the story, Harry, Ron, and Hermione each get a chance to use their talents to overcome the obstacles to reaching the Sorcerer's Stone. In the movie, Hermione's talent is summed up by defeating the vicious plant Devil's Snare because she remembers its botanical qualities: "Lucky Hermione pays attention in Herbology," Harry says.[1]

But we fans of the books know that this is just the *first* obstacle Hermione helps the Trio overcome in the quest for the Stone, certainly not the only one, nor the most important or challenging one. In the book, hers is the last obstacle before Harry can continue to the Mirror of Erised, which houses the Stone. Presented with a series of potions, Hermione must decipher a riddle crafted by Potions Master (and another serious nerd) Severus Snape. With sinister purple flames leaping behind them and black flames ahead, Hermione must solve the riddle so that Harry can drink the potion to allow him to go forward and she can

---

[1] A similar line appears in the book, too, but unlike in the film it is not the sum total of Hermione's contribution to the quest (*Sorcerer's Stone*, 278).

drink the one that will allow her to go back and send for Dumbledore. After reading Snape's scroll, Hermione sighs and smiles:

> *"Brilliant,"* said Hermione. "This isn't magic—it's logic—a puzzle. A lot of great wizards haven't got an ounce of logic, they'd be stuck here forever."
>
> "But so will we, won't we?"
>
> "Of course not," said Hermione. "Everything we need is here on this paper."
> (*Sorcerer's Stone*, 285-286)

And of course, she's right. She finds the correct solution to the puzzle, and both she and Harry fulfill their roles so that the Stone is safe from Voldemort's grasp. Dumbledore publicly recognizes Hermione's achievement in the final ceremony, awarding Gryffindor fifty points for Hermione's use of "cool logic in the face of fire" (305).

It bothers me that, with the elimination of this scene, Hermione's intelligence, her "cool logic," and her analytic prowess are reduced in the film to paying attention in class. That is not Hermione's great talent, and it's not what makes nerds, nerds.

We nerds are not just paying attention (though that is important, too). Crucially, we also know how to decipher what's on the page. As you'll see in this volume, we Harry Potter Nerds know how to figure things out based on careful reading and solid reasoning. And what we're figuring out provides keys to understanding pivotal ideas about justice, love, integrity, death, truth, and friendship. It tells us how to go forward or how to go back.

It's not accidental that Hermione's most important contribution in the final Harry Potter book, *The Deathly Hallows*, also requires her to decode and decipher written words on paper. This time, her riddle comes in the form of a children's story, a fairy tale, but one which holds the very real answer to secrets Harry, Ron, and Hermione have been pursuing for the entire book. Dumbledore, knowing Hermione's literary and logical acumen, in his will left her his copy of *The Tales of Beedle the Bard*, which contains the story of "The Deathly Hallows." This is a tale of ambition, yearning, fear, and death. The filmmakers, incidentally, get this one just right, telling the story in beautiful silhouette images, poignantly narrated by Hermione herself. The Hallows, it turns out, prove not to be just the imaginary creations of a fairy story but real objects that wield enormous power. For readers of the Harry Potter books, this tale encapsulates the core themes of the entire seven-book series. Those of us who, like Hermione, give our full, analytic attention to this story, and to all the Harry Potter books, stand to receive a wealth of wisdom, "everything we need," from what appears on the books' pages.

Our analyses of the books seek to uncover such wisdom, for our delight and edification. The chapters in Part I, "Nerds at Hogwarts," explore in depth the characters, relationships, symbols, and humanistic appeal of the Harry Potter stories. All of these authors provide careful readings of the books, use literary and thematic analysis, and seek a thorough understanding of Rowling's created fantasy world.

Deborah M. Chan's "Love is the Strongest Family Tie," leads our quest with an examination of the "found families" in the series, suggesting Rowling's belief that blood and "purity" are weak links compared to the strength of real love and emotional connection. In successive chapters, targeted character studies reveal Rowling's subtle but rich human understanding and empathy. Katherine Sas, in "'Shabby Robes' and a 'Swift Smile,'" analyzes the wide appeal of the flawed hero Remus Lupin. She argues that readers love Lupin not despite his imperfections, but because of them—and because of Rowling's sensitive and psychologically nuanced portrayal of a man who lives in the shadows. Carol Eshleman in "Twin Core" explains not only the importance of Weasley twins Fred and George, but also the symbolic twinning of other characters and even objects, as a way to understand major themes across the entire Harry Potter series. My own "'Real House-elves' of J.K. Rowling" uses feminist theory to understand the complexities of house-elf liberation, and sees this liberation as necessary for overcoming the fear of death and conquering the forces of evil.

The next two chapters, Kelly Orazi's "Gothic Meets Comic" and Rochelle Deans's "The Dark Lord's Descent," explore the books' treatment of death and the quest for eternal life (and its enormous pitfalls). Neither the ghosts nor Voldemort have the answer to the secrets of death, but both provide vital insights into what it is to live, and why there may be "things much worse than death" (*Order of the Phoenix*, 814). In "The Second War Was Won on the Quidditch Pitch of Hogwarts," Emily Strand provides a compelling case for reading the baffling sport of Quidditch as symbolic of the plot's narrative arc and the "positions" of characters in the central action. And finally, Hayley and Michael Burson remind us that neither Quidditch nor the Harry Potter fan experience is dead at all, with their advice on "Surviving the Potter-pocalypse."

Drawing on insights from the realm of fantasy, the authors in Part II, "Hogwarts Nerds in a Muggle World" use the Harry Potter books to illumine problems and injustices in our own world and to find their solutions. Kris Swank sets the tone of this section when she points out how Rowling's books fit into a rather disturbing genre in "*Harry Potter* as Dystopian Literature." Surveillance, forced self-incrimination, bureaucratic entrapment, silencing dissent and eradicating difference, media indoctrination—and the consequent difficulty of resisting powerful monoliths—abound in the wizarding world; the books serve as both a cautionary tale and as inspiration to rebels.

You'll find these dystopian themes reflected in several chapters in this section, including Amy H. Sturgis's "Seeking Dumbledore's Mother," which evokes the parallel between the fantasy world of wizards and the Native-American experience of alienation and dislocation in the United States and Canada. Alison R. Jones's "A Librarian's View of Madam Pince" demonstrates the problems for real-world librarians when their imaginary-world counterparts conform to certain unpleasant stereotypes, as does the Hogwarts librarian. Repudiating Vernon Dursley's notion that wizards are nothing but unemployed "layabouts" (*Deathly Hallows*, 35), Madelyn V. Young's exploration of "Work in the Wizarding World" uses the Harry Potter stories to explain the modern capitalist system of labor and reflect on the quandary of wizard poverty.

Turning toward politics and philosophy, the next chapters in the book delve into issues of resistance, power, and what is really "fair" (or ethical) in the context of war—even a war against the vilest sort of evil. Mad-Eye Moody repeatedly demands "Constant Vigilance!" against the forces of dark magic and repression, but what does this entail? Carrie-Ann Biondi's careful reading of both John Locke's work and *Harry Potter* Book 5 in "Un-Locke-ing *The Order of the Phoenix*" reveals Rowling's intuitive understanding of modern democratic theory and the social contract. When do governments become illegitimate and what does it take to make rebellion legitimate? The strategy of nonviolent resistance is the topic of my chapter "Dumbledore's Army and the White Rose Society," which draws a parallel between the student resistance fighters of Hogwarts and a group of German students at the University of Munich who spoke out against Hitler during World War II. Laura Lee Smith examines both the moral dimension and the effectiveness of truth-telling and lying in "Who Deserves the Truth?" When is a lie acceptable? What truths matter most? Finally, the roles of watchers and the watched are turned to a more positive purpose in Robb A. McDaniel's "Watching the Defectives," an investigation of how Squibs (among others) promote the idea of virtue through surveillance, bearing witness, transformation, and the crossing of invisible boundaries. One of those boundaries separates the Muggle (real) world from that of wizards. All of us, as readers, are like the Squibs in a way, as we navigate between these two realms and attempt to "see" the justice and injustice in both.

Traveling back and forth across the imaginary and the real, we nerds who have contributed to this volume believe that fantastic stories have power, that they have wisdom to impart, that they remind us of our own lives and struggles, that they show us—like Snape's riddle and Beedle the Bard's tales—the way forward and the way back. At the end of the final book in the series, at the ethereal intersection at King's Cross station, Harry asks the image of Dumbledore, "Is this real, or has this been happening inside my head?" Dumbledore's response, which Rowling has called her favorite line from all the books, emphasizes the importance of fantasy and imagination: "Of course it is happening inside your head, Harry, but why on earth should that mean it is not real?" (*Deathly Hallows*, 723). There is perhaps one thing that young Hermione did not get quite right in her first year: this logic *is* a kind of magic.

Works Cited

Harry Potter and the Sorcerer's Stone. Distributed by Warner Home Video, 2011. Film.

Rowling, J.K. *Harry Potter and the Deathly Hallows.* New York: Scholastic Books. 2007. Print.

_____. *Harry Potter and the Sorcerer's Stone.* New York: Scholastic Books. 1997. Print.

PART I
Nerds at Hogwarts

CHAPTER 1

Love is the Strongest Family Tie

Deborah M. Chan

In *Harry Potter and the Order of the Phoenix*, Harry and his friends come across a room in the Department of Mysteries to which they can't gain entry. Hermione's "Alohomora!" fails, and when Harry tries Sirius Black's knife on the door, it not only remains closed, but melts the knife's blade.

We don't learn anything more about the room or encounter it again. However, after the disastrous Ministry battle in which Sirius dies, Dumbledore says to Harry, after explaining Lily's blood sacrifice,

> "There is a room in the department of Mysteries that is kept locked at all times. It contains a force that is at once more wonderful and more terrible than death, than human intelligence, than forces of nature. It is also, perhaps, the most mysterious of the many subjects for study that reside there. It is the power held within that room that you possess in such quantities and which Voldemort has not at all. That power took you to save Sirius tonight. That power also saved you from possession by Voldemort, because he could not bear to reside in a body so full of the force he detests." (843-844 OotP; all references are from the Scholastic editions)

It's not hard to conclude that this mysterious room contains love.

In J.K. Rowling's seven book saga, love is ever the most powerful force, and its influence and impact is felt throughout the story. One way Rowling explores the power of love is through the diverse wizarding families she creates. She even makes family relationships a central theme of the books.

Her families reflect real world changes that have redefined the meaning of family over the last half-century. Until that time, the word "family" was considered typically to mean the idealized "traditional" or nuclear family—a father, mother and their biological (and adopted) children living together in one family residence. In its narrow definition, the father was the financial provider and the stay-at-home mother cared for the children. After World War II, due to many social changes, the definition of family evolved over the decades. Divorce, remarriage, cohabitation, absentee parents and other factors have resulted in an enlarged understanding of family—blended families with step-parents and step- or half-siblings; single-parent and unmarried-parent families; grandparent families (grandparents raising grandchildren); extended families (related people, including grandparents and sometimes other relatives living together); gay parent families; childless families, and "found families" of unrelated people, whose camaraderie and shared values unite them in a familial group. Today's definition of family includes all of these familial ties.

Embracing the idea that families come in all shapes and sizes, Rowling saturates her books with diverse family dynamics and bonds, upending the adage that "blood is thicker than water." To make a point of it, only four Harry Potter families—the Weasleys, Dursleys, Malfoys and Grangers—are traditional, intact, nuclear blood families.

What's important in the books isn't so much the type of family, but family dynamics and how members treat each other. Through her families, Rowling reveals the impact of healthy and dysfunctional behavior.

Unconditional love, respect and acceptance are the key qualities of a healthy family, exemplified by the Weasleys. Individuality is recognized as good and natural, and loyalty and humility are a given. Parents work together as a team, live their values and are patient with their children. Communication is good, conflicts are worked out and problems can be discussed freely. When a wrong is done to another, there is forgiveness. There is no preferential treatment or "golden child" against whom siblings are found wanting. Everyone knows they are loved, heard and valued.

Unhealthy families are rife with intolerance, disrespect, injustice and damaging expectations that cause lasting emotional wounds, and sometimes, as with Sirius Black, bitter estrangement. In dysfunctional families parents may abuse their authority, with children forced to embrace the parents' values and beliefs or risk rejection. Parents may display favoritism that engenders sibling rivalry and competition for affection, making children feel devalued (Harry Potter, Sirius Black, Ron Weasley to some degree). There may be mental illness (the Black and

Gaunt extended families), physical and/or emotional abuse (the Dursley, Black and Snape families), alcohol or drug abuse (possibly the Snapes), and other assorted ills. Communication is poor, and problems are neither acknowledged nor discussed, with the stress of secrecy maximizing damage and ensuring further fracture.

All of Rowling's families exhibit complex combinations of these positive and negative traits, because none of them is perfect.

Yet Rowling makes it clear that the nature of a family structure, or how it functions, doesn't determine a child's future. As Dumbledore declares in *Goblet of Fire*, ". . . It matters not what someone is born, but what they grow to be!" (708 GoF)

Our families are the most critical relationships we have, and it's easy to see ourselves in Rowling's families filled with selfish, noble, immature, wounded, aspiring, sacrificial, unkind, generous, bitter, loving, cruel, nutty, fallible people. Restoration, when it occurs, is hopeful but flawed—sometimes satisfying and sometimes incomplete—and tragic when it doesn't. Such honesty about family dynamics is one of the most powerful aspects of the story. Rowling portrays families as they *are*, rather than how we'd like them to be. And this reality rings true.

In every conceivable manner, the family is link to our past, bridge to our future. —Alex Haley

Let's examine three traditional blood families—the Weasleys, Malfoys, and Dursleys—and two modern families.

The Weasleys

The Weasleys are a healthy, loving family. Easygoing, eccentric Arthur and earth-mother Molly are a happy couple, and this is reflected in their family life. They're good parents, raising children who know they are unconditionally loved, and for the most part they encourage their children's interests and careers. Apart from normal sibling bickering and rivalry, the Weasley siblings mostly get along well and enjoy each other's company. Arthur and Molly pass on good values, such as embracing Muggles and Muggle-born rights, although they hold a few prejudices toward other magical beings, usually repeated by Ron to Harry.

But even the Weasleys aren't immune to some dysfunction. Ron and Ginny struggle over their place in the family, and with feelings of loneliness and inferiority. Once he's working for the Ministry, son Percy not only rejects his family's politics, he makes it personal by rejecting the family itself, even coldly returning his mother's handmade Christmas gift. He also abuses their desire to see him merely to corral Harry for his boss's agenda. Continually wounded by this crushing behavior, Arthur and Molly still hope for a loving reunion. Percy's disgusted siblings aren't so generous. But when Percy finally returns to the fold and humbly confesses his hurtful behavior, the entire family forgives and embraces him.

The inclusive Weasleys have a large welcome mat and generously porous family boundaries. They quickly absorb Harry and Hermione into their clan. Harry receives Christmas gifts equal to Ron's; Molly calls him "as good as" her son (90 OotP) and gives him her martyred brother's watch for his seventeenth birthday. The Weasleys also offer extended family to lonely Remus and others, and are a family home base for the Order of the Phoenix, whether at the Burrow or House of Black.

The Malfoys

Although we aren't privy to as much about the Malfoys, Lucius, Narcissa and pampered son Draco exhibit unconditional family love for each other. Although he can be demanding, Lucius has a close relationship with his son, who in turn idolizes him. Enraged at his father's imprisonment in Azkaban and eager to avenge him, Draco becomes a Death Eater, and when he does, Narcissa frantically begs Severus Snape to protect her son. During the Battle of Hogwarts, the Malfoy parents' one concern is Draco's safety. Narcissa even betrays Voldemort to learn that her son is alive.

Yet in Lucius's and Narcissa's obsession with status, wealth and blood purity, they demonstrate snobbery and indifference toward anyone they regard as inferior, and teach these values to Draco. Even though the Weasleys are pure-bloods like themselves, the privileged Malfoys constantly insult them for their poverty and embrace of Muggle-borns. Longtime members of Voldemort's inner circle, the Malfoys gladly serve a psychopathic murderer and enjoy tormenting Muggles. Lucius and Draco use Unforgivable Curses on others, and Lucius has no scruples about exploiting and torturing children. The Malfoys are cruel to their house-elf Dobby, and Draco apes his father's cowardice and bullying, especially toward the vulnerable who can't fight back. Lucius bribes his way into Ministry influence and position, as well as onto the Hogwarts Board of Governors, and buys Draco's position on the Slytherin Quidditch team. Arrogant Narcissa disregards lower-class Severus Snape's soul in comparison to her son's. And Draco, without a qualm, endangers fellow students and others at Hogwarts to carry out Voldemort's task—murdering Dumbledore and getting Death Eaters into the school.

Though their appalling values, cruelty, and indifference to others' lives are repugnant, the Malfoys aren't a dysfunctional family. Still, their sacrificial love is only for each other, as ingrown as themselves.

The Dursleys

The Dursleys are a dysfunctional family. Petunia and Vernon have no compassion for the orphan nephew left on their doorstep. Instead, they and their spoiled son Dudley maltreat Harry and keep him an outsider at the family hearth. Relegated to sleeping under the stairs, Harry is punished for magical abilities he can't understand or control, and is callously treated like a servant. A quintessential "Cinderfella," Harry never experiences one moment of familial love with the Dursleys.

Consumed with jealous hatred, and never moving on from past hurts, Petunia continues waging war on her magically gifted and—in her mind—favored sister Lily by reversing the Evans family dynamic to a shocking degree. In Petunia and Vernon's family, the non-magical son is favored, while the magical child suffers a loveless life of misery and abuse, with himself and his parents continually disparaged. Petunia and Vernon do show Dudley unconditional love, but to an indiscriminate and ruinous degree that is never in his best interests.

Despite her aversion to magic, Petunia unwittingly and ironically provides two services to the wizarding world she so hates. First, by grudgingly providing the barest minimum of a physical, if not emotional, home to Harry, she ensures that her sister's sacrificial blood charm keeps his protection from Voldemort intact. Second, by taking Harry in, she unknowingly ensures both the magical world and Muggle world a savior. The great tragedy of Petunia is that she *does* have the capacity for magic, since love is the most powerful magic of all. As Dumbledore says, "It is our choices, Harry, that show what we truly are, far more than our abilities." (333 CoS) Petunia squanders her potential under bitter hatred and cruelty, instead of choosing love that would have made her a hero to a grateful wizarding world.

Unfortunately, generous and sacrificial love is completely foreign to the Dursleys.

Now let's look at two nontraditional families.

The Lovegoods

The Lovegoods are a single-parent family. Luna and her father Xenophilius have a loving relationship that seems more adult than parent-child in nature, likely due to the loss of Luna's mother, and they travel the globe together doing research. Luna is her peculiar father's staunchest defender, and he sacrifices his integrity and beliefs—even the future of the wizarding world—in his desperation to save his beloved daughter from Voldemort's clutches.

The Longbottoms

In a more complex situation, Neville Longbottom lives in a grandparent family with his grandmother Augusta. Though she loves Neville, Augusta is overly enamored of her son Frank's magical abilities and heroism; her unreasonable expectation that Neville be a carbon copy of his father continually undermines Neville's confidence and self-worth. Knowing he's a disappointment and failure, Neville fears his grandmother because her approval is conditional. Not until he heroically leads the student rebellion at Hogwarts does Neville win her unqualified praise, but as always, in comparison to his father. Augusta fails to see that Frank's magical prowess dims in comparison to the power of Neville's sacrificial love, loyalty and courage.

Every child should have a caring adult in their lives. And that's not always a biological parent or family member. It may be a friend or neighbor. Often times it is a teacher. — Joe Manchin

There are some important parental figures in the books, including some who care for Harry even before he joins the wizarding world.

Fathers

Along with Arthur Weasley and warmhearted Hagrid, Harry has three key father figures who are flawed, but show him unconditional love.

Albus Dumbledore's fatherly love for Harry wars with what Harry's future requires. Albus must allow Harry to grow up in an abusive home to protect the boy's life and, at the same time, ironically, plan for Harry's death to save the world. Dumbledore's secretive nature and failure, out of his affection, to tell Harry important truths, actually causes harm, leaving Harry lacking critical knowledge he needs to find Voldemort's Horcruxes and with disillusioned distrust in Albus's love. Albus confesses his failures to Harry in part after the Ministry Battle and in full at King's Cross where he asks Harry's forgiveness.

Godfather Sirius Black and teacher Remus Lupin are damaged father figures who love Harry and try hard to do the right thing. As Sirius has difficulty distinguishing where James Potter ends and Harry begins, he's an odd blend of brother and father to Harry. Still, with Sirius Harry finally knows parental care. Remus is a more balanced mentor, teacher and friend. Harry thrives with their love and support.

Harry, Remus and Sirius have all lived outside both a family circle and society for different reasons. The Black family's pure-blood mania made teen Sirius so unhappy that he ran away, and his mother disowned him; then his friend Peter Pettigrew framed him for murder. Once a jocular and fun-loving boy, his long imprisonment in Azkaban and fugitive status has turned Sirius into a depressed, embittered man. It's only when he connects with Harry and Remus that he finds hope and meaning for a fresh start. Remus comes from a good wizarding family, but he was brutally attacked by werewolf Fenrir Greyback as a young child. Since then, his lycanthropy has made him a dangerous societal outcast, and as an adult Remus has lived a lonely, hardscrabble, hand-to-mouth existence. Unable to have their own families, both men welcome a relationship with James and Lily's son Harry, an abused boy who's never known family love or friendship until going to Hogwarts. It's no surprise that these three have such a bond. They're the ones who understand a life ruled by injustice, cruelty, alienation and loneliness. The deaths of Sirius and Remus, who understand him so well, are a profound loss for Harry.

Mothers

We've already looked at Molly Weasley, Narcissa Malfoy and Petunia Dursley. But given pride of place in the books is Harry's mother Lily Potter, who died refusing to sacrifice her son and thus ensured him a lingering blood protection against Voldemort. Through otherworldly means in the Little Hangleton graveyard and the Forbidden Forest, Lily speaks love and encouragement to Harry and he finds strength in her.

Another good mother is single woman, Order member, and Squib Arabella Figg, who faithfully watches over Harry in his dull suburb for seventeen years, with only her cats for company. In addition to protecting him, Arabella sacrificially shows her motherly love as restraint, sadly making sure Harry never enjoys being with her. She also courageously testifies on his behalf before a hostile Wizengamot, after the Dementor attack in Little Whinging.

Curiously, three mothers—including an anti-mother figure—are insane.

The pathetic, abused Merope Gaunt, Tom Riddle's inbred mother, bewitches Tom's father, bears his son and then chooses to die, abandoning her child. Sirius Black's mother Walburga, with whom we become acquainted through her portrait at the House of Black, spews raving vitriol to those (including her outcast son Sirius) she considers unworthy by blood or values to enter her home. Bellatrix Lestrange, a sociopath without children herself, is a perverted anti-mother who considers it an honor to sacrifice a son to certain death, enjoys torturing children while talking baby talk to them, and revels in her murderous fights against them at the Ministry and Hogwarts. She is defeated by the power of true motherhood in Molly, who will fight to the death for her own and any other child.

If you want to do really important things in life and big things in life, you can't do anything by yourself. And your best teams are your friends and siblings. —Deepak Chopra

Some of the most important bonds formed in the story are devoted sibling-type relationships.

Going back in time, we have the Marauders—confident James Potter, disaffected pure-blood Sirius Black, secret lycanthrope Remus Lupin, and sycophantic Peter Pettigrew—whose brotherly bond results in secret adventures as undercover Animagi. After Peter defects to the Death Eaters, his betrayal causes James and Lily Potter's death, Sirius's false imprisonment and Remus's isolation as Remus believes Sirius is to blame. When Sirius and Remus are reunited in the Shrieking Shack during Harry's Third Year, their bond is restored.

Harry and Hermione fit easily within the Weasley family, spending as much time as possible with them. With the happy, boisterous Weasleys, only child Hermione gains siblings and becomes an older sister to Ginny, and Harry finally has a family who loves him. Fred and George give Harry the Marauder's Map and he gives them his Tri-Wizard Cup winnings as a startup for their joke shop. Learning of Harry's generous act, Ron, who normally grumbles about the pains of poverty, selflessly applauds the decision.

Two other people exemplify devotion to sibling bonds—Neville Longbottom and Luna Lovegood.

Luna's parents have raised a remarkably compassionate, confident child, a faithful friend and consoling light. This lonely, ostracized girl is patient and forgiving of other students, including those in her Ravenclaw house family, who mistreat her. She finds family in the D.A. (Dumbledore's Army) and fights Death Eaters with them at the Ministry and Hogwarts. Once captured by Voldemort, Luna selflessly cares for his other prisoners. On her home bedroom ceiling she paints a beautiful tribute to her friends—her found siblings.

Neville is a hapless, insecure boy who, like Luna, is ridiculed by other students, even within his Gryffindor house. The unpopular Neville continually shows loyalty, dignity, bravery and perseverance, qualities that strengthen over time and eventually make him the brilliant, revered leader of those who formerly dismissed him. Neville also builds bonds in the D.A., and fights at the Ministry and Hogwarts. Leading the resistance during Voldemort's rule at the school, he is a big brother who protects the weak and suffers for it. At the Battle of Hogwarts Neville defies Voldemort, slays the Horcrux Nagini, and is a beloved hero to all.

At the beginning of Fifth Year, Harry is embarrassed by Luna and Neville, wishing he was surrounded instead with "very cool people." (187 OotP) But one year later, he boasts of these friends; Neville and Luna are family.

Friends are family you choose for yourself. —Author Unknown

Rowling peoples her universe with those who find or create found families with no blood ties. She continually demonstrates that such family ties, based on propinquity, love, friendship and shared ideals and goals, are as robust and tightly knit as in traditional families.

Two specific examples are the Order of the Phoenix and the Death Eaters. The Order, composed mostly of biologically unrelated people, is an extended family united by a cause—defeating Voldemort and his blood purity agenda. A hallmark of the Order is inclusivity, and the diversity of its male and female members—pure-bloods, half-bloods, Muggle-borns and Squibs of all ages and abilities—are an example of the unity the Sorting Hat adjures and Dumbledore works to build throughout the wizarding world. (In addition to the Order, Dumbledore forges alliances with centaurs, Merpeople and other beings.) Order headquarters is at the Black house and some members lodge there, while others come and go. In *Order of the Phoenix* we see Order folks cleaning house under Molly Weasley's direction, celebrating Christmas, eating together, squabbling, and having fun like any family. There's even a family portrait—the photograph of the first Order that Moody shows Harry, which includes Harry's parents, Molly's slain brothers and the tortured Longbottoms.

The Death Eaters, sycophantic servants to Voldemort, are his henchmen and enforcers, a brotherhood like the Klan or the Mafia. A "good ole boys" brotherhood, it has only one female member, Bellatrix Lestrange. In stark contrast to the Order, this exclusive group consists of pure-bloods (and some secret half-bloods) who are blood purists, although they recruit beings they consider inferior—giants and werewolves such as Fenrir Greyback—who can further their agenda. Wearing robes and masks, they bear the Dark Mark tattoo which summons them to their master. They freely use dark magic and Unforgiveable Curses, even on children, and are responsible for murder, mayhem, torture, permanent injuries and disappearances. Voldemort neither loves nor respects them, and plays them against each other, with several believing they are his "most trusted." Death Eaters are rightly afraid of their master and it's a family no one can leave. At eighteen their sons are expected to join the "family firm."

On a wider scale, Hogwarts is the formative training ground for British wizards and forges lifetime bonds. It should be one big family where everyone makes friends with those of differing ideologies and backgrounds; sadly, most students seem to leave school with their prejudices intact. The frictions of the four Hogwarts Founders perpetuate in the permanent Sorting of students into four houses according to character, personality and predilection—and at a very young age. The Sorting Hat worries about such artificial division and warns that unity must prevail to save the wizarding world's way of life, or "we'll crumble from within" against "external, deadly foes." (206-207 OotP) Dumbledore also pleads for unity and tells Severus Snape in "The Prince's Tale" that "I sometimes think we sort too soon," instead of giving children time and opportunity to find their own direction and prove themselves. (680 DH)

The four houses, where the students reside, provide a more intimate setting. "While you are here," says Professor McGonagall, "your house will be something like your family within Hogwarts." (114 SS) Each house quarters in a different area of the castle and students share the same dormitory room during their seven-year tenure. The constant competition between these houses maintained through teacher favoritism, house rewards and Quidditch fails to encourage inter-house bonds.

One important family at Hogwarts arises from desperation—Dumbledore's Army. Like the Order, the D.A. is a diverse group with differing bloodlines, backgrounds and abilities, with some of the members being "the least likely to succeed." Students from Gryffindor, Ravenclaw and Hufflepuff work together to learn defense against the Dark Arts from Harry, in a unity that would delight Dumbledore and the Sorting Hat. In some ways the group patterns the dynamic of the Death Eaters—members sign an oath of secrecy, meet in a secret room for training and have secret coins (marks) to inform them of meetings. Yet the D.A. family is supportive of its weakest members, with everyone cheering each other on. The bonding goes further for some who have struggled with loneliness, including faithful Neville, Luna and Ginny who keep their coins at hand and thus alert the school when Death Eaters invade. The D.A. regroups under Neville during the Trio's absence in *Deathly Hallows*, stands against Voldemort's rule at the school and fights in the Battle of Hogwarts.

Many family bonds in the wizarding world, as in the Muggle world, transcend bloodlines and race. Whether these ties are healthy and holy, or twisted and dangerous, they are powerful.

To us, family means putting your arms around each other and being there. —Barbara Bush

The most shining and ideal example of an unconventional loving family is exemplified by the Trio—Harry, Ron and Hermione, three friends from very different backgrounds, temperaments, blood purities and abilities. Their deep, abiding, sacrificial bond of love is continually tested, refined and purified by friction from within and without. When they're in harmony, things go well; otherwise they're weak, floundering, and vulnerable to disaster. In spite of occasional fireworks and estrangements, Harry, Ron and Hermione are a unified team, supporting and forgiving each other. When the formerly jealous and angry Ron reaches out to Harry after Harry's near-death experience with the Hungarian Horntail during the Tri-Wizard Cup, both boys quickly make up with few words. The same thing happens when Ron returns after his defection in *Deathly Hallows*, though Hermione is slower to forgive. Despite initially opposing the Ministry rescue mission, Hermione and Ron go with Harry to save Sirius, even fearfully riding on flying Thestrals they can't see. They fight valiantly and never reproach Harry for being wrong, even though they're both grievously wounded in the fiasco. Ron and Hermione also selflessly accompany Harry without question on his Horcrux mission.

Because Harry has been abused and neglected by his blood family, he greatly treasures his bond with Hermione and Ron, his found family, with their Three Musketeers sensibility of "all for one and one for all."

This is why it's so painful and humiliating when Harry comes to the Black house in *Order of the Phoenix* and discovers that Ron and Hermione have been there together for weeks, with access to information he's been denied. It taps into his childhood as a devalued outsider denied knowledge of his magical heritage. Once again Harry's kept in the dark and this time by the ones he most trusts—his *real* family. He's infuriated, yet eventually works through his feelings of betrayal with Ron and Hermione.

Ron knows he's always sidekick to Harry, yet they're like brothers from the moment they meet. When the locket Horcrux reveals Ron's jealousy and insecurity over Harry and Hermione's relationship, Harry reassures Ron that he loves Hermione only as a sister. This frees Ron to become the person he's always wanted to be—a confident leader. Hermione, who probably lacked friends until coming to Hogwarts, now has two friends who aren't intimidated by her brilliance, even when they get annoyed with her devotion to scholarship and rules. Through all travails—and there are many—the family relationship of the Trio is secure and extends through their marriages and children. Such is love at its most powerful.

"A loving and nurturing family structure—which the Trio has—can also allow for genuine conflict, growth, and reconciliation," says Carrie-Ann Biondi, Blogengamot member at The Hog's Head. "Understanding this will only help to clarify why other family units are unable to heal long-standing wounds." (Biondi)

Loneliness is the ultimate poverty. —*Pauline Phillips*

Those in the series who function in the least healthy manner are loners without family—blood or found—or with very little in the way of family ties. Brothers Albus and Aberforth Dumbledore grew up in a good family, until tragedy and bitterness tore it, and them, apart at a young age. Now, tormented by anguished memories, secretive Albus plots alone, with no equal to offer valuable insight on his schemes. Though the brothers, according to Albus, have come to some kind of peace, we learn how bitter Aberforth remains when he unloads the Dumbledore history to the Trio just before the Battle of Hogwarts.

Two men who found family with the Marauders are forced as adults into lonely existences. Though lycanthrope Remus Lupin is able to bond, he's banned from human society and refuses to join other werewolves, preferring a solitary existence in poverty. Sirius Black suffers alone in Azkaban for thirteen years; afterward he's a roving fugitive and depression causes him to sometimes withdraw from even temporary family life with the Order at the Black house. His longtime enemy Severus Snape is a lonely double agent who exacts his pain and bitterness on helpless students, especially Harry, refusing healing connection. Instead of being true brothers in arms for the same cause, Sirius and Severus suffer from delayed adolescence, unrepentantly nurturing old grudges and constantly needling each other. If Severus could choose to love Harry like a son for Lily's sake, and if he and Sirius could nobly transcended childish hatred, how much better their lives—and others'—would be. Instead, they stay locked in old, isolating roles.

Retired Auror Alastor "Mad Eye" Moody is a pivotal member of the Order and interacts fairly well with the others. However, scarred and maimed from many past battles with dark wizards, Moody tends to detach himself, paranoid of everything and everyone.

The most extreme soloist is Tom Marvolo Riddle, Lord Voldemort. A narcissist who exhibits antisocial and cruel behavior at an early age, he grows up a full-blown murdering psychopath who mocks even the idea of love. Others exist merely as tools to carry out his grandiose plans for world domination, pure-blood wizardry and eternal physical life. Although he surrounds himself with his Death Eaters, many having served a long time, Voldemort has no affection for these fawning flunkies who are terrified of him. They're merely tools, easily punished or dispatched without regret.

Though all these individuals are *technically* in various families and some, such as Remus and Sirius, welcome such bonds when they're possible, soloists in the story usually avoid or have difficulty with healthy relationships. Yet five Order loners will sacrificially and heroically die for the found family that claims them—Albus, Moody, Remus, Sirius and Severus.

United we stand, divided we fall. –Aesop

In *Chamber of Secrets*, Hagrid says, "There are some wizards—like Malfoy's family—who think they're better than everyone else because they're what people call pure blood." (115-116 CoS) For the entire wizarding family, the defining division is over blood purity. This controversy broke up the Four Founders of Hogwarts, brought about both Grindelwald's and Voldemort's rise to power in Germany and Britain, respectively, and produced the first and second Voldemort wars.

Blood purists are pure-bloods of unalloyed wizarding descent who believe that all but pure-bloods are inferiors to be excluded from the wizarding world despite equal talent. The purists despise half-bloods (wizards with one Muggle and one wizard parent), Muggle-borns (wizards born of two Muggle parents, derogatorily called Mudbloods), Squibs (those with wizard parents who themselves lack magical abilities), and even pure-bloods who embrace these groups. They also treat other magical beings as lesser and deny them full rights in the community. We see concrete examples of this ideology in the Ministry's Fountain of Magical Brethren portraying all magical beings as subservient to wizards, the Magic is Might sculpture in which Muggles are crushed under wizards' feet, and the Muggle-Born Registration Commission under Voldemort.

Prideful and besotted with blood purity, the purists' zeal blinds them to the value of others' abilities and the importance of diversity to a healthy community. For example, the blood-obsessed Gaunt family is inbred to the point of insanity (Voldemort is Marvolo Gaunt's grandson and Merope Gaunt's son) and so is the Black family, whose motto is *Toujours Pur* ("always pure"). (111 OotP) Sirius's parents are second cousins and his first cousin is the deranged Bellatrix Black Lestrange. The Blacks, Gaunts, and Malfoys regard themselves as the wizarding elite, viewing the pure-blood Weasleys and others who hold pro-Muggle views as blood traitors. However, Sirius Black tells Harry that almost all contemporary wizard families have Muggle ancestors, though some strenuously deny it, and Ron Weasley tells Harry, "Most wizards these days are half-blood anyway. If we hadn't married Muggles we'd've died out." (116 CoS)

Rowling makes a strong case throughout the story that the insistence on blood purity is a corrupted way of thinking about kinship and family, and uses the issue as a metaphor for any kind of prejudice. As with the unhealthy family, prejudice demeans, ostracizes, denies rights and places higher value on some people and beings over others. Those whom wizards regard as inferior are hectored ("Mudbloods"), used (giants and werewolves), compartmentalized (the goblins), isolated (centaurs and merpeople), and abused (house-elves). Such select thinking and discrimination breeds division, injustice and ultimately civil war, weakening or even destroying the wider collective family/social structure.

Former blood purist Albus Dumbledore fights an uphill battle for half-blood and Muggle-born rights, insisting to Minster of Magic Cornelius Fudge, "You place too much importance, and you always have done, on the so-called purity of blood! You fail to recognize that it matters not what someone is born, but what they grow to be!" (708 GoF)

Just as the Sorting Hat exhorts Hogwarts students that Gryffindors, Hufflepuffs, Ravenclaws and Slytherins best function together in unity, those of varying blood purities and races together build a healthy and vigorous wizarding world. Blood purists who refuse to recognize the necessity of heterogeneity are to learn painful lessons about trust in exclusive blood purity, the weakness and impotency of an ingrown community, and how much the diversity they despise will ultimately matter.

Great things are done by a series of small things brought together. —Vincent van Gogh

Because in the end it's not blood purity that saves the world or creates a better one.

It's the Trio—a pure-blood, half-blood and Muggle-born—who heroically and steadfastly fight together for seven years against Voldemort and his evil.

It's Albus Dumbledore, who has, in the face of scorn and expulsion from wizarding world authority, courageously and faithfully led the fight against Voldemort for decades.

It's the mixed-blood Order of the Phoenix and D.A., underground resistance groups ever at the ready to battle against the Dark Lord and his Death Eaters.

It's formerly disaffected Aberforth, who watches over Harry through the two-way mirror, sends house-elf Dobby to rescue him and others at Malfoy Manor, allows the D.A. to use a secret tunnel from his pub to the school and overcomes his resentments to fight in the Battle.

It's the students, parents, teachers and others of all blood purities who refuse to surrender Harry under Voldemort's deadly ultimatum, who fight, suffer injury, and sacrifice their lives.

It's weak and dreamy Sybill Trelawney, who finally puts her crystal balls to good use, hurling them at Death Eaters. And Horace Slughorn, Head of Slytherin, who stays to fight.

It's Narcissa Malfoy who, in a stunning turnabout, lies to Voldemort and protects Harry upon his return to consciousness in the Forbidden Forest. And surprisingly, it's all three Malfoys who defect and sit out the Battle, rather than joining forces with the other Death Eaters.

It's Slytherin and double-agent Severus Snape, who refuses to reveal to Voldemort that Draco (he thinks) has the Elder Wand and thus dies, saving the boy's life; who with his last breaths desperately unloads his memories—both favorable and unfavorable—to Harry, giving him the critical information he needs—memories that reveal Severus's love for Lily, his part in the Potters' deaths, his service to Dumbledore and his double life.

It's those considered lesser beings—centaur Firenze who leaves his herd to become a Hogwarts teacher, and then with his centaur brethren fights bravely at the Battle; the Hogwarts house-elves who defend their home with kitchen implements; childlike giant Grawp who gets his half-giant brother Hagrid and Fang into the castle, and then helps defeat Voldemort's giants. And it's werewolf Remus, who fights and dies for the wizarding world that rejected him—what greater love than this?

Together as one family, of mixed-blood status, social position, wealth, ability, race and bond, they purge the world of Voldemort and expose blood purity fallacies.

Lily's blood running in Harry's veins defeated Voldemort the first time and offered her son protection from Voldemort through her loving, sacrificial death. In the final showdown with Voldemort at the Battle of Hogwarts, Harry is able to do "what my mother did" through his own loving, sacrificial death—he's able to protect from Voldemort his entire magical family with whom he has no blood tie at all. (738 DH)

The ties created by love win. The Sorting Hat and Dumbledore were right all along.

When everything goes to hell, the people who stand by you without flinching—they are your family. –Jim Butcher

At the end of Fifth Year, Harry, depressed and filled with grief over Sirius's death, leaves the Hogwarts Express, facing a lonely, miserable summer with his blood relatives. But as he exits Platform 9 ¾, he's surprised to be greeted by a reception committee—Mad-Eye, Tonks, Remus, Arthur, Molly, Fred and George. "We thought we might have a little chat with your aunt and uncle before letting them take you home," says Remus. Hermione leaves her own parents and with Ron joins the group, which then approaches the Dursleys with a threat. ". .

. If we get any hint that Potter's been mistreated in any way, you'll have us to answer to," declares the intimidating Mad-Eye. He turns to Harry.

> "So, Potter . . . give us a shout if you need us. If we don't hear from you for three days in a row, we'll send someone along . . . ."

> Harry nodded. He somehow could not find words to tell them what it meant to him, to see them all ranged there, on his side. Instead he smiled, raised a hand in farewell, turned around, and led the way out of the station toward the sunlit street, with Uncle Vernon, Aunt Petunia, and Dudley hurrying along in his wake. (868-870 OotP)

Harry knows who his real family is. It's the one bonded by love.

Works Cited

Biondi, Carrie-Ann. June 13, 2012. "Family Ties in Harry Potter and the Order of the Phoenix—Part 3." http://thehogshead.org/

Rowling, J.K. 1997-2007. *Harry Potter.* Vol. 1-7. New York: Scholastic.

CHAPTER 2

"Shabby Robes" and a "Swift Smile":

Remus Lupin's Nuanced Characterization in *Harry Potter and the Prisoner of Azkaban*

Katherine Sas

The character of Remus Lupin is one of the most beloved in the Harry Potter saga. Between the interviews with author J.K. Rowling archived on the websites *Accio Quote!* and *Remus-Lupin.Net*, I count no fewer than ten interviews in which she lists him as her favorite or one of her favorite characters in her seven-work saga, three which list him as the best teacher in the books, and one in which she chooses him as the character she would most like to meet. Harry Potter film alumni such as actor Matthew Lewis, producer David Heyman, and director David Yates have all singled Lupin out as their favorite in the series (see Wigler, Hill, and "Mugglecast Transcript 237"). *Empire Online's* poll of fans and readers to determine the top twenty-five "greatest" characters in the entire story place Lupin at number six. In light of the considerable length of the Harry Potter series and the several hundred characters readers are presented with, this consistent popularity and enduring fascination is quite notable.

Despite these facts, little work has been done by scholars to analyze the role and nuances of Remus Lupin as a character in the story. Top *Harry Potter* scholars such as John Granger and Travis Prinzi make little more than passing references to him at such moments that he affects the main plot of the story. A few longer studies have been done, such as Andrea Schutz's article "Beings and the Beast,"

Brent Stypczynski's doctoral dissertation "Evolution of the Werewolf Archetype from Ovid to Rowling," and Siamak Tundra Naficy's "Werewolf in the Wardrobe" chapter of *The Psychology of Harry Potter*. All three, however, focus almost solely on how Rowling uses lycanthropy and werewolves symbolically or as metaphors for another condition or state of being, only looking at Lupin's individual character in light of his status as "werewolf in residence" or as a foil to the "bad werewolf" Fenrir Greyback. Rather than use Lupin to discuss werewolves, this essay will examine Lupin as a fully rounded character in his own right. This is not to say that his werewolf nature is not integral to his character development, nor to deny it is a fascinating and fruitful area of study. But it is by no means the only aspect of his character and by itself does not explain the draw he holds for readers. On the contrary, his popularity can be attributed to the incredible detail and believable psychology with which he has been consistently drawn by creator J.K. Rowling. This essay examines Lupin's role and arc through the first book in which he appears, *The Prisoner of Azkaban*, and shows through that close reading that what readers respond to is above all a well-drawn and compelling character study.[1]

Professor R.J. Lupin first appears on the Hogwarts Express in chapter five of *The Prisoner of Azkaban*. The fact that we do not find out Lupin's first name (Remus) until the climactic Shrieking Shack scene at the end of the book is significant, for this is also the point at which his back-story and true nature are fully revealed. For the astute reader, however, quite a lot of information is packed into Lupin's name. Demonstrating Rowling's deftness at creating suspense, she hides Lupin's first name which helps to deflect readers from guessing his werewolf identity. Put together, both his first and last name point to his lupine nature and would be a bit of a giveaway: Remus, the legendary twin brother of Romulus, was raised by wolves; *Canis Lupus* is of course the Latin name for the wolf family. Though accounts differ on the cause of death, every version of the mythical founding of Rome agrees that Remus died before the completion of Rome's con-

---

[1] This essay will focus on Lupin's role and characterization in *The Prisoner of Azkaban*, but will make occasional reference to his appearances in books five through seven of the series, showing how *Prisoner* both prefigures and foreshadows future development.

struction, perhaps hinting that Rowling's choice of this name reflects his mythical namesake's tragic nature. More subtly, in traditional French folklore there are two words for werewolf, each designating a different type of behavior: "lubins or lupins [which in French folklore were characterized as] female and shy in contrast to the aggressive loup-garous" ("Werewolf France"). Of the two werewolves we see in any detail in the Harry Potter series, the withdrawn and gentle Remus Lupin would certainly resemble his namesake, whereas the violent and animalistic Fenrir Greyback adheres more closely to the more conventionally monstrous loup-garous.

All of this is only clear in hindsight, however. Indeed, the plot of *Prisoner* is largely driven by the mystery of Lupin's character, and the way in which his choices and history have affected not only the current plot of Harry's third year at Hogwarts but the larger history of the Wizarding World and the First War. Lupin is, quite literally, a figure who illuminates the past for Harry and readers. He first appears in deep sleep aboard the Hogwarts Express, but wakes to protect the children from the dementor, conjuring "a handful of flames" in his hand which "[illuminate] his tired, gray face" (83). He faces down the dementor and tells Harry and his friends its name and nature, passing out blocks of comforting chocolate. This first appearance which brings light, warmth, recovery, and information is a concise visual metaphor for Lupin's enlightening and reassuring role in the novel. He largely continues this role in future books, frequently explaining difficult concepts and histories to Harry and the reader. See, for example, his key role as Harry's mentor and the leader of the Advance Guard in chapter three and his schoolboy reminiscences in chapter twenty-nine of *Order of the Phoenix*. He seems keen to reprise this role in chapter eleven of *The Deathly Hallows* by joining Harry, Ron, and Hermione on their quest to destroy the Horcruxes, but by that point his newly-found role as father and husband complicates things and causes Harry to reject him.

Books Three and Five (*Prisoner of Azkaban* and *Order of the Phoenix* respectively, hereafter *Prisoner* and *Order*) are the two in the series to dwell most fully on the back-story of the Marauders, Harry's parents' generation, and as such Harry spends a lot of time with the only two remaining "faithful" Marauders, Lupin and Black, in the course of those books. Due to its title and the central mystery of its plot, *Prisoner* is often referred to as "the Sirius Black book," but this is far more appropriate to *Order*. *Prisoner* is truly dominated by Lupin. One need only look at the amount of time spent with each character in the respective novels to come to this conclusion, but more importantly the books are influenced by their respective moods and personalities. According to John Granger, *Order* is the "nigredo" of the series (named for the black stage of alchemy) in which Harry is stripped down and purified by fire (Granger, ch. 15). The book is dark and edgy, and Harry himself fluctuates between violent anger and crushing depression, not unlike his mercurial godfather Sirius Black, whose name invokes the black stage, a good example being chapter twenty-two of *Order* where Harry notes both the "whiff of stale drink about him" (implying his battles with depression) and, two pages later, how he "looked for a moment as though he would quite like to hit Fred" (475-477).

Though similarly melancholy, the tone of *Prisoner* as a narrative far more closely embodies the reflective and sensitive character of Professor Lupin, with whom Harry spends so much time. In contrast to Sirius's emotional volatility, Lupin is characterized by a restrained and even dispassionate approach. Where Sirius wears his emotions on his sleeve and must visibly control himself, Lupin's emotions stay well below the surface. His true feelings are often only apparent when he chooses to show them verbally or demonstratively, for instance the moment when he hugs Sirius, demonstrating his mingled forgiveness and apology (344). In reflection, Harry is correspondingly reserved with his emotions in this book, going so far as to hide his tears from Lupin during their boggart session (240-241).

The pain Harry experiences in *Prisoner* is less acute and damaging than in *Order*, and also more therapeutic, even cathartic. Indeed, at times the lines between suffering and joy become blurred, as when Harry both longs for and fears to hear his dead parents' voices:

> Harry felt drained and strangely empty, even though he was so full of chocolate. Terrible though it was to hear his parents' last moments replayed inside his head, these were the only times Harry had heard their voices since he was a very small child. But he'd never be able to produce a Patronus if he half wanted to hear his parents again...
>
> "They're dead," he told himself sternly. "They're dead and listening to echoes of them won't bring them back."   (243)

Contrast the poignancy of this moment with the disillusionment of the corresponding memories of his parents in *Order* which cause Harry to "[feel] cold and miserable at the thought of [his father James]" and James's troubling relationships with Lily and Snape (654). In *Order* the perspective of the past subscribed to by both Harry and Sirius is one of bitterness, regret, and anger. These memories and revelations are not pleasurable for Harry in any way. In contrast, Harry experiences the past in *Prisoner* as bittersweet and nostalgic, echoes he simultaneously misses dreadfully and yet is grateful to have experienced. Indeed, the above paragraph from Harry's Patronus lesson in *Prisoner* perfectly embodies the concept of the word nostalgia, which comes from a Greek compound combining the noun "nostos" (homecoming) with the combining form –algia (indicating pain) (OED). Lupin's presence during these one-on-one Patronus lessons during which Harry hears the voices of his departed parents ensures his influence on the overall tone of the sessions.

This tonal difference is relevant to Lupin because, to put it bluntly, Harry, as something of an Everyman, often conforms to those around him. He sees the past this way because Lupin, his mentor and major adult influence in the third book, sees the past this way. Though the first-time reader does not know this until the very end, Lupin is going through a parallel transformation throughout the book. Though he tries his best to hide his personal investment in Harry's Patronus lessons, as John Granger points out it is quite obvious in retrospect that Lupin is also "pained by the experience...No doubt the analyst is experiencing some catharsis" (148-149). These scenes are subtly and carefully drawn by Rowling, who notes that Lupin looks "paler than usual," speaks in a "strange voice," and "look[s] as though he were doing this against his better judgment" (239-241). On several occasions, he gently suggests that they abandon the effort. After twelve years of unconfronted guilt and suppressed memories, the examination of the circumstances surrounding Harry's parents' death is not something he is keen to dwell on.

Most telling are the moments when he is caught off guard and accidentally reveals his inner anxiety, such as when Harry asks if he knew Sirius Black:

> "Professor Lupin?" he said. "If you knew my dad, you must've known Sirius Black as well."

> Lupin turned very quickly.
>
> "What gives you that idea?" he said sharply.
>
> "Nothing—I mean, I just knew they were friends at Hogwarts too...."
>
> Lupin's face relaxed.
>
> "Yes, I knew him," he said shortly. "Or I thought I did..."(242-243)

Once again, the reader must return to this moment after the story is finished and carefully read between the lines to understand the full significance of the inter-change and Rowling's cleverness in misdirecting the reader. Lupin is, of course, paranoid of being thought in league with the dangerous fugitive Black due to their old friendship (as Snape, and no doubt others, explicitly believe) and is star-tled by the notion that Harry might have made this association. On a slightly deeper level, Lupin is of course actually helping Sirius implicitly as he knows of Sirius's animagus ability which assisted in his escape from prison. This is both a clue to the reader of Lupin and Sirius's history and true natures, and also some-thing of a red herring. It must be remembered that in the first two books of the series, the Defense Against the Dark Arts teacher was ultimately revealed to be villainous. Though Lupin breaks this tradition, the first-time reader is invited to suspect his intentions.

Naturally intuitive and trusting, Harry does not suspect him, and this is a pointer to more than Harry's naïveté. Though Lupin has several character flaws and often makes questionable decisions, his good nature is undeniable. Indeed, it would not be an overstatement to say that his major personality trait, that which he personifies more than anyone else in the entire seven books, is kindness. In addition to being personally invested in Harry's attempts to repel dementors and produce a Patronus, Lupin is undeniably troubled for Harry himself.

Harry frequently perceives, in *Prisoner* and throughout the series, that Lupin seems to be a mind-reader. When Harry tells him in a "would-be casual voice" that he has been left out of the Hogsmeade visit, Lupin "consider[s] Harry for a moment" and then invites him into his office for tea and conversation, presuma-bly to distract him from his disappointment (153). Barely a page later, he teases Harry about Professor Trelawney's prediction, calling out and correctly guessing Harry's anxiety about this and the boggart lesson (154-155). After Harry falls from his broom during the Quidditch match, Lupin once again anticipates Harry's thoughts:

> [Harry] hesitated, and then the question he had to ask burst from him before he could stop himself. "*Why?* Why do [the dementors] affect me like that? Am I just—?"
>
> "It has nothing to do with weakness," said Professor Lupin sharply, as though he had read Harry's mind. "The dementors affect you worse than the others because there are horrors in your past that the others don't have."
>
> A ray of wintery sunlight fell across the classroom, illuminating Lupin's gray hairs and the lines on his young face. (187)

Continual references are made throughout the series to this apparent mind-reading. In *The Half-Blood Prince*, he laconically answers Harry's unspoken question of who his "equals" are ("'Werewolves,' he added, at Harry's look of incomprehension") and a short time later causes Harry discomfort with his perception of Harry's hopes of his father being the Half-Blood Prince ("[Harry] tried to sound casual, as though this was a throwaway comment of no real importance, but he was not sure he had achieved the right effect; Lupin's smile was a little too understanding") (334, 336). Whether this insightful quality is wholly innate or partially magical (has he studied legilimency, perhaps?) or a mixture of both is never explicitly confirmed.

The conspicuous mention of Lupin's "gray hairs and the lines on his young face," however, suggest an innate source of his perceptiveness: his empathy, which seems to be a direct product of his lifelong suffering. Rowling draws attention to his prematurely gray hair and lined face because they point to his suffering and the fact that he has been made old before his time (much like Harry) due to his condition and difficult life. Even the adjective "wintery" in the above passage suggests age and despondency. The reader is invited to imagine that from experience Lupin understands Harry's suffering and his embarrassment about being thought weak. Similarly, when asked by Harry to teach him to defend himself against the dementors, Lupin responds with, "I don't pretend to be an expert at fighting dementors, Harry...quite the contrary" (189). This may be simple modesty, but more likely this is a literal statement. Like Harry, Lupin has experienced "horrors" which set him apart from everyone else, making him particularly vulnerable to their influence. One can imagine that, as a young man training alongside his friends in the Order of the Phoenix, Lupin would have felt self-conscious of his seeming vulnerability to such creatures as boggarts and dementors, and perhaps even struggled to repel them as Harry does.

In her address to the 2008 graduating class of Harvard University, Rowling made explicit her high regard for what she eponymously called "The Fringe Benefits of Failure and the Importance of Imagination." She sees these two things as being inextricably related. "Failure," she explains, "taught me things about myself that I could never have learned any other way...." According to Rowling, the unexpected fruit of personal hardship can teach the individual the virtuous power to empathize with others, the ability to imagine oneself into the lives and hardships of other people:

> [H]umans can learn and understand, without having experienced. They
> can think themselves into other people's places.... What is more, those who
> choose not to empathize enable real monsters. For without ever committing an
> act of outright evil ourselves, we collude with it, through our own apathy....
> What we achieve inwardly will change outer reality.... We do not need magic
> to change the world, we carry all the power we need inside ourselves already:
> we have the power to imagine better.

In Rowling's ethical worldview, empathy for others and the ability to imagine oneself into the position of another stands as the highest virtue. The innate human magic of the imagination shapes the world for the better. As detailed in Rowling's speech, Lupin's intense suffering and his choice to identify with and have compassion for others are mutually reinforcing.

Lupin's experience of suffering enables him to identify with others and treat them as he wishes to be treated, making him a model of the Golden Rule. Unfortunately, this generosity of spirit is often not reciprocated once his status as a werewolf becomes known. Lupin's wry and somewhat humorous attempts to kill Snape with kindness fall on deaf ears, such as in chapter eight when he repeatedly thanks Snape for brewing him the Wolfsbane Potion. Indeed, despite the fact that Lupin has never intentionally done Snape any harm, Snape seems to feel at least as threatened by him as by the "known murderer" Sirius Black. When he captures them with the intention of handing them over to the dementors, Snape only incapacitates Lupin, not the notorious mass murderer Black, suggesting that he feels Lupin to be the bigger physical threat. Likewise, he completely ignores the fact that in the eyes of the law it is only Black that the dementors have been authorized to kiss, remarking that, "Perhaps the dementors will have a kiss for [Lupin] too—" (359-360).

This prejudice and unlawful behavior may say more about Snape than anything else, but it seems to be predicated on the treatment of werewolves by Wizarding society in general. Ron, who, as Travis Prinzi notes, is ever the voice of "dysconscious" prejudice (ch. 13), spits at Lupin, *Get away from me, werewolf!* when Lupin moves to help him stand up, to which Lupin "stop[s] dead" in compulsive obedience (345). Hagrid, normally the first to defend supposedly dangerous magical creatures, also registers no surprise that Lupin would leave Hogwarts after he is "outed" by Snape, suggesting how deeply ingrained the discrimination against werewolves lies in the Wizarding World (422). Dumbledore notes that Lupin's testimony to Black's innocence will "count for very little" in the Wizarding legal system (392). In the pseudonymous Newt Scamander's *Fantastic Beasts and Where to Find Them*, the werewolves' XXXXX level classification by the Ministry of Magic (indicating "known wizard killer/impossible to train or domesticate," the highest classification possible) is qualified in a footnote to only refer to the werewolf "in its transformed state," but one imagines that not many average wizards read or regard the footnote (41). Scamander's creation of the Werewolf Register in 1947, in any case, subtly implies his own fascistic views on the matter (vi).

All of this stigmatization and scapegoating affect Lupin in very interesting ways, and this undeserved status of social pariah informs both his greatest strengths and weaknesses. However, rather than allowing the character to merely become a symbol of the undeservedly oppressed werewolf race and conform to generalization and stereotypes, Rowling also allows Lupin's individual choices and character to dictate his actions, resulting in a fully rounded identity. He is shown to be his own person, unlike any other individual (full human or werewolf) that readers meet in the series.

Rather than respond in anger by embracing his capability for violence and perpetuating the vicious revenge cycle (as Fenrir Greyback does), in the entire series he is never seen to rebuke anyone for their treatment of him or their prejudice. He even goes so far as to take responsibility for it and suggest that it is in some way deserved. Lupin takes responsibility for his actions despite the fact that he cannot control himself while in his transformed state. When Snape "outs" him as a werewolf, Harry expresses his disbelief that Lupin would leave Hogwarts "just because of that." Instead of retaliating with a public account of Snape's own irresponsible behavior, or even criticizing him privately in front of Harry, Lupin merely "smile[s] wryly," admitting that he understands why parents "will not want a werewolf teaching their children." He admits that "after last night, I see their point. I could have bitten any of you…That must never happen again" (423). Lupin seems to view his own lycanthropy as analogous to original sin as depicted in Romans 7:15: "I do not understand what I do. For what I want to do I do not do, but what I hate I do" (NIV).[2] Lupin understands that his own inability to prevent his transformations does not absolve him of responsibility. In this way, lycanthropy can be read as a metaphor for original sin, something common to all human beings, which (in Christian tradition) is paradoxically both inborn and transgressive.

Lupin's ability to understand parents' fears for their children's safety inoculates him to the bitterness felt by many others of his kind who, as he says in *The Half-Blood Prince*, habitually "[shun] normal society and live on the margins," believing that "under [Greyback's] rule, they will have a better life"(334). "It has been difficult to gain their trust," he admits. "I bear the unmistakable signs of having tried to live among wizards…. I cannot pretend that my own particular brand of reasoned argument is making much headway against Greyback's insistence that we werewolves deserve blood…." (334-335). Ironically, this refusal to retaliate and insistence on trying to understand and forgive his oppressors make him an outcast in both societies.

---

[2] Lycanthropy as used by Rowling has also been examined as a metaphor for physical disease (especially multiple sclerosis and HIV/AIDS), self-harm or "cutting," and homosexuality, among others. While all of these get at part of the truth, I find each explanation dissatisfying on its own and am inclined to think that Rowling did not mean it as a stand-in for any one particular real-world condition but a fictional or mythic condition all its own which bears resemblances to these and other real issues.

Part of what makes Rowling's characterization of Lupin (and, to be fair, many of her characters) so compelling is that she portrays each personality trait honestly, admitting both its potential strengths and weaknesses. Although Lupin's willingness to put the feelings and wishes of others before himself and not deny his flaws is certainly admirable, this can occasionally morph into a self-imposed martyrdom and angsty self-loathing. Some readers have criticized Lupin's final decision in *Prisoner* to flee Hogwarts as cowardly and self-serving, wishing that he would face the criticism of parents and colleagues with dignity and the knowledge of his own innocence and good intentions. Indeed, it is difficult to imagine any amount of scorn from the school board of directors convincing Professor Dumbledore or Sirius Black to abandon Harry to the mercies of yet another potentially dangerous Defense Against the Dark Arts teacher, not to mention the fact that Lupin's decision to leave also deprives Harry of one of his only remaining connections to his parents. Lupin's instinct for flight over fight in this instance is not as altruistic as it first appears, but on second glance looks tellingly thin-skinned. His instinct for self-denial blends imperceptibly into a kind of selfishness, preferring to hide himself away in the name of the comfortable status quo to the more difficult choice to defend himself and his actions publicly.

Though less dramatic, Lupin's choice here serves as a telling foreshadowing of his even more self-centered actions in *The Deathly Hallows*, in which he briefly abandons his wife and unborn child. Interestingly, Rowling makes it clear that his fears for them are legitimate and sympathetic. "I should never have married [Tonks]," he explains. "I've made her an outcast! [...] how can I forgive myself, when I knowingly risked passing on my own condition to an innocent child?" (213) However, despite the genuine danger, Lupin's reckless decision to leave them out of a mistaken belief that his presence puts them in more danger is unequivocally criticized by Harry and (implicitly) by Rowling. Though Harry concedes that Lupin is no coward, he maintains that "he's acting like one," indicating that he believes Lupin to be capable of more noble action and even hoping that his harsh words will serve to help him change his mind. One wonders if he felt similarly disappointed in Lupin's actions at the end of *Prisoner* but lacked the maturity and critical faculties to adequately express this. Though trauma and suffering can lead to increased wisdom (as Rowling's Harvard commencement speech makes clear), Lupin's behavior in these instances demonstrates how it can also

lead to compulsive, unhealthy, and fear-driven behavior. By showing these negative fringe detriments, Rowling avoids romanticizing the suffering experienced
by Lupin and others. While failure and affliction can strengthen, they also undeniably cause irrevocable damage and evil.

As with many fictional characters, and indeed real people, origins for Lupin's
behavior can be found by looking at his childhood. Reticent as ever to talk about
himself, Lupin's explanation of his childhood solutions to his disease are disturbing but so subtle as to be easily overlooked. His statement that his "parents tried
everything, but in those days there was no cure" is implicitly ominous: To what
lengths his parents went in search of a cure, and what this communicated to their
young son about the value of his "diseased" life, the reader is left to imagine (352).
Lacking a cure but having been awarded a place at Hogwarts by the open-minded
and progressive new headmaster Dumbledore, the solution was to lock himself
away at the full moon.[3] "Separated from humans to bite," he explains, "I bit and
scratched myself instead" (353). For an eleven-year-old boy to willingly go
through this traumatic ordeal on a monthly basis, and for his parents and teachers
to have confidence in his ability to handle himself physically, emotionally, and
mentally, speaks for itself regarding his preternatural moral character and self-
possession even at this young age, and stands in stark contrast to the only other
werewolf we are presented with in any detail, Fenrir Greyback, who intentionally lets himself loose in order to kill, main, and contaminate others. Like the
gifted teacher Lupin, Greyback "specializes in children." But whereas Lupin im-
prisons and injures himself to keep his classmates and students safe, Greyback
goes out of his way to "bite them young...and raise them away from their parents...to hate normal wizards" (*Prince* 334-335). While Greyback uses and revels
in his loss of control and violent abilities, Lupin's full moon boggart suggests that
these are his greatest fears (*Prisoner,* ch. 7 and 22). If Greyback fears being controlled by others, Lupin fears not being able to control himself, a subtle but significant difference of emphasis.

---

[3] As far as is known, Lupin was and remains the only werewolf in history to attend
Hogwarts. Why he was so singled out is never explained, but could point to his remarkable
character even as a child, and certainly underscores the mutual respect between himself
and Dumbledore throughout the series.

If lycanthropy were merely an allegorical stand-in for some real world counterpart, it would be very easy to make Lupin, the afflicted and ostracized werewolf, a one-dimensional character: a melancholy and self-sacrificial scapegoat. Rowling, however, works hard to make him realistic and well-rounded, and well-rounded characters, like people, are complex and often contradictory. Unexpectedly, apart from noting his "shabby" dress, ill appearance, and obvious poverty, by far the most frequently referenced physical characteristic is his smile. Between his first "small smile" for the frightened kids on the train and his final departure in which he leaves Harry with a nod and a "swift smile," Lupin gives the impression of inner peace. He takes things in stride, making the best of bad situations and finding humor in everything (86, 425).[4] He even has smiles for Peeves and Snape, who go out of their way to bait and insult him in front of his students (131, 156). These references to his smile continue into later books, such as his "warm" smile to comfort Harry while telling Harry about his experience living with the werewolves in *Prince* (334) or his "beaming" smile when delivering the news of his son's birth (*Hallows* 514).

Related to this physical characteristic is a more general attitude of cheerfulness, even in otherwise stressful or unpleasant situations. Indeed, this humor can, at times, be quite black and even a little bit disturbing. Most notably, he conducts the interrogation of their traitorous friend Peter Pettigrew in the Shrieking Shack with his characteristic politeness and dry humor: He addresses Peter "pleasantly, as though rats frequently erupted into old school friends around him," and pointedly dismisses Peter's denials of guilt by explaining, "I must admit Peter, I have difficulty in understanding why an innocent person would want to spend twelve years as a rat" (369). His methodical calmness in this scene serves as a brilliant contrast to the emotional and volatile Sirius.

In addition to being generally cheerful and unflappable, Lupin is often portrayed as something of a mischief-maker. Though lacking the flashy and attention-seeking flair for troublemaking displayed by the Weasley twins or Sirius, Lupin is strongly and consistently connected with humor. When good manners fail, Lupin often has cutting jabs for Snape: he suggests that Neville dress him in

---

[4] The adjective "swift" also seems to me particularly lupine and appropriate to a wolf.

drag when he realizes how Neville is bullied by the Potions Master (135); his eloquent "Moony" avatar in the Marauders Map "presents his compliments to Professor Snape, and begs him to keep his abnormally large nose out of other people's business" (287); most subtly of all, the "vampire essay" assignment which he casually mentions in front of Snape may be a small retaliation against Snape, who is often likened to a vampire bat, and his werewolf essay assignment (289). Central to the issue of humor, of course, is his identity as Moony in the Marauders, his own generation's equivalent of the mischievous Weasley twins. Despite his great respect for Dumbledore and the knowledge of his own precarious place in the Wizarding world, the teenage Remus, it seems, frequently chose to break rules, ordained by governmental and school law, in order to sneak out and have fun with his friends. Though he rebukes Harry for doing the same with Black on the loose, his final act as he leaves school is to give Harry the Marauder's Map and hint that it is right that Harry should use it for that very thing (424-425). Despite his suffering and frequent self-denial, Lupin is not presented merely as a navelgazing ascetic. Like his fellow Marauders, he places a high value on fun and community. He says that in his reckless youth he was "happier than [he] had ever been in [his] life," and "always managed to forget [his] guilty feelings [for breaking Dumbledore's rules] every time [they] sat down to plan [the] next month's adventure" (354-356).

Humor and optimism in general are also connected with Lupin's role as teacher. The two main lessons we see him teach are the Patronus and Riddikulus Charms, which defend against depression and fear, respectively, as symbolized by dementors and boggarts (see *Prisoner of Azkaban* chapters seven and twelve especially). The essential ingredients to make these particular charms work effectively are powerfully happy memories and laughter. Harry finds dementors and boggarts particularly crippling given his difficult past, and notably it is Lupin, who Rowling calls a "damaged person, literally and metaphorically," who helps Harry learn to ward them off using these positive and empowering tools ("What Jo says about Remus Lupin").

To further flesh out the character, Rowling does not hesitate to show the negative aspects of his personality and choices, and as with his strengths these seem to be part and parcel of the life he has lived. The natural consequence of a life spent in hiding is the tendency towards secrecy, and Lupin is no exception.

SHABBY ROBES" AND A "SWIFT SMILE" • 41

He is a good liar, as evidenced by the fact that he has managed to keep his were-wolf identity out of the public eye until the events of *Prisoner* when he is thirty-four years old. He manages to hide the truth about the Marauder's Map from Snape, a known legilimens (a type of Wizarding mind-reader), and Harry notes his "odd, closed expression" and the fact that he seems to be "doing some very quick thinking" when attempting to deceive Snape (288). All of this secrecy and the ability to blend into the crowd unfortunately play into and perhaps even con-firm the popular fears and stereotypes of werewolves as "sleeper cells," dangerous monsters who can appear normal and hide in plain sight. Painful though it is to imagine, these abilities to effectively lie and manipulate others possibly lay at the root of Sirius's suspicions of Remus in the First War, which resulted in the mis-trust among the formerly close-knit group and the resulting deaths of Harry's parents.[5]

When his secret is discovered, Lupin's knee-jerk reaction is one of flight. Fol-lowing the traumatic events of Halloween 1981, he keeps himself out of young orphan Harry's life for twelve years despite being the last of his parents' close friends. As *Harry Potter* fan fiction author Victoria P. notes, "Remus's besetting sin is inaction," a motif that will continue and flourish in later books, such as his initial refusal to reciprocate the relationship with Tonks despite returning her feelings in *Prince*. Though there is perceptible "self-disgust" at his own actions, and he himself describes them as "cowardly," Lupin cannot bring himself to con-fess to Dumbledore what he knows about Sirius's Animagus abilities because of what it might imply about his own lack of trustworthiness (356). When the truth is finally revealed, rather than face the world with honesty and confidence in his own innocence, he easily folds under the threat of parental disapproval, giving Harry the impression that he "want[s] to leave as quickly as possible" (425). Though in many ways a role model and worthy of the respect of Harry and read-ers, Rowling does not sanitize the realities of Lupin's condition and shows the damaging as well as the ennobling consequences of his illness.

---

[5] Rowling never gives Sirius's reasons for this mistrust definitively, but this seems to me the most logical conclusion given Remus's character. See pp. 372-373 of *Prisoner* for the only discussion of these events.

By the end of *Prisoner*, the extremely well-crafted and nuanced character of Remus Lupin has elevated the Harry Potter novels. From the earlier books in which many of the adult characters were portrayed as caricatures, Rowling's introduction of the more nuanced adult character of Lupin cues readers to the growing maturity and complexity of the series, paving the way for the later psychological development of the young characters and the growing understanding of the complexities of adult characters such as Dumbledore, Sirius, and Snape. Presented with a sympathetic, likeable, but believably shaded character, readers and fans have responded with enthusiasm, making him one of the most effective and memorable characters of the series, if not the most famous, and this seems to suit Lupin's withdrawn yet influential character perfectly. Lupin will reappear in *The Order of the Phoenix*, *The Half-Blood Prince*, and *The Deathly Hallows*, but it is *The Prisoner of Azkaban* that lays the groundwork for readers' understanding of him and his motivations, setting the stage for one of the most fascinating and moving character arcs in the series.

Works Cited

Granger, John. *How Harry Cast His Spell: The Meaning Behind the Mania for J.K. Rowling's Bestselling Books.* Carol Stream: Tyndale House Publishers, Inc., 2008. Print.

Hill, Erin. "Producer David Heyman: 'Harry Potter Has Been the Gift of all Gifts.'" *Parade.com.* 13 Jul. 2011. Web. 8 July 2014.

"JK Rowling on Remus." *Remus-Lupin.net.* Web. 8 July 2014.

"Werewolf France." *Werewolves.monstrous.com.* Web. 24 August 2014.

"Mugglecast 237 Transcript." Mugglenet.com. Web. 8 July 2014.

"nostalgia, n." *OED Online.* Oxford University Press, June 2014. Web. 8 July 2014.

Prinzi, Travis. *Harry Potter & Imagination: The Way Between Two Worlds.* Zossima Press, 2009. Print.

Rowling, J.K. *Fantastic Beasts and Where to Find Them.* New York: Scholastic Inc., 2001. Print.

Rowing, J.K. "The Fringe Benefits of Failure and the Importance of the Imagination." *Harvard Gazette.* 5 Jun. 2008. Web. 31 Aug. 2014.

Rowling, J.K. *Harry Potter and the Deathly Hallows.* New York: Scholastic Inc., 2007. Print.

Rowling, J.K. *Harry Potter and the Half-Blood Prince.* New York: Scholastic Inc., 2005. Print.

Rowling, J.K. *Harry Potter and the Order of the Phoenix.* New York: Scholastic Inc., 2003. Print.

Rowling, J.K. *Harry Potter and the Prisoner of Azkaban.* New York: Scholastic Inc., 1999. Print.

Schutz, Andrea. "Beings and the Beast: Free Will, Destiny and Contagion for Animagi and Werewolves." *Accio 2008 Conference.* Web. 8 July 2014.

Stypczynski, Brent. A. "Evolution of the Werewolf Archetype from Ovid to J.K. Rowling." Diss. Kent State University, 2008. Web. 8 July 2014.

"The 25 Greatest Harry Potter Characters." *EmpireOnline.com.* Web. 8 July 2014.

Tundra Naficy, Siamak. "The Werewolf in the Wardrobe." *The Psychology of Harry Potter: An Unauthorized Examination of the Boy Who Lived.* Ed. Neil Mulholland. Dallas: BenBella Books, Inc., 2006. Print.

Victoria P. "'When It Alteration Finds' Commentary." *Unfitforsociety.net.* Web. 8 July 2014.

"What Jo says about Remus Lupin (aka 'Moony')." *Accio Quote!* Web. 8 July 2014.

Wigler, Josh. "Harry Potter World Cup: Matthew Lewis Summons Bracket Predictions." *MTV Movies Blog.* MTV, 5 Jul.0 2011. Web. 8 July 2014.

CHAPTER 3

Twin Core:

An Exploration of Twins in the Wizarding World

Carol Eshleman

In May of 2007, two months before the release of *Deathly Hallows,* I sat in a hotel room at the Phoenix Rising Conference in New Orleans with the members of Pottercast as well as several other loyal members of the Potterverse. As part of a book discussion to be aired on the Borders website, we covered what we believed would happen in book seven. Of course, the question arose: who was going to die? In stating our various theories, I put forward my belief that one of the Weasley twins would be killed—an opinion that was immediately met with horror. Even when stating that I believed the Weasley twins were literary descendants of the Greek twins Castor and Pollux (close brothers who are tragically separated when one of them dies) and that Fred and George's strong magical abilities and line of defense products were setting them up to take a fighting role in the war, the idea was still unpopular. I found out how widely unpopular when I read the Mugglenet book *What Will Happen in Harry Potter 7* and saw that the staff of Mugglenet considered the possibility of a Weasley twin death as basically a non-issue. In fact, the Mugglenet crew stated, "Unless J.K.R. does the unthinkable, only one destiny could possibly await them: jokes, jokes, and more jokes" (183). I felt so certain, however, that something had been missed. Thus, I began the investigation that has now become this essay. My intention was to discover textual clues and foreshadowing of a twin death, which I did indeed find in abundance. Two months later, my theory was proven valid, but in the meantime I had also found a larger message in the series that J.K. Rowling had used twins to tell.

It is a fairly common device of authors to speak of duality and to create various pairings in their fictional worlds. Light versus dark and good versus evil are dichotomies that are familiar across broad spectrums of readers. J.K. Rowling's explorations within this framework, however, go much deeper. The Wizarding World does not have casual, intermittent symbols of duality; Rowling's world is one absolutely riddled with pairings of numerous varieties—twins of all sorts. There are identical twins, evil twins, parasitic twins, missing twins, and even twins that are inanimate objects. What appears when these symbols are deciphered is an intricate thematic foundation. Rowling's twin imagery provides the infrastructure for the saga's message about the importance of choice and the wholeness of true friendship.

Rowling has stated that the deaths in particular had great significance to the overarching plot. Back in 2000, when *Goblet of Fire* had just been released, Rowling said that she had decided who was on the chopping block: "I know all of them who are going to die, yeah...There are reasons for the deaths in each case, in terms of the story. So that's why I'm doing it" ("J.K. Rowling Interview"). The foreshadowing of Fred's death thus becomes an important literary device. It gives the audience clues as to what precisely is at stake. Rowling cleverly makes this foreshadowing through a masterful display of narrative misdirection.

In *Sorcerer's Stone*, when we hear the Hogwarts school song (the only time we hear it in the series), we learn that there is no one accepted tune to accompany it. Everyone picks whatever pace and beat he or she prefers. We are not told how other students choose to sing, but we do get a description of Fred and George's rendition: "At last, only the Weasley twins were left singing along to a very slow funeral march" (128). This scene takes place in the Hogwarts great hall, which becomes the repository for Fred's body as well as other victims during the final battle in the seventh book.

We begin to gain a sense in *Chamber of Secrets* that Fred's attitude towards death is slightly more nonchalant than George's. Before the critical Gryffindor versus Slytherin Quidditch match, Oliver Wood has some ominous words for Harry:

"Get to that Snitch before Malfoy or die trying, Harry, because we've got to win today, we've got to."

"So no pressure, Harry," said Fred, winking at him. (167)

This could possibly be regarded as merely an example of Fred's sarcasm if it were not for George's reaction to this same comment after Harry is being attacked by the rogue Bludger: "'This is all your fault,' George said angrily to Wood. ' "Get the Snitch or die trying," what a stupid thing to tell him....'" (170). Clearly, unlike Fred, George thinks death is no joking matter.

Prisoner of Azkaban sees no change in Fred's attitude. When Ron believes Crookshanks has eaten Scabbers, Fred tries to comfort Ron with words that eerily echo his own eventual fate: "It was probably better for him to snuff it quickly—one swallow—he probably didn't feel a thing" (253). Fred does indeed "snuff it quickly."

In *Goblet of Fire* and onwards, the foreshadowing becomes increasingly vivid and dark. In this book we learn of Fred and George's ambition to open their own joke shop, which has a major impact on the plot of all further novels. Using the Weasley twins' invented Extendable Ears in *Order of the Phoenix*, Harry learns that he could possibly be possessed by Voldemort. With the aid of Fred and George's Peruvian Instant Darkness Powder, Draco makes his escape in *Half-Blood Prince*. Harry breaks into Umbridge's office in *Deathly Hallows* with the help of some Weasley Decoy Detonators. Looking back at the involvement Fred and George had through their joke shop, it's no wonder Mrs. Weasley saw that the twins were venturing into dangerous waters: "It's not as though they haven't got brains...but they're wasting them, and unless they pull themselves together soon, they'll be in real trouble" (*Goblet of Fire* 58-59). They do indeed get into real trouble shortly afterwards.

When the Dark Mark makes an appearance at the Quidditch World Cup, Molly is naturally concerned about her family. Mrs. Weasley shocks her kids (but not careful readers) when her first concern is Fred and George after they return home:

"I shouted at you before you left!" Mrs. Weasley said, starting to sob.

> "It's all I've been thinking about! What if You-Know-Who had got you, and the last thing I ever said to you was that you didn't get enough O.W.L.s? Oh Fred... George...." (146)

As in *Chamber of Secrets*, Fred once again turns death into a joke, shortly afterwards:

> "You wouldn't be thinking of restarting Weasley's Wizard Wheezes, by any chance?"
>
> "Now, Mum," said Fred, looking up at her, a pained look on his face. "If the Hogwarts Express crashed tomorrow, and George and I died, how would you feel to know that the last thing we ever heard from you was an unfounded accusation?"
>
> Everyone laughed, even Mrs. Weasley. (153)

Fred's nonchalant attitude is reiterated after the Triwizard Tournament is announced. He's quite eager to get his name in the Goblet despite the age limit:

> "People have died, though!" said Hermione in a worried voice ...
>
> "Yeah," said Fred airily, "but that was years ago, wasn't it? Anyway, where's the fun without a bit of risk?" (190)

Bringing up death numerous times, while making the reader laugh over and over about the prospect of Fred dying is a fantastic display of Rowling's use of narrative misdirection. By the second half of the series, the reader is convinced that the idea of a twin death is purely laughable.

In *Order of the Phoenix*, the comedic foreshadowing begins to have a much darker tone, and it becomes increasingly specific as to the manner of Fred's demise:

> "Headless Hats!" shouted George, as Fred waved a pointed hat decorated with a fluffy pink feather at the watching students. "Two Galleons each—watch Fred now!"
>
> Fred swept the hat onto his head, beaming. For a second he merely looked rather stupid, then both hat and head vanished. (540)

This passage is foreboding once the actual manner of Fred's death is revealed—a head injury while in mid-laugh.

Yet even after all of this foreshadowing, the argument could still have been made that many of these passages could refer to either one of the twins. The beginning of *Deathly Hallows*, however, sealed Fred's fate. George's injury in Harry's escape marked him for mourning: "As the lamplight fell across George's head, Ginny gasped and Harry's stomach lurched: One of George's ears was missing" (69). Notice that George's injury is not a cut or a slash that would leave a scar, an addition to his appearance. It's a subtraction. A part of him is missing. Throughout the books, we have seen Fred and George constantly being mistaken for each other. George's injury finally makes this impossible. This is the most definitive and grim foreshadowing: George is finally defined because of the absence of his ear. Because George and Fred were always considered a unit, for the remainder of his life, George will be defined by the absence of his twin. George will never figuratively or literally be whole again.

It's interesting that Harry and all those on his side hardly portray any sense of purity or wholeness. Harry is a half-blood and an orphan. Hermione is Muggle-born. Lupin is a werewolf, putting him on the outs of magical society. Tonks is half-blood, and to emphasize her non-singular qualities, is shown with a constantly altering appearance. Sirius is the outcast of his family and an accused criminal. The Weasleys, though pure-bloods, are marginalized by their poverty. Neville's magical prowess is less than stellar (despite his pure-blood status), and with his parents mentally absent, he is practically an orphan. Dumbledore's pure-blood family is nearly all dead except for his one goat-loving brother with whom he maintains an icy relationship. How do any of these people become examples of wholeness? This is where Rowling's use of twin imagery comes into play.

There are a multitude of dualistic images in the series, but they can be simply categorized by the distinction of natural or unnatural. Some characters have natural, in-born dualistic qualities or relationships that represent a natural partnership. Other characters attempt unnatural experiments in duality that force them to supersede their own inherent natures. This is the distinction that guides the reader to determine wholeness among the characters. The obvious place to begin is with the natural twinships of the series.

Identical twins occur biologically when a single fertilized egg splits in two and each half develops into a complete embryo, creating two complete people who are genetically the exact same person. Fred and George Weasley fall into this category, and these two tricksters make it difficult to even consider them as separate entities. During their very first appearance in the series, their first joke is to toy with their mother over which twin is which:

> "Fred, you next," the plump woman said.
>
> "I'm not Fred, I'm George," said the boy. "Honestly, woman, you call yourself our mother? Can't you *tell* I'm George?"
>
> "Sorry, George, dear."
>
> "Only joking, I am Fred," said the boy, and off he went. (92)

The twins are still using this gag in *Deathly Hallows* when they pull the same joke on Mad-Eye Moody:

> … "Arthur and Fred—"
>
> "I'm George," said the twin at whom Moody was pointing. "Can't you even tell us apart when we're Harry?"
>
> "Sorry, George—"
>
> "I'm only yanking your wand, I'm Fred really—"
>
> "Enough messing around!" snarled Moody. (52)

Even Fred's and George's extracurricular activity does nothing to earn them each a singular identity as they play the same position on their Quidditch team. Their position as Beaters is central to their characterization. Every other Quidditch position is singular (Seeker or Keeper) or in the instance of Chasers, tripled. Beaters are in pairs and serve the basic purpose of bringing chaos to the game by knocking around the two most unpredictable of the four Quidditch balls, the Bludgers. When Harry seems afraid of being gravely injured by the Bludgers, Wood reassures him, "Don't worry, the Weasleys are more than a match for the Bludgers—I mean, they're like a pair of human Bludgers themselves" (169). Fred and George fit naturally into this mold. It's this teamwork and friendship that make it even more heartbreaking when Fred is killed. Fred and George are separate but whole, a natural complete pair.

Yet, Fred and George are not the only pair of identical twins at Hogwarts. Parvati and her sister Padma are also identical twins. However, their relationship is nothing like that of Fred and George. Despite being biologically identical, they are not what could be considered a unit. The Sorting Hat places them in two different houses, Gryffindor and Ravenclaw respectively, whereas Fred and George are both in Gryffindor. Harry and Hermione marvel at this peculiarity:

> "Brothers and sisters usually go in the same Houses, don't they?" [Harry] said. He was judging by the Weasleys, all seven of whom had been put in Gryffindor.
>
> "Oh no, not necessarily," said Hermione. "Parvati Patil's twin's in Ravenclaw, and they're identical. You'd think they'd be together, wouldn't you?" (*Goblet of Fire* 174)

Parvati and Padma are mentioned briefly as twins in book one, but the reader may well have forgotten that Parvati has an identical twin until the fourth book when they accompany Harry and Ron to the Yule Ball. When Parvati and Padma are finally shown together they don't behave as a unit like Fred and George.

Why is there such a discrepancy? What is Rowling trying to point out by providing the reader with two sets of identical twins that behave in two completely different ways? A comparison of these sets of twins shows their importance. In the case of Parvati and Padma, their similarity lies in their biology alone. In behavior and friendship, Fred and George and Parvati and Padma are completely opposite. Fred and George act identical while Parvati and Padma behave as separate entities. Thus, it is behavior that the reader is meant to associate with twinship, not biology. Fred and George are a unit. Parvati and Padma are not. The twins' names also emphasize this message as Fred and George, the more "identical" twins, have names that begin with two different letters, while Parvati and Padma's names are more physically similar, both beginning with "Pa." Rowling's message is clear: actions determine wholeness—not appearance or genetics.

Based on this model of twinship, we can determine other pairs who Rowling would group together as natural twins. Harry and Ron form a twin pair as their friendship mirrors that of Fred and George. In the Epilogue, Ron and Harry are literally brothers. Harry and Ginny's marriage is much more the case of Harry becoming a Weasley than of Ginny becoming a Potter.

Another pair of non-biological natural twins is Hogwarts's first pair of tricksters, James and Sirius. Although Slughorn speaks of Sirius and Regulus as a "set" (*Half-Blood Prince* 70), it is James who is Sirius's true sibling. When we first hear of James and Sirius's friendship, Rowling also slips in a comparison to Fred and George:

> "Black and Potter. Ringleaders of their little gang. Both very bright, of course—exceptionally bright, in fact—but I don't think we've ever had such a pair of troublemakers—"
>
> "I dunno," chuckled Hagrid. "Fred and George Weasley could give 'em a run fer their money."
>
> "You'd have thought Black and Potter were brothers!" chimed in Professor Flitwick. "Inseparable!" (*Prisoner of Azkaban* 204)

The twin pair of Harry and Ron can also be compared to James and Sirius. Harry's and Ron's Patronuses mirror James's and Sirius's Animagus forms: Harry's Patronus is a stag while Ron's is a dog.

Lupin is an interesting study in twinship in that he represents both missing duality and an unnatural twinship. The key lies in his name—Remus Lupin. Remus is famous in mythology as the twin brother of Romulus, founder of Rome. As legend goes, these twins were raised by wolves. Clearly, this is a fitting name since Lupin (also a name referring to wolves) is a werewolf, a condition that plagues him in the Wizarding World, placing him on the margins of society. Because of his first name, there has been speculation in the Harry Potter fandom that Remus had a twin – a theory that Rowling debunked on her website (Rowling, "Professor Lupin"). The question then arises, why give Remus Lupin a name pointing to twinship if he doesn't have a twin? Further, if Rowling simply wanted to make an allusion to the mythical wolf twins, why not use Romulus instead of Remus? Either name is a reference to the same myth. The answer is because, like his mythical namesake, Remus Lupin is not a whole man. He has been plagued by his werewolf condition from a young age, separating him and cutting him off as a full member of society.

Rowling christens him Remus instead of Romulus because he does not believe in his own ability to do great things. He thinks of himself as broken and tries to use this as an excuse to not begin a relationship with Tonks when she professes her feelings for him. Arguing with Molly and Arthur Weasley, Lupin responds, "Tonks deserves somebody young and whole" (*Half-Blood Prince* 624). Although Lupin does eventually marry Tonks, it is clear that he hasn't completely gotten over his insecurities. When Tonks becomes pregnant with his child, Lupin runs away, fearing the consequences of founding a line that begins with his condition. Harry admonishes Lupin to return to Tonks, whose duality is inborn and natural, unlike Remus's unnatural werewolf alter-ego, which is the result of an outside infection. It is significant that the next time Harry hears of Lupin after their confrontation, he has since returned to Tonks and accepted his fatherhood, taking his place as the founder of a line. Listening to Potterwatch, Harry learns Remus has chosen the pseudonym "Romulus." Remus and "Romulus" are a single unit. Having accepted his wife and his unborn child, Lupin considers himself a greater man, and as a member of a family unit, Lupin is now whole.

Neville, like Lupin, is also a would-be twin. While Harry is the Boy Who Lived, Neville serves as the Boy Who Could Have Been. Neville is very much a foil to Harry. Harry's parents die, but Harry is able to see and connect with images of them via the Mirror of Erised, Priori Incantatem, and the Resurrection Stone. Neville can see, hug, and speak to his parents, but there is no true communication because of their mental incapacitation. When pondering Neville's situation, Harry considers it even sadder than his own. Harry and Neville both live with their overbearing next of kin, and while Harry's aunt and uncle attempt to squash the magic out of him, Neville's grandmother is concerned he may not be magic enough. In fact, it could be said that Neville was bullied into magic.

Neville's isolation is furthered by his ignorance of the prophecy and what could have been his fate instead of Harry's. Harry's full knowledge of the prophecy's contents identifies Neville as the severed twin, and Harry is left solo to contemplate their lives in reflection. Neville and Harry's connection is solidified in *Deathly Hallows* when Harry imparts the knowledge of the final Horcrux to Neville: "Dumbledore had died knowing that three people still knew about the

Horcruxes; now Neville would take Harry's place: There would still be three in the secret" (696). Neville serves as Harry's double in this respect.

Dumbledore is also a severed twin. His twinship with Grindelwald is an example of that very common device known as "the evil twin." Similar to the Sirius/Regulus relationship, Albus Dumbledore physically resembles his brother Aberforth. Harry even mistakes Aberforth's eye for Albus's in the sliver of Sirius's broken mirror. Albus's true partner, however, was Grindelwald, who Rowling referred to as Dumbledore's "dark twin" (Anelli). Both brilliant and both looking to right wrongs against wizard kind, Dumbledore and Grindelwald are equally ready to act for "the greater good." The tragedy of Arianna's death pulls Dumbledore back from the extremes of Grindelwald's quest for power, at which point Dumbledore severs their friendship. He never ceases to recognize in himself the likeness of Grindelwald, however, and keeps himself away from too much power in the event that this darker side of himself would once again surface. The severed connection is further represented by Dumbledore's winning of the Elder Wand from Grindelwald. During their friendship, they were connected by their quest for the Deathly Hallows. The Elder Wand ends its allegiance to Grindelwald during their duel, cutting off Grindelwald from power and leaving Dumbledore to emerge as the victorious but much humbled twin.

Wands throughout the series serve as inanimate twins of the wizards and witches that wield them. Though they are objects, Rowling portrays them with the ability to choose whose power they allow themselves to channel. She revealed, "I see wands as being quasi-sentient, you know.... As close to it as you can get in an object because they carry so much magic" (Anelli). For wizard-kind this is a natural connection, and the attempt to use a wand other than one's allied wand produces less than desired results and a feeling of unnaturalness. Harry experiences this feeling with a wand Ron wins after Harry's own wand is broken in his escape from Voldemort: "The new one felt intrusively unfamiliar, like having somebody else's hand sewn to the end of his arm" (*Deathly Hallows* 392). This unnaturalness is the source of this attempted twinship's failure.

The loss of a wand in the Wizarding World is portrayed as a type of bereavement. The reader is meant to feel pity and sympathy for a wandless witch or wizard. It also represents a severing of the witch or wizard from normal magical society. As readers, we're outraged when Muggle-born witches and wizards are portrayed as thieves of "real" witches' and wizards' wands in *Deathly Hallows*. We know the prejudice towards Muggle-borns has reached a crescendo when their natural magical right to wand twinship is in question.

Rowling cultivates sympathetic feelings towards Hagrid by likewise showing him as wandless. Hagrid's status of being half-giant, which we learn of in book four, is merely a confirmation that he is not a fully accepted member of his community. Our pity for Hagrid begins in book one when it's shown that Hagrid's wand was snapped when he was expelled. The comic treatment of Hagrid's wand being hidden inside a pink umbrella mirrors his treatment by the majority of society. Hagrid's ineptitude is generally the object of laughter.

Like Hagrid, Ron is a character to be pitied because early in the series he breaks his wand. Harry and Ron have just crashed into the Whomping Willow, but the state of the car isn't Ron's first concern:

> "My wand," said Ron, in a shaky voice. "Look at my wand—"
>
> It had snapped, almost in two; the tip was dangling limply, held on by a few splinters. (*Chamber of Secrets* 74)

The Weasleys' financial status often elicits great sympathy from Harry and feelings of inadequacy from Ron. In *Chamber of Secrets*, Ron's wand is damaged but not fully broken, making it useable but not reliable, much like Ron's behavior throughout the series. His fits of jealously and self-pity make him the most volatile member of their group. Yet, in the end, Ron's loyalty wins out, and he finds new stamina and optimism, as symbolized by his replaced wand and the new wands he provides the Trio after returning in *Deathly Hallows*.

Of course, Harry's wand is the most curious in the series. Its connection with Voldemort's wand is an obvious mirroring of Harry's own connection with Voldemort through Harry's scar horcrux, and the mystery of their twin cores is a central mystery in the series, one that Rowling clearly wants us to ponder. She uses the term "twin core" eight times in *Deathly Hallows*. Like the cores, the telepathic connection that Harry and Voldemort share is one that neither of them anticipated and which Voldemort is eager to overcome. In both cases (telepathic and wand), Harry becomes aware of the connection before Voldemort. Harry realizes both connections in the first novel, but Voldemort is not aware of the core connection until book four and not aware of the mind connection until book five.

The twin core problem and Harry's and Voldemort's reactions to the connection reflect the attitudes of Harry and Voldemort to their mental connection as well. In the beginning of *Goblet of Fire*, Harry's wand is used as a beacon to announce the Dark Lord's rising strength just as, later in the novel, Harry's blood is used as an ingredient to accomplish Voldemort's resurrection. Harry accepts his wand's connection to Voldemort as a forgivable aspect of its inherent nature. Harry uses that connection and its effect to his advantage to escape Voldemort in *Goblet of Fire* and ultimately to defeat Voldemort in *Deathly Hallows*. Even though the Holly-Phoenix wand is not used in Harry and Voldemort's final duel, the two wands used both share an allegiance to Harry and thus can be said to be equivalents of the Holly-Phoenix wand. The Elder and Hawthorn wands essentially have the same connection as the Yew and Holly wands. They are both representations of a single allegiance.

Voldemort's whole attempt to gain the Elder Wand in the first place is driven by his desire to circumvent the Phoenix core connection. This desire is the reason Voldemort kidnapped the wandmaker Ollivander. Ultimately, Voldemort's desire to side-step the twin core problem leads to Harry's advantage in their final duel, much like attempting to undo the prophecy results in its fulfillment and Harry's scar horcrux, which provides their mental connection. Voldemort's use of this connection in *Order of the Phoenix,* which resulted in Sirius's death, is really the only instance of Voldemort using the link. After this instance, Voldemort uses Occlumency to block Harry and doesn't attempt to plant mental images in Harry's head again, which is quite strange given the success that Voldemort had in using it. Harry, however, easily uses the link to locate Voldemort in *Deathly Hallows*, which leads him to Snape's death scene and the answer to Voldemort's defeat. Although the idea of this infection disgusts Harry, he's still willing to use it if it will assist in undermining Voldemort, much like Harry accepts his wand despite its twin core.

Yet Harry's wand is not only a connection to Voldemort. The phoenix feather in the wand comes from Dumbledore's phoenix, Fawkes, so it also just as greatly represents a connection to Dumbledore. In *Chamber of Secrets* Fawkes represents loyalty to Dumbledore, which Harry shows greatly until Voldemort's return. In *Goblet of Fire*, Harry's wand is stolen, which foreshadows how Harry's faith in his headmaster will soon be tested. In *Deathly Hallows*, the breaking of Harry's wand mirrors his test of faith in Dumbledore. Harry's discovery of Dumbledore's earlier temptations of power makes him question his trust in his mentor's larger plan. He is even drawn to considering whether Dumbledore had any plan at all. It is at this lowest point that Harry's wand is shown broken, and Harry's situation looks similarly irreparable:

> Dumbledore had left them to grope in the darkness, to wrestle with unknown and undreamed-of terrors, alone and unaided: Nothing was explained, nothing was given freely, they had no sword, and now, Harry had no wand (351).

The incident at Malfoy Manor and Dobby's death force Harry to reconsider, and Harry chooses to trust Dumbledore again. During the escape from Malfoy Manor, Harry wins the loyalty of Draco's wand. Although "Malfoy" is French for "bad faith" (Colbert 116), Harry regains his loyalty because of this incident and the acquisition of Malfoy's wand. His faith is returned and restored.

Through this encounter with Draco, Harry simultaneously wins the allegiance of the Elder Wand, an allegiance that Voldemort clearly did not understand. When Voldemort turns the Elder Wand on Harry, the readers have been fully prepared for the final result. The refusal of the Elder Wand to destroy its own master ultimately seals Voldemort's fate. The Elder Wand then enables Harry to fully repair his original phoenix wand. Harry's first, natural wizard-wand twinship is whole once more.

What is Voldemort's great fallacy on all of these occasions? Why does he make all these mistakes that lead so pointedly to his downfall? Answering these questions ties in Rowling's framework of wholeness to the story's overarching theme. It is the natural tendency to speak of Harry and Voldemort in the realm of evil twins, but discussing them along this line leads to a greater discussion of their differences instead of putting the focus where Rowling wishes it—on their likenesses. If Harry and Voldemort can be described through likenesses, the focus narrows to their choices alone. Through the twin motif Rowling has encouraged seeing their similarities but noting their different behavior. Practiced on minor characters, this structure provides readers the tool kit with which to analyze the main characters.

While Harry's Fawkes-feather wand represents a connection with Dumbledore, given Harry and Voldemort's identical status this connection must apply to Voldemort's wand as well. Yet how can Voldemort's wand represent a loyalty to Dumbledore when Voldemort has never shown any inclination to accept Dumbledore's ideals or tutelage? The answer goes back to Dumbledore's acknowledgement of the existence and importance of choice. Voldemort had the same opportunity as Harry to choose Dumbledore's guidance, and Voldemort consistently chose to go it alone. Choice depends on an acceptance of natural duality, the existence of multiple options, but Voldemort over and over again refuses to acknowledge his natural duality. Thus, Voldemort's decision to believe the prophecy truly represents a disbelief in choice. This is Voldemort's gravest mistake. Harry, unlike Voldemort, heard the whole prophecy. Contemplating it in its entirety, Harry accepts its dual nature.

Dumbledore recognized Voldemort's weakness the first time he encountered young Tom Riddle in the orphanage, and Dumbledore felt this weakness should be shared with Harry as part of his education in fighting Voldemort:

> "...I hope you noticed Riddle's reaction when I mentioned that another shared his first name, 'Tom'?"
>
> Harry nodded.
>
> "There he showed his contempt for anything that tied him to other people, anything that made him ordinary. Even then, he wished to be different, separate, notorious. He shed his name, as you know, within a few short years of that conversation and created the mask of 'Lord Voldemort' behind which he has been hidden for so long.
>
> "I trust that you also noticed that Tom Riddle was already highly self-sufficient, secretive, and, apparently, friendless? He did not want help or companionship on his trip to Diagon Alley. He preferred to operate alone. The adult Voldemort is the same. You will hear many of his Death Eaters claiming that they are in his confidence, that they alone are close to him, even understand him. They are deluded. Lord Voldemort has never had a friend, nor do I believe that he has ever wanted one." (*Half-Blood Prince* 277)

Voldemort's great weakness is his quest for power through the embracing of unnatural singularity. This is where Harry has the upper hand, as Dumbledore informs him: "...[Voldemort] was in such a hurry to mutilate his own soul, he never paused to understand the incomparable power of a soul that is untarnished and whole" (*Half-Blood Prince* 511). This is why Fred Weasley was clearly marked as a victim, because the twins represent the exact things that Voldemort is out to destroy, that which is naturally dualistic yet whole.

Voldemort denies his own inherent duality, his half-blood status. He is disgusted with his own name, one that represents duality ("Thomas" means "twin"), yet Tom is his true identity—his wholeness. Dumbledore insists on referring to Voldemort as Tom, indicating his hope that Voldemort would return to that which is natural and whole. Harry, in his final confrontation with Voldemort, also addresses him as "Tom" (*Deathly Hallows* 738) and, in this exchange, is extending to Voldemort a final offer of wholeness. Of course, Voldemort refuses to take it. Only in the realm of horcruxes did Voldemort accept duality, but the duality that he strove for in this case was unnatural and thus an abomination.

Harry represents the strength and power of love, but most importantly, he represents what is natural and whole. He accepts his dual nature—his choices—and through that acceptance is able to maintain his wholeness while extracting the unnatural. Harry recognizes that family and friendship (natural dualities) are additions and not subtractions from one's own natural wholeness. He acknowledges the existence of choice and with this great power, Harry chooses faith. This is the core meaning of Rowling's images of twinship. Many are always greater than one. A true, natural, unified whole will always triumph over that which is unnatural and in essence, divided.

Works Cited

"Anelli, Melissa and Emerson Spartz. 'The Leaky Cauldron and Mugglenet Interview Joanne Kathleen Rowling: Part Three,' *The Leaky Cauldron*, 16 July 2005." *Accio Quote!* Web. 2 Jan. 2012.

"Barnes & Noble chat transcript, *Barnes&Noble.com*, September 8, 1999." *Accio Quote!* Web. 16 Dec. 2011.

"Barnes and Noble interview, March 19, 1999." *Accio Quote!* Web. 15 Dec. 2011.

Bulfinch, Thomas. *Myths of Greece and Rome.* New York: Penguin Books, 1981.

Print.

Colbert, David. *The Magical Worlds of Harry Potter: A Treasury of Myths, Legends, and Fascinating Facts.* New York: Berkley Books, 2002. Print.

"Comic Relief live chat transcript, March 2001." *Accio Quote!* Web. 28 Dec. 2011.

Crimmons, Julia. "Vieira, Meredith. 'JK Rowling One-On-One: Part One.' *Today Show (NBC)*, 26 July 2007." *Accio Quote!* 27 Jul. 2007. Web. 3 Jan. 2012.

Damerell, Lorie. "TLC's 'Harry Potter and the Order of the Phoenix' Press Junket Report." *The Leaky Cauldron.* 22 Jun. 2007. Web. 3 Jan. 2012.

De Nooy, Juliana. *Twins in Contemporary Literature and Culture: Look Twice.* Houndmills: Palgrave Macmillan, 2005. Print.

Eric and Melissa. "Mzimba, Lizo, moderator. *Chamber of Secrets* DVD Interview with Steve Kloves and J.K. Rowling, February 2003." *Accio Quote!* Web. 2 Jan. 2012.

Evslin, Bernard. *Heroes, Gods and Monsters of the Greek Myths.* New York: Bantam Books, 1975. Print.

"Fraser, Lindsay. 'Harry Potter – Harry and me,' *The Scotsman*, November 2002." *Accio Quote!* 12 Feb. 2007. Web. 2 Jan. 2012.

Granger, John, Colin Manlove, Amy H. Sturgis, and James W. Thomas. *Hog's Head Conversations: Essays on Harry Potter.* Travis Prinzi Ed. Allentown: Zossima Press, 2009. Print.

Granger, John. *Harry Potter's Bookshelf: The Great Books Behind the Hogwarts Adventures.* New York: Berkley Books, 2009. Print.

Granger, John. *How Harry Cast His Spell: the Meaning Behind the Mania for J.K. Rowling's Bestselling Books.* Carol Stream: SaltRiver, 2008. Print.

Granger, John. *Looking for God in Harry Potter.* U.S.A.: SaltRiver, 2004. Print.

Granger, John. *The Deathly Hallows Lectures.* Allentown: Zossima Press, 2008. Print.

Hamilton, Edith. *Mythology: Timeless Tales of Gods and Heroes.* New York: Mentor, 1969. Print.

"'Harry Potter: Everyone's Wild About Harry,' *CNN News*, 18 November, 2001." *Accio Quote!* Web. 29 Dec. 2011.

"Hulbert, Dan. Just wild about Harry: Dedicated fans of a young wizard have

Scottish scribe J.K. Rowling to thank,' *The Atlanta Journal and Constitution*, October 22, 1999." *Accio Quote!* Web. 28 Dec. 2011.

"'J.K. Rowling Interview,' *CBCNewsWorld: Hot Type*, July 13, 2000." *Accio Quote!* Web. 27 Dec. 2011.

"'JK Rowling talks about Book Four,' *cBBC Newsround*, July 8, 2000." *Accio Quote!* Web. 27 Dec. 2011.

Josee, Super Alex, and Lisa Bunker. "An Evening with Harry, Carrie and Garp: Readings and questions #1, August 1, 2006." *Accio Quote!* Web. 2 Jan. 2012.

Kronzek, Allan Zola and Elizabeth Kronzek. *The Sorcerer's Companion: A Guide to the Magical World of Harry Potter*. New York: Broadway Books, 2001. Print.

Leeming, David. *The Oxford Companion to World Mythology*. Oxford: Oxford University Press, 2005. Print.

Matthew, Roonwit, and Lisa Bunker. "Living with Harry Potter." *Accio Quote!* Print. 2 Jan. 2012.

Meann. "Viera, Meredith. 'Harry Potter: The Final Chapter' *Dateline (NBC)*, 29 July 2007." *Accio Quote!* 1 Aug. 2007. Web. 3 Jan. 2012.

"MuggleNet's Interview with John Granger." *MuggleNet*. Web. 2 Jan. 2012.

Ortiz, Meann. "Anelli, Melissa, John Noe and Sue Upton. 'PotterCast Interviews J.K. Rowling, part two.' PotterCast #131, 24 December 2007." *Accio Quote!* 28 Dec. 2007. Web. 3 Jan. 2012.

Roob, Alexander. *The Hermetic Museum: Alchemy & Mysticism*. Koln: Taschen, 2001. Print.

Rowling, J. K. *Harry Potter and the Chamber of Secrets*. New York: Scholastic Inc., 2000. Print.

Rowling, J. K. *Harry Potter and the Deathly Hallows*. U.S.A.: Arthur A. Levine Books, 2009. Print.

Rowling, J. K. *Harry Potter and the Goblet of Fire*. New York: Scholastic Inc., 2002. Print.

Rowling, J. K. *Harry Potter and the Half-Blood Prince*. New York: Scholastic Inc., 2006. Print.

Rowling, J. K. *Harry Potter and the Order of the Phoenix*. New York: Scholastic Inc., 2004. Print.

Rowling, J. K. *Harry Potter and the Prisoner of Azkaban.* New York: Scholastic Inc., 2001. Print.

Rowling, J. K. *Harry Potter and the Sorcerer's Stone.* New York: Scholastic Inc., 1999. Print.

Rowling, J. K. *Harry Potter and the Half-Blood Prince.* New York: Scholastic Inc., 2006. Print.

Rowling, J. K. "In what way is 'Harry Potter and the Half-Blood Prince' related to Harry Potter and the Chamber of Secrets'?" *J.K. Rowling Official Site.* Web. 15 Dec. 2011.

Rowling, J. K. "Professor Lupin has a twin." *J.K. Rowling Official Site.* Web. 15 Dec. 2011.

Rowling, J. K. "We learned in book six that Merope Gaunt staggered into the orphanage of New Year's Eve and gave birth to Tom Riddle 'within the hour'. Was Voldemort born on December 31ˢᵗ or January 1ˢᵗ?" *J.K. Rowling Official Site.* Web. 15 Dec. 2011.

Rowling, J. K. "What is the significance of Neville being the other boy to whom the prophecy might have referred?" *J.K. Rowling Official Site.* Web. 15 Dec. 2011.

Schoen, Spartz, Gordon, Stull, Lawrence, and Laura Thompson. *Mugglenet.com's What Will Happen in Harry Potter 7.* Berkeley: Ulysses Press, 2006. Print.

"Simpson, Anne. 'Face to Face with J K Rowling: Casting a spell over young minds,' The Herald, 7 December 1998." *Accio Quote!* Web. 15 Dec. 2011.

"Spoiler alert! Rowling discusses Harry's fate here." *USA Today.* Ed. Brent Jones. 25 Jul. 2007. Web. 3 Jan. 2012.

Thomas, James, Travis Prinzi, and John Granger. *Harry Potter Smart Talk: Brilliant PotterCast Conversations About J.K. Rowling's Hogwarts Saga.* Unlocking Press, 2010. Print.

"Treneman, Ann. 'J.K. Rowling, the interview,' The Times (UK), 30 June 2000." *Accio Quote!* Web. 26 Dec. 2011.

CHAPTER 4

The "Real House-Elves" of J.K. Rowling:

The Elfin Mystique Revisited[1]

Kathryn N. McDaniel

Near the entrance to the Ministry of Magic sits a golden fountain, we're told in *Harry Potter and the Order of the Phoenix*. A golden witch and wizard stand in the center of a pool, with the figures of a centaur, a goblin, and a house-elf arranged around them, gazing up at the witch and wizard in rapt adoration. The Fountain of Magical Brethren, as it is called, symbolizes the harmony among magical folk in the wizarding world, a harmony that is achieved through the dominant, protective leadership of humans and the grateful, obedient support of nonhuman magical creatures. But as Harry gets a closer look at the fountain on his way out of the Ministry of Magic, he sees that the "noble-looking" wizard actually appears "weak and foolish," the beautiful witch "vapid": "and from what Harry knew of goblins and centaurs, they were most unlikely to be caught staring this soppily at humans of any description. Only the house-elf's attitude of creeping servility looked convincing" (127, 156). In

---

[1] This is a revised and expanded version of "The Elfin Mystique: Fantasy and Feminism in J.K. Rowling's *Harry Potter* Series," which appeared in *Past Watchful Dragons*, ed. Amy H. Sturgis (Mythopoeic Society Press, 2007). Many thanks go to the several McDaniels who read versions of this work, as well as Amy H. Sturgis (its first champion), and John Granger and Keith Hawk whose conversation with me about the house-elves on a MuggleNet Academia podcast greatly helped my thinking about the house-elves in the final two books.

short, Harry realizes that these statues present a fiction: goblins and centaurs do not simply bow to the dominion of wizarding folk, and in believing that they do (or should) witches and wizards reveal their own foolishness.

Rowling's description of the Fountain of Magical Brethren demonstrates her recognition that not everything in her fantasy world is ideal: not the relationships among the different magical peoples, and not the wizarding world's understanding of the "reality" of those relationships. But readers of fantasy fiction often expect such imaginary worlds to be ideal worlds as well—places where the everyday problems, inequalities, and injustices of our own world are resolved. They expect to see the world as the Fountain of Magical Brethren portrays it and not as Harry actually sees it, filled with tension, discrimination, resentment, and oppression. Importantly, for the fantasy writer the reader's ability to see the flaws in the fantasy world (as they perhaps cannot in their own) may serve to highlight those aspects of the "real world" that need to be attended to and changed. Rowling, through the symbol of the fountain at the Ministry of Magic, seems to be calling on readers to identify those elements of the magical world that are not, in fact, ideal. Two strong critiques of Rowling's fantasy world focus on her depictions of female characters and the house-elves; in both instances, readers have argued that she spoils the integrity of her fantasy world by injecting real-world prejudices that undermine her central message.

Rowling's books emphasize liberal values: equality, diversity, freedom of action and freedom of thought. Thus, her tendencies to depict female characters in occasionally stereotypical ways and the images of the house-elves as "happy slaves" are not only troubling, but perhaps also fundamentally contradictory to her liberal fantasy. Significantly, Harry finds neither the gendered quality of the witch nor the subservient character of the house-elf to be counter to his own experiences, as he does when looking at the goblin and centaur. By looking at the house-elves through the lens of gender (and particularly through the lens of second-wave feminism), we can understand how Rowling's view of gender roles fits into her liberal world view. Rowling does suggest that all the peoples of her world—male and female—should be equal and free, but she is not naïve about the many difficulties in accomplishing true equality, even in the realm of fantasy. What her treatment of these issues shows is that, although she writes in the genre of fantasy, she is committed to portraying the sometimes unsettling realities of the "unfantastical" world in which her readers live.

The House-Elf Problem

The house-elves indeed create a serious problem for Rowling's liberal fantasy. Her portrayal of these magical creatures suggests that they are not only servants but slaves. Magical ties bind them and their descendants to serve their masters for all of their lives without pay, vacations, or even the right to complain about their situation. Failures to serve properly are met with harsh and sometimes arbitrary punishments. Yet, though they are arguably the most oppressed nonhuman magical creatures, house-elves, as we hear repeatedly in Books 4 and 5, are quite happy in their subservient position. Attempts to liberate them from this subjection—or to convince them that they should even desire liberation—repeatedly meet with resistance, fear and, worst of all, laughter. Is Rowling contradicting her own egalitarian themes in suggesting that there are "natural" slaves? Especially to Americans thinking of African enslavement in a country founded on liberal principles, the notion that some slaves embrace their subjugation is deeply repugnant.

But we make a mistake when we read the house-elves only in this context. Liberation is not a simple or straightforward process and often encounters reluctance from both those who enslave and those who are enslaved. There are multiple analogues for the house-elves that might prove useful for analysis: looking at them as servants, slaves, immigrants, or members of the working class, for example. But one of the most developed areas of inquiry on the complexities of liberation, and domestic liberation in particular, is feminist theory. If we think of the house-elves not as African-American slaves, but as "unliberated" women, shackled by the chains of tradition to a circumscribed role in the domestic sphere, we can perhaps understand the source of their ambivalence and thus how they fit with Rowling's larger view of the world—as it is and as it should be.

Reading the house-elves as symbolic of women generally does not require an interpretive stretch. Despite the fact that house-elves appear to be both male and female, there is actually some confusion about their gender. When Harry first meets Dobby, he thinks of him as "it," since the elf's gender is obscured by characteristics like his "high-pitched voice," androgynous apparel (a pillowcase), and the fact that he appears to be a "large and very ugly doll" (*The Chamber of Secrets*, 12-13). Winky similarly is called "it" initially, though Harry mistakes her for Dobby. Eventually, Harry comes to think of Winky as female ("though it was very hard to tell with a house-elf") (*The Goblet of Fire*, 97). House-elves, with their small stature, diminutive names, and high voices are feminized as a group.

The house-elves correspond to house-wives in many respects, including their name itself. Other magical creatures have names we recognize from traditional fairy tales and folk tales: goblins, mermaids, giants, gnomes, centaurs, trolls, and so on. But we don't have simple "elves" in the world of Harry Potter; they are, rather, *house*-elves, like "house-wives" defined specifically by their domestic role, a role in which they are the caretakers of the home, guardians of children, keepers of the family secrets. Like many twentieth-century house-wives, the house-elves are constrained within this domestic role: some like it, others do not. But no matter: they are all equally bound and equally unable to change their situations. Because of the nature of their subjugated roles, they are also separated from each other, denied a real community of their own and thus, similar to married women, "sleeping with the enemy," as has been a common phrase in the women's liberation movement.[2]

The house-elves, however, are not without power. Dobby displays the magical potential of house-elves in *The Chamber of Secrets*. Their more subtle power over the families they serve becomes evident in *The Goblet of Fire* and *The Order of the Phoenix*. Yet, as Fred Weasley says, "house-elves have got powerful magic of their own, but they can't usually use it without their master's permission" (*The Chamber of Secrets*, 28). Because of their tradition-based bondage, they do not use their powers, magical or otherwise, to gain their liberation. They are not free,

---

[2] We know from *The Goblet of Fire* that Hogwarts is about the only place that can support more than one house-elf at a time, and even there the house-elves do not appear to have their own rooms. We can infer this from the fact that Dobby seeks out the Room of Requirement for Winky to "sleep off" her drunken binges—if she had her own room, such a room would not be "required." This, of course, corresponds neatly to Virginia Woolf's argument that women need "a room of one's own" in order to develop as individuals.

but what is it, exactly, that keeps them enslaved? Their chains are invisible; they are bound by some ancient magical tradition that is never precisely identified. Many house-elves, like many twentieth-century house-wives, derive enjoyment, a sense of purpose, the very core of their identity from their service to home and family, and so have no wish to be "liberated." In fact, their freedom usually comes in the form of a "divorce" from their families that is often considered shameful, frightening—even punishment of a most severe kind. Although the house-elf Dobby, liberated from his "barefoot" status by being given a sock, finds joy in his freedom, Winky feels cast out, bereft of everything that made her useful, and so descends into butterbeer-induced alcoholism. The key similarity between house-elves and twentieth-century women rests in this problem of liberation: that it is not unequivocally desired, that it can be devastating, that it does not always seem to be a "true" liberation at all, and that many in fact derive satisfaction from their status as "helpmeet," subordinate though it may be.

Critics of the Harry Potter series have often expressed frustration (one that twentieth-century feminists would recognize) that the house-elves do not desire or even accept freedom. None, however, has examined the house-elves from this gendered perspective. Rather, they tend to view the house-elves as symbols of racial or class prejudices. For example, in "Images of the Privileged Insider and Outcast Outsider," Elizabeth E. Heilman and Anne E. Gregory suggest that the house-elves are representative of the working class and that Rowling's depiction of the house-elves "reinscribes and normalizes the marginalized status of the immigrant or dialectic speaker," thereby promoting the idea that "oppressed people can and should be satisfied with their lot" (244-245). They look at the statue of the house-elves and, like Hermione, believe that this should not be so. The house-elves' refusal to contradict this image is troubling.

Most scholars who touch on the subject of house-elf liberation view the house-elves as African-American slaves. In "Crowning the King: Harry Potter and the Construction of Authority," Farah Mendlesohn argues that Rowling has created a "world of apartheid" in which discrimination and slavery lie at the foundation of hierarchical power, and "in which the slaves are presented as happy, simple souls who merely wish to serve their families to the best of their ability" (178-179). Mendlesohn rightly finds this, and what she calls the image of the "happy darky," "difficult to accept" (178-179). She concludes that, even if the house-elves are eventually freed in the Harry Potter series, by presenting the notion that slaves may be content in their bondage, Rowling does irreparable harm to her liberal message (181). Mendlesohn's concerns reveal an unsubtle approach to the problem of liberation. Freedom is not always perceived as an absolute good, even by those who would be liberated. Rowling should not be criticized for portraying such subtleties, no matter how disturbing readers may find them. Nor should we simply accept the vision that her magical world seems to reinforce, that house-elves enjoy their slavery and that it is natural to them.

Curiously, at least one interpreter of *Harry Potter* has denied that we should be troubled by the image of the happy servant. In *The Hidden Key to Harry Potter*, John Granger identifies prejudice and tolerance as central themes in the books. But because Rowling does not depict house-elf liberation as an absolute good, Granger excludes the house-elves from those whose status should be changed. He suggests that readers should take the fact of their "creeping servility" at face value. Referring to Hermione's attempts to free the house-elves as an exercise in satire, he says, "while the house elves are nominally slaves, they are delighted in that condition congenitally" (36-37). Granger's interpretation is ultimately unsatisfying. The house-elves are not "nominally slaves"; they are in fact enslaved; they are an unfree people. This sets up a contradiction in Rowling's message which is too serious to be dismissed as a running joke in the series.

Mendlesohn, Heilman and Gregory, and others have used this contradiction as a way to demonstrate supposed fault-lines in Rowling's liberal, democratic perspective and have blamed her for such inconsistency. But all of these critics have made the crucial error of believing, like Granger, that the house-elves delight in their servitude "congenitally." There are nuances in Rowling's world that present challenges to facile ideas about liberty and equality, all of which correspond to challenges in the feminist liberation movement of the twentieth century. Yes, there are happy house-elves depicted here, ones who conform to the attitude displayed in the Fountain of Magical Brethren. On the other hand, all four of the house-elves we know as individuals—the only ones we know by name—give lie to this view: Dobby, Winky, Hokey, and Kreacher are all miserable because of their circumscribed roles, for a variety of reasons.

Free Dobby

Dobby is the first house-elf we meet in the series, and so it is worth beginning with an examination of his particular situation, which corresponds most closely to a liberal understanding of subjection and freedom. Harry meets Dobby when the house-elf appears unexpectedly in Harry's bedroom at the Dursleys'. When Harry politely invites him to sit, Dobby bursts into tears. "Dobby has *never* been asked to sit down like an *equal*—" the house-elf sobs in gratitude (*The Chamber of Secrets*, 13). Dobby understands that he is a slave "bound to serve one house and one family forever" with no chance for freedom (14). Harry asks him why he wears a ratty pillowcase, and Dobby responds, "'Tis a mark of the house-elf's enslavement, sir. Dobby can only be freed if his masters present him with clothes, sir" (177). From the little Dobby reveals of his life—most of which he must punish himself for, since he is not allowed to speak critically of his family—it is clear that he spends his time in a routine of drudgery, punished severely when he makes mistakes. He feels bound to this life, and yet he derives no satisfaction from it. He tells Harry that the young boy's defeat of Lord Voldemort years before provided hope for the house-elves, who were even more bitterly oppressed at that time, that there might be something more for them, a better life for "the lowly, the enslaved, we the dregs of the magical world!" (178). Thus, although Dobby has internalized his position as a creature without rights, he does not enjoy this position and we can see even from these small moments that Dobby would like to be free, that he deserves to be free, that he *must* be free for there to be justice in the magical world.

Dobby's liberation is a moment of triumph in *The Chamber of Secrets*. Harry tricks Lucius Malfoy—Dobby's master—into giving the house-elf a sock, and thus his freedom. Realizing that he holds in his hands the ticket to his freedom, Dobby regards it "as if it were a priceless treasure."

> "Got a sock," said Dobby in disbelief. "Master threw it, and Dobby caught it, and Dobby—Dobby is *free.*"

> Lucius Malfoy stood frozen, staring at the elf. Then he lunged at Harry.

> "You've lost me my servant, boy!"

> But Dobby shouted, "You shall not harm Harry Potter!"

> There was a loud bang, and Mr. Malfoy was thrown backward. He crashed
> down the stairs, three at a time, landing in a crumpled heap on the landing be-
> low. He got up, his face livid, and pulled out his wand, but Dobby raised a long,
> threatening finger.
>
> "You shall go now," he said fiercely, pointing down at Mr. Malfoy. "You
> shall not touch Harry Potter. You shall go now." (338)

Amazingly, the powerful dark wizard Lucius Malfoy does go. Dobby's freedom is
a victory for the side of good over the side of evil, and for the oppressed against
their oppressors. Once liberated, Dobby comes fully into his powers, powers
strong enough to challenge even the wizard's wand. He is obviously overjoyed
with his freedom. "Harry Potter freed Dobby!" he cries. Given only this view of
house-elf enslavement and liberation, it appears that Rowling's message is unequivocally liberal. Slavery is a horrific state of being, those who enslave are evil,
those who are enslaved wish nothing more than their own liberation.

The problem is that this is not the end of Dobby's story. He reappears in *The
Goblet of Fire* amid a troubling new view of the house-elves. When Harry meets
Winky, he learns from her that Dobby has had a difficult time. Dobby, it seems,
does not want to be the slave to another family; instead, he wants to be paid for
his labor. This, thinks Harry, seems reasonable. But Winky explains to him that
there is no room in the world for a free house-elf:

> "House-elves is not paid, sir!" she said in a muffled squeak. "No, no, no. I
> says to Dobby, I says, go find yourself a nice family and settle down, Dobby. He
> is getting up to all sorts of high jinks, sir, what is unbecoming to a house-
> elf. You goes racketing around like this, Dobby, I says, and next thing I hear
> you is up in front of the Department for the Regulation and Control of Magical
> Creatures, like some common goblin." (98-99)

Winky makes it clear that there is something internally, definitionally contradictory about a "free house-elf." Enjoying his independence, Dobby betrays his true
nature as a house-elf: house-elves settle down with nice families, they do not get
into trouble with the law (like goblins), and they do what they are told. This is
what it is to be a house-elf, and Dobby's liberation is dangerous, not just for him,
but potentially for all house-elves who get "ideas above [their] station" (98).

There is more going on in this passage than the politics of class differences. House-elves are tied to families, as Winky points out. Without a family,

Dobby is an oddity in a way that he was not even in his most degraded position with the Malfoys. This attitude is reminiscent of the belief some have that even an abusive marriage is better for women than spinsterhood or divorce. Moreover, Dobby cannot get a job and so is struggling economically as a result of his freedom. House-elves are not paid, Winky says, but why not? If we take a gendered perspective on the house-elves' working lives, Winky's perspective begins to make sense. A proper home is the only context for a house-elf, service to family is a house-elf's chief duty, and the domestic work of the house-elf does not warrant a salary. Each of these beliefs parallels ideas about women that gained force in the nineteenth century and remained powerful throughout the twentieth century.

These ideas originated in the context of middle-class industrial and urban development in Europe and the United States and are generally organized around the concept of "separate spheres" for men and women. Many nineteenth-century writers articulated the distinctions between the woman's sphere of home and family and the man's sphere of business and market activity.[3] Woman's domestic sphere came to be seen as a wonderful shelter from the cold realities and brutal competition of the industrial-capitalist marketplace.[4] Consequently, work done in the home could not be tied to market values (Boydston, 155-161). From this perspective, naturally, no one wants to pay Dobby for doing housework—which, for that matter, house-elves should want to do anyway since it is part of their natural role. Dobby has stepped out of his proper sphere and, as a result, he has no place to go to be free, no way to support himself in his freedom.

---

[3] There are too many to list them all, but Tennyson's *The Princess,* John Ruskin's *The Sesame and the Lilies,* and Sarah Stickney Ellis's *Women of England* provide good examples of this view. Significantly, there were many women like Ellis who upheld the notion of separate spheres.

[4] Historian Jeanne Boydston has analyzed this view in the context of the antebellum United States, pointing out that "the presumed contrast between the sexes permitted Woman-in-the-abstract to be defined as the embodiment of all that was contrary to the values of and behaviors of men in the marketplace, and thus, to the market. Against its callousness, she offered nurturance. Against its ambition, she pitted her self-effacement and the modesty of her needs. Against its materialism, she held up the twin shields of morality and spiritual solace" (155).

Other house-elves clearly share this view that housework should not be paid. Winky, as we know, finds it shameful, as do the house-elves who work at Hogwarts, which turns out to be the only place Dobby can find employment. Winky refuses payment when, cast off from her family early on in *The Goblet of Fire*, she also seeks employment at Hogwarts. She equates payment for work with the dishonor of freedom: "Winky is a disgraced elf, but Winky is not yet getting paid! . . . Winky is not sunk so low as that! Winky is properly ashamed of being freed!" (*The Goblet of Fire*, 379). Dobby (who has sunk so low as to demand wages) has had real difficulty finding a job. When Harry finds Dobby working in the Hogwarts kitchen, Dobby explains that he "traveled the country for two whole years, sir, trying to find work! . . . But Dobby hasn't found work, sir, because Dobby wants paying now!" At these words, the other house-elves look away "as though Dobby had said something rude and embarrassing" and begin "edging away from Dobby, as though he were carrying something contagious" (378).

Dobby, too, has reservations about his new-found economic freedom. He explains that when he told Professor Dumbledore he was free and wanted to be paid for his domestic labor, Dumbledore offered him "ten Galleons a week and weekends off." Dobby shudders and explains to Hermione that he persuaded Dumbledore to *lower* the salary and benefits: "Dobby likes freedom, miss, but he isn't wanting too much, miss, he likes work better" (379). When Hermione suggests to the house-elves who work in the Hogwarts kitchen that they might be free like Dobby, they react in horror. "You've got the right to wages and holidays and proper clothes, you don't have to do everything you're told—look at Dobby!" she says, linking their material independence to their individual freedom. The house-elves' friendly, gracious demeanor fades; they regard Hermione "as though she were mad and dangerous" (538-539). Even Dobby is embarrassed by Hermione's statement. He says uneasily, "Miss will please keep Dobby out of this" (538).

Despite the fact that Dobby cherishes his freedom, his experiences reveal that it is not enough to be liberated. He still must survive in this world, and the skills that he bears from his life of domestic servitude are not generally recognized as worthy of wages. Moreover, Dobby himself has qualms about his freedom. He takes pride in dressing himself in his own clothes instead of the detritus of domestic life (doilies, pillowcases, tea-cozies), but he shudders at the idea of an independence equal to that of wizards. Dobby would not know what to do with such luxury, such autonomy, such spare time. He is at this point, in a way, still trapped in the dominant view of house-elves, a view that defines house-elves as purely domestic and servile creatures. The way he punishes himself for daring to challenge the bonds of his servitude (punishments which persist even when he is free) are a clear sign of his internalization of what we might call, with a nod to Betty Friedan, the "Elfin Mystique." Dobby remains tied to this powerful image of the ideal house-elf that suggests house-elves ought to be content in the security of their domestic identity. Even though he is liberated in the most important way, he is not yet fully free.

Winky Scorned

The house-elf Winky, whom we meet in *The Goblet of Fire*, is an even more complex reminder of the ambiguities involved in liberation from the domestic sphere. Unlike Dobby, Winky does not welcome her liberation; in fact, it nearly destroys her. She was as subjugated within her family, the Crouches, as Dobby was with the Malfoys (though perhaps less abused). Yet for her freedom is no triumph of justice, but the supreme punishment. Having disobeyed Mr. Crouch, she is told, *"This means clothes!"* She begs not to be given this marker of freedom, but Crouch says coldly, "I have no use for a house-elf who disobeys me" (138-139). Winky is thus cast out of the shelter of the home and into the world. Luckily, Dobby seeks her out and together they venture to Hogwarts for employment in the only place that could support more than one house-elf and the only place where a free house-elf might find work.

But Winky does not adapt to her new role. She seems to cry all the time and is obsessed with what may be happening to her family in her absence: "My poor Mr. Crouch, what is he doing without Winky? He is needing me, he is needing my help! I is looking after the Crouches all my life, and my mother is doing it before me, and my grandmother is doing it before her . . . oh and what is they saying if they knew Winky was freed? Oh the shame, the shame!" (381). Later, when Hermione says to Ron and Harry that she thinks Winky will get over her desolation and see "how much better off she is without that Crouch man," Ron replies skeptically, "She seems to love him" (383). This doesn't sound like the devotion of a slave for her master, but rather the devotion of a wife for her husband. No matter that he was abusive and unforgiving, no matter that he abandoned her with no regard for her future welfare, Winky still feels the strong emotional ties that her service to Mr. Crouch created in her. Winky links herself to a chain of female relatives, none of whom were exiled as she has been, and feels the burden of her inability to hold on to her prescribed role.

On the second occasion the children meet Winky in the Hogwarts kitchens, she has developed a debilitating addiction to butterbeer (536). Dobby explains that she is "pining" for Mr. Crouch, whom she still considers her master. Indeed, Winky is only roused when Mr. Crouch's name is mentioned, and she soon reveals that she was not only a housekeeper for her former master, she also bore his secrets, a trust which even now she will not break: "Winky keeps—hic—her master's secrets. . . . Winky is a good house-elf—hic—Winky keeps her silence" (538). Winky's definition of a "good house-elf" is significant. In her inebriated state, she obviously does not do much housework at Hogwarts. But she is still a good house-elf because she retains her loyalty to her family. Though divorced from them through little fault of her own, she still retains her identity as the Crouches' house-elf. This is an identity that provides her with a link to the past (through her female relatives who had the same identity), a purpose in the present (through protection of family secrets), and hope for the future (through the expectation that she may yet be needed by those she served so faithfully). It is all the identity she has, and she clings to it fiercely.

The tendency has been for critics of the *Harry Potter* series to blame Rowling for displaying in Winky such passivity, such lack of independence, imagination, and spirit. Mendlesohn claims that Rowling's message appears to be "house-elves do not want freedom and servants should be kept away from alcohol: everyone knows that house-elves cannot cope on their own" (180). Granger sees in Rowling's portrayal of the elf a critique of self-indulgent grief, chiding Winky for her "paralyzing self-pity" and blaming "her hysterical and selfish way of mourning" for the deaths of the very masters she claims to love (60). But Rowling is more subtle here than her critics have discerned.

Winky's attitude is frustrating and destructive, true enough. Nevertheless, it is not at all clear that we can blame her for clinging to the "Elfin Mystique" she has absorbed, especially if we draw from the discourse of second-wave feminism. Even after women achieved the vote in most western societies, second-wave feminists believed women were still not culturally free from the bonds of domestic servitude. In *The Feminine Mystique* Betty Friedan points out what she believes to be a common pattern of over-eating, alcoholism, and drug addiction among suburban house-wives with no identity beyond the everyday routine of their domestic lives. Friedan also articulates the difficulty of relinquishing the identity provided by the Mystique: "It is not strange that women who have lived for ten or twenty years within the mystique, or who adjusted to it so young that they have never experienced being on their own, should be afraid to face the test of real work in the real world and cling to their identity as housewives—even if, thereby, they doom themselves to feeling 'empty, useless, as if I do not exist'" (252-253). Winky, still unpaid and sheltered within the domestic space of the Hogwarts kitchen, has not really dared to consider herself free. Her fear of freedom is natural, even reasonable, though not perhaps insurmountable.

The Hogwarts house-elves are embarrassed by Winky's intemperance, quickly bundling her up in a tablecloth and apologizing to the students. Hermione wonders why they don't try to cheer Winky out of her unhappiness "instead of covering her up," and she is told, "house-elves has no right to be unhappy when there is work to be done and masters to be served" (*The Goblet of Fire*, 538). Despite Winky's own feeling that she is still a good house-elf, the other house-elves see her as transgressive: not as Dobby is—his freedom is dangerous, but unlike Winky he is a hard worker. Forced into freedom as she is, Winky simply refuses to perform the domestic tasks she is given at Hogwarts. As a result, she is in a state of protest of her condition that she herself does not seem to recognize. Her depression and alcoholism in some ways constitute an even more wrenching protest than Dobby mounts against the limitations of the house-elf's role.

We discover at the end of *The Goblet of Fire* that Winky was actually very important in the Crouch household, not just for the housework she performed, but because of the way she was "keeper and caretaker" to young Barty Crouch, Jr. in his mother's absence, using her influence to get him special treats from his father, including the disastrous trip to the Quidditch World Cup. Barty explains that "she said my mother would have wanted it. She told my father that my mother had died to give me freedom" (685-686). In spite of Winky's own enslavement, she is still capable of lobbying for the freedom of others, though her love for her family makes her a poor judge of character in the case of Barty Crouch. Winky also shows the power that house-elves possess—not only her magical powers, which she uses to try to control Barty when he goes astray, but her powers of influence, which she derives from her domestic role and her substitution for Mrs. Crouch in the household. [5]

Can we blame Winky for having pride in her role in the Crouch family? Having fully internalized the wizarding community's idea of what it is to be a house-elf, Winky has no idea what she could be outside this circumscribed and subordinate position. Even though she was enslaved, she had a purpose in her life with the Crouches, she had power and influence, and she could take pride in who she was and how she served her family. Now that she is free, she has none of this. In objecting to this loss, Winky displays and protests the true insecurity and transience of the house-elf's position in the magical world. Through Winky's "bad" behavior as an exiled house-elf, and her joining a large community of house-elves, Rowling opens the door to a better life for her. But Winky will have to take the step toward true liberation for herself; by the end of the series, it is not clear whether she will ever do so. Winky's story thus illustrates the prolonged tragedy of internalizing the Mystique.

Treacherous Kreacher

The third house-elf *Harry Potter* readers come to know as an individual is as miserably constrained by the limitations of his identity as Dobby was in *The Chamber of Secrets* and as Winky is in *The Goblet of Fire*. In *The Order of the Phoenix*,

---

[5] Winky seems to parallel the kind of harmful mothering that Friedan spoke of in *The Feminine Mystique* as "symbiosis," in which parents—particularly mothers who are denied independent action outside the home—attempt to live vicariously through their children (288-305). They develop unhealthy attachments as a result that harm both themselves and the children. Winky's advocacy for Barty's freedom may be the closest she can come to asserting her own repressed desire to be autonomous. She is bound to young Barty, but if he can be free, she can perhaps share in that freedom as well.

Kreacher is the house-elf who presides over number twelve, Grimmauld Place, the former home of the Black family—who were, with the exception of the present head-of-house Sirius Black, Voldemort supporters and elitists—and the current home to the Order which seeks to defeat the revived Dark Lord. The house itself is a mess. Harry sees the mounted, shrunken heads of former house-elves hanging on the wall and hears that the presiding house-elf has "gone round the twist, hasn't cleaned anything in ages" (83).

Kreacher is a malevolent old house-elf who says whatever he thinks, no matter how racist or insulting, without seeming to realize that others can hear him. Although he hasn't been much of a housekeeper in recent years, he is in a significant way the keeper of Black family traditions. He bows low to Sirius, his present master, but he does not really respect or honor his service to this man who represents the opposite of what his former Mistress believed. "Whatever Master says," Kreacher says obsequiously and then mutters, "Master is not fit to wipe slime from his mother's boots, oh my poor Mistress, what would she say if she saw Kreacher serving him, how she hated him, what a disappointment he was—" (109). Under the guise of cleaning, Kreacher is in reality attempting to protect the remaining contents of the household from destruction by the house's new occupants. Accused of "sneaking" things out of rooms so they can't be thrown out, Kreacher grumbles, "Mistress would never forgive Kreacher if the tapestry was thrown out, seven centuries it's been in the family, Kreacher must save it, Kreacher will not let Master and the blood traitors and the brats destroy it—" (110).

In Kreacher's mad fascination with the material remains of the family he once served, he represents the kind of pathological obsession with the domestic that Simone de Beauvoir discussed in The Second Sex. Constrained within the domestic sphere, women become "queens" of this realm. Surrounded by the fabrics and furniture and knick-knacks that define the "counter-universe" in which they must live, women gradually begin to doubt the reality of that outer world, the nondomestic realm into which others may venture. They invest all of themselves, their power, their identity, into this closed material existence (Beauvoir, 449-452). Beauvoir sees a compulsion for cleaning—removing all signs of dirt and decay from the house—as the chief manifestation of this domestic obsession: "Women's fate is bound up in perishable things; in losing them, they lose all. Only a free subject, asserting himself as above and beyond the duration of things, can check all decay; this supreme recourse has been denied to woman" (602). Kreacher's reverse compulsion, his conviction that cleaning will destroy his realm, is merely the other side of this same coin. He fears the decay of the material world that comprises his existence and the existence of his beloved mistress.

As in Winky's case, Kreacher's identity is bound up in the family he serves. Yet in contrast to Winky, it is not the relationships with those family members he most tries to preserve, but the material manifestations of their existence, his domain as the domestic servant of the house. And so he vainly tries to save the tapestry bearing the family tree and a host of other objects from destruction at the hands of the "blood traitors" who stand in opposition to everything the Black family formerly held dear. His service to Sirius cannot provide continuity; only the domestic stuff which surrounds him can help keep him linked to the chain of house-elves mounted on the wall. In the absence of these household artifacts, Kreacher loses himself, his existence has no meaning, and he can see neither past nor future for himself.

Despite the fact that he is an unpleasant obstruction to the Order's work in Grimmauld Place, he cannot be freed because he knows too much about the Order's secrets. Kreacher feels confident of his continued position in the house as well; threatened with clothes, he replies, "Master will not turn Kreacher away, no, because Kreacher knows what they are up to, oh yes, he's plotting against the Dark Lord, yes, with these Mudbloods and traitors and scum . . ." (118). Kreacher, though wretched in his current state, cannot begin to contemplate freedom, and the masters he now serves cannot free him because he knows too many of their secrets. Unlike Winky, Kreacher cannot be trusted to maintain the secrets of the house if he is set free.

As it turns out, Kreacher cannot be trusted anyway. Kreacher's misery and feelings of oppression are audible each time he appears. His new master thwarts his attempts to preserve the traditions of the house at every turn. Kreacher's frustrations with his domestic impotence echo those of women which Beauvoir articulated in the mid-twentieth century:

> The heavy curse that weighs upon her consists in this: the very meaning of her life is not in her hands. That is why the successes and the failures of her

conjugal life are much more gravely important for her than for her husband . . . her work does not take her out of her situation; it is from the latter, on the contrary, that her work takes its value, high or low. Loving, generously devoted, she will perform her tasks joyously; but they will seem to her mere drudgery if she performs them with resentment. (456-457)

Care of the house—for Kreacher, not in the form of cleaning, but preserving—is the sum of his life; denied agency even in this realm, Kreacher becomes a resentful drudge. Kreacher is as conscious of his servile status, his unfree position, as Dobby was in *The Chamber of Secrets*. And like Dobby, Kreacher proves to be equally willing to bend the rules of house-elf loyalty to do what he believes is right. In doing so, he launches his own revolt against the bonds that bind him in servitude.

Kreacher essentially finds a loophole in the terms of his enslavement, a technicality through which he can leave Grimmauld Place in order to betray the secrets of his master in an indirect but significant way. This betrayal is Kreacher's great act of treachery, and because he works for the side of evil instead of the side of good, we readers, like Harry, blame him bitterly for it. Yet this is precisely the same kind of rebellious act that prepared Dobby for the exhilarating acceptance of freedom. Kreacher's treachery toward Sirius demonstrates again that house-elves have the power to create change, even if those changes are morally repugnant in the universe of the Harry Potter stories. It is also not clear that Kreacher should bear the full blame for what he has done. When Harry and Dumbledore discuss Kreacher's betrayal at the end of *The Order of the Phoenix*, Dumbledore says, "Kreacher is what he has been made by wizards, Harry. . . . Yes, he is to be pitied. His existence has been as miserable as your friend Dobby's. He was forced to do Sirius's bidding, because Sirius was the last of the family to which he was enslaved, but he felt no true loyalty to him. And whatever Kreacher's faults, it must be admitted that Sirius did nothing to make Kreacher's lot easier—" (832).

Thus Dobby, Winky, and Kreacher are all engaged in some form of protest of their oppressed and circumscribed condition. That they do not all protest in the same way, or even in productive or moral ways, reveals the complexity with which Rowling understands not just the fantasy world she has created, but the real world as her readers experience it. None of these enslaved house-elves has "delighted in that condition congenitally," as Granger observed. Each of their stories belies the open adoration the golden house-elf statue displayed in the Fountain of Magical Brethren.

Happy House-Elves

There are, however, happy house-elves in the magical world, though they are not individualized, and we know less about their particular situations. They are the house-elves who serve Hogwarts and who provide the chorus of disapproval to the idea of liberation from the traditional house-elf role. They are the ones who deny that house-elves may demand wages, that house-elves may indulge their grief, and that there is anything but shame to be had as a liberated house-elf. They are also the biggest obstacle to Hermione's attempts to gain a wider liberation for house-elves, as they seem to disprove the imperative she witnesses in Dobby, Winky, and Kreacher, that house-elves ought to be free. Contrarily, the Hogwarts house-elves also offer the greatest hope for house-elf liberation: as the only community of house-elves presented in the magical world, they have a potential collaborative power that other house-elves do not possess, isolated as they are in individual homes. Hogwarts's happy house-elves reveal the difficulty of battling deeply held cultural mores and suggest the troubling notion that some find contentment in subjugated positions. The problems of domestic liberation are most subtly portrayed through their rejection of Hermione's attempts to organize them in protest.

Hermione's encounter with Winky in *The Goblet of Fire* provides the spur for her to take action in defense of house-elves. She witnesses Mr. Crouch's cruel treatment of the poor house-elf and sees the injustice inherent in Winky's powerlessness. "You know, house-elves get a *very* raw deal!" she says to Ron and Harry. "It's slavery, that's what it is! . . . Why doesn't anyone *do* something about it?" Ron answers her by saying that the house-elves are happy and enjoy "being bossed around," to which Hermione responds, "It's people like *you*, Ron, . . . who prop up rotten and unjust systems, just because they're too lazy to—" (125). Hermione has conversations similar to this one, which are consistently interrupted, throughout the fourth book. When Hermione complains to Mr. Weasley about Winky's treatment, he tells her that, although he agrees with her, "now is not the time to discuss elf rights" (138-139). Her discovery that there are over a hundred house-elves in service at Hogwarts reveals to her that she, too, is implicated as an oppressor in this situation, and so she forms an organization designed to lobby in an overtly political way for house-elf rights. Calling her organization the "Society for the Promotion of Elfish Welfare" (S.P.E.W.), she enlists the aid of Ron and Harry to rectify the problem that the elves are "shockingly underrepresented" in the magical community (224-225). Her friends reluctantly join but have no true passion for this cause.

Everyone else whom Hermione tries to persuade to join S.P.E.W. refuses for a variety of reasons that, nevertheless, always point to the happy house-elves who seem not just content with their lot but downright thrilled with it. Ron, the Weasley twins, and Hagrid all make this argument. For Hagrid, it is simply in the nature of house-elves to "look after humans," and freeing them, even paying them for what they do, would be an "unkindness" and "insultin'" to them. Confronted with Dobby, the counter-example to all of these happy house-elves, Hagrid replies, "Yeah, well, yeh get weirdos in every breed. I'm not sayin' there isn't the odd elf who'd take freedom, but yeh'll never persuade most of 'em to do it . . . ." (265). At every turn, Hermione is met with resistance and ridicule. But this does not mean that Rowling thinks Hermione's end is either futile or foolish.

The most significant obstacle to Hermione, and the one which others repeatedly raise, is the house-elves' own happiness in their subordinate position. The Hogwarts house-elves seem to reflect perfectly the image Harry sees in the fountain. They bristle at the idea of wages, cringe at freedom, and seem most delighted when they are serving others in the domestic realm by feeding them and picking up after them. The house-elves will not join S.P.E.W. and do not appreciate that Hermione has formed this group. Faced with the failure of her political organization, Hermione hopes for their liberation by other means: perhaps they will see how gleeful Dobby is in his freedom and will want to join him (383), or perhaps they can be forced into freedom by inadvertently picking up the elf-hats that Hermione has strewn around the Gryffindor Common Room. Yet these strategies, too, do not have any measurable success. In fact, all the house-elves but Dobby refuse to continue cleaning Gryffindor Tower because they find the hats scattered about to be, as Hagrid might have predicted, insulting (*The Order of the Phoenix*, 385).

The house-elves' docility has attracted most of the criticism Rowling has faced on this issue. But the acceptance of powerlessness, the internalization of subordination, is not uncommon among marginalized groups. In *Power and Powerlessness: Quiescence and Rebellion in an Appalachian Valley,* John Gaventa has determined that quiescence often results from the "third dimension" of power, in which the dominant group manages to persuade the subordinate group that they deserve their subjected position or that their wants are identical to those of the dominant group. When severe inequalities persist, the powerless, because of their high level of dependence on the powerful, develop a "culture of silence" that prevents them from developing an "authentic voice" or even a real consciousness of their situation (Gaventa, 15-19). The house-elves, who clearly live in such a state of extreme inequality and dependence, have been manipulated by the culture of the magical world to believe that they should be happy, and therefore they reflect those attitudes which keep them in a state of bondage. They see the statue in the Ministry of Magic, they see the mounted heads of other house-elves on the wall, they see a chain of "happy house-elf" relatives extended back through history, and they believe that this is their destiny. In vain does Hermione sputter that they are brainwashed and uneducated (*The Goblet of Fire,* 239). [6] To happy house-elves, Hermione is at best misguided and condescending, at worst dangerous to their very way of life.

Quiescence has also been a problem for the feminist movement, as both Friedan and Beauvoir have explained. Recognizing the pervasive influence of

---

[6] A related point is the separation of house-elves from their own history. They are attached to the past only through models of the "Elfin Mystique," as we see in Winky's recollection of her relatives and Kreacher's connection to the house-elves mounted on the wall in 12 Grimmauld Place. Such a narrow view of the past prevents them from being able to envision a different future and helps perpetuate the idea that house-elves have always been and will always be domestic slaves. This alienation from history parallels the experience of western women. In *The Creation of Feminist Consciousness,* Gerda Lerner has argued that History has worked to prevent women from knowing of strong, independent women in past eras, and that therefore they must reinvent their liberation in successive generations without being able to build from what previous women have done before. Hermione notes the invisibility of house-elves in the history books—specifically *Hogwarts: A History,* which she thinks should be renamed *"A Highly Biased and Selective History of Hogwarts, Which Glosses Over the Nastier Aspects of the School"* (*The Goblet of Fire,* 238).

culture in shaping womankind, Beauvoir says, "One is not born, but rather becomes, a woman. No biological, psychological, or economic fate determines the
figure that the human female presents in society; it is civilization as a whole that
produces this creature" (267). Civilization dictates what woman will be, and
woman's own internalization of that idea shapes her existence. Breaking free of
these notions is a frightening proposition, as women are convinced that their
subordination gives them security. Beauvoir explains that women continue in
their subjection because it is actually easier to do so than to risk becoming
free: "Man-the-sovereign will provide woman-the-liege with material protection and will undertake the moral justification of her existence; thus she can
evade at once both economic risk and the metaphysical risk of a liberty in which
ends and aims must be contrived without assistance" (xxi). A few decades later,
Friedan writes that the "chains that bind [the suburban housewife] in her trap
are chains in her own mind and spirit. They are chains made up of mistaken
ideas and misinterpreted facts, of incomplete truths and unreal choices. They are
not easily seen and not easily shaken off" (31). Women (like house-elves) are
securely bound to their roles, but their bonds are hidden within themselves and
cannot simply be broken by an external force. In one of her most forceful metaphors, Friedan imagines the suburbs as a "comfortable concentration camp" in
which isolation, boredom, and domestic routine steadily dehumanize women,
making them dependent and passive and reinforcing the legitimacy and even
safety of their subjection (307). Women's subordination is bound up in the invisible strands of culture that pervade everyday life, and so their complete liberation is a strikingly complex process.

Both Friedan and Beauvoir critique the notion of women's happiness in their
assigned domestic roles. Beauvoir suggests that "happiness" is just a mislabeling
of stagnation and can be thus an obstacle to achieving liberation. Similarly,
Friedan says, "Surely there are many women in America who are happy at the
moment as housewives . . . but happiness is not the same thing as the aliveness
of being fully used" (155). It is not enough to be "happy"; this is not the goal of a
truly realized life. Moreover, the supposed happiness of subjugated people is not
enough to deny them independence and autonomy. Rowling, who often speaks
through the voice of Hermione, also seems to reject this idea; yet she recognizes
it for the powerful obstacle that it is. Through the Fountain of Magical Brethren

Rowling demonstrates the role of culture in promoting the image of the happy house-elf. However, at the end of *The Order of the Phoenix*, the golden fountain lies in ruins, and Dumbledore—always the voice of truth and wisdom—tells Harry, "The fountain we destroyed tonight told a lie. We wizards have mistreated and abused our fellows for too long, and we are now reaping our reward" (834).

House-Elves in Perilous Times

This shattering of the Fountain of Magical Brethren symbolizes the breakdown of the magical world upon Voldemort's return at the end of *The Order of the Phoenix*. In the final two books of the Harry Potter series, magical peoples will choose up sides and fight among themselves. The ultimate goal will indeed not be happiness, but rather the triumph of good over evil. The house-elves, too, have their valuable roles to play in this struggle and have even, these two last books reveal, already served in important ways as servants of power or resistance. Their actions during this epic struggle suggest the critical importance of true liberation and also the liberating effect that crisis can have on subjected peoples.

In *The Half-Blood Prince* readers meet a new house-elf, Hokey, who has inadvertently aided Voldemort's initial quest for power. Hokey's appearance is brief and tragic, demonstrating clearly the sad fate of a house-elf who has so thoroughly internalized her subject status that she does not even know or trust herself. We see Hokey only through her memories, collected by Dumbledore and stored in his Pensieve, then shown to Harry as Dumbledore teaches him about Voldemort's quest to create Horcruxes out of objects connected to the Hogwarts founders. Hokey is the house-elf of Hepzibah Smith, an aging collector of antiquities who falls prey to Tom Riddle's (a.k.a., Voldemort's) charms. Hepzibah's orders keep Hokey dashing about during Riddle's visit, serving tea cakes and bringing out Hepzibah's treasures, which include her two greatest possessions: Helga Hufflepuff's cup and Salazar Slytherin's locket. Dumbledore explains to Harry that Hepzibah died a mere two days later: "Hokey the house-elf was convicted by the Ministry of poisoning her mistress's evening cocoa by accident." Harry replies, "No way!" and Dumbledore agrees, but says that Hokey confessed. Harry insists that Voldemort must have modified her memory, and again Dumbledore agrees, explaining that "the Ministry was predisposed to suspect Hokey"—and Harry finishes—"because she was a house-elf." Harry then reflects that he "had rarely felt more in sympathy with the society Hermione had set up, S.P.E.W." After Hokey was convicted of the murder, Hepzibah's family discovered the cup and locket had been stolen, but by then it was too late and "that was the last that was seen or heard of Tom Riddle for a very long time" (438-439).

This is the end of Hokey's tale. But this small glimpse into her life shows us how complete her subjugation was and how damaging in the struggle between good and evil. Hokey's guilt seems clear to herself, despite the fact that even Harry, who has only seen Hokey for a few minutes, knows instinctively that she could not have poisoned her mistress, accidentally or not. This internalizing of guilt is a consistent theme of modern feminist scholarship, particularly as it relates to women's caretaking roles. Friedan acknowledged the "career woman's guilt syndrome," which caused one woman to feel responsible for her son's injury in a car accident, even though she was not present—in fact, *because* she was not present (353). In recent years a proliferation of studies about "maternal guilt" reveal it as a psychological problem to be taken seriously, one which results from a conflict between expectations of being a perfect caretaker contrasted with failures to live up to this ideal (Rotkirsch 100). Hokey's guilt then can be seen as a natural outgrowth of the Mystique, even though she is mistaken in believing herself capable of such an extreme error. Hokey's story is even more tragic than that of the other house-elves because she does not even have the self-possession to protest her condition; she does not even realize the injustice done to her. Unlike Dobby, Winky, or Kreacher, she does not act out against the Mystique in any way, and her life is forfeit as a result. Significantly, the absence of protest allows Voldemort to get away with his crime, assisting him in his quest for domination. Through her passivity and self-abnegation, through her acceptance of a kind of "maternal guilt," Hokey is thus not only a victim but also an unconscious agent for evil.

Kreacher also demonstrates the house-elf's ability to participate unwittingly in Voldemort's quest for power. In *The Deathly Hallows* "Kreacher's Tale" shows how a house-elf could be used effectively by either side of the approaching conflict. We learn that Kreacher was first summoned by Voldemort to help him take the locket—now a Horcrux—to its hiding place in the cave. Voldemort chose an elf to serve him in order to test the magical protections he had created, and so Kreacher rides with him across a sea of Inferi, drinks a basin full of poison, and then is left to perish. Much to the surprise of Harry, Ron, and Hermione, to whom he tearfully tells this story, Kreacher successfully returns to Grimmauld Place, his beloved Mistress and her son, Regulus Black. He returns because Regulus has ordered him to do so. Once Regulus understands the implications of Voldemort's actions, however, he determines to claim and destroy the locket, again enlisting Kreacher's help for the journey into the cave. This time, it is Regulus who drinks the poison, telling Kreacher to go home, keep quiet, and destroy the locket. Despite his love for his master, Kreacher leaves Regulus to die, fulfilling his orders to the extent that he can, though he finds himself unable to destroy the locket. Notably, we have Kreacher to thank for saving the locket from being disposed of during cleaning so that it may later be destroyed by Ron wielding the sword of Gryffindor.

Hermione sees Kreacher's tale quite clearly in terms of Kreacher's subject status. Voldemort's treatment of Kreacher, and his ignorance of the fact that a house-elf could Disapparate from the cave, reveal his utter contempt for house-elves and their magical powers. Harry can't understand why, given this harrowing experience, Kreacher would pass along information to the Death Eaters as he did in *The Order of the Phoenix*. But Hermione explains, "What do wizard wars mean to an elf like Kreacher? He's loyal to people who are kind to him, and Mrs. Black must have been, and Regulus certainly was, so he served them willingly and parroted their beliefs. . . . I've said all along that wizards would pay for how they treat house-elves. Well, Voldemort did . . . and so did Sirius" (*The Deathly Hallows*, 198). Subjected as he is, Kreacher has no thought for the greater good, only personal, familial loyalties. After this moment, Harry begins to treat Kreacher with kindness and respect, and as a result, Kreacher becomes an ally. He acts purely out of loyalty to Harry, though, not out of an independent understanding of what is right and good. Even as he leads the Hogwarts house-elves in the Battle of Hogwarts at the end of the book, his war cry speaks of this narrow sense of purpose: "Fight! Fight! Fight for my Master, defender of house-elves! Fight the Dark Lord, in the name of brave Regulus! Fight!" (734).

Neither Hokey nor Kreacher represents a fully liberated agent; instead, they are used by others to accomplish aims the elves themselves may not agree with. As a result, their achievements past and present, like those of the Hogwarts house-elves, are comparatively small. By the end of the series, Kreacher demonstrates the *potential* for independence and the *potential* for good, appearing on the scene as he does in the Battle of Hogwarts in a leadership position, though he is apparently back to making sandwiches in the aftermath of the great battle (749). We are uncertain, though we may be hopeful, about what his future will be.

On the other hand, Dobby, our lone example of the house-elf as a fully self-actualized agent for moral good, clearly proves in the final book the importance of his independence, courage, and goodness in his ultimate sacrifice. Called upon to help rescue Harry and others from their imprisonment in Malfoy Manor, Dobby uses his power to save multiple lives, then returns to save more. Dobby steps right into the wizards' conflict upon his return, despite the fact that he is frightened and trembling as he confronts his former masters. He drops a chandelier on the formidable Bellatrix Lestrange and disarms Narcissa Malfoy. Bellatrix rages, "How dare you take a witch's wand, how dare you defy your masters?" Instead of attesting to his loyalty to someone else (Harry), Dobby declares, "Dobby has no master! . . . Dobby is a free elf, and Dobby has come to save Harry Potter and his friends!" (*The Deathly Hallows,* 474). Having successfully saved the lives of those who have the power to defeat Lord Voldemort, Dobby is mortally wounded. Harry personally and nonmagically digs Dobby's grave and writes on his tombstone "Here Lies Dobby, A Free Elf" (481).

Dobby's sacrifice is possible because he is free, because he has no master, because he is able to think beyond the cultural expectations imposed on house-elves. This liberation must be enabled by circumstances and opportunity, but at base it can only occur from within, a revelation of one's true power to enact good in the world and a conscious decision to act on that revelation without regard for one's security or for what others might say. This existential imperative is mirrored in *The Second Sex* and *The Feminine Mystique*, as both Beauvoir and Friedan argue that women cannot be fully self-actualized, fully free, or "transcendent," until they unchain themselves from the notion of passive, obedient womanhood inculcated into them. Dobby's story also confirms the ultimate theme of Rowling's series, that the fear of death itself must be defeated to allow for the triumph of good. And so in the final books of the series, by following the house-elves into perilous times, we see that house-elf liberation is far from being a humorous side-plot or a hopeless enterprise that demonstrates the existence of "natural" slaves. Instead, it reveals Rowling's conviction that freedom, equality, and self-possession are essential for the victory of good over evil.

The House-Elf Liberation Front

At the end of the series, the readers of *Harry Potter*, like Hermione, are left in the same quandary about the house-elf situation as second-wave feminists were about the house-wife problem in the mid-twentieth century. How can those who have internalized the legitimacy of their subordination, who even derive happiness from this position, gain liberation? From the specific examples presented of miserable house-elves, and particularly from the example of the wonderfully free Dobby, it is clear that Rowling believes house-elf liberation is necessary for the growth of democracy and equality in the wizarding world. It also seems clear from the depiction of the house-elves' domestic servitude that, despite the fact that Rowling has been roundly criticized for her portrayal of female characters, she has a feminist orientation.[7] She understands the complexities of feminine liberation, however, and can acknowledge that although liberation is ideal for all creatures, not everyone will respond to it with enthusiasm. Some will deny its possibility, some will fear it, others will abuse it, still others will embrace it wholeheartedly. Many of Rowling's critics seem to wish she were more "fantastic" in depicting the world as they believe it should be and not in the full light of its real paradoxes and contradictions.

---

[7] For an example of the feminist criticisms of Rowling's female characters, see Elizabeth E. Heilman, "Blue Wizards and Pink Witches: Representations of Gender Identity and Power," *Harry Potter's World: Multidisciplinary Critical Perspectives* (New York: RoutledgeFalmer, 2003), 221-239.

Given that Rowling demonstrates a general belief in the values of tolerance, equality, respect for others, and fulfillment of individual potential, and given her nuanced yet unquestionable application of these principles to the subjugation of the house-elves, it is legitimate to wonder exactly how house-elf liberation might occur. Hermione's strategies—attempting as an outsider to convince the house-elves that they should want to be free, forming a political organization through which to invite other outsiders to support house-elf liberation, tricking house-elves into an enforced freedom—seem not only ineffective but also alienating to the house-elves. Notably, however, Harry and Ron both achieve a new consciousness of the house-elves' subjection, which has a lot to do with Hermione's advocacy through S.P.E.W. Harry feels in sympathy with S.P.E.W.'s aims after he hears Hokey's story, and Ron insists on trying to evacuate the house-elves from Hogwarts before the battle begins. "We don't want any more Dobbies, do we? We can't order them to die for us—" he says, only to be interrupted by an adoring Hermione's embrace (*The Deathly Hallows*, 625). Perhaps S.P.E.W.'s purpose is not to "raise the consciousness" of the house-elves but of wizards and witches, those in the powerful positions to effect change, so that they understand the inequalities in their world and rectify them. Such recognition of intolerance and prejudice among wizards and witches could produce real change and could promote better relationships among all magical creatures. The bitter goblin Griphook, a character necessary for locating one of the Horcruxes, is at first unwilling to help Harry because of his disgust with wizard superiority. Harry says, "This isn't about wizards versus goblins or any other sort of magical creature" to which Griphook replies, "But it is, it is about precisely that! As the Dark Lord becomes ever more powerful, your race is set still more firmly above mine! Gringotts falls under Wizarding rule, house-elves are slaughtered, and who among the wand-carriers protests?" Hermione says, "We do!" and then explains, "Did you know that it was Harry who set Dobby free? . . . Did you know that we've wanted elves to be freed for years?" (*The Deathly Hallows*, 488-489). In this sense, S.P.E.W. could in fact be effective in not only house-elf liberation, but also more generally producing tolerance and fairness in the wizarding world as a whole. As feminists have commonly said, liberation and equality for women also correlates to liberation for men. Instead of seeing the two sexes, or the groups of magical peoples, necessarily in conflict, great work can come with cooperation and the spirit of equal participation in society. [8] To facilitate house-elf liberation, the wizarding community could continue to do what Dumbledore, Hermione, Harry, and Ron have begun: recognize the lie of the Elfin Mystique; offer the house-elves wages for the work they perform; liberate the house-elves from their enslavement and grant them legal and political equality.[9]

There is no quick and easy resolution to this problem of domestic liberation, and it cannot come exclusively from above or outside. Second-wave feminism emerged in the aftermath of the first-wave movement's success in gaining women the vote, political and legal equality. But they were still not really equal, bound as they were by cultural expectations of womanhood that they themselves accepted. Consequently, mid-twentieth-century feminist authors like Friedan and Beauvoir argued that liberation is a collective and individual process that must come from within womankind. If the chorus of those happy in their subordination is to be quieted, more individuals must discover the source of their bondage and have the courage to face their own autonomy. Beauvoir explains, "When women are called upon for concrete action, when they recognize their interest in the designated goals, they are as bold and courageous as men" (602-603). We see this perhaps reflected in the Howarts house-elves' defense of the school in the Battle of Hogwarts, despite Ron's intention to evacuate them. Strangely, they do not use their magic to fight but rather "carving knives and cleavers" with which they stab at the legs of the Death Eaters (*The Deathly Hallows*, 734-735). Domestic tools related to their subjection have been turned

---

[8] Such a claim was made by nineteenth-century feminist Margaret Fuller Ossoli in *Woman in the Nineteenth Century* (1855): "We would have every arbitrary barrier thrown down. We would have every path laid open to Woman as freely as to Man. Were this done, and a slight temporary fermentation allowed to subside, we should see crystalizations more pure and of more various beauty. We believe the divine energy would pervade nature to a degree unknown in the history of former ages, and that no discordant collision, but a ravishing harmony of the spheres, would ensue" (37).

[9] J.K. Rowling in an interview said that after Hogwarts Hermione went to work for the Ministry's Department for the Regulation and Control of Magical Creatures, "where she was instrumental in greatly improving life for house-elves and their ilk." She also explained that Winky had participated with other Hogwarts house-elves in the Battle of Hogwarts ("J.K. Rowling Interview").

into bloody weapons, though they seem to make the house-elves a less effective fighting force than if the elves unleashed their full magical potential.

The house-elves' centrality to this wizards' war—and their vital roles on either side of the conflict—undermine the validity of the Elfin Mystique and demonstrate its dangers. The experience of the world wars in the first half of the twentieth century did much to raise American and European women's awareness of their political, social, and economic potential, individually and collectively. It may be that the house-elves will similarly feel empowered by their central participation, individually and collectively, in the defeat of Voldemort. We may speculate that Hogwarts might become a refuge for other Dobby-types who recognize their subjection and want freedom.

At any rate, the next generation of house-elves will now have a significant hero in Dobby, "A Free Elf," through whom they can re-envision their own possibilities. Perhaps the Fountain of Magical Brethren's image of the house-elf will be replaced with iconic statues of Dobby and other house-elves whose participation in the war made such a difference. The invisible chains of the Mystique can only be broken by the house-elves themselves, and while Rowling does not assure us that this will happen any time soon, her story compels readers to see the strength of those chains as well as the necessity of shaking them off. For those who uphold, sometimes without conscious thought, the cultural forces promoting inequality and enslavement, as well as those who internalize such attitudes for themselves, it is past time to shatter such images as those portrayed in the Fountain, whether in the magical realm or the real.

Works Cited

Boydston, Jeanne. "The Pastoralization of Housework." *Women's America: Refocusing the Past.* Ed. Linda K. Kerber and Jane Sherron De Hart. 6th ed. New York: Oxford University Press, 2004. 153-164.

De Beauvoir, Simone. *The Second Sex.* Trans. H. M. Parshley. New York: Alfred A. Knopf. 1957.

Friedan, Betty. *The Feminine Mystique.* New York: W. W. Norton and Company, Inc. 1974.

Heilman, Elizabeth E. "Blue Wizards and Pink Witches: Representations of

Gender Identity and Power." *Harry Potter's World: Multidisciplinary Critical Perspectives.* Ed. Elizabeth E. Heilman. New York: Routledge-Falmer. 2003. 221-239.

_____ and Anne E. Gregory. "Images of the Privileged Insider and Outcast Outsider." *Harry Potter's World: Multidisciplinary Critical Perspectives.* Ed. Elizabeth E. Heilman. New York: RoutledgeFalmer. 2003. 241-260.

Gaventa, John. *Power and Powerlessness: Quiescence and Rebellion in an Appalachian Valley.* Chicago: University of Illinois Press. 1980.

Granger, John. *The Hidden Key to Harry Potter.* Hadlock, WA: Zossima Press. 2002.

Lerner, Gerda. *The Creation of Feminist Consciousness: From the Middle Ages to Eighteen-Seventy.* New York: Oxford University Press. 1993.

Mendlesohn, Farah. "Crowning the King: Harry Potter and the Construction of Authority." *The Ivory Tower and Harry Potter: Perspectives on a Literary Phenomenon.* Ed. Lana A. Whited. Columbia: University of Missouri Press. 2002. 159-181.

Ossoli, Margaret Fuller. *Woman in the Nineteenth Century.* Freeport, New York: Books for Library Press. 1972.

Rotkirch, Anna. "Maternal Guilt." *Evolutionary Psychology.* 8:1. 2009. 90-106.

Rowling, J. K. *Harry Potter and the Chamber of Secrets.* New York: Scholastic Press. 1999.

_____. *Harry Potter and the Deathly Hallows.* New York: Scholastic Press. 2007.

_____. *Harry Potter and the Goblet of Fire.* New York: Scholastic Press. 2000.

_____. *Harry Potter and the Half-Blood Prince.* New York: Scholastic Press. 2005.

_____. *Harry Potter and the Order of the Phoenix.* New York: Scholastic Press. 2003.

_____. "J.K. Rowling Interview." *The Deathly Hallows Web Chat.* MuggleNet. July 2007. www.mugglenet.com/jkr/interviews/dh-webchat.sthml

Westman, Karin E. "Specters of Thatcherism: Contemporary British Culture in J. K. Rowling's Harry Potter Series." *The Ivory Tower and Harry Potter: Perspectives on a Literary Phenomenon.* Ed. Lana A. Whited. Columbia: University of Missouri Press. 2002. 305-328.

CHAPTER 5

When Gothic Meets Comic:

Exploring the Ghosts of Hogwarts Castle

Kelly Orazi

As a series largely concerned with the crossing of physical and spiritual boundaries, J.K. Rowling's Harry Potter novels naturally play host to a number of supernatural spirits and liminal beings. From Voldemort, who occupies a physical space but never a wholly spiritual one, to the many thinking and talking—but never living—portraits that line the walls of Hogwarts, Rowling's supernatural beings inhabit a world between life and death. Some of the most significant liminal characters in the Harry Potter series are the ghosts of Hogwarts castle. These spiritual beings are all in some way between life and death; they are neither "here nor there" as Nearly Headless Nick puts it.[1] While Rowling herself has said that death "is one of the central themes in all seven books,"[2] the ghosts' significance to the Harry Potter series as a whole can be easily overlooked. Ghosts like Sir Nearly Headless Nick and the Grey Lady may reside in the background of Hogwarts, but as prevalent and accessible inhabitants of the in-between world, they have a profound influence over Harry's developing attitude towards death.

The nature of Rowling's ghosts in the *Harry Potter* series is complex, as their liminal status is twofold: not only are they textually in between life and death, but

---

[1] J.K. Rowling, *Harry Potter and the Order of the Phoenix* (New York: Scholastic Inc. 2003), 861.

[2] Malcolm Jones, "Why Harry's Hot," *Newsweek,* July 16, 2000, accessed 11 May 2012, http://www.newsweek.com/why-harrys-hot-162001.

they are also in between two literary conventions. By their nature, ghosts are deeply rooted within the Gothic tradition. The ghosts of Hogwarts, however, are friendly, ubiquitous, and comical and thus do not often evoke the traditional terror of the Gothic. To explore the ghosts' unique role throughout the series then, we must turn to the first tradition Rowling is pulling from: the Gothic. Originating in the mid 18th century, Gothic literature became popularized in works like Horace Walpole's *The Castle of Otranto*, Ann Radcliffe's *The Mysteries of Udolpho*, and Mary Shelley's *Frankenstein*. Traditional Gothic literature features

> accounts of terrifying experiences in ancient castles — experiences connected with subterranean dungeons, secret passageways, flickering lamps, screams, moans, bloody hands, ghosts, graveyards, and the rest. By extension, it came to designate the macabre, mysterious, fantastic, supernatural, and, again, the terrifying.[3]

Gothic stories almost always include what Ann Tracy, author of *Patterns of Fear in the Gothic Novel*, calls "superficial trappings"[4] like ghosts, castles, and flickering candles. In *Harry Potter's Bookshelf*, John Granger states, "Gothic stories are usually set—obviously enough—in a Gothic manor or castle...probably a ghost or two will show up eventually."[5] In the Harry Potter series, the Hogwarts castle is teeming with touches of this Gothic scenery. In fact, Harry's contact with the Gothic happens almost simultaneously with his first arrival at the school. When Harry approaches Hogwarts he sees a "vast castle with many turrets and towers"[6] and once inside, he notices that its "stone walls were lit with flaming torches."[7] Only moments later, "pearly-white and slightly transparent"[8] ghosts glide through the

---

[3]"The Romantic Period: Topics," *Norton Anthology of English Literature*, accessed March 10, 2015. http://www.wwnorton.com/college/english/nael/romantic/topic_2/welcome.htm

[4] Ann Tracy, *Patterns of Fear in the Gothic Novel, 1790-1830* (Ayer Publishing, 1930), Travis Prinzi, "Story Shapes: Grotesque," *The Rabbit Room*, last modified October 17, 2011, http://www.rabbitroom.com/2011/10/righteous-horro/

[5] John Granger, *Harry Potter's Bookshelf* (New York: Berkeley Publishing Group 2009), 73-74.

[6] J.K. Rowling, *Harry Potter and the Sorcerer's Stone* (New York: Scholastic Inc. 1997), 111.

[7] Ibid., 113.

[8] Ibid.

walls of the Great Hall to greet Harry. From the very first moment he steps foot in Hogwarts, then, Harry is immediately and deeply immersed within a traditional Gothic setting.

Gothic touches such as the ones we see in Hogwarts are meant to foster what Tracy calls "nameless fears" and "familiar anxieties."[9] While a large, poorly lit castle may not be a frightening aspect in and of itself, such a setting is perfect for producing the essential atmosphere of fear in a Gothic novel. This is a type of fear that is distinguished from something merely momentarily scary. For instance, a loud noise in an otherwise quiet moment produces only a brief moment of fear followed by a sigh of relief. Instead, fear in the Gothic tradition is centered on the unknown. It is something that, as Granger states in *Harry Potter Smart Talk*, "heightens all of your senses, makes you aware of who you are and what you're all about."[10]

This type of terror plays a significant role throughout the Harry Potter series. Even as early as the *Sorcerer's Stone*, Harry has a memorable Gothic encounter when he first meets Voldemort in the Forbidden Forest:

> Harry had taken one step toward it when a slithering sound made him freeze where he stood. A bush on the edge of the clearing quivered…Then, out of the shadows, a hooded figure came crawling across the ground like some stalking beast. Harry, Malfoy, and Fang stood transfixed. The cloaked figure reached the unicorn, lowered its head over the wound in the animal's side, and began to drink its blood.[11]

The type of "nameless fear" Harry experiences here is fundamentally Gothic. Harry becomes paralyzed and completely aware of his surroundings as he watches an enigmatic—but deeply frightening—scene unfold. The dead unicorn and the beastly, yet human-like figure drinking its blood evoke subtle, familiar anxieties of purity, death, and dehumanization.

---

[9] Granger, *Bookshelf*, 73.

[10] Tracy, quoted in John Granger, Travis Prinzi, James Thomas, *Harry Potter Smart Talk* (Unlocking Press 2010 Kindle eBooks), location 687, paragraph 30.

[11] Rowling, *Sorcerer's Stone*, 256.

At the heart of this paralyzing fear is, in fact, death. As Granger states, "it makes you more sensitive to the way you think about death which...is the hallmark and point of the Gothic."[12] When the protagonist of a Gothic novel encounters this sort of terror, death and its immediacy become emphasized. No type of Gothic encounter does this more than the supernatural one. Meetings with ghosts blur the lines between the worlds of the living and the dead. In *The Gothic Imagination*, scholar Linda Bayer-Berenbaum states, "Gothicism insists that what is customarily hallowed as real by society and its language is but a small portion of a greater reality of monstrous proportion and immeasurable power."[13] The spirits and ghosts of the Gothic both awaken our fear in the unknown and bring us closer to understanding a greater reality than our own.

The ghosts of Hogwarts, however, have a rather complex relationship with the Gothic. Harry's first encounter with them briefly hints at their Gothic nature:

> Then something happened that made him jump about a foot in the air—several people behind him screamed...He gasped. So did the people around him. About twenty ghosts had just streamed through the back wall...they glided across the room talking to one another and hardly glanced at the first years.[14]

The ghosts not only add to the Gothic setting of the castle, but also seem to strike a chord of fear of their own. It's no surprise that Harry, who has grown up in a Muggle household, should be alarmed at seeing ghosts. But the narrator makes sure to note that many of Harry's schoolmates are startled as well. Even to many of the first-years who are already familiar with the wizarding world (and are thus probably familiar with ghosts as well) the ghosts' appearance nonetheless strikes a natural, nameless fear.

The following moment, however, complicates this would-be Gothic scene; for there doesn't seem to be anything actually frightening about the Hogwarts ghosts. In fact, the students seem to momentarily alarm *them*. Nearly Headless Nick is busy talking to the Fat Friar until he "suddenly notices" the first years and

---

[12] Granger, Prinzi, Thomas, *Smart Talk*, location 686, paragraph 30.

[13] Linda Bayer-Berenbaum, *The Gothic Imagination* (New Jersey: Associated University Press, Inc. 1982), 21.

[14] Rowling, *Sorcerer's Stone*, 115.

interrupts himself, asking, "—I say, what are you all doing here?"[15] Harry and his fellow first-years put their guard up for the Gothic encounter but soon realize that it is quite unnecessary. The Fat Friar even welcomes them to school and wishes them well, excitedly stating, "Hope to see you in Hufflepuff! My old house, you know."[16] The ghosts, despite evoking an initial fear, do not instill the lasting, slow-building fear of the Gothic. Instead, they are helpful, friendly, and eager to get along with the students.

If the heart of the Gothic fear is the unknown, then the Hogwarts ghosts do not seem to be fully Gothic. The ghosts and the students often have open discourse. The students may not know exactly what the ghosts are, but they are always able to ask questions and receive answers in turn. One of the first things Harry and his fellow first-years do is ask Nick the very personal question of, "how can you be *nearly* headless?"[17] Despite taking slight offense to such a direct question, Nick answers by demonstration. He even freely gives personal details of his beheading to Harry in *Chamber of Secrets*, stating that he got "hit forty-five times in the neck with a blunt axe."[18] In addition to developing a personal relationship with some of the ghosts of Hogwarts, every student is actually required to have open (if not personal) discourse with a ghost: the History of Magic class is taught by Professor Binns, a long time Hogwarts teacher, who also happens to be a ghost.

Thus the Hogwarts ghosts far from add to the atmosphere of fear. But Rowling even goes one step further—the ghosts are not only harmless, but they are also comical. As Harry's relationship with Nick grows in *Chamber of Secrets*, he attends his deathday party where he meets numerous ghosts that reside outside of Hogwarts. Here, readers are invited to laugh not only at Harry, Hermione, and Ron's awkwardness of being surrounded by ghosts, but also at the ghosts' attempts to embrace death and fearsomeness. For instance, we know that Nick is not intimidating or very frightening. But it soon becomes clear that among *other* ghosts, Nick feels the need to prove that he is indeed quite fearsome. He asks

---

[15] Ibid., 115.

[16] Ibid., 116.

[17] Ibid., 124.

[18] J.K. Rowling, *Harry Potter and the Chamber of Secrets* (New York: Scholastic Inc. 1999), 123.

Harry, "Do you think you can possibly mention to Sir Patrick how *very* frightening and impressive you find me?" [19]The deathday party makes it clear that the ghosting community either wants to or feels a duty to be frightening and macabre. The ghosts embrace nicknames like "the Wailing Widow,"[20] dance to an orchestra that sounds like "a thousand fingernails scraping an enormous blackboard,"[21] and put out plates of "large, rotten fish" and "maggoty haggis."[22] Even Nick, despite obviously having a good time, puts on a mournful demeanor to his ghostly guests.[23] As a whole, the deathday party is a ritual to celebrate and embrace death. But it is clear that the ghosts have to go to great lengths to embrace death in a Gothic manner.

Although the ghosts are likeable and at times laughable, they should not be mistaken for a full parody of the Gothic. They may be slightly mocking of the genre, but what Rowling does is distinguishable, as scholar Amy Sturgis states, "from the way that, say Jane Austen did, with *Northanger Abbey*...Rowling is much more playful than that, lovingly playful."[24] In *Northanger Abbey*, Catherine Morland has read so many Gothic novels that when she gets invited to spend time at the Abbey, she quickly imagines herself as the heroine of a traditional Gothic novel, suspecting terror and deceit at almost encounter. But in the end she realizes it was "all a voluntary, self-created delusion."[25] The closest Rowling gets to this sort of parody is with Harry's obsession with the Grim in *Prisoner of Azkaban*. But Rowling also uses the Gothic very seriously (particularly in *Prisoner of Azkaban*). Sturgis suggests that Rowling "tends to be on the whole more serious about the Gothic than playful or critical."[26] Though Rowling's ghosts have a distinct humor throughout the series that continually makes light of their Gothic roots, the humor never actually rises to a full parody the genre.

---

[19] Ibid., 130.

[20] Ibid., 135.

[21] Ibid., 131.

[22] Ibid., 133.

[23] Ibid., 136.

[24] Granger, Prinzi, Thomas, *Smart Talk*, location 754, paragraph 26.

[25] Jane Austen, *Northanger Abbey* (Project Gutenberg. 1816. Kindle eBooks), location 2528, paragraph 1.

[26] Granger, Prinzi, Thomas, *Smart Talk*, location 736, paragraph 26.

Thus the ghosts, hovering somewhere between being frightful by nature and comical in character, have a unique influence over Harry throughout his time at Hogwarts. Although they may be more silly than scary in Harry's first few years at Hogwarts, the end of *Deathly Hallows* takes the ghosts and their Gothic role very seriously. In the middle of the chaotic battle of Hogwarts, Harry turns to the Ravenclaw ghost for help in finding the diadem-turned-Horcrux. Harry stops to listen to the Grey Lady, whose lost diadem is wrapped in a Gothic romance story:

> "He tracked me to the forest where I was hiding. When I refused to return with him, he became violent. The Baron was always a hot-tempered man. Furious at my refusal, jealous of my freedom, he stabbed me."
>
> "The *Baron*? You mean—?"
>
> "The Bloody Baron, yes...when he saw what he had done, he was overcome with remorse. He took the weapon that had claimed my life, and used it to kill himself. All these centuries later, he wears chains as an act of penitence."[27]

In his whole time at Hogwarts, Harry has never known this about the Grey Lady and the Bloody Baron. Even Nearly Headless Nick has "never bothered to ask"[28] about the stains of blood on the Bloody Baron's robes. This is exactly what makes this moment so crucial. The Grey Lady's story makes us re-examine the ghosts of Hogwarts; their deaths, their reasons for becoming ghosts, and what it means to be ghosts all become essential to understanding their role in the series.

In the beginning of the series, the ghosts are presented as more alive than dead. After all, they do more than just walk and talk: they participate in Hogwarts events, they have their own celebrations, they recollect their former lives, and they seem to maintain their personalities. Except for having no actual physical bodies, the ghosts seem alive and human. This is at least, how Harry views them during his first five years at school. But after Sirius dies at the end of *Order of the Phoenix*, Harry truly faces death. He has difficulty accepting that Sirius is actually gone: "He did not believe it, he would not believe it...Sirius was hiding, simply

---

[27] J.K. Rowling, *Harry Potter and the Deathly Hallows* (New York: Scholastic Inc. 2007), 616.

[28] Rowling, *Sorcerer's Stone*, 124.

lurking out of sight—"[29] Even a bit later, after Harry has accepted the fact that Sirius has died, he turns to Nick in desperation:

> "You died, but I'm still talking to you…. You can walk around Hogwarts and everything, can't you?"

> "Yes," Nick said quietly, "I can walk and talk, yes."

> "So you came back, didn't you?" said Harry urgently, "People can come back, right? As ghosts. They don't have to disappear completely."[30]

The ghosts have been so "alive" that Harry has not really stopped to think of them as quite dead. He never really considered why anyone would not want to stay behind as a ghost because he never gave too much thought to why anyone might want to die. But at the end of *Order of the Phoenix*, Harry must ultimately rethink what death—and what escaping death—truly means. There must be a reason why there aren't more than twenty ghosts roaming around Hogwarts. It could be that many, like the Bloody Baron, punish themselves to ghost-hood as a sort of penance. Others, like Nick, could be merely afraid of death. Others still may lack faith in the world of the dead.[31] No matter the case, it is clear that becoming a ghost is an unpopular choice for a reason. Nick states, "I know nothing of the secrets of death, Harry, for I chose my feeble imitation of life instead."[32] It becomes clear that the ghosts, having chosen *not* to move on, are neither living nor dead. Their state, as it turns out, is worse than either.

Thus the ghosts are not frightening because they have died, but because they represent the inability to move on after death. Throughout the series, Dumbledore repeats "there are things much worse than death."[33] It has always seemed that this idea was directed at Voldemort and (as we later find out) his creation of Horcruxes. It is entirely possible, however, that Dumbledore also had in mind the

---

[29] Rowling, *Order of the Phoenix*, 807.

[30] Ibid., 860.

[31] Professor Binns is a possible example of this. His refusal to believe in anything other than what he can see in front of him, of "solid, believable, verifiable *fact*" (*Chamber of Secrets,* 152), may have led him to become a ghost.

[32] Rowling, *Order of the Phoenix*, 861.

[33] Ibid., 814.

ghosts. Travis Prinzi states that the Gothic involves "wanderings, temptations, and delusions."[34] Who does this describe more so than the ghosts? Tempted by life after death, the ghosts now roam the mortal wizarding world, wishing for death or else deluded they are still alive.

Harry's conversation with Nick in *Order of the Phoenix* is the first moment he truly examines death. It is also ultimately his first step in accepting death. In *Deathly Hallows*, we learn that becoming the master of death does not mean to become immortal, but rather to accept death. But Harry does not, and perhaps cannot, accept death until he understands the price anyone—not just Volde-mort—pays in denying it. The ghosts of Hogwarts have been exemplary in this from the moment Harry first arrived at Hogwarts. They illustrate that one *does not have to be evil to fear death*. It is easy to turn to Voldemort, who murders others to stay alive, as an example of the wrongness of escaping death. The ghosts are an example of that same wrongness, but they instead show the fears of the ordinary witch or wizard. They are never directly compared to Voldemort, but their unwillingness to move on stems, like Voldemort's, from their fear of death. This is part of the reason the ghosts are at first made out to be more comical than fearsome.

As Harry grows to like them, particularly Nick, he is more easily able to both pity them and relate to them. Nick admits to Harry, "I was afraid of death … I chose to remain behind. I sometimes wonder whether I oughtn't to have."[35] This is perhaps the clearest moment in which the ghosts illustrate how important is it to accept death. Harry learns that wizards who choose to escape death through magic end up having a "feeble imitation of life"[36] rather than an extension of it. Throughout the Harry Potter series the ghosts of Hogwarts do more than simply add to the comedic and Gothic tones of the series. By being liminal characters that are both in-between two worlds and in-between two literary conventions, they open up the dialogue on what it means to die and ultimately broaden Harry's understanding of death. From knowing the Hogwarts ghosts, Harry can accept and perhaps even appreciate death.

---

[34] Travis Prinzi, *Gothic Tales and Other Mysteries—Hog's Head Pubcast,* Podcast audio, October 7 2011, accessed May 2012.

[35] Rowling, *Order of the Phoenix,* 861.

[36] Ibid., 861.

Works Cited

Austen, Jane. *Northanger Abbey*. Project Gutenberg, 1816. Kindle eBooks.

Bayre-Berenbaum, Linda. *The Gothic Imagination*. New Jersey: Associated University Press, Inc. 1982.

Granger, John. *Harry Potter's Bookshelf*. New York: Berkeley Publishing Group. 2009.

Granger, John. Prinzi, Travis. Thomas, James. *Harry Potter Smart Talk*. Unlocking Press, 2010. Kindle eBooks.

Jones, Malcolm. "Why Harry's Hot." *Newsweek Magazine*. July 16, 2000. Web 11 May 2012. http://www.newsweek.com/why-harrys-hot-162001.

Prinzi, Travis. *Gothic Tales and Other Mysteries—Hog's Head Pubcast*. iTunes Podcast, accessed May 2012.

---. "Story Shapes: Grotesque." *The Rabbit Room*, last modified October 17, 2011, http://www.rabbitroom.com/2011/10/righteous-horro/

Rowling, J.K. *Harry Potter and the Sorcerer's Stone*. New York: Scholastic Inc. 1997.

---. *Harry Potter and the Chamber of Secrets*. New York: Scholastic Inc. 1999.

---. *Harry Potter and the Order of the Phoenix*. New York: Scholastic Inc. 2003.

--- *Harry Potter and the Deathly Hallows*. New York: Scholastic Inc. 2007.

"The Romantic Period: Topics." *Norton Anthology of English Literature*. Accessed March 10, 2015, http://www.wwnorton.com/college/english/nael/romantic/topic_2/welcome.htm.

CHAPTER 6

The Dark Lord's Descent:

How Voldemort Falls from Soul to Body as a Result of Reverse Alchemy

Rochelle Deans

The language of alchemy has been a staple of English literature for hundreds of years, stretching back to the days of Chaucer. Its colors and symbolism translated well to the world of books. However, unlike many symbols, which have static meaning, alchemy's purpose in literature has transformed on numerous occasions. While recent forays into literary alchemy by such authors as C.S. Lewis, J.R.R. Tolkien, and even Suzanne Collins have used what John Granger calls "traditional" symbolism,[1] in the Harry Potter series J.K. Rowling brings alchemy back to its oft-forgotten roots in satire in the character arc of Tom Riddle.

Alchemy itself, as a science and an art form, has been around for thousands of years in cultures across the world. However, the use of alchemy in fiction began during the Middle Ages. Most people point to Chaucer's *Canterbury Tales* as the first finite example of alchemy in literature. In the beginning, "alchemy in literature" just meant "a story involving an alchemist."

Stanton J. Linden, author of several books about alchemy and editor of the journal *Cauda Pavonis: Studies in Hermeticism,* explains that alchemists homed in on "the process from decay to growth, from death to resurrection" as a way to

---

[1] John Granger, *Unlocking Harry Potter: Five Keys for the Serious Reader* (Wayne, PA: Zossima Press, 2007), 52.

relate to Christ's death, burial, and resurrection through the transmutation of metals.[2] They were interested in turning lead into gold and creating the Philosopher's Stone for which the first Harry Potter book is named. The process involved three main stages: the black stage, called the Nigredo, the white stage, the Albedo, and the red stage, the Rubedo. Alchemy was not only intended to bring riches and eternal life to the alchemist. Even in failing, it was a way of relating to the death, burial, and resurrection of Jesus Christ.

In early alchemical literature, though, not all alchemists were considered good, and not all were after the spiritual benefits of identifying with the risen Lord. In fact, much early alchemical literature is satirical, invoking alchemists not as "good guys" to be emulated, but the "bad guys" to be avoided. "Alchemy is splendidly equipped to represent moral transformation and transmutation," writes Linden, "sometimes from evil to good, but also, in works belonging to the satirical tradition, *from good or potential good to evil.*"[3]

According to Frances Yates, it doesn't matter whether alchemy is used for personal gain or religious—the methods are the same. However, in literature, when alchemy is used for a perverse purpose, the typical method, working from lead to gold, from black to white to red, is reversed. Granger notes in *Unlocking Harry Potter* that the whole of alchemy can be summed up in Titus Burckhardt's words: "to make of the body a spirit and of the spirit a body."[4] The second part of this phrase quite literally sums up the first four books of the *Harry Potter* series— from the perspective of Tom Riddle.

The work from good or potential good to evil, from spirit to body, is typical in sixteenth-century uses of alchemy as satire. In fact, it was so common that a "stereotype emerges, according to which the complexities of the art [of alchemy] are reduced and simplified to the point where it is viewed as little more than a crude form of deception; its practitioners came to be universally known as cheats and imposters."[5] On the stage, having an alchemist in the play was a kind of shorthand for a quick laugh, perhaps in a similar way to slapstick lawyer jokes today.

---

[2] Stanton J. Linden, *Darke Hieroglyphicks: Alchemy in English Literature from Chaucer to the Restoration* (Lexington, KY: University Press of Kentucky, 1995), 9.

[3] Ibid., 24. Emphasis added.

[4] Granger, *Unlocking Harry Potter*, 51.

[5] Linden, 63.

This version of the alchemist was a far cry from the later works that evoked alchemy to transform a character's soul and create a cathartic experience within the audience as they related to the protagonist. But it was out of these satirical ashes that John Donne, George Herbert, and William Shakespeare rose. They were among the first to see alchemy's potential as symbolism for change and growth rather than just stock comedy. Donne and Herbert especially "tend to use alchemy with an understanding of...its potential in meeting the intellectual, spiritual, and imagistic demands of the metaphysical poetry they were creating."[6]

These three poets likely drew on an underappreciated aspect of Chaucer's *Canterbury Tales*, especially the Yeoman's tale. While Chaucer's use of an actual alchemist in a storyline was common by Shakespeare's day, the Yeoman's story actually also uses alchemy as symbolism. But in his story, it is not a movement from coarse to pure. In fact, "The Yeoman's seven years of apprenticeship have been an exercise in futility. He has lost all the money he ever possessed and is now deeply in debt for money borrowed; he reiterates the transformation that his appearance has undergone, *a kind of reverse alchemy from 'freesh and reed' to leaden.*"[7]

John Donne uses this reverse process in his poems "Twicknam Garden" and the "Nocturnall."[8] There is even an example of literal reverse alchemy in the story *[An Historical Account] of a Degradation of Gold Made by an Anti-Elixir: A Strange Chymical Narative*, where, as the title suggests, gold is transmuted into lead via an anti-elixir.[9]

In *Harry Potter*, Rowling combines the satire of reverse alchemy with the sacred process of literary alchemy, using traditional satire to highlight a spiritual process: the Dark Lord's descent. If there is anyone who did *not* want to identify with the death, burial, and resurrection of Jesus, it's Tom Riddle. Death, after all, is his biggest fear, and Jesus is love personified; Rowling makes it clear that Tom has no grasp on the concept of love. The sacred process of alchemy requires the alchemist to be in a holy state of mind or it will not work: "Because alchemy is an

---

[6] Ibid., 155.

[7] Ibid., 47. Emphasis added.

[8] Ibid., 181.

[9] Ibid.

'art of purification,' it follows that the presence of things of 'leprous nature' will retard the process, whether they exist in base metals or in the adept himself."[10] In the case of Tom Riddle, no one can doubt that he is an adept. As Ollivander says, Tom has done "Great things. Terrible things, but great." [11]However, he certainly has things of "leprous nature" inside of him.

In George Starkey's seventeenth-century alchemical *Pyrotechny*, Starkey, aware of the caricatures of alchemy in literature, presented "The Character of a Praeposterous search after Natures secrets." This character is the "deluded adept" common in alchemical satire: "His pride inspires him only to the highest ends, but incapable of attaining them for reasons of impatience and contempt for requisite training and preparation, '...resolving to appear nothing, unless he may equal the highest, he lives all his life in obscuritie, care, and anxiety.'"[12] This quote, while referencing *Pyrotechny*, applies surprisingly well to Tom Riddle. When he couldn't obtain the Philosopher's Stone to bring himself back to life, he resolved to remain a spirit, searching for a way to be what he considered the highest form—a human body. Alchemy has no place for him, but he pursues it anyway. All his attempts to achieve greatness via alchemy end up working in reverse, and dissolve him from spirit to lead in a four-book alchemical process.

We know only a few key things about Voldemort's life before the books open. He rose to power in the 1970s, spread fear throughout Britain, and felt threatened by the imminent birth of a baby. He had created his first Horcrux years before his rise to power, and most likely intended to create his last with Harry's death. This backfired and his body died, leaving him as merely a maimed soul.

Although much of this backstory wasn't revealed until *Half-Blood Prince*, this pre-story gives many hints of the reverse alchemy to come. The point of alchemy for the alchemist is the movement from body to spirit and from spirit to body. Here, before the story begins, Voldemort moves from body to spirit. For our corrupt alchemist, however, the remaining soul is broken, torn because of the murders he had committed. In alchemical terms, this cursed life was the closest Voldemort ever got to perfection, since alchemical perfection is the attaining of

---

[10] Ibid., 80.

[11] J.K. Rowling, *Harry Potter and the Philosopher's Stone* (London: Bloomsbury, 2010 edition), 65.

[12] Linden, 30.

an eternal spirit from an imperfect body. While Rowling does mention Tom briefly sharing the bodies of animals, Rowling's focus in the narrative is on his lack of body. This "perfection" lasted between October 1981 and the death of his soul-host, Quirinus Quirrell in 1992.

In traditional alchemy, there is both a subject and an object. The subject, a human, works on the object, lead, to transform the lead into gold and him- or herself into a better person. In literature, the alchemist is a mentor and the object is usually the protagonist. For instance, in Harry's alchemical process[13] in books five, six, and seven, Dumbledore is the alchemist and Harry is the object. He consciously shapes Harry from volatile teenage boy to a man willing to sacrifice himself for what is truly the greater good.

Voldemort, however, does not have the same alchemist for the entire process. He has three: Quirinus Quirrell in book one, Lucius Malfoy in book two, and Wormtail in book four. Since Voldemort works through the stages backwards, his first alchemist, Professor Quirrell, aligns with the Rubedo in *Harry Potter and the Philosopher's Stone*. He is host to Voldemort's tarnished soul, feeding on unicorn blood in order to sustain it, acting as the body that pursues the literal Philosopher's Stone.

Like the many black/white/red symbols in books five, six, and seven, respectively, alchemical imagery is not lacking in the first four books. William Sprague, in a guest post on HogwartsProfessor.com, points out many of these connections as they relate to Harry.[14] My interest in expanding his research involves how these symbols apply to Voldemort.

There are hints in Quirinus Quirrell's name that point to the Rubedo. Quirinus is an ancient Roman god of war, predating Rome's adoption of the Greek gods. While there is no direct connection between the gods Quirinus and Mars, Quirinus's popularity died out when Greek gods became popular, which makes

---

[13] Harry's alchemical process is well documented by John Granger on his website (www.hogwartsprofessor.com) and in his books *How Harry Cast His Spell, Unlocking Harry Potter: Five Keys for the Serious Reader,* and *The Deathly Hallows Lectures.*

[14] William Sprague, "Guest Post: The Connection of Ring Composition and Literary Alchemy in the Layout of the Seven Book Harry Potter Series," Hogwarts Professor, August 20, 2011, accessed January 26, 2015, http://www.hogwartsprofessor.com/guest-post-the-connection-of-ring-composition-and-literary-alchemy-in-the-layout-of-the-seven-book-harry-potter-series/

Mars Quirinus's indirect replacement. Not only is Professor Quirrell an instigator in the second wizarding war, his name invokes the name of the *red* planet. Quirrell, while as much of a nonsense word as Quidditch, sounds similar to the word *quarrel*, strengthening the war/red planet connection.

At the end of *Philosopher's Stone*, Voldemort says, "See what I have become?... Mere shadow and vapour.... I have form only when I can share another's body."[15] From where his alchemical journey began after attempting to murder Harry, he has dropped from being "mere" spirit—the goal of traditional alchemy—to sharing a body with another. This is a step down in the transformation process, like going from gold to silver.

Like the bleeding colors between the last three books (to gray between black and white, to pink between white and red), the colors bleed in reverse in the first four books. In the main fight scene between Quirrell and Harry, the transition from red to white begins, with the colors shown in the face of Voldemort himself: "[His face] was chalk white with glaring red eyes and slits for nostrils, like a snake."[16]

This blending of colors brings us to *Chamber of Secrets*, the most obviously alchemical book of the first four in the series. In this book, Voldemort finds his alchemist in Lucius Malfoy. "Lucius Malfoy (a white haired, pale fellow) is the initiator...; the reverse Alchemist is wicked."[17] His looks are an obvious match for the Albedo, and he instigates the events of *Chamber of Secrets* by putting the diary in Ginny's bag before school started. While he has no interaction with Voldemort or Tom Riddle's memory during this time, Lucius's presence is felt throughout, as his son, Draco, plays a large role in the book, and he returns at the end.

In traditional alchemy, the Albedo represents the purity of the object as it becomes closer to gold and further from lead. One of its main symbols, and one central to the second Harry Potter book, is water. The chamber itself is accessed via a faucet in a bathroom, and the inside is wet like a sewer. As Sprague points

---

[15] Rowling, *Harry Potter and the Philosopher's Stone*, 213.

[16] Ibid., 212.

[17] Sprague.

out, "the water that is present is the means by which the serpent moves. The water itself is impure as a result."[18]

While the typical Albedo stage is about inner purity, this definitely isn't a part of young Tom Riddle's journey through the book. However, purity is—or at least was—one of his goals. In his final confrontation with Harry inside the Chamber of Secrets itself, Tom says, "Haven't I already told you that killing Mudbloods doesn't matter to me anymore?"[19] The most important word in this sentence is the last one. The purity of Hogwarts was, then, Tom Riddle's original goal. Instead of seeking *inward* purity through his own perfection and becoming more Christlike, he sought *outward* purity by ridding his school of all Mudbloods.

Midway through the book, Ginny understands the danger of the Diary and tries to get rid of it: "A great flood of water stretched over half the corridor, and it looked as though it was still seeping from under the door of Moaning Myrtle's bathroom."[20] There are many methods Ginny could have chosen for destroying the Diary. The one she chooses? Flushing it down a toilet. It only takes a quick thought regarding the size of plumbing to note that even in a magical school this probably wasn't the best idea. The toilet seemed to agree and regurgitated the book, causing the flood mentioned above. The Diary was "washed out" again. This flushing and regurgitation serves as a crude and backwards baptism into the waters of the pipelines that provide the Basilisk's path through the school.

The Diary makes two other interesting appearances with regard to flooding. The first is when Harry's book bag gets ink spilled all over it: "All his other books were drenched in scarlet ink. The diary, however, was as clean as it had been before the ink bottle had smashed all over it."[21] The books were soaked with this ink, but the diary itself absorbs the liquid and shows no sign of it. Later on, when Harry finally destroys the Horcrux-holding Diary, the book is the one to *create* the flood, perhaps regurgitating all the ink it had absorbed: "Ink spurted out of the diary in torrents, streaming over Harry's hands, flooding the floor."[22] Tom's

---

[18] Ibid.

[19] J.K. Rowling, *Harry Potter and the Chamber of Secrets* (London: Bloomsbury, 2010 edition), 230.

[20] Ibid., 171.

[21] Ibid., 179.

[22] Ibid., 237.

soul, through the Diary, has been baptized into his impure ways, and through the Diary's power, Tom has become memory-made-flesh, which is even closer to his eventual goal of reincarnation.

Harry Potter and the Prisoner of Azkaban is the only book that doesn't involve Voldemort in its plot. Instead, its story is setup for the plot of *Goblet of Fire*, which is a key turning point for Voldemort just as much as or more than it is for Harry. In *Prisoner of Azkaban*, we have two hints as to what is to come. The first is the Dementors, who are a perfect symbol for the Nigredo, with their darkness, despair, and the chill they bring to those around them. Sprague notes that "Dementors are black beings that play a sort of reverse Nigredo on the object of their kiss: they take away *everything except the body*."[23] The second is Peter Pettigrew, the alchemist in *Goblet of Fire* and arguably the most important alchemist of the series.

Voldemort in his present-day form is absent from both *Chamber of Secrets* and *Prisoner of Azkaban*. The last we saw him, he was thrown out of Quirinus's dying body and escaped into the world as a soul. Since Rowling does not draw attention to Voldemort's second life as just-soul, this state has little significance to the story and does not affect Voldemort's on-page transformation from soul to body. Indeed, he has spent this interim period securing his important alchemist in Wormtail.

Peter Pettigrew has few concrete connections to the Nigredo. Unlike Sirius, a main alchemical symbol in *Order of the Phoenix*, Pettigrew's name has no connection to black, and he has neither the black hair nor the fiery personality of the friend he once framed. However, Wormtail is also the most straightforward of the three reverse alchemists. He is the one who performs the spell that returns Voldemort to his body. Like Harry is nurtured at the very beginning of his journey, Wormtail nurtures Voldemort at the very end of his.

When *Goblet of Fire* opens, we find out the whereabouts of Voldemort, not Harry. Rowling decides to start the crux of the Harry Potter series with a baby-like creature, a rat, and a snake in Little Hangleton. Voldemort is pleased with Wormtail's work in getting him a rudimentary body (yet another step closer to

---

[23] Sprague, emphasis in original.

his leaden incarnation), and tells him he will have a task for his "faithful servant" that the rest of his followers would give their *right hands* to do.[24]

On the surface level, of course, this is simply foreshadowing for what will happen in the graveyard during the climax. It is also proof that Voldemort knew exactly what he was doing, and what spell they were preparing for. If he didn't, he would have used the common expression, to give one's right *arm*. He knew the end game, and Wormtail was a pawn to get him there. He even tells Harry near the end of the book that his search for alchemical meaning had reversed: "There was no hope of stealing the Philosopher's Stone any more...but *I was willing to embrace mortal life* again, before chasing immortal."[25]

Harry hadn't seen or heard from Voldemort himself in three years by the time the Dark Lord says that line. For Tom Riddle, the storyline from the summer of 1992 to the summer of 1995 is summed up in the above quote. The Philosopher's Stone was destroyed, Quirrell was dead, and he spent the next two years searching for a way to get a body of his own. By the time Wormtail finds him in the summer of 1994, he has discovered a method for doing so and guides Pettigrew in the process of creating the ugly, baby-like creature he had become.

At the end of *Prisoner of Azkaban*, Professor Trelawney predicts that "the Dark Lord will rise again with his servant's aid, greater and more terrible than ever before...."[26] The beginning of the prediction depicts Voldemort as "alone and friendless, abandoned by his followers."[27] This description is indicative of the Nigredo.

Like a typical Nigredo, Voldemort will rise from this state. But instead of rising out of it into a higher state of being, he rises *into* it, taking on Nigredo-made-flesh. Because he chooses to rise via incarnation during a Black Mass, he does not rise into a purer state of being, but a cruder one. It isn't *his* blood, *his* flesh, or *his* bone that make up his new body. His reincarnation isn't a purer form of himself; instead, it's a crude representation of the human body, torn apart by his soul-

---

[24] J.K. Rowling, *Harry Potter and the Goblet of Fire* (London: Bloomsbury, 2010 edition), 15. Emphasis added.

[25] Ibid., 569. Emphasis added.

[26] J.K. Rowling, *Harry Potter and the Prisoner of Azkaban* (London: Bloomsbury, 2010 edition), 238.

[27] Ibid.

splitting actions, and stitched together, Frankenstein-like, with physical elements stolen from others.

In fact, this Black Mass is the pinnacle of the series, and it is brimming with alchemical imagery from beginning to end. In just a few pages, the creature Wormtail created becomes a man, and Rowling spends a lot of time describing the event. Many of her descriptions center on color and other typical alchemical symbols such as water and darkness. The symbolism moves backward through the stages of alchemy, one at a time. Voldemort begins as an ugly, unformed thing, a mix between the Nigredo (first) and the Rubedo (last) stages:

> The thing Wormtail had been carrying had the shape of a crouched human child, except that Harry had never seen anything less like a child. It was hairless and scaly-looking, a *dark, raw, reddish black*. Its arms and legs were thin and feeble, and its face – no child alive ever had a face like that – was flat and snake-like, with gleaming red eyes.[28]

Here, Rowling presents us with a raw creature, as would be expected at the beginning of an alchemical work. But instead of a raw black, which would convey the symbolism of the Nigredo, Voldemort is a raw red, with red eyes. He is, in this sense, the imperfect, failed Philosopher's Stone. As Harry stares at the thing in the cauldron, he wishes nothing more than to let it drown, appropriate symbolism for the Albedo stage. The thing does not drown, though.[29] Instead it turns a "burning red," bright enough for Harry to see through closed eyes. This further represents the reverse Rubedo.

Wormtail then collects Harry's blood to add to the potion. Harry's red blood is added to the "burning red" solution and "the liquid within turned, instantly, a blinding white."[30] As noted in relationship to *Chamber of Secrets*, Rowling often uses nonsensical descriptions and actions (such as Ginny flushing the Diary) in ways that truly only make sense within the framework of alchemy. This red plus red equals white description is an apt example.

---

[28] Rowling, *Harry Potter and the Goblet of Fire*, 555-556. Emphasis added.

[29] Ibid., 556.

[30] Ibid., 557.

Wormtail's Black Mass continues, combining other people's body parts into the mixture in order to resurrect his master: "The cauldron was simmering, sending its diamond sparks in all directions, so blindingly bright that it turned all else to velvety blackness."[31] While the potion here does remain white and shining like diamonds, the next color Rowling introduces is a velvety blackness, one that represents the Nigredo, right as Tom Riddle rises again.

The anti-Mass, this evil alchemist's ultimate potion, physically goes through the colors of alchemy in reverse. When the incarnation is complete, Lord Voldemort returns in black robes, white skin, and red eyes.

As Sprague notes, "The reverse process is completed when Voldemort is incarnated, and the true Alchemy (books 5-7) results in his final destruction."[32] While Sprague is adept at tying alchemy to ring composition and noticing the colors prominent in the first four books, his theory reaches fuller potential when connecting this reverse alchemy with Voldemort's journey, rather than Harry's. The first four books of the Harry Potter series take Tom Riddle from spirit to body, from gold to lead, in a way that brings to mind the satirists who first used alchemy in literature. Rowling's artistry, however, goes beyond simply an attempt to poke fun at corrupt alchemists. By using Tom Riddle as Harry's doppelganger, she could contrast the process of alchemy as it was used for evil versus how it was used for good.

As much as Voldemort was interested in alchemy for evil purposes, he did not intend to go backwards through the stages. Just as he never understood the true power of the Deathly Hallows and focused his attention on the Elder Wand, he never understood the true power of alchemy. He sought eternal life via alchemy, first intentionally through attempting to steal the Philosopher's Stone, and then unintentionally as he completed the alchemical stages in reverse, thinking that resurrecting his body and possessing Horcruxes would be enough to keep him alive indefinitely.

Unlike early alchemists who searched for something positive—a connection with their Savior, eternal life in him, a purer spirit, or even riches and fame, like the alchemists who were satirized—Tom instead sought to protect himself from

---

[31] Ibid.

[32] Sprague.

what he feared. Creating a new body in which to house his mangled soul could prevent his death. Tom's alchemy was motivated not by desire but by fear.

If Voldemort were to treat his soul and its eternal properties with the reverence souls deserve, he would have understood that eternal life is only achieved through death. By privileging body, his goal could never be attained. Voldemort's only desire was to protect his own life, and it was his attempt to protect it (via Horcruxes and his unintentional reverse alchemy) that cost him his life in the end. Conversely, Harry was willing to sacrifice his life for the sake of others, and because of this, he was able to keep it. The two characters perfectly illustrate Matthew 16:25: "For whoever wants to save his life will lose it, but whoever loses his life for me will find it."

CHAPTER 7

The Second War was Won On the Quidditch Pitch of Hogwarts:

Quidditch as a Symbol Set in the *Harry Potter* Narrative[1]

Emily Strand

> *I cordially dislike allegory in all its manifestations, and always have done so since I grew old and wary enough to detect its presence. I much prefer history, true or feigned, with its varied applicability to the thought and experience of readers. I think that many confuse "applicability" with "allegory"; but the one resides in the freedom of the reader, and the other in the purported domination of the author.*
>
> *J.R.R. Tolkien, The Fellowship of the Ring (Foreword to the Second Edition)*

In J.K. Rowling's *Harry Potter* series, the dominant sport among witches and wizards is Quidditch: the game from Queerditch Marsh.[2] The game is played on broomsticks; two teams of seven players each score points with the Quaffle, avoid beatings by Bludgers, and cheer on each team's Seeker as he or she tries to catch the Golden Snitch. The game, a product of the author's imagination, is charmingly quixotic, but its impracticality points to the possibility that Quidditch may be something more than a cultural adornment on the story world, dreamed up by a less-than-sport-savvy author. Rather than perennially frustrating us, the quirks of Quidditch could instead send us searching for the

---

[1] Many thanks to early readers of this text: Jessica O'Brien and Amy Sturgis. I am also grateful to the editors and to John Granger and Kelly Orazi for suggestions which greatly enhanced the text.

[2] J.K. Rowling, *Quidditch Through the Ages* (New York: Scholastic Press, 2001), 7.

sport's "applicability," as Tolkien called it in the passage above: the way in which Quidditch resonates not simply with the thought and experience of readers, but with the larger narrative of the Harry Potter series itself. The search for Quidditch's applicability may well reward the diligent Seeker by shedding light on important truths about the series' characters, their overarching goals, and how they attain them.[3]

The Problem with Quidditch (and its Solution)

Quidditch is an exhilarating sport. Rowling created a game for her magical community that possesses all the features fans want in a popular sport: fast-paced action, suspense, drama, and … four balls to keep track of? Two almost totally separate spheres of play, one of which seems disproportionately consequential? However well Quidditch functions to flesh out the culture of Rowling's magical world, many Muggle readers and reviewers struggle with this quirky game. Harold Bloom, in his infamous review of the series, calls the sport "bizarre"[4] and A.S. Byatt deems Quidditch one "caricature" among many in the series.[5] Even apart from these and other higher-than-thou-brow literary voices, average readers also have a hard time with the game. A simple Google search of the phrase "Quidditch doesn't make sense" yields, alarmingly, more than 2 million results. Many are blog posts and comments whose authors grumble fluently about nearly everything Quidditch-related. In a post on the humor site *Cracked* dated July 14, 2009, Chris Bucholz likens Quidditch to a game of American football, with the addition of two guys playing tetherball in the middle of the field. *11 Points* blogger Sam Greenspan complains, on March 8, 2011, that Quidditch both is too visually difficult for spectators to follow, and requires equipment too complex and specified

---

[3] N.B.: This study does not suggest that Quidditch as a sport does not have an important function in the narrative; it is, on a basic, literal level, an effective cultural adornment of Wizarding and especially Hogwarts culture and, at this literal level, lends interest, character development and suspense to the narrative. But this study hopes to show that Quidditch functions symbolically in the narrative as well. This is not to say that every Quidditch-related event or reference in the text has symbolic meaning.

[4] Harold Bloom, "Can 35 Million Book Buyers Be Wrong? Yes," *Wall Street Journal*, 11 July 2000, A26.

[5] A.S. Byatt, "Harry Potter and the Childish Adult," *New York Times*, 7 July 2003, A13.

to permit amateur play. Tony Manfred on *Business Insider* calls Quidditch "the dumbest sport ever," arguing that "Quidditch is not a team sport, it's an individual sport masquerading as a team sport" (July 15, 2011).

This perceived over-emphasis on the role of the Seeker in Quidditch is a common thread running through many critiques of the fictional sport. Even Steve Vander Ark, creator of the *Harry Potter Lexicon*, admits on the site's blog that the point reward for catching the Snitch is "crazy" and "doesn't make sense" (June 17, 2014). Readers seem to feel this pervasive frustration with Quidditch most acutely with regard to the strangely consequential action of catching the Golden Snitch, which both ends the game and adds 150 points to the score of the successful Seeker's team. This means that, in certain cases, catching the Snitch will cause the triumphant Seeker's team to *lose* the game, if they trail their opponent by more than 150 points. This inauspicious event in fact occurs in the series at least once: during the Quidditch World Cup in *Harry Potter and the Goblet of Fire*.[6] This pitfall of the Quidditch scoring system may be what Rowling was referring to when she told *The Telegraph* that Quidditch "infuriates men."[7] It may infuriate men, but its quixotic scoring system seems to confound Muggles regardless of gender. This is evidenced by a key adaptation to Quidditch by real-world Muggles for collegiate play; in the official US Muggle Quidditch rulebook, version 8.2, while catching the Snitch still ends the game (except in the event of a tie), the point value of the Snitch-catch has been reduced from 150 to 30 points.[8]

In the same *Telegraph* article in which Rowling admits to the infuriating potential of Quidditch, she also says: "I had been pondering the things that hold a society together, cause it to congregate and signify its particular character and knew I needed a sport."[9] This information points the discerning reader to a

---

[6] J.K. Rowling, *Harry Potter and the Goblet of Fire* (New York: Scholastic, Inc., 2000), 113-114.

[7] Hannah Furness, "J.K. Rowling invented Quidditch after a row with her boyfriend," *The Telegraph*, 18 May 2013, accessed 11 July 2014. http://www.telegraph.co.uk/culture/books/10065868/JK-Rowling-invented-Quidditch-after-a-row-with-her-boyfriend.html. Rowling says this maddening aspect of Quidditch (for men, apparently) satisfies her since she invented the game after quarreling with her then-boyfriend.

[8] US Quidditch Rule book, Eighth Edition, Second Version, http://www.usquidditch.org/about/rules/. Accessed on 19 September 2014.

[9] Furness, "J.K. Rowling invented Quidditch after a row with her boyfriend."

deeper *sense* in Quidditch. It is not necessary for Quidditch to make perfect sense as a workable sport because it serves a larger purpose in the story world of *Harry Potter*; Quidditch *signifies the particular character* of the Wizarding world. The sport signifies the character of Rowling's magical world in at least three key ways. Firstly, it is played on broomsticks: that stereotypical symbol of witches and wizards, held over from medieval Muggle suspicions and old wives' tales. Secondly, in Quidditch, the play is rough, the game is fast-paced and, because played in flight, necessarily dangerous. This portrays the character of life in the magical community; at least as it is represented in the seven Harry Potter books, there is never a dull or "safe" moment in this universe. Lastly, at the same time, Quidditch play—and the life of the magical community which it signifies—is a thrilling, fulfilling and unique experience. It is in this world-signifying sense that Dumbledore, in his forward to *Quidditch Through the Ages*, says of the sport:

> Anyone who plays or watches Quidditch regularly will relish Mr. Whisp's book, as do those of us interested in wider wizarding history. As we have developed the game of Quidditch, so it has developed us…[10]

While Quidditch works well as a general emblem of life in the Wizarding world, this understanding of the game does not exhaust Quidditch's symbolic power in the series. To extract more meaning out of Quidditch as a symbol (or even a symbol set) in the *Harry Potter* world, we must contextualize the series within the tradition of the British School Days novel. This genre enjoyed enormous popularity in the UK and elsewhere, beginning with Hughes' *Tom Brown's School Days* in 1857, even up until the early 1940s, when paper rationing during the Second World War proved an obstacle to the stories' continued dissemination in popular boys' weeklies.[11] The genre initially gained popularity due in part to the universality of its subject matter among its readership, and also to its many resonant conventions, which make story after story within the genre feel comfortable to the reader. The genre is tied tightly to notions of the British Empire, and especially the British "public" school system, which was entrusted with the training and formation of future bureaucrats, who would prop up the Empire

---

[10] Rowling, *Quidditch Through the Ages*, vii.

[11] Susan Hall, "School Ties, House Points, and Quidditch," in *Harry Potter and History*, ed. Nancy R. Reagin (Hoboken, NJ: John Wiley & Sons, Inc., 2011), 214.

across many lands, over many generations. Scholar Susan Hall states, "the purpose of the Muggle public schools during the nineteenth and early twentieth centuries was to create and nurture a ruling elite."[12] But this seminal part of the story of the British Empire was told from the inside out: from small to great, that is, from the point of view of the students, not the bureaucrats they would become, or even the teachers who ruled over them. The British School Days novel (or chapter, episode, interlude, etc.) tradition was a genre that celebrated—and, for some authors, helped to process—the intense, glorious, painful and usually exilic experience of acquiring an education.

The role of sport in the British School Days story was important, and this helps explain why Rowling knew she "*needed* a sport" for the Wizarding world; she must have known by that point that what she was writing was, in large part, a British School story. Hall says sport in British public schools was an important means of class elevation, pressuring students to abandon more common sports played at home (such as British football) and conform to school sports such as rugby and cricket.[13] James Gunn adds to this understanding an emphasis on morality as expressed in sport in the British public school tradition. In novels like *Tom Brown's School Days*, morality emerged from team sports, and the values one learned through sport were essential in shaping the English gentleman.[14] Interestingly, Potter expert Amy H. Sturgis adds that sport in the School Days tradition miniaturized the world of politics, war, and leadership thereof which awaited the student after school, serving as a training ground for service to the Empire.[15] So, claims Sturgis, when Lucius Malfoy buys his son a place on the Slytherin Quidditch team by purchasing the whole team new top-of-the-line broomsticks in Harry's second year, this is not simply a lesson that money can buy power and position in the world of Quidditch, but that this principle operates in the larger world as well, for better or worse. It is this world-imitating reality of sport in the British public school tradition (and its immortalization in novels

---

[12] Ibid., 196.

[13] Ibid., 204-205.

[14] James Gunn, "Harry Potter as School Days Novel," in *Mapping the World of Harry Potter*, ed. Mercedes Lackey (Dalla, TX: Benbella Books Inc., 2005), 147-148.

[15] Amy H. Sturgis, "Rowling and the British School Story," (lecture presented as part of LL511a "Taking Harry Seriously" course for Mythgard Institute, Summer 2014).

like *Tom Brown's School Days*) that fueled the popularity of the famous quote, attributed to the Duke of Wellington: "The Battle of Waterloo was won on the playing fields of Eton."[16]

Thus it seems that solving the "problem" of Quidditch—its quirky rules and somewhat illogical scoring—is a matter of thinking of Quidditch not as a mere sport in the Wizarding world, but as a unique training ground which effectively prepares the characters for life in the Wizarding community, and their particular roles therein. As Dumbledore put it in *Quidditch Through the Ages*, Quidditch "develops" the players in particular ways. Moreover, the reader can readily forgive the quixotic nature of Quidditch and deepen his or her understanding of the text by appreciating what Tolkien would call the *applicability* of Quidditch: not simply to the world outside the novel (though its lessons resonate there as well), but to the larger story line *within* the books. Quidditch is an important symbol system that both prefigures and reflects the important events that will lead to the defeat of Voldemort and his Death Eaters, and the roles main characters will play in bringing about these events.

The Symbolic Function of Quidditch

In Shakespeare's *Hamlet*, the main character stages a play which, he supposes, tells the true story of his father's murder, so that he may "catch the conscience" of his uncle, the new king.[17] Without reproducing the scheming and mockery of Prince Hamlet's play, Quidditch echoes this dramatic miniaturization of the larger plot of the *Harry Potter* series in its rules, player positions and even equipment. It is something akin to Hamlet's "play within a play." However, in Quidditch, the game's miniaturization of the story world does not recreate past events, but offers insight into contemporary situations in the story, and at times prefigures events yet to come.

---

[16] Ibid., also referenced in Hall, "School Ties, House Points, and Quidditch," 193. There is some legitimate doubt that the Duke of Wellington actually made this statement, including the fact that he hated his time at the school and during it there were no playing fields at Eton.

[17] William Shakespeare, *Hamlet*, Act 2, Scene 2.

The rules. Seven players make up a Quidditch team. Seven is a significant number in many cultures; in the Judeo-Christian tradition it symbolizes spiritual perfection. Even an underage Tom Riddle understands something of the number seven's great significance to witches and wizards when he asks Slughorn: "I mean, for instance, isn't seven the most powerfully magical number...?"[18] Perhaps most importantly, however, the story of Harry Potter unfolds in seven volumes, or over seven years of Harry's life. All these factors combine to suggest that having seven players on a Quidditch team was not an arbitrary choice by the author.

The sport's structure of play is also important symbolically. In Quidditch, there are two "spheres" of play, with little overlap. In one sphere of play, the Chasers try to score goals against the Keepers. In the other sphere of play, each team's Seeker searches for the Golden Snitch. The Bludgers create the overlap between the two spheres; they may harass either Seekers or Chasers, and, consequently, the Beaters may be called upon to protect either or both positions. This reality of two spheres of play which overlap only at certain times is an expression of the two spheres of action throughout the Harry Potter series: the Trio's sphere (which becomes Harry's sphere) and everyone else's. From the Trio's obsession with the Sorcerer's Stone and their *sans*-adult adventure to rescue it in Book 1, to Harry, Ron and Hermione's long exile hunting for Horcruxes in Book 7, in each book the Trio works discreetly to resolve the conflict, and at some point toward the end, Harry has to act alone. This "two spheres of play" reality, of which Quidditch play is a strong emblem, is most pronounced in *Harry Potter and the Deathly Hallows*. In this final book, the Trio is wholly removed from the rest of society, alone and in exile in their hunt for Horcruxes, while, in the other sphere of play, points are scored on either side of the fight against Voldemort (that is, between the Order of the Phoenix and Voldemort's Death Eaters).

Harry and his friends cannot participate in this other sphere of play, however; Dumbledore has given them a task and they must stick to it, because everything is riding on it. The all-important nature of the task of the figurative Seeker in the narrative (Harry/the Trio) is represented by the high number of points awarded to the one who catches the Golden Snitch. 150 points can help a team snatch an

---

[18] J.K. Rowling, *Harry Potter and the Half-Blood Prince* (New York: Scholastic Inc., 2005), 498.

un-looked-for victory out of the depths of their Quidditch despair; they could be down by 140 points (or 14 goals) and yet win if they catch the Snitch. No matter the score in the war against Voldemort, Harry and his friends, in their hunt for Horcruxes, have the power to end the game—the power to win it all—if only they can find and destroy the Horcruxes. Alternatively, if the Seeker catches the Snitch too late for the resultant points to clinch the win for that Seeker's team, then the Seeker's moment of triumph means little. But as Harry reflected on Krum's Snitch-catch at the Quidditch World Cup, catching the Snitch remains a moment of dignity for the Seeker and those he represents: "'He knew they were never going to catch up!' Harry shouted back over all the noise, also applauding loudly. 'The Irish Chasers were too good.... He wanted to end it on his terms, that's all....'"[19]

The players. This idea which Harry expresses—the importance of the freedom and dignity of the Seeker, even in the face of defeat—is an important lesson for Harry as a Seeker: not just as the Seeker of the Gryffindor Quidditch team, but as the Seeker of Voldemort's Horcruxes. It also provides a window of insight into how the player positions within Quidditch are applicable to the characters in *Harry Potter* and their various roles in the war against Voldemort. Witnessing Krum's Quidditch World Cup decision helped to prepare Harry for an important revelation about his own freedom as the Horcrux Seeker in *Half-Blood Prince*:

> But he understood at last what Dumbledore had been trying to tell him. It was, he thought, the difference between being dragged into the arena to face a battle to the death and walking into the arena with your head held high. Some people, perhaps, would say that there was little to choose between the two ways, but Dumbledore knew—*and so do I*, thought Harry, with a rush of fierce pride, *and so did my parents*—that there was all the difference in the world.[20]

And later, as Harry walks to the Forbidden Forest to lay down his life before Voldemort, it is without bitterness that he thinks: "The long game was ended, the Snitch had been caught, it was time to leave the air..."[21] This reference to

---

[19] Rowling, *Goblet of Fire,* 114.

[20] Rowling, *Half-Blood Prince,* 512.

[21] J.K. Rowling, *Harry Potter and the Deathly Hallows* (New York, Scholastic Inc., 2007), 698.

Quidditch shows, in true British School Story and Tolkienian form, the lessons Harry has learned from Quidditch are highly applicable to life in the larger context of the plot. Like Viktor Krum's World Cup Snitch-catch, for Harry the Horcrux Seeker, even defeat is an expression of his freedom and dignity. It is surely by the author's careful design that, at this very moment, Harry is carrying the Golden Snitch from his first Quidditch match. [22]

Perhaps it was the freedom and dignity of the Seeker on the Quidditch pitch that prepared another Seeker, Regulus Arcturus Black, to make a difficult but totally free choice to sacrifice himself for the greater good of defeating Voldemort. In his note to the Dark Lord, he says with great dignity, "I face death in the hope that when you meet your match, you will be mortal once more."[23] Harry identifies the younger Black brother as a Seeker from his old Quidditch team photograph, and indeed, given the lonely and brave task that lay ahead of him of finding and destroying the locket Horcrux, he could not have played any other Quidditch position. In the cases of Harry Potter and Regulus Black, experience as a Quidditch Seeker prepared them for a lonely, brave and self-sacrificial choice for the good of the whole Wizarding community. It taught them that there is dignity in having the freedom to choose, even if it means each Seeker's own personal defeat.

Another Quidditch position which seems to resonate strongly with character roles in the larger narrative is that of Keeper. *Quidditch Through the Ages* quotes Zacharias Mumps's 1398 description of the Keeper position:

> The Keeper should beware of straying too far toward the other end of the pitch, in case his baskets come under threat in his absence. However, a fast Keeper may be able to score a goal and then return to his baskets in time to prevent the other team equalizing. It is a matter of the individual conscience of the Keeper.[24]

The idea of a player position that is both primarily responsible for the protection of the goal hoops and yet also expected to score points on behalf of his team is one of those practical quirks of Quidditch that exasperates sports-savvy readers.

---

[22] Ibid.

[23] Rowling, *Half-Blood Prince*, 609

[24] Rowling, *Quidditch Through the Ages*, 24.

It just doesn't seem realistic or wise to expect the Keeper to play both offensive and defensive roles.[25] However, if readers see Quidditch as miniaturizing the character roles and events of the larger *Harry Potter* narrative, the idea becomes coherent. In a Tolkienian sense, Mumps's description of the Keeper is highly applicable to the role of Albus Dumbledore in the war against Voldemort, especially as Dumbledore is depicted in *Harry Potter and the Half-Blood Prince*. Dumbledore is relentlessly hunting Horcruxes by Book 6, and periodically leaves his school unprotected (by him) in his pursuit of these all-important "goals" in the fight against Voldemort. Harry confronts him on this abandoning of his post:

> "You're leaving the school tonight, and I'll bet you haven't even considered that Snape and Malfoy might decide to—"

> "To what?" asked Dumbledore, his eyebrows raised. "What is it that you suspect them of doing, precisely?"

> "I... they're up to something! ... He's trying to mend something dangerous in there and if you ask me, he's fixed it at last and you're about to just walk out of school without—"

> "Enough," said Dumbledore. He said it quite calmly, and yet Harry fell silent at once; he knew that he had finally crossed some invisible line.... "Please do not suggest that I do not take the safety of my students seriously, Harry."[26]

As Mumps suggests, the decision of a Keeper to leave his goal posts is a matter of individual conscience. Dumbledore's choice here is firm and confident, because he assumes that he himself is the sole target of Malfoy and Snape's plotting. And, given Dumbledore's often comically high opinion of himself, he likely considers that if any "Keeper" is fast enough to make it back to his goals in time to protect them, it will be himself.

The parallels between Mumps's description of the Keeper and Dumbledore's role as the "Keeper" of Hogwarts are clear. But the connection between Dumbledore and Quidditch in the storyline is not. Within the books there is no mention

---

[25] *Quidditch Through the Ages* clarifies that this dual expectation of Keepers was revised as Quidditch evolved as a sport, and Keepers are now advised to stay within their team's scoring area for the most part.

[26] Rowling, *Half-Blood Prince*, 550.

of Dumbledore ever having played Quidditch, much less Keeper, during his time at Hogwarts; if he had, we could reasonably expect Elphias Doge to have mentioned it in his *Daily Prophet* remembrance.[27] We know, both from his presence at Hogwarts Quidditch matches and from Dumbledore's foreward to *Quidditch Through the Ages*, that the headmaster does follow Quidditch.[28] But Aberforth Dumbledore's bitter description of his brother as a young man in *Deathly Hallows* all but precludes the idea that the elder Dumbledore ever graced a Quidditch pitch as a player:

> "...Albus, he was always up in his bedroom when he was home, reading his books and counting his prizes, keeping up with his correspondence with 'the most notable magical names of the day,'" Aberforth sneered.[29]

However, this lack of evidence of Dumbledore literally playing Keeper in the story should not dissuade us from the applicability of Mumps's description of the Keeper in *Quidditch Through the Ages* to Albus's role in the Second War. The fact that Dumbledore was never a literal Keeper in the narrative points to the reality that, at a more fundamental level in the world of *Harry Potter*, Quidditch is less a game to be taken literally (though it is also that) than a reflection of the larger plot and those who bring about its major events.

By far the strongest connection between Albus Dumbledore and the Quidditch Keeper position comes in *Deathly Hallows*. It manifests in chapter seven, "The Will of Albus Dumbledore," wherein the Trio learns of the personal bequests made to each of them by their late headmaster. Perhaps the most baffling bequest—to both the characters and the reader—is that of Dumbledore's Deluminator to Ron. The Minister of Magic asks Ron suspiciously:

> "If you were not very close to Dumbledore, how do you account for the fact that he remembered you in his will?..."

---

[27] Rowling, *Deathly Hallows*, 16-20.

[28] Rowling, *Quidditch Through the Ages, viii.* Dumbledore wishes Puddlemere United a good season. Presumably his favorite team, Puddlemere United's symbol, according to the same text, is "two crossed golden bulrushes." (36) The bulrush is a symbol associated, in the Judeo-Christian tradition, with Moses.

[29] Rowling, *Deathly Hallows*, 565.

"I ... dunno," said Ron. "I ... when I say we weren't close ... I mean, I think he liked me."[30]

Dumbledore only says, in his will, *"To Ronald Bilius Weasley, I leave my Delumina-tor, in the hope that he will remember me when he uses it."*[31] Despite their evasive statements to Scrimgeour, the Trio is truly puzzled by this last act of Dumbledore, as is evidenced by their unproductive conversation about it a few pages later.[32] However, the reader can deduce from that rare, perhaps singular canonical mention of Ron's middle name, "Bilius," that Dumbledore (or rather, his author) is making a sly reference to that character trait to which Ron's middle name points: Ron's propensity for irritability or bad-temperedness. Dumbledore may indeed have liked Ron Weasley, but, more importantly, he understood him. He somehow grasped that Ron's sometimes bilious nature would lead him to make a mistake that Dumbledore, through the bequest of his Deluminator, hoped to give him the power to correct.

This foresight of Dumbledore with regard to Ron's actions is that of one (figurative) Keeper to another. From the first book in the series, Dumbledore must have observed and made assumptions about Ron's role in the Trio, despite his lack of one-to-one interactions with Harry's red-headed friend. Ron's self-sacrifice in the enchanted chess game in *Sorcerer's Stone*, his lame-brained decision to fly a car to Hogwarts in *Chamber*, his injuries from Sirius Black in *Prisoner*, and especially his desire, despite his insecurities and nerves, to serve Harry's Quidditch team as Keeper: all these point Dumbledore to Ron's place, not as the brains of the outfit (obviously that's Hermione), but as the protector. And it is especially Ron's performance as Gryffindor Keeper which gives Dumbledore (and the reader) the needed insight to see Ron would require the Deluminator at some point in their hunt for Horcruxes. On the Quidditch pitch, Ron is a good player, but one with insecurities that dangerously threaten his team's chances of success. As Harry tells Ron in *Half-Blood Prince*, "you can save anything when you're on form, it's a mental problem you've got!"[33] These same qualities, the good and the

---

[30] Ibid., 124.

[31] Ibid., 125.

[32] Ibid., 132-133.

[33] Rowling, *Half-Blood Prince*, 291.

bad, accompany Ron as he becomes the figurative Keeper of his friends in *Deathly Hallows*. Dumbledore understands Ron's loyalty yet insecurity, and he also understands, more than anyone, what the Trio will face as it seeks to find and destroy Voldemort's Horcruxes.

Recall Mumps's admonition in *Quidditch Through the Ages*: "The Keeper should beware of straying too far toward the other end of the pitch, in case his baskets come under threat in his absence." As Dumbledore must have predicted, in *Deathly Hallows*, Ron makes the unwise decision to abandon his friends (his "baskets") whom he had sworn to protect and help. Consistent with Mumps's warning, Ron ultimately abandons his friends, not totally out of Horcrux-induced ill-temper, but also out of a legitimate frustration with their seeming inability to "score" in their theater of the war against Voldemort. His frustration had been building, predictably, ever since they began the wandering exile caused by their near-capture at the Ministry of Magic:

> "So where next?" was [Ron's] constant refrain. He did not seem to have any ideas himself, but expected Harry and Hermione to come up with plans while he sat and brooded over the low food supplies.[34]

He becomes somewhat obsessed with Harry's visions of Voldemort's doings, solely because they might give him some insight into the well-being of his loved ones.[35] This is evidence that Ron's head is not in the right sphere of play; he is neglecting his duties as "Keeper" in favor of his interest in what's going on at the other end of the pitch. His desire to "score" is clearest in the final confrontation before he abandons his friends. He says to Harry:

> "I just hoped, you know, after we'd been running round a few weeks, we'd have achieved something."…

> "I thought you knew what you'd signed up for," said Harry.

> "Yeah, I thought I did too."

---

[34] Rowling, *Deathly Hallows*, 288.
[35] Ibid., 291.

> "So what part of it isn't living up to your expectations?" asked Harry. ... "Did you think we'd be staying in five-star hotels? Finding a Horcrux every other day?"
>
> "We thought you knew what you were doing!" shouted Ron ... "We thought Dumbledore had told you what to do, we thought you had a real plan!"[36]

Ron's frustration combines with his bilious nature and he walks out on his friends, seemingly for good—not because of Ron's stubbornness but because the deep cover under which Harry and Hermione would continue to travel would make it impossible for Ron to find them again. However, thanks to Albus Dumbledore's enigmatic bequest of the Deluminator, Ron possesses the exact tool that will help him find his otherwise unplottable friends again:

> "He knew what he was doing when he gave me the Deluminator, didn't he? He—well," Ron's ears turned bright red and he became engrossed in a tuft of grass at his feet, which he prodded with his toe, "he must've known I'd run out on you."
>
> "No," Harry corrected him. "He must've known you'd always want to come back."[37]

From one Keeper to another, Dumbledore entrusts this unlikely tool in the fight against Voldemort to Ron Weasley. Both Harry and Ron are right in their assumptions about the reason behind this gift; Dumbledore suspected Ron would be tempted to abandon his post, as it were, and yet also knew he would wholeheartedly desire to return to his most important duty: guarding and helping his friends in their pursuit of the Horcruxes: *"To Ronald Bilius Weasley, I leave my Deluminator, in the hope that he will remember me when he uses it."*[38] Perhaps Dumbledore wished Ron to remember that Dumbledore, too, abandoned his baskets (Hogwarts) to score an important goal (collecting the locket Horcrux), but, sadly, realized his mistake too late to keep his students, members of the Order and himself out of harm's way.[39]

---

[36] Ibid., 307.

[37] Ibid., 391.

[38] Ibid., 125

[39] Rowling, *Half-Blood Prince,* 581.

The Beater position in Quidditch holds symbolic significance in the larger story as well. Harry's first Quidditch Captain, Oliver Wood, describes Beaters Fred and George Weasley as "like a pair of human Bludgers themselves,"[40] making them perfectly disposed to be Beaters. But unlike Slytherin Beaters Crabbe and Goyle, the Weasley twins use as much brains as brawn to keep the Bludger from taking out their team mates (especially Harry).[41] This is true both on and off the field. The Weasley twins protect Harry from myriad opponents (some much worse than Bludgers) by freely passing him the Marauders' Map in Book 3. "'It's a wrench, giving it to you,' said Fred, 'but we decided last night, your need's greater than ours.'"[42] This map becomes an invaluable aid to Harry in escaping danger and fighting against the Dark Lord and his followers throughout the rest of the series, particularly during the Battle of Hogwarts.

The Weasley twins also assist Harry, not once but twice, in breaking into Dolores Umbridge's office. Consistent with their Beater role, in both incidents, the twins do not assist Harry directly with the task at hand, for, as in Quidditch, Beaters do not help catch the Snitch. Rather the twins simply remove obstacles that, much like Bludgers, get in the way of what Harry seeks to accomplish. The first incident is at Hogwarts in *Order of the Phoenix*; the Weasley twins purposely coordinate their mayhem-making with Harry's need to use the Floo Network in Umbridge's office. Fred reasons, "if we're going to be causing a bit of uproar, why not do it so that Harry can have his chat with Sirius?"[43] The resultant swamp in the east wing is not only an impressive piece of magic, it is also the twins' last act as Hogwarts students, for remaining at the school will mean torture at the hands of Filch, with the permission of Umbridge.[44] In order to remove the obstacle (Umbridge) that stands in Harry's way, the Weasley twins have willingly made

---

[40] J.K. Rowling, *Harry Potter and the Sorcerer's Stone* (New York: Scholastic, Inc., 1997), 169.

[41] *Quidditch Through the Ages* notes that "Seekers are most likely to be fouled by members of the opposition," and receive the worst injuries as they are often targeted specifically by Beaters. (27)

[42] J.K. Rowling, *Harry Potter and the Prisoner of Azkaban* (New York: Scholastic, Inc., 1999), 191.

[43] J.K. Rowling, *Harry Potter and the Order of the Phoenix* (New York: Scholastic, Inc., 2003), 658.

[44] Ibid., 673.

themselves outcasts. They flee the scene lightheartedly on the broomsticks Umbridge herself had confiscated when she banned them from Quidditch. On one broomstick, the iron peg of its imprisonment still hangs, "swinging dangerously" (much like an iron Bludger might) as they exit the building and fly into the sunset.[45] This glorious escape expresses the insuppressible resonance of the Weasley twins' role in the narrative with their role on the Quidditch pitch.

The second time the Weasley twins assist Harry in breaking into Umbridge's office occurs at the Ministry of Magic. Again, their assistance is indirect, and involves the creation of a diversion to nab the attention of those who would prevent Harry from his task. Earlier in book 6, the twins, now proprietors of Weasley's Wizard Wheezes, give Harry a couple of their Decoy Detonators. "'I can't do that!'" says Harry when the twins refuse his money. "'You don't pay here,' said Fred firmly, waving away Harry's gold."[46] Both their generosity and their choice of product serve Harry well. In *Deathly Hallows*, the Weasley twins' Decoy Detonator is just what Harry needs to divert the attention of the dozen Ministry workers making pamphlets right outside Umbridge's office, so he can sneak in under the Invisibility Cloak.[47] Again the twins' indirect assistance is invaluable to Harry in his role as Seeker of the locket Horcrux.

The twins' willingness, through diversionary tactics, to remove obstacles that stand in the way of Harry's success and safety is also evident when each twin becomes one of the "Seven Potters" in *Deathly Hallows*. The goal is for Harry to escape Privet Drive before his seventeenth birthday, when the protection of his aunt's blood will expire.[48] The obstacles are the many Death Eaters who, the Order of the Phoenix rightly suspects, await them as soon as they leave the magically-protected home. The diversion is Polyjuice Potion. The twins use their keen senses of humor to deflect Harry's protests against this risky plan. And although the operation is successful, Harry's concerns are justified—George Weasley is permanently disfigured as a result.[49] Clearly, the role of the Weasley twins in the

[45] Ibid., 675.

[46] Rowling, *Half-Blood Prince*, 120.

[47] Rowling, *Deathly Hallows*, 250.

[48] Rowling, *Deathly Hallows*, 46.

[49] Rowling, *Deathly Hallows*, 71. And of course Mad-Eye Moody is killed.

series extends beyond comic relief; as Beaters, their role is one of unswerving protection and assistance to their Seeker, Harry Potter.

On the other hand, Beaters Crabbe and Goyle, as Draco Malfoy's henchmen, do nothing but hinder Harry, both on the Quidditch pitch and in Harry's series-long fight against darkness. An interesting Beater parallel unfolds in *Deathly Hallows'* "The Battle of Hogwarts"; in this chapter, one each of the opposing sets of Beaters—Crabbe and Goyle versus Fred and George—is killed hindering or protecting Harry respectively, as per their Beater role. Crabbe, in attempting to hamper Harry's mission to find the diadem, becomes his own undoing in the Room of Requirement after setting Fiendfyre to the place. This act by Crabbe is consistent with his role as Beater: one that often, in repelling Bludgers, attempts to simultaneously thwart members of the opposing team. Crabbe's act of conjuring the Fiendfyre in the Room of Requirement is like the figurative lobbing of a mortal deterrent—a demonic, fiery Bludger—at his opponent. But, in the end, Crabbe should have paid more attention to Kennilworthy Whisp's cautionary description of Bludgers in *Quidditch Through the Ages*:

> Bludgers are bewitched to chase players *indiscriminately*. If left to their own devices, they will attack the player closest to them, hence the Beaters' task is to knock the Bludgers as far away from their own team as possible.[50]

The Fiendfyre, set by Crabbe, leads to Crabbe's own destruction (and nearly that of his "teammates"), but only temporarily hampers Harry from finding the Diadem Horcrux.[51] The Beater parallel comes when Fred Weasley dies moments later: a tragic casualty of the Hogwarts army. Fred, true to his Beater identity, seems more cognizant of Whisp's warning about the figurative Bludger which approaches, for he is standing his ground, attempting to repel the Death Eaters who seek to deliver Harry to Voldemort.[52] This intriguing parallel points to the enduring quality of characters' Quidditch positions, which shape their roles in the story well beyond the edge of the Quidditch pitch.

---

[50] Rowling, *Quidditch Through the Ages*, 23. Emphasis added.

[51] Rowling, *Deathly Hallows,* 634.

[52] Ibid., 637.

Quidditch Through the Ages reports that "Chaser is the oldest position in Quidditch, for the game once consisted wholly of goal-scoring."[53] This points to the symbolic significance of two particular Chasers in the larger *Harry Potter* narrative. First, it points to the reality that war and the defeat of tyrants were simpler before Voldemort's experimental attempts to defy mortality through the creation of multiple Horcruxes.[54] While it is unclear precisely when Dumbledore begins to suspect that Voldemort has created Horcruxes, it can be assumed that Chaser James Potter had no idea that any other sphere of play existed except the one at hand: Dumbledore and the Order of the Phoenix versus Voldemort and the Death Eaters. The First War, for James, was a matter of goal-scoring, as it were: one side against the other. His life, thrown in front of Voldemort to buy time for his wife and child's escape, is just another point scored by Voldemort in this evil game. In death James is rendered impotent in the game. Another Quidditch Chaser, Ginny Weasley,[55] is rendered impotent in the "game" against Voldemort as well; she is banned by her parents (and Harry) from fighting in the Battle of Hogwarts. But this ban proves ineffective, and James Potter's Seeker son will, in the higher and more important sphere of play which has developed (seeking and destroying Horcruxes), offer his own life, as Chaser James before him, so that Ginny Weasley, and so many others, might live to continue the fight.

The equipment. A look at the Quidditch equipment in light of literary alchemy confirms that Quidditch has a symbolic function in the larger narrative of the *Harry Potter* series. Other authors have established that literary alchemy, to an appreciable extent, helps structure both the individual books and the series as a whole. If Quidditch acts as an emblem of the larger plot of the series, then it makes sense to look for alchemical symbols and elements on the Quidditch pitch

---

[53] Rowling, *Quidditch Through the Ages*, 25.

[54] We know from Voldemort's speech to his Death Eaters in *Goblet of Fire* (653) that he believes himself to be the first wizard ever to create so many Horcruxes. There is nothing in the series to contradict this belief.

[55] On page 575 of *Order of the Phoenix*, Ginny states her preference for goal-scoring (Chaser) over Seeking. Due to this stated preference, we can also take her character as symbolically more akin to Chaser than Seeker, although on the Quidditch pitch she plays both positions.

as well as within the narrative. This search pays off, especially with regard to the various equipment used in Quidditch and its purpose.

John Granger says all narratives structured upon the alchemical model have black, white and red stages, and these stages can be clearly identified in the *Harry Potter* series.[56] The black stage or *nigredo* "is the stage in which the subject is broken down, stripped of all but the essential qualities."[57] This black stage corresponds to the Bludgers in Quidditch: two iron balls described as "jet black,"[58] and whose sole purpose is to unseat and disorient the players. Indeed, Wood tells Harry in his first Quidditch lesson, that Bludgers are known to break players' jaws,[59] and Harry's own arm is broken by a Bludger in *Chamber of Secrets*. If the black Bludgers correspond to the black stage of alchemy, then the red Quaffle must correspond to the red stage or *rubedo*, in which there is a resolution of opposites. As the Quaffle is the ball used by each team in turn to score upon the opposite team's goals, this correspondence pattern holds nicely.

But what of the stage which comes between black and red in alchemy? The element corresponding to the white stage or *albedo* is more subtle in Quidditch; no "white" equipment is mentioned as part of the game. But Harry's first broomstick is the Nimbus 2000, and "nimbus" means a luminous cloud or aura. This corresponds well as a symbol of the *albedo*, which is a stage of purification. It is on a broomstick that Harry *becomes* a Seeker; he is a natural from his first kickoff, and his broomstick (whether this or subsequent models) is a vehicle toward his victory over Voldemort's schemes in countless instances throughout the series. Besides facilitating his many victories on the Quidditch pitch, Harry uses a broomstick to find the winged key in his pursuit of the Sorcerer's Stone, to outrun the dragon in the First Task of the Triwizard Tournament, to depart Privet Drive safely in *Order of the Phoenix* and to recover the Diadem Horcrux in the Room of Requirement. Broomsticks are not for everyone; Fleur is not fond of brooms,[60] and Hermione and Neville, Harry supposes in Book 1, are too fearful

---

[56] John Granger, *The Deathly Hallows Lectures* (Cheshire, CT: Zossima Press, 2008), 18.

[57] Ibid., 19.

[58] Rowling, *Sorcerer's Stone*, 168.

[59] Ibid., 169.

[60] Rowling, *Deathly Hallows*, 53.

in their approach to flying to properly command their broomsticks.[61] But Harry knows how to fly on instinct:

> ... in a rush of fierce joy he realized he'd found something he could do without being taught—this was easy, this was *wonderful*. He pulled his broomstick up a little to take it even higher, and heard screams and gasps of girls back on the ground and an admiring whoop from Ron. ... Malfoy looked stunned.[62]

Flying on a broomstick is a purifying, transformative experience for Harry Potter. On the school broomstick and later on his Nimbus 2000 and Firebolt, his uncertainties and feelings of being an outsider in the Wizarding world melt away. On a broomstick, Harry becomes who he is meant to be: the Gryffindor Seeker, and the Seeker of Horcruxes in the war against Voldemort.

Finally, both the golden goal hoops and the Golden Snitch correspond well to the pure gold which a complete alchemical process is said to produce. This is true both on the Quidditch pitch (scoring goals through the golden hoops and catching the Golden Snitch are both means of winning the game), and in the larger arc of the narrative (the Golden Snitch Harry carries throughout *Deathly Hallows* bears the inscription: "*I open at the close*,"[63] or when the Seeker's work is complete). Additionally, John Granger has pointed out the striking similarity between the form of Rowling's Golden Snitch and the alchemical "winged sphere": the symbol of the *prima materia* or base material that, in one 17th-century illustration, represents the completion of the alchemical process.[64] Interestingly, Granger describes the final stage of alchemy, in which the Philosopher's Stone (the stone that brings immortality) emerges from within this *prima materia* (the winged sphere). Rowling leans heavily on this alchemical imagery with the emergence of the Resurrection Stone (which brings back loved ones from the grave, if imperfectly) from within the Golden Snitch as Harry walks to the Forest in *Deathly Hallows*, when his own work as the Seeker of Horcruxes is complete.

---

[61] Rowling, *Sorcerer's Stone*, 146.

[62] Ibid., 148-149.

[63] Rowling, *Deathly Hallows*, 698.

[64] John Granger, *Unlocking Harry Potter* (Cheshire, CT: Zossima Press, 2007), ii.

The Game Goes on: 2014 Quidditch World Cup

Despite Harry the Seeker's work being indeed complete at the end of *Deathly Hallows*, and despite the many avowals from J.K. Rowling that she would write no more stories about the Boy (Man?) Who Lived, in 2014, Potter fans received a slew of newly-composed writings by Rowling on *Pottermore*, the author's Potterverse-encyclopedia-meets-fandom-social-media website. The new material, a series of short reports on the 2014 Quidditch World Cup in Patagonia, was penned from the perspectives of sport correspondent Ginny (Weasley) Potter and gossip columnist Rita Skeeter. Though ostensibly written for fun, these new writings bring fresh insights about the continuing interplay between Quidditch and the story of Harry Potter.

If Quidditch is a symbol set for the larger arc of the Harry Potter narrative, it may at first seem strange that Rowling should be willing to write new material about the sport, while holding to her claim that Harry's story is complete. However, we must remember what Dumbledore says of Quidditch in his forward to *Quidditch Through the Ages*: anyone interested in general wizarding history (and presumably culture) will be interested also in Quidditch. Dumbledore's words reflect Rowling's own motive, stated in the *Telegraph*, for creating Quidditch: the need for an element which would hold her magical society together, cause Wizarding folk to assemble and signify the particular character of Wizarding society and culture. There is ample support for the notion that Quidditch in the Harry Potter series is highly applicable to the larger plot of the seven books, but although the story within those books has ended, Quidditch goes on. In fact, given the growing popularity, professionalism and proliferation of collegiate Muggle Quidditch leagues, one could certainly say that, even apart from the books that gave birth to the sport, Quidditch has taken on a life of its own.

The new stories about the 2014 Quidditch World Cup communicate clearly that Quidditch is not shackled to the Potter plot, in a somewhat tongue-in-cheek manner. The organization of the numerous national teams involved, the number of matches and reports (25 reports – some lengthy – on 13 matches) as well as the attention to detail within the reports (which was, at times, too much for this non-sporty Potter fan) all help portray Quidditch as something that can firmly stand independent from Harry Potter in the Wizarding world (and perhaps beyond). The tongue-in-cheek aspect of this message is, not surprisingly, provided by Rita Skeeter's contributions, which amount to nothing but gossip bordering on slander about Harry and his family and friends, who show up to watch the finals. The Quidditch event of the decade is going on all around Skeeter, and despite the thousands of fans ravenous for details of the matches, she reports that Harry Potter has a cut under his right eye.[65] Perhaps this is Rowling's comical way of confirming that Harry's story is indeed complete in essentials, despite the media's fixation on him. At the same time, Rowling also expresses that the world she created around Harry Potter continues to be a vibrant, magical place.

If these new reports on *Pottermore* show us the vibrancy of Quidditch independent from the *Harry Potter* plot, they conversely show that the story of Harry Potter cannot boast such independence from Quidditch. As this essay has discussed, in so many ways, the Second War *was* won on the Quidditch Pitch of Hogwarts; Quidditch was an essential means of articulating the values, character roles and strategies that ultimately helped win the war. But notably, the 2014 World Cup event draws Harry Potter and his gang to the *sidelines*, not to the pitch. He offers no dialogue in the reports, and Rita Skeeter's obsessive observations of his every movement in the VIP box tell us far more about the sour, fixated reporter than about Harry. Despite Skeeter's attempts to make his presence headline news, unless Harry is on the pitch (both literally and figuratively), he is not scoop-worthy. Those who hoped these new writings would be Harry's big comeback are, I fear, bound for disappointment. The only character making a comeback at the 2014 World Cup is Viktor Krum, who returns triumphantly as Seeker for the Bulgarian national team.[66] In the 2014 Quidditch World Cup reports, readers find a totally new relationship between Harry Potter and Quidditch: one where Harry is a mere spectator to the action. In this way, we can see that Quidditch is still at work as a symbol of the larger story of Harry's life; in Harry's adulthood, he is removed from the most intense realms of danger and war. Those roles are now reserved for others, and Harry's part is to cheer them

---

[65] J.K. Rowling, "Dumbledore's Army Reunites at Quidditch World Cup Final," *Pottermore*, July 8, 2014. Pottermore.com. Accessible only to registered users.

[66] Ibid.

on as one of the crowd (if a rather notable one). Harry's appearance, happy and healthy with his family, in the stands at the 2014 Quidditch World Cup is another way for Rowling to express that all is well.

Conclusion

Even before the release of these new World Cup writings, fans of the Harry Potter books knew Quidditch to be clever enough an invention to appreciate merely on its own, literal terms. But Quidditch skills, rules, players, lessons and accoutrements bear significantly upon the larger narrative, and a conscientious reader can choose to see a more sublime meaning for Quidditch than what's on the surface. True to the British School Story tradition, Quidditch in *Harry Potter* miniaturizes the larger story world, helping characters learn important lessons about their roles in the narrative, such as Harry's appreciation for his own freedom and dignity as Seeker despite being the "Chosen One." In a Tolkienian sense, the rules, playing positions and even equipment used in Quidditch are highly *applicable* to character roles and motifs within the larger narrative arc of the story, such as the "two spheres of play" and the literary alchemy to which the Bludgers, Quaffle, Nimbus 2000 and Golden Snitch all point. At times, elements and events within the Quidditch narrative even prefigure events that will take place as the crisis of the series unfolds, such as both Dumbledore's and Ron's decisions to abandon and reclaim their posts as figurative "Keepers." Moreover, the lessons and skills he has learned on the Quidditch pitch help Harry the Seeker to defeat Lord Voldemort, and, in retrospect, each time Harry catches the Golden Snitch in a Quidditch match seems to prefigure the all-important moment in this epic tale:

> And Harry, with the unerring skill of the Seeker, caught the wand in his free hand as Voldemort fell backward, arms splayed, the slit pupils of the scarlet eyes rolling upward. ... Voldemort was dead, killed by his own rebounding curse, and Harry stood with two wands in his hand, staring down at his enemy's shell.[67]

---

[67] Rowling, *Deathly Hallows*, 744.

150 points—that absurdly high award—go to Harry's team: the side of good, the side of life and light. Despite the goals the Death Eaters may have scored against Harry's team throughout the long game—and there were many, and they were tragic—Harry's last catch heals all. Well played, Potter.

CHAPTER 8

Surviving the Potter-pocalypse
Keeping the Magic Alive in a Post-Potter World

Hayley Burson and Michael Burson

On July 21, 2007, the final Harry Potter novel (*Harry Potter and the Deathly Hallows*) was released. Thousands of fans donned their robes and brandished their wands to attend midnight release parties held in bookstores across the globe. Girls dressing as Hermione wore curly brown wigs and toted stuffed, orange cats. Boys put on circular glasses and drew lightning bolt scars on their foreheads. The sensation of getting ready for a Harry Potter book release was invigorating. Everyone participating that night would be among other Harry Potter fans, which meant they were among friends.

Everyone was feverous to get their hands on the orange-covered book, rabid to know how the saga, a decade long love affair, would come to an end. Much of the excitement came from an urge to know the answers to burning questions: Was Snape good or evil? Was Dumbledore truly dead? How would the Horcruxes be destroyed? Would Harry survive to see the end of the series? Soon, all of these questions would be answered.

At the book release parties, the excitement reached its zenith as the midnight countdown began.

10. This was it.
9. It was really happening.
8. We were finally going to get the book.
7. This was the end.
6. There were no more books after this.
5. This was the last time we would be at one of these events.

4. When will we ever wear these robes again?

3. Sure, there are the movies, but that's not quite the same.

2. It's really all over.

1. How will I survive the end of Harry Potter?

Does My College Supply List Include a Standard Size 2 Pewter Cauldron?

Michael started his freshman year at the University of North Carolina at Charlotte in the fall of 2008. Like so many other college freshman, he was in the position of trying to figure out how he would make a place for himself in a new environment, especially since he did not know anyone attending the same school. He had brought all seven of his hardback Harry Potter books, still fresh from a furious summer reread, to reside on his small dorm bookshelf. In high school, he had bonded and made friends with the other Harry Potter fans around him. In college, there was no way of knowing who liked the books or had even read them. He had never really been active on the online side of the fandom (dial-up Internet at his parents' house had deterred him from spending hours on forums) so how was he to find other people like himself to meet and hang out with? With no means accessible, he decided to create his own.

After visiting the student government office, he got the information on how to form a student organization. It seemed like a good idea: make a club where Harry Potter fans can come together and talk about the books and films. Intramural Quidditch was just starting to become popular in colleges around the country, so the idea of an organization dedicated to his favorite book series did not seem completely far-fetched. It was not to be a club solely for studying the literary and academic aspects of the books, like some clubs professors had created at other universities. It was to be a casual, fun, social organization where anyone, from the people who had only seen one of the films to the people who knew the whole series by heart, should feel at home. He decided to call the club Potter Watch after the name of the magical wireless show that told what was really going on in the wizarding world.

In order to start a student organization at UNC Charlotte, there have to be at least eight people who are willing to join and become members. In order to get these eight, Michael held an interest meeting in one of the smaller conference rooms on campus. He expected that the fliers he had put up a few days before might bring in a handful of die-hard fans. He would talk to them for a bit, try to convince them to bring their friends to join, and wrap up the meeting within 20 minutes.

Boy, was he wrong. Looking back, Michael can understand how Harry felt in the Hogshead the moment a few dozen people wandered in wanting to join his new club. The room was packed. Many had to stand because the room was too small to fit them all. Those who had come all had different personalities and backgrounds. There were introverts who barely spoke the entire meeting, and some who were so talkative that he had to ask them to keep it down. Each of them had come to hear the ideas for how a Harry Potter club would function, from plans for everyone to be sorted into Houses to throwing Deathday Parties and Yule Balls. They wanted to know what they were going to talk about at meetings, what the ideas for activities and discussions were. Most of all, they wanted to know when the new club would start!

The meeting adjourned, leaving Michael with a feeling of accomplishment and hope. The people who had come really wanted to keep the magic going. Some of those who attended that first meeting would spend their entire college careers as regular members. After amassing a list of willing new participants, he went before the student organization senate and Potter Watch, the Official Harry Potter Club of UNC Charlotte was born.

That next summer, Hayley was perusing the list of student organizations at UNC Charlotte and stumbled onto Potter Watch. A life-long fan herself, she was thrilled to get the chance to geek out with some fellow Potter nerds. She had had a group of friends who had all grown up with the books and, being drama students, had come up with some impressive, themed, group costumes for the later book releases (Disco Dumbledore, Hip Hermione, Regular Ron). In her teens, she had been an active participant on the Mugglenet Interactive forums and was eventually made a prefect moderator. She even participated in the post-*Hallows* chat with J.K. Rowling, asking about Regulus Black's change of heart in regards to Kreacher (the fact that she helped add to the Harry Potter canon is still a point of great pride for her).

Hayley messaged Michael to find out more about the club. Michael obliged with his standard cut-and-paste response to potential members, telling her about the meetings and events. Undeterred by this all-business response, she attended the first meeting the next fall, and every meeting after that. She ran for Secretary of the club, and with Michael and the other officers, they continued to lead the club for three more years.

A Harry Potter Club?

Anytime Michael told anyone he was the president of a club dedicated to Harry Potter, the first thing anyone said was, "Wait, there's a Harry Potter club here?" followed by, "What do you even *do* in a Harry Potter club?" At first, the weekly meetings were just about sharing news and discussing aspects of the books everyone enjoyed. Everyone was sorted into Houses by either simply joining their favorite House or taking a 120 question sorting quiz online. By bringing in discussion topics, baking Potter-themed treats, or sharing their merchandise for "show and tell," members could gain points for their Houses. We logged onto some of our favorite Potter news sites and would discuss updates to the filming of the last remaining movies, which took up most of the meetings (*Half-Blood Prince* was due out the summer of 2009, and it was not even fathomed *Deathly Hallows* would be split into two films).

With the steady flow of casting updates, movie stills, and trailers, there was still so much to be excited about, even though the books were finished. There was even the thrilling news about *The Tales of Beedle the Bard* being published in December 2008, and a few members stayed up until midnight to pick up the book in an attempt to relive the excitement. Unfortunately, there was no grand spectacle at the particular book store we had chosen to attend like previous book releases, so our copies were quietly collected and we left the store as quickly as possible, while receiving a few stares and sniggers for being in our robes.

During the first meetings, in addition to following film updates, discussions were mostly focused on theories and unanswered questions. We would save time at the end of each meeting for discussions, some of which became rather heated. How did moving portraits work, and how did they see the world from inside their frames? Was it possible or advisable to wield more than one wand in a duel? What exactly was Peeves, and how was he different from the other specters of Hogwarts? There had been so few post-*Deathly Hallows* interviews, and certainly no Pottermore, to give these answers, so we talked, shared ideas, laughed over some of the more outlandish theories, and just hung out and talked Potter.

As the club began to grow, and the membership seemed to be expanding at an exponential rate, the club began to organize several events. At first, these events were small and rather unspectacular. That changed during the second year when Hayley joined the club. Beside being a devout Harry Potter fan, she enjoyed planning events and parties. She enjoyed them so much that when she was eventually elected Secretary (or as we called that position in the club, the Head of House) she created the Party Planning Committee to help make our events even better. As there were several parties and events to model after in the book series, Potter Watch members were eager to enjoy them in the Muggle world following midterm papers and final exams, just as they do in the wizarding world. So, as a club working together, we decided to have an annual Deathday Party, Yule Ball, Triwizard Tournament, and End-of-the-Year Feast.

Our Own Hogwarts

Though they started out small initially, the Potter Watch events grew to become one of the most exciting aspects of the club. The first annual event was the Deathday Party, named, of course, after events ghosts hold to celebrate the anniversary of their deaths. Around Halloween we turned an unused classroom into a dungeon ballroom, complete with stone walls (plastic, party-store, wall coverings), floating Jack-O-Lanterns (you could barely see the fishing line holding up the plastic pumpkins), and spooky snacks (it was amazing what you could come up with walking down the Dollar Store aisles). Everyone would wear their Halloween costumes, Potter-themed or otherwise, and play games like Pin the Scar on the Harry, which involved blindfolding, spinning, and taping a paper lightning bolt onto a poster of Daniel Radcliffe, and the Pumpkin Painting Contest, where each House would work together to paint a pumpkin to show scenes from the books. Entries included all the characters who died in the series holding hands with little X's for eyes, a black skull Dark Mark pumpkin, and a Whomping Willow pumpkin complete with a "Ford Anglia" Rice Krispy treat painted blue and stuck to the side with a toothpick.

After everyone returned from holiday break, we held the Yule Ball, a winter formal with a potluck dinner followed by dancing. We usually held it after the holidays because everyone was either stressed out with finals or heading home right afterwards, so the first few weeks of the new year were a great time to get back together and welcome the new semester. In a room decorated in white tablecloths and ice blue streamers, members danced to classical music before "letting their hair down," as Professor McGonagall would say, and getting down to more modern favorites. Many of the girls brought out their high school prom dresses, happy for an excuse to wear them again, while the boys wore the jackets and ties they had bought for their college interviews.

As soon as Spring Break ended, we organized the Triwizard Tournament, a three-day contest where members of the four Houses would compete against each other for House points, and, of course, ultimate glory. On Day One, there was the Mental Challenge, usually made up of book trivia and mental puzzles that would test House members' canon knowledge. A High Inquisitor acted as an impartial judge and question master, asking each House in turn increasingly difficult trivia questions, from "What is the spell to open locks? " (Answer: Alohomora) all the way to "What is the name of the Muggle weather man who talks about seeing shooting stars over Kent in the first book?" (Answer: Jim McGuffin).

On Day Two, the Physical Challenge was held, a collection of physical tests to prove the most athletic and nimble House (yes, even Harry Potter nerds can do athletic stuff). Challenges were made up of anything we could think of, from "De-Gnoming the Garden" (hurling potatoes with faces painted on them and little paper cone hats as far as we could), to "The Golden Egg Hunt" (dozens of Easter eggs spray-painted gold thrown out over a field; whoever got the most eggs won), to a 4-way Capture the Flag game (it was just as complicated as it sounds). Each House wore their respective colors and each year the games got more and more competitive. The night before the Physical Challenge held the third year of the club, the Slytherin team drove around to the other House members' apartments and tagged their cars with "Slytherin Rulz!!" in washable green car paint.

On Day 3 there was the Final Challenge, a massive scavenger hunt where buildings across the UNC Charlotte campus became different themed locations: classrooms for different subjects at Hogwarts the second year, departments in the

Ministry of Magic the third, or shops in Diagon Alley the fourth. By following a series of riddles and clues, each House would "Brew a Potion" (combine some pinches of Kool-Aid into an original concoction), "Write Legislation for the Department of Magical Creatures" (draft a new law for the treatment of a particular magical beast), and "Intern at Ollivander's" (create a new wand out of sticks, ribbons, glitter, and beads). Once all the tasks had been completed, each House was judged on creativity in completing each task. After all the points were added from the three challenges, the winner was announced and presented with a light-up Triwizard Cup replica (Ravenclaw has won every Triwizard Tournament to date).

The final and perhaps most anticipated event of the year was the End of Year Feast. After spending a year building up House points from making good discussion topics, baking Harry Potter themed treats, bringing in merchandise, and winning games and contests, the winner of the House Cup was announced. The room where the Feast was held would be festooned in the winning House's colors, and everyone was expected to wear those colors in honor of the victors. Everyone brought dishes and drinks to celebrate a successful year of hanging out and enjoying Harry Potter with friends.

DIY Potter Events

All of these events and parties were created through imagination and hard work. If you are reading this chapter and are thinking, "I wish I could do something like that with my friends/group/club/association/team/society/guild" then we have four suggestions for you:

One: Foster buy-in

The thing about getting people to come to events is that if you do not give them a good reason for being there, they will not come. Think about what you are hoping to provide and who you want to show up. If you are a librarian or teacher, take care in deciding on the age group you want to target and try to give them incentive for showing up (extra credit in English class, library fee waiver vouchers, take-home crafts and activities). If you are targeting a college-aged or community-based population, try to create events that foster a sense of community and togetherness. Many of those who grew up with Harry Potter are still looking for a way to connect. Giving them the chance to socialize, play some games, and have perhaps more grown up discussion about the series is a great place to start.

Two: Select your events carefully

When Michael and Hayley were running Potter Watch, they were constantly asking the members for feedback. What parts of the meetings and events did they enjoy? What did they not enjoy? What worked and what did not? How could we improve the things that did not go over well? It was that feedback that helped us prune away activities and features that members found boring and promote new and interesting ideas to create better events. For example, for every Potter Watch meeting for three years we started with a news update from Potter fan sites. It was not until the fourth year that the members spoke up and said that going over the scant updates was a waste of time because there was so little to share and everyone had already seen anything that was big enough to matter on Mugglenet or Facebook before the meeting. We would have kept plowing along if no one had said anything. Afterwards we were able to devote more time to more interesting things like activities and contests which the members enjoyed much more.

Three: Magical substitutions

As hard as we may wish, we are not witches and wizards; thus, we cannot wave our wands and produce spells nor can we hop on our broomsticks and fly around campus. It therefore becomes necessary to use some creativity and imagination to get as close to the real experience as we can. Falling short of that, we tried to make whatever we were doing fun. The Internet is filled with crafts and projects from people who have already done most of the work for us. Want to make some Butterbeer? There are dozens of recipes online. Need a wand and can't shell out the galleons for licensed replicas? Chopsticks, brown paint, and some strategically placed hot glue for texture will work just fine, all for less than $5. Making these items and treats yourself is not only usually less expensive than buying the premade versions, but they will also be more special because they have your heart and creativity added in.

Four: Friendly competition

A major factor in keeping a Potter club or event relevant and to keep participants coming back is a level of friendly competition. Creating a sense of accountability and community encourages participation, buy-in, and a feeling of responsibility and fun to any event or organization. Getting sorted into one of the Houses is usually the easiest way to do this, but groups can also be divided by Death Eaters and Order of the Phoenix members, students against professors, Muggles against wizards, or any other system you can imagine. Rewarding participation with House points and playing up the value of winning the House Cup or similar competition fuels the fire of being part of something exciting and bigger than the individual. In Potter Watch, House members all created secret Facebook groups or text chats where they would remind each other to bring in items or food for House points each week. Each House could be separated to work on games and challenges during the meetings where there was plenty of attempted sabotage and trash talking across the room. Creating an atmosphere where all of this can be done in good fun means that people will come back time and again to defend their House or group.

Whether it is a child's birthday party, an hour-long event at a school or library, or a weekend festival celebrating all things Potter, the most important thing is to make it fun. Veteran fans are looking to relive the magic they grew up with. Those new to the Harry Potter fandom are trying to learn what it is like to be part of something bigger than just words on a page. The sense of community, whether online or in person, is what makes Potter special. You do not need to recreate the Great Hall in seamless detail in order to have great event. Bringing people together to celebrate something they love with other people who love the same thing is all that is required.

The Potter-pocalypse

Potter Watch went on much the same way for the first three years. Membership was always growing, meaning that larger and larger classrooms had to be reserved in which to hold the weekly meetings. The competition for the House Cup became an all-out battle for dominance with each House doing all they could to win games and bring in items and food to earn House points. More games and contests were proposed, such as writing scathing Rita Skeeter articles or designing American wizard robes, all for heaps of House points for the most creative submission.

Discussion was lively as November 19, 2011 approached, meaning the midnight premiere of *Deathly Hallows, Part 1* was nearly at hand. It would be the first movie release since the club's creation, meaning that costumes had to be made and carpools had to be organized. Celebrating the fandom by watching the midnight showing together was more than just a film release: it meant that the fandom was living on, and the club's members were perpetuating that.

As the high from seeing Harry fight off the Malfoys had worn off and the tears from watching Dobby perish had dried, the excitement for *Part 2* began. Speculations for what would be included in the final film began as soon as we left the theater. Yet as the weeks wore on, it began to dawn on many: this would be the last, truly last, Harry Potter event that we would ever attend. After all was said and done, would this be the Potter-pocalypse?

We were diverted from answering this question by travelling to Florida to visit the Wizarding World of Harry Potter. After months of fundraising, taking extensive advantage of group hotel rates, and cramming everyone into as few cars as possible, the eight-hour drive took us to the gates of Hogwarts on earth. It is difficult to describe the feelings of elation and pure joy that accompanied strolling through the streets of Hogsmead for the first time, of seeing the scarlet Hogwarts Express puffing smoke, or the awe felt by standing before the edifice of Hogwarts castle. It is also difficult to say just how many butterbeers we drank. Being in the park was like being inside the books and movies, like walking onto a film set that in many ways had always partially existed in our minds. The group spent all of two days in absolute paradise, and everyone was disappointed when it was time to return to the Muggle world.

All too soon, the semester was over and summer had begun. July 15th now loomed ahead, both a point of thrilling excitement and impending doom. After 13 years of experiencing the Harry Potter books and films for the first time, this would be the last midnight party, the last time to wear robes (at least in public), the last time to see the Warner Brothers logo fly through those dark clouds. The members that were still nearby, or a least willing to drive back from wherever they spent their summers, gathered together in the lobby of the movie theater in a nearby mall. All had come in costume. Some costumes had been worn before, while others were created especially for the occasion. All of the members shared a common purpose: to enjoy each other's company while watching the last Harry Potter film. The Potter-pocalypse was here at last, and we were prepared to weather it together.

A Fandom Moving Forward

Before the premiere of *Deathly Hallows Part 2*, a couple of local news channels sought out Potter Watch for interviews. Most of their questions focused on what it meant that the series was ending, and what Harry Potter fans were to do now that there was nothing to look forward to. The answer to the first question was obvious: it was the end of an era. For nearly all our lives, at least the parts we could remember, Harry Potter had been there, and there had always been something more to look forward to. Whether a new book or a new film, the prospect of newness, new questions, new theories, and new mysteries, had always been there as a kind of security blanket, just so we could always be sure that Harry Potter was not going to end. Not only was the book series a source of entertainment, but it also provided an outlet to meet other fans and introduced other types of literature. Yet, alas, all good things must come to an end; the Hogwarts saga had ended, and we had to accept that.

The second question we were asked, however, is one many Harry Potter fans struggle with to this day: What do we do with ourselves now that there is nothing to look forward to? Surely, the legions of devoted fans will have no choice now but to disappear back into their cupboards under the stairs, to the time before there was any Hagrid to knock down the door and boom his way into our lives, too big to be allowed. But the strange thing, and what fans everywhere are finding out, is that there is simply no going back after the journey that we have all been on together. We will no longer be content to sit in History of Magic class after we have faced Death Eaters and destroyed Horcruxes. Dinner with the Dursleys will no longer satisfy after sampling Molly's treacle tart and feasting in the Great Hall. Our own Dementors do not seem quite so frightening after we learned to cope using our own Patronus charms. The stories are now part of us, and there is no abandoning something that touches our hearts and minds so deeply.

Smart Talk, Meet-Ups, and Wrock & Roll

There is still so much to look forward to. Harry-Potter-themed academic conferences are popping up all over the county. Now that fans can look back on the series and study it in its entirety, academics are leaping at the chance to talk about the series from an intellectual perspective. As is made clear by any of the other authors published in this collection or other collections of essays, J.K. Rowling's magical world was created with great intention and care for detail. Symbolism, language, composition, character names and traits, references to classical mythology, and much more are all there on the pages for academics to obsess over, trying to find each detail in the narrative that points back to Rowling's inspirations. The fact that the novels are composed in a ring composition (see John Granger's writings on this subject) alone prove their merit for literary discussion.

Due to the fact that there is so much material to analyze and discuss, many conferences and events have come into being. Potter Watch has been able to host two conferences to date, Potter Watch 2011 and 2013, both of which have had participants from over a dozen different universities and from across six states. A large variety of individuals were able to submit papers for these conferences; anyone from published professors, like keynote speakers Dr. Amy Sturgis and John Granger, who connect Potter to literary classics, to novices, who feel like they have something to say about the series, have all been able to share their thoughts.

Much larger gatherings and conferences are flourishing around the world. Perhaps one of the largest is LeakyCon, now named GeekyCon in order to expand their programming to cover more than just Potter (www.GeekyCon.com). Hosted by the Harry Potter fansite The Leaky Cauldron, LeakyCon began in 2009 and has held annual conventions nearly every year since, even holding an additional convention in London in 2013. The conventions have gained enough recognition to be able to headline leading and supporting actors from the Harry Potter films as well as celebrated performing artists like Team Starkid, the wizard wrock band Harry and the Potters, and the Harry Potter Puppet Pals. While the programming changes year-to-year at these conventions, discussions and activities usually focus on the many enjoyable aspects of the fandom, including "shipping" discussions (of various Potter relationships), craft tutorials, dance parties, meet-ups, performances, and much more. A tagline for the conference reads "[LeakyCon] is a place where fans can, finally, be themselves."

LeakyCon is not the only conference put together by hardworking, dedicated fans. Other gatherings include MistiCon in Laconia, New Hampshire (www.misti-con.org), The Harry Potter Festival and Academic Conference in Philadelphia, Pennsylvania (www.harrypotterconference.com), CONjuration in Atlanta, Georgia (www.conjuration.com), and many more. Potter fans are also taking over other conventions like DragonCon in Atlanta, Georgia, where areas like the young adult literature groups are typically invaded by participants in black robes and round glasses. All of these gatherings accomplish the same goal: getting people together who all love the same thing and giving them the chance to bond over and share it with one another. Whether a convention or an academic conference, fans are able to focus their creativity and hard work into producing something that hundreds of individuals get to enjoy.

Quidditch Through the Campuses

The phenomenon of Intercollegiate Quidditch has taken off (not literally, unfortunately) across the world, and continues to grow despite the assumed notion that the fandom is now is in its decline. Started in 2005 by a group of students at

Middlebury College in Vermont, the sport has since spread across the world. Currently, there are some 300 registered Quidditch teams in colleges, high school, and communities in over 20 countries around the world (http://iqaquidditch.org/). There are 14 governing bodies that maintain regional organization and support for these teams from Australia to Belgium. The North American branch of the IQA is about to hold its eighth Quidditch World Cup, a tournament that has grown from a small gathering of nearby college teams into a nationwide, weekend-long competition of players and spectators numbering in the thousands.

Perhaps the most remarkable thing about Quidditch is the players. Some may normally think of themselves reclusive, bookish, unphysical-types; yet on the pitch, they are beasts playing a game they already love. In addition to getting individuals more physically active, the IQA has made social advocacy a large part of their organization, especially with gender equality (http://iqaquidditch.org/). This is exemplified by the initiative Title 9 ¾ which requires that all teams have no more than four members of one gender playing on the team at a time. In addition, they openly support trans* individuals and those with non-binary gender expressions and identities (i.e., identities other than just male and female, both, or neither) being able to play as whichever gender they decide. They also encourage teams to promote literacy and reading among their players and within their community, particularly with young people. These important humanitarian efforts aim not only to encourage the members of each team to do their best to be supportive and inclusive, but also to inspire other club sports and community organizations to do the same.

Being able to play Quidditch in the real world, even in its modified or Muggle-fied form, is not only a fantastic example of fandom expression, but is an excellent opportunity for fans across states, countries, and continents to meet and socialize. The phenomenon started with just a few people coming together with an idea for something they liked and, with creativity and hard work, turned into something thousands of people now enjoy. With the trend of new teams being formed each year, Intramural Quidditch will give fans the chance to keep Potter alive for years to come.

Keeping the Magic Alive

There is still so much for Harry Potter fans to look forward to. *Fantastic Beasts and Where to Find Them* is being adapted into a series of films with screenplays written by Rowling herself. A West End stage production is in development for a musical showing Harry's life with the Dursleys pre-*Philosopher's/Sorcerer's Stone*. Universal Studios Hollywood is opening yet another Wizarding World of Harry Potter in California to partner the parks in Orlando and Tokyo. Pottermore features continue to be released and updated. Intramural Quidditch and Harry Potter conferences and conventions continue their annual festivities. And then, of course, there are the random gems of information that Rowling posts on Twitter.

What connects these events and organizations are three things: creativity, hard work, and a love of something held dear. Potter Watch was started as a way of bringing fans of the books and films together. To this day, both of us agree that Potter Watch is the best thing we ever did through our college years. Not only did we meet some of our closest friends through the club, but we met each other. Now almost at our two-year wedding anniversary (we were married June 21, 2013, which happened to be the 10th anniversary of Order of the Phoenix being published, a happy coincidence), we can both agree that without both being part of this fandom, there is no guarantee that we would ever have met.

We are the Harry Potter generation, and there is still so much to look forward to. Potter Watch, the organizations mentioned here, and hundreds of other group and individual efforts were started as a way to bring fans together, and that is just what we have done. We have all been touched by Harry's story, and now that the books and films are over, thousands of fans are asking themselves, What do I do now? How do I survive the Potter-pocalypse? The answer is to keep the magic alive, to keep having fun, and to keep celebrating the things we love most.

PART II
Hogwarts Nerds in a Muggle World

CHAPTER 9

Harry Potter as Dystopian Literature

Kris Swank

Even magical worlds have their issues. When readers are first introduced to J.K. Rowling's world in *Harry Potter and the Sorcerer's Stone*,
the wonders and marvels crowd the margins. But as the series progresses, readers come to realize that all is not liquorice wands and pumpkin fizz
in Wizarding Britain. There is slavery of house-elves, prejudice between races,
cruel and unusual punishment, and a government bureaucracy that hinders more
than it helps. In fact, by the time the series reaches *Order of the Phoenix*, the Ministry is using increasingly draconian measures to monitor its citizens, control the
press, and keep itself in power. Just about the time Hogwarts "High Inquisitor"
Dolores Umbridge begins banning student organizations, meting out sadistic
punishments and restricting free speech, readers of George Orwell's *1984* should
be sensing a bit of *déjà vu.*

There are already some excellent studies of the ways in which Wizarding
Britain resembles "some despotic central African nation" (Barton 34) or historical
fascist states, such as Nazi Germany (Castro 122). Thomas draws an analogy between Fudge's policy of Voldemort-denial and Neville Chamberlain's appease-
ment policies toward Hitler in the buildup to World War II (Part 5), while Prinzi
compares Britain's growing surveillance capabilities to those of Rowling's Ministry of Magic. What has been less examined are the many ways in which Harry's
society resembles the totalitarian states found in literary works such as *1984* and

Ray Bradbury's *Fahrenheit 451*, works belonging to the genre of "dystopian fiction."

Granger, Gunn, Hardy, Schaubert, Steege, and Sturgis (among others) have explored how Rowling draws from various traditions in the English literary canon to imbue her works with an incredible depth and richness. Alongside the influences of authors like Tolkien, Dickens, Spenser and Austen, dystopian authors such as Zamyatin, Boye, Orwell, Burgess and Bradbury may be added to the list. Throughout the Harry Potter series, Rowling engages fully with common dystopian tropes and themes such as government surveillance, information control, the absence of democratic institutions, and the use of cruel and unusual punishment. However, unlike most dystopian literature, the defeat of Voldemort and his pure-blood regime suggests there may be ways to halt a society's decline into a fully-realized totalitarian dystopia.

Writing about imagined societies is a human activity that reaches at least as far back as the Greek philosopher Plato who, in his *Republic* (c.380 BC), considered the elements of the ideal state and the roles of its citizens. But the word "utopia" was not coined until the Renaissance by English statesman Thomas More in his 1516 work of that name. Possibly derived from the Greek οὐ ("not") and τόπος ("place"), the term can be used to describe both imagined and real planned communities. "Utopian literature" is a form of "social dreaming" (Sargent 9). Many authors since the time of Plato have imagined societies which are considerably better than the ones in which they lived, so-called "eutopias," while other have imagined societies considerably worse than their own, or "dystopias." Dystopian literature serves as a warning of what might come to pass if certain negative elements in a society are allowed to proceed unchecked. Dystopias can be drawn from any contemporary societal concern such as artificial intelligence (e.g., *The Terminator*), environmental disaster (e.g., *WALL-E*), or organ donation (e.g., *Never Let Me Go*). Political dystopias, like those depicted in George Orwell's *1984* and *Animal Farm*, became a particular focus of early twentieth-century literature, reflecting their authors' concerns over the rise of totalitarian states such as Nazi Germany, Fascist Italy and Communist Russia. The central features of this type of dystopia include the oppression of the majority by a ruling elite and the regimentation of all aspects of the society (Clute and Grant). In his introduction to Karin Boye's *Kallocain*, Richard B. Vowles describes the totalitarian dystopia:

"The state is everything, the individual is nothing, regulation prevails, and that which cannot be regulated is outlawed or extirpated" (xviii).

As readers first encounter the Wizarding World, it is still grappling with the fallout of the tyrannical Voldemort's first attempt to take power. As the series progresses, the fear over Voldemort's re-emergence brings to the forefront the debate between Wizarding society's security and the rights of its individual citizens. This is the same debate going on in western nations in the wake of terrorist attacks that occurred during the period Rowling was penning her later volumes, and the same debate carried on in the wake of World War II and the rise of totalitarianism. In the Harry Potter series, Rowling extrapolates the same issues and concerns addressed by the authors of twentieth-century dystopian fiction. Yevgeny Zamyatin's Russian novel *We* (1921), Karin Boye's Swedish novel *Kallocain* (1940), and Ray Bradbury's American novella *Fahrenheit 451* (1951) follow the disillusionment of one-time loyal government supporters as they become rebellious malcontents against totalitarian regimes. George Orwell's *Animal Farm* (1945) and *1984* (1949) explore the abuse of power by government elites and their efforts for total societal control. British author Anthony Burgess's *A Clockwork Orange* (1962), with its ultra-violent street gangs extrapolated from the youth movement of the 1960s, connects with Harry Potter's world in its treatment of crime, punishment and propaganda. By drawing comparisons between the Wizarding World and the dystopian societies in these classic works, it's evident that Rowling has woven several themes from this genre into her magical tapestry.

An over-arching theme in dystopian literature is the use of "panopticon surveillance" (Clute and Grant), or the ability of a government to spy on its citizens anywhere and everywhere. Meaning "all-seeing" the term *panopticon* is derived from a model prison designed (though never built) by British Utilitarian philosopher Jeremy Bentham in 1787. The building would be circular, with the inmates occupying cells along the interior circumference, each one isolated from the others by opaque partitions. A guard stationed in a watchtower at the center of the circle could observe any prisoner at any time. Unaware exactly when they were being observed, inmates would be discouraged from attempting misbehavior or escape. Isolation from one another would additionally render the prisoners unable to form coalitions or conspiracies. In addition to its use as a prison, Bentham believed the Panopticon could be adapted for a variety of institutions, including "work-houses, or manufactories, or mad-houses, or hospitals, or schools" (Letter I). French philosopher Michel Foucault posited that "panopticism" applied to an entire society would include a ruling power which had infiltrated, or at least undermined, all other aspects of the culture (216). In the words of Orwell's *1984* government, BIG BROTHER IS WATCHING YOU (5).

1984 features the ubiquitous telescreens, installed in every home and business. Protagonist Winston Smith writes that "any sound above the level of a very low whisper would be picked up by it, moreover, so long as he remained within the field of vision which the metal plaque commanded, he could be seen as well as heard" (6). In Boye's *Kallocain*, homes and offices are likewise equipped with surveillance devices, police-ears and police-eyes "that saw and heard the most intimate acts of the fellow-soldiers [i.e., citizens] day and night, as well as listened to their most private conversations" (97). In both *We* and *1984*, roving police patrols snoop into people's windows. Winston Smith, echoing Bentham's views, illustrates how control relies not on the omnipresence of the enforcers, but only on the threat of their omnipresence:

> There was of course no way of knowing whether you were being watched at any given moment. How often, or on what system, the Thought Police plugged in on any individual wire was guesswork. It was even conceivable that they watched everybody at all times. But at any rate they could plug in your wire whenever they wanted to. You had to live—did live, from habit that became instinct—in the assumption that every sound you made was overheard, and, except in darkness, every movement scrutinized. (6)

Kolding and Greenbrier describe how nothing is really private in Harry Potter's world, either. Magic lets anyone spy on everyone: "A read through the series reveals at least one new way to go undercover per book: invisibility cloaks, potions that will let a stranger perfectly imitate your friend or family (or your pet, or any passing animal), mind control that will take over your best friend and force him to relay back what he hears." The Marauder's Map, Kolding and Greenbrier note, allows the possessor to know who is engaged in the most intimate acts in any bathroom or bedroom inside the castle. Yet some of this magical surveillance can be seen as beneficial. Molly Weasley's clock lets her monitor the safety of each family member when they are away from home. Molly trades individual privacy for security when it's a family matter, as does any parent who uses a GPS app to track the whereabouts of his or her child.

But when it's the government doing the tracking, instead of a parent, the debate over privacy versus security changes tone. Potter scholar Travis Prinzi advances the argument that the government in *Harry Potter* also employs pervasive surveillance of the magical community. Prinzi found that in later volumes "the growing arm of influence of the Ministry of Magic can be paralleled to Foucault's concept of modern society as a Panopticon." The Ministry employs a web of benign-sounding intrusive decrees to monitor such magical practices as underage sorcery, the misuse of Muggle artifacts and dark magic, and the activities of other magical races like house-elves and goblins. Established as safety measures to protect the society, in the wrong hands, these practices could be used for illicit monitoring. This close surveillance is most evident in the Ministry of Magic's monitoring of underage sorcery. Young witches and wizards have the "Trace" put on them, a charm used to detect spells performed outside of Hogwarts, which are forbidden under the Ministry's Decree for the Reasonable Restriction of Underage Sorcery. Harry violates (or is accused of violating) this decree at least three times. When Dobby the house-elf uses a Hover Charm in the Dursleys' kitchen in *Chamber of Secrets*, Harry soon receives an official warning from the Ministry (20-21). In *Prisoner of Azkaban*, when Harry uses an Inflating Charm on Aunt Marge, Minister of Magic Cornelius Fudge is immediately aware of the violation (45). In *Order of the Phoenix,* Harry's use of the Patronus Charm to save himself and Dudley from Dementors results in Harry's immediate expulsion from Hogwarts as well as a disciplinary hearing (26-27). The Trace supposedly breaks on a wizard's or witch's seventeenth birthday, but when Death Eaters easily locate Harry, Ron and Hermione in a café in *Deathly Hallows*, Hermione wonders if Harry still has the Trace on him. Ron argues, "He can't have … The Trace breaks at seventeen, that's Wizarding law, you can't put it on an adult." But Hermione is more cynical, "As far as you know" (168). As it turns out, the Death Eaters have created a Taboo which allows them to track anyone (of any age) who utters the word "Voldemort" (389-90). When Death Eaters infiltrate the Ministry of Magic—as Remus Lupin says, "to all intents and purposes they're the same thing now" (*Deathly Hallows* 206)—it is literally the magical government monitoring the private conversations of its citizens, just as Big Brother does with *1984*'s telescreens, and the Worldstate with *Kallocain*'s police-ears.

If such measures seem fantastic, consider the British Parliament's introduction of a data communications bill in 2012, dubbed the "snooper's charter," requiring Internet service providers to track the records of every subscriber, including web browsing history and social networking site messages, to store that data for 12 months, and to allow police access to the records without a warrant (Gray). Also in 2012, the U.S. Department of Homeland Security was ordered to release a list of keywords its analysts were tracking in social networking sites and online media for potential security threats. Alongside words such as "Al Qaeda" and "dirty bomb" were the benign-seeming "pork," "erosion" and "Tucson" (Miller, and U.S. Dept. of Homeland Security). As the Death Eaters were using the word "Voldemort" to identify potential enemies, so Homeland Security was using its long list of keywords. Added to the Trace and Taboos, students at Hogwarts are constantly under threat of surveillance by Mr. Filch, his cat Mrs. Norris, Peeves the Poltergeist, and even some of the castle portraits, which effectively become Ministry tools when Hogwarts is infiltrated by the Ministry in *Order of the Phoenix* and *Deathly Hallows*.

As in the Panopticon, these dystopian societies also employ isolation as a technique to quash conspiracies. In *We*, each cipher lives alone in a glass-walled apartment, only occasionally being granted visitation from friends and lovers. Children are raised not by parents but in state-sponsored nurseries. In *Kallocain*, young children are moved to youth camps at age seven. In *1984*, families are allowed to cohabitate, but the state's tendency to approve marriages only between couples who are *not* attracted to one another results in many Party members, like Winston Smith, living alone. In *Kallocain*, *1984*, and *Fahrenheit 451*, neighbors and family members are obliged to report any illegal activity committed by another individual or risk arrest themselves.

In *Half-Blood Prince*, a Ministry pamphlet entitled "Protecting Your Home and Family Against Dark Forces" enlists the public to report any "family member, colleague, friend, or neighbor ... acting in a strange manner" to the Magical Law Enforcement Squad (42). Remus Lupin explains that many people "daren't confide in each other, not knowing whom to trust" (*DH* 208). Leo Kall, the protagonist of *Kallocain*, spins this as a virtue: "If there were cause and reason for confidence among individuals, the State would never have come into existence. The sacred and essential foundation for the State is our mutual and well-founded suspicion of each other" (100-101).

The government trains children to be informers in *Kallocain*'s youth camps and *1984*'s Youth League and Spies, analogues of the real-world German Youth and League of German Girls which operated in Nazi Germany from the 1920s to 1945. In *1984*, Winston Smith thinks how "It was almost normal for people over thirty to be frightened of their own children [...] hardly a week passed in which *The Times* did not carry a paragraph describing how some eavesdropping little sneak [...] denounced its parents to the Thought Police" (22). No stretch of the imagination is required to equate these groups with the Inquisitorial Squad created by Hogwarts High Inquisitor Dolores Umbridge in *Order of the Phoenix*. As Draco Malfoy gleefully informs Hermione, the Inquisitors are a "select group of students who are supportive of the Ministry of Magic" (626), and who have the power to report and punish all student infractions.

The Inquisitorial Squad is also tasked with opening and reading mail into and out of Hogwarts (631). Further, Umbridge ensures that "All channels of communication in and out of this school are being monitored. A Floo Network Regulator is keeping watch over every fire in Hogwarts... And Mr. Filch is observing all secret passages in and out of the castle" (*Order of the Phoenix* 631). D-503, the protagonist of Zamyatin's *We*, risks his life merely possessing a pile of incriminating notes (164). In *1984*, Winston Smith's diary is a compromising possession, "Even with nothing written in it" (9). "As for sending a letter through the mails," Smith writes, "it was out of the question. By a routine that was not even secret, all letters were opened in transit" (88).

Education itself becomes a target in dystopias. In *Order of the Phoenix*, Hermione learns that she and her fellow students "are being prevented from learning Defence Against the Dark Arts because Fudge is scared we'll use spells against the Ministry" (303). Dangerous knowledge is also the key theme in Bradbury's *Fahrenheit 451*, where the general populace—fed on a daily diet of cheap television and glossy magazines—Is suspicious of "examiners, critics, knowers, and imaginative creators, the word 'intellectual,' of course, became the swear word it deserved to be" (37). Hermione Granger is well-known for memorizing and quoting the contents of the tomes she has read. In *Fahrenheit 451*, Guy Montag, one of the city's "firemen" who track down and burn illicit books, meets Granger, the leader of a clandestine group who memorize the contents of important books before they can be burned. Is it coincidence or is Rowling tipping her hat that in both *Harry Potter* and *Fahrenheit 451* a character closely-associated with memorizing books is named "Granger"?

Limitation of the free expression of ideas also extends to the media in dystopian societies. As the society in *Fahrenheit 451* burns books to keep its populace "safe" from information, *1984's* Winston Smith, working for the ironically-named Ministry of Truth, expurgates newspapers of any information contradictory to the official Party line. Rowling's *Daily Prophet* also quickly gets behind the Ministry of Magic's campaign to quash rumors of Voldemort's return. Lupin tells an incredulous Harry, "the Ministry is leaning heavily on the *Daily Prophet* not to report any of what they're calling Dumbledore's rumor-mongering, so most of the Wizarding community are completely unaware anything's happened" (*Order of the Phoenix* 94). John Granger notes that "When the Ministry goes under the Dark Lord's control in Harry's seventh year, the *Prophet* falls into line as well... The media, in Rowling's satirical treatment, is joined at the hip to the powerful, the bozos, and to parasites on the body politic" (163). One hold-out against government pressure is the *Quibbler*, the tabloid magazine published by Luna Lovegood's father Xenophilius. In *Order of the Phoenix*, the *Quibbler* runs Rita Skeeter's interview with Harry Potter on the rebirth of Lord Voldemort at the same time the *Daily Prophet* is supporting Fudge's policy of Voldemort denial. After the Death Eaters takeover the Ministry of Magic in *Deathly Hallows*, the *Quibbler* continues to publicly support Harry until Death Eaters kidnap Luna, and Xenophilius is coerced to print anti-Harry propaganda. Finally, the only remaining independent outlet becomes "Potterwatch," the roving pirate radio station whose news-readers are constantly under threat of capture by the Death Eaters.

Such methods are standard fare for literary dystopias, but they are present in the literature because of their analogues in the real world. The measures exerted by the Ministry of Magic increase throughout the Harry Potter series just as real-world events during the period Rowling was writing the series, such as the terrorist attacks in the U.S. on September 11, 2001 and the London Underground on July 7, 2005, increased the tension between advocates of free speech and national security. High-profile protesters Noam Chomsky and Icelandic politician and WikiLeaks campaigner Birgitta Jonsdottir argued the United States' National Defense Authorization Bill, signed by President Barack Obama at the end of 2011, would "effectively broadened the definition of 'supporter of terrorism' to include peaceful activists, authors, academics and even journalists interviewing members of radical groups" (Harris). Ex-*New York Times* reporter Chris Hedges told a judge he feared arrest for interviewing or even meeting with Islamic radicals. "I could be detained by the US military, held in a military facility—including offshore—denied due process and incarcerated until 'the end of hostilities' whenever that is," he said (Harris). In 2005, the International Federation of Journalists warned that "anti-terror legislation being prepared independently by Britain and Australia could endanger democracy and press freedom and are 'chilling for the exercise of journalism'" (International Federation of Journalists). Yet such concerns are ever-present in any society. In an article for the *New Republic*, Ritika Singh and Benjamin Wittes trace the debate between privacy and security to the founding of the United States in documents such as the Constitution and the Alien and Sedition Acts of 1798, passed in anticipation of potential conflict with France.

Limits on individual free expression further extend to the suppression of free association. In *Kallocain*, it is against the law to form any organization outside the State's control (99), and a significant portion of the novel concerns efforts to interrogate members of a group whose only crime seems to be that they meet without permission. Leo Kall and Police Chief Karrek demand, "what kind of revolution do you have in mind? [...] You must want something—" (80). In *Order of the Phoenix*, Umbridge also forbids all unauthorized student organizations at Hogwarts, and makes participation in them grounds for expulsion. When she uncovers the secret meetings of "Dumbledore's Army," she and Fudge believe Dumbledore is planning to overthrow the Ministry. The irony is that Harry and his classmates initially had no intentions of fomenting rebellion; they simply wanted to practice defensive magic in case Voldemort started a war. In *Kallocain*, the clandestine group that Kall uncovers likewise has a no revolutionary agenda.

While on the surface it might not seem as if the Harry Potter books have much in common with the ultra-violent brutality of Burgess's *A Clockwork Orange*, there are a few striking parallels. Alex's violent gang of droogs and Fenrir Greyback's snatchers are both violent gangs which operate outside the law. Both governments attempt aversion therapy to alter unwanted behavior—via the "Ludovico technique" with Alex, and via Umbridge's Blood Quill with Harry. Both governments seek to use Alex and Harry as propaganda tools. Once a violent criminal, Alex's "cure" makes him a desirable poster boy of a government eager to prove its aversion therapy technique works (even though it doesn't). The Minister of the Interior or Inferior (the "IntInfMin") offers Alex a job in the middle of a hospital-bed publicity photo shoot: "I and the Government of which I am a member want you to regard us as friends. Yes, friends. We have put you right, yes? You are getting the best of treatment.... When you leave here... you will have no worries. We shall see to everything. A good job on a good salary. Because you are helping us...Smile!" (Burgess 112). Similarly, in the *Half-Blood Prince*, the new Minister of Magic Rufus Scrimgeour attempts to recruit Harry as his poster boy in the fight against the resurrected Voldemort, "the point is, you are a symbol of hope for many, Harry... you might consider it, well, almost a duty to stand alongside the Ministry, and give everyone a boost" (345). Both governments show no qualms about using young men—boys, really—to give a positive spin to failed policies.

Dystopian literature also often exposes an absence of democratic institutions in the societies portrayed. In *We*, the One State has succeeded in completely perverting free elections, as can be seen in D-503's explanation:

> Tomorrow is the day of the annual election of the Benefactor.... It goes without saying that this does not resemble the disordered, disorganized elections of the Ancients, when—it seems funny to say it—the result of an election was not known beforehand.... They say that the Ancients conducted elections in some kind of secrecy, hiding like thieves.... For us, there is nothing to hide and nothing to be ashamed of: we celebrate election day in the daytime, openly and honestly. I see everyone vote for the Benefactor; everyone sees me vote for the Benefactor. (141)

In *1984*, there is not even the farcical election presented in *We*. Orwell's mustachioed Big Brother is the unopposed dictator of the Party. Big Brother has always been the dictator. Big Brother will always be the dictator. It hardly matters that even Party insiders aren't certain if there is, or ever was, a real man called Big Brother. In Orwell's other great dystopian work, *Animal Farm* (1945)—which Rowling named as one of the top ten books every child should read (Higgins)—a group of animals ousts their drunken human farmer, opting instead to establish their own egalitarian society where "All animals are equal" (43). But there are no democratic processes as the pigs soon elevate themselves to positions of authority from where they enjoy special privileges and oppress the other animals. They even revise the farm's prime commandment to read, "All animals are equal but some animals are more equal than others" (133).

There may be no democratic process in Harry's world either. As Barton points out, when Cornelius Fudge is replaced as Minister of Magic by Rufus Scrimgeour in *Half-Blood Prince*, there is no mention of an election being held. A parliamentary or legislative process is never mentioned, and the Wizengamot high court appears to be controlled by the Minister himself: "There are thus no governmental bodies outside the Ministry of Magic to act as a check upon government abuses" (Barton 42-43). And when the Death Eaters take over the Ministry, their pure-blood agenda seeks to oppress Muggles, "mud-bloods," and non-human magical creatures just as the *Animal Farm* pigs oppress non-pigs (as well as any dissenting pigs).

The totalitarian dystopias of twentieth-century literature also uniformly have justice systems which lack due process. To be accused is to be guilty in *Kallocain* and *1984*. Judgments are made, not by a court system, but on the spot by the firemen in *Fahrenheit 451*. There is a notable lack of due process in the Wizarding world, as well. When Harry violates the Decree for the Reasonable Restriction of Underage Sorcery in *Order of the Phoenix*, he is instantly expelled from Hogwarts and ordered to appear at a disciplinary hearing. He is not provided with defense counsel, nor is he told that wizard law gives him the right to present witnesses. The Ministry even attempts to exclude Dumbledore from the proceedings by providing him with the wrong time for the hearing. But Harry turns out to be lucky considering that both Hagrid, in *Chamber of Secrets*, and Stan Shunpike, in *Half-Blood Prince*, are incarcerated in wizard prison without any sort of trial.

Emerging from an age of unprecedented technological and chemical advances, twentieth-century dystopian authors were also exceedingly imaginative in their creation of cruel and unusual punishments. Orwell's Winston Smith is subjected to horrific brainwashing techniques, as is Burgess's Alex in *A Clockwork Orange*. In Bradbury's *Fahrenheit 451*, an old woman is left to burn alive with her illegal library. D-503 in *We* is forced to undergo "The Great Operation," a lobotomy that restores "100% Happiness" by removing his imagination, and thus, his will to rebel. Harry Potter's world has equally inventive, and horrific, punishments. In *Order of the Phoenix*, Harry is punished with Dolores Umbridge's Blood Quill. She orders him to write *"I must not tell lies"* on parchment while the magic of the quill literally etches that message into Harry's skin, an excruciating process which permanently scars the fifteen-year-old boy. Remus Lupin explains that the wizard prison, Azkaban, is a fortress "set on a tiny island, way out to sea, but they don't need walls and water to keep the prisoners in, not when they're all trapped inside their own heads, incapable of a single cheerful thought. Most of them go mad within weeks" (*Prisoner of Azkaban* 188). This is due to the prison's guards, the Dementors, who "drain peace, hope, and happiness out of the air around them…. Get too near a Dementor and every good feeling, every happy memory will be sucked out of you" (*Prisoner of Azkaban* 187). Hagrid says, the Dementors are not concerned with justice, "Long as they've got a couple o' hundred humans stuck there with 'em, so they can leech all the happiness out of 'em, they don' give a damn who's guilty an' who's not"(*Prisoner of Azkaban* 221). Those reckoned irredeemable are subjected to the "Dementor's Kiss," the sucking out of one's very soul.

An interesting analogue between Boye's *Kallocain* and Rowling's *Harry Potter* series is the use of truth drugs. In the real world, modern democratic societies protect individuals against self-incrimination. In Britain, the right for criminal suspects to remain silent was well established in common law from the seventeenth century. The Fifth Amendment to the United States Constitution protects witnesses from being forced to incriminate themselves. In the 1996 case of "John Murray v. The United Kingdom," the European Court of Human Rights stated "there can be no doubt that the right to remain silent under police questioning and the privilege against self-incrimination are generally recognised international standards" (§45). But the totalitarian dystopia recognizes no such privilege. Leo Kall, a chemist employed in the Worldstate laboratory invents a pale green, injectable fluid which causes subjects to disclose their innermost secrets. Kall views his eponymous "Kallocain" as the solution to the prevalence of false testimony being presented in court cases: "my discovery will solve this problem in a trice. Not only can witnesses be controlled now—indeed, no witnesses will be required, since the criminal will confess, happily and without reservation, after one single little injection" (46). It is a matter of mere days before police begin using this truth drug on suspects not even charged with a crime, as well as political rivals. In *Goblet of Fire*, Albus Dumbledore uses the magical potion *verita serum* (literally "truth serum") to force a confession from Barty Crouch, Jr. But who is Dumbledore anyway? Not a police officer or a prison official, but a high school headmaster who doses Crouch without so much as a judicial hearing. Umbridge, in her capacity as Head of Hogwarts, attempts to use the potion on Harry in *Order of the Phoenix*. Even Harry's moral compass goes astray when he suggests secretly using *verita serum* on Horace Slughorn in *Half-Blood Prince*.

After the real-world terrorism events of the new millennium, western societies have debated the appropriate balance between national security and human rights in matters like compelled self-incrimination. Those charged with protecting their societies may not believe terrorism suspects should be given the same human rights as their own society's citizens. Human rights advocates warn of the slippery slope which leads from suspending the rights of terrorism suspects (some of whom *are* citizens), to suspending the rights of the very citizens interrogators are charged with protecting. In *Kallocain*, Leo Kall's supervisor Edo Rissen recognizes the implications of using truth drugs in interrogations, "This much at least is certain—the last vestige of our private lives will then be gone," that is, a person's private thoughts. Kall chuckles in reply, "Well, *that* is not too important!" (51).

Words of Warning

John Granger writes that "Ms. Rowling's political and social allegory within and beneath her story line are not as dark as Orwell's picture of 1948 reality projected into his nightmare *1984* or even his relatively comic portrayal of political revolution in *Animal Farm*" (164). And this is true. A major difference between the protagonists of these twentieth-century dystopian works and the Harry Potter series is that Harry has a (mostly) happy ending, while the others are crushed beneath the heel of their totalitarian states. Winston Smith and D-503 are tortured into submission. Kall, Montag and Alex face uncertain futures. Only Harry makes a significant difference in his society, defeating an evil that threatens to establish the sort of totalitarian nightmare states seen in *1984* and the other works.

What Harry and his allies confront is really a *nascent* totalitarian state, its tentacles reaching out in all directions, but not yet completely strangling all resistance. There are still good people in the Ministry of Magic, like Arthur Weasley and Kingsley Shacklebolt, willing to take great risks to stop Voldemort and the Death Eaters. There are still enough students at Hogwarts willing to defy the likes of Umbridge and the Carrow siblings, and still just enough space to make defiance possible. There is no such space in Orwell's, Boye's or Zamyatin's societies; it's too late. Big Brother is already inside every office, bedroom, and interpersonal relationship. Occasional rebels like Winston Smith and D-503 are soon identified and quashed. But the net is closing in on the Wizarding World, and the pivotal moment, beyond which resistance would be futile, is the Battle of Hogwarts.

Herein lies Rowling's point. If a faction such as D-503's and his allies had made their stand earlier in that society's movement toward totalitarianism, could it have been stopped? Rowling says "yes," as evidenced by Harry's victory at the Battle of Hogwarts. What a comparison of the Harry Potter series to *We* and other dystopian literature suggests is that the time to stand up for one's liberties is not after the regime is entrenched, but at the first signs of its emergence.

The purpose of dystopian literature is to highlight disturbing aspects of real-world societies. Rowling's portrayal of a Wizarding society with pervasive surveillance, for instance, is a reflection of modern-day Britain, which has greatly increased its ability to collect and monitor information about individuals. In 2007, the same year that *Deathly Hallows* was published, Henry Porter commented in the *British Observer* on the increasing ability of the British government to monitor its citizens since 9/11:

> The ID card database, the national surveillance of vehicles and retention of information about every individual motorway journey, the huge number of new criminal offences, the half million intercepts of private communications every year, the proposed measures to take 53 pieces of information from everyone wishing to go abroad, which will include powers to prevent travel.... (quoted in Prinzi).

When readers can see the correlation between increased surveillance in the Wizard World and in their own—when, for instance, readers can see the correlation between a Ministry that puts you on a watchlist for saying "Voldemort" and a government that might put you on a watchlist for typing "pork," "erosion," or "Tucson" into a social media site—then readers can see the correlation between the dystopian society and what their own society *could become*" if the negative elements proceed unimpeded. The message in all dystopian literature, and one of the most powerful Rowling sends to her readers, is that people are, ultimately, responsible for the governments they have. It's up to the average citizen to halt government abuses *as they begin*, no matter how hard that may be, no matter if the effort appears hopeless. The protagonists of *We, Kallocain, 1984, Fahrenheit 451* and *A Clockwork Orange* all suffer greatly for defying their respective governments. Harry suffers greatly, too. That he is ultimately victorious does not mean that Rowling's message is less dire. Hers is, in fact, a powerful warning about what average citizens can (and should) do to halt budding totalitarian governments before it's too late.

Works Cited

Barton, Benjamin H. "Harry Potter and the Half-Crazed Bureaucracy." *The Law and Harry Potter*. Eds. Jeffrey E. Thomas and Franklin G. Snyder. Durham, NC: Carolina Academic Press, 2010: 33-47. Print.

Bradbury, Ray. *Fahrenheit 451*, 60th anniversary ed. Intro. Neil Gaiman. New York: Simon & Schuster, 2013. Print.

Burgess, Anthony. *A Clockwork Orange*. New York: W. W. Norton, 1986. Print.

Boye, Karin. *Kallocain*. Intro. by Richard B. Vowles. Trans. Gustaf Lannestock. Madison: University of Wisconsin Press, 1966. Rpt. in *The Literature Collection*. University of Wisconsin Digital Collections Center, 2004. Web.

"Case of John Murray v. The United Kingdom (Application no. 18731/91)." *The European Court of Human Rights.* 8 Feb. 1996. British and Irish Legal Information Institute database. Web.

Castro, Adam-Troy. "From Azkaban to Abu Graib: Fear and Fascism in Harry

Potter and the Order of the Phoenix." *Mapping the World of the Sorcerer's Apprentice: An Unauthorized Exploration of the Harry Potter Series Complete Through Book Six.* Ed. Mercedes Lackey, with Leah Wilson. Dallas: BenBella Books, 2006: 119-132. Print.

Clute, John and John Grant, eds. *Encyclopedia of Fantasy* London: Orbit, 1997. Rpt. in *SFE: The Encyclopedia of Science Fiction.* 1999. Web.

Granger, John. *Harry Potter's Bookshelf: The Great Books Behind the Hogwarts Adventures.* New York: Berkley Books, 2009. Print.

Gunn, James. "Harry Potter as Schooldays Novel." *Mapping the World of the Sorcerer's Apprentice: An Unauthorized Exploration of the Harry Potter Series Complete Through Book Six.* Ed. Mercedes Lackey, with Leah Wilson. Dallas: BenBella Books, 2006: 145-155. Print.

Hardy, Elizabeth Baird. "Horcruxes in Faerie Land: Edmund Spencer's Influence on Voldemort's Efforts to Elude Death." *Harry Potter for Nerds: Essays for Fans, Academics, and Lit Geeks.* Ed. Travis Prinzi. [United States?]: Unlocking Press, 2011. Kindle e-book.

Harris, Paul. "US anti-terrorism law curbs free speech and activist work, court told." *The Guardian* (U.K.). 29 Mar. 2012. Web.

Higgins, Charlotte. "From Beatrix Potter to Ulysses ... what the top writers say every child should read." *The Guardian* (U.K). 30 Jan. 2006. Web.

International Federation of Journalists. "Terror law 'chilling for democracy and press freedom,' warns IFJ." *IFEX.* 7 Nov 2005. Web.

Kolding, Micah and Michael Greenbrier. "6 Horrifying Implications of the Harry Potter Universe." *Cracked. com* 14 Mar. 2012. Web.

Miller, Daniel. "Revealed: Hundreds of words to avoid using online if you don't want the government spying on you (and they include 'pork', 'cloud' and 'Mexico')." *Daily Mail (U.K.) Online.* 26 May 2012. Web.

Orwell, George. *1984.* Boston: Houghton Mifflin Harcourt, 1983. Nook e-book.

——. *Animal Farm.* New York: Penguin, 1996. Print.

Prinzi, Travis. "The Ministry as Panopticon." *The Hog's Head.* TheHogsHead.org, 09 Aug. 2007. Web.

Rowling, J.K. The *Harry Potter* series [hardcover editions]. New York: Arthur A. Levine, Scholastic, 1997-2007. Print.

Sargent, Lyman Tower. "The Three Faces of Utopianism Revisited." *Utopian*

Studies 5. 1 (1994): 1-37.

Schaubert, Lancelot. "Mars is Bright Tonight: A Deeper Look at J.K. Rowling's Use of Dante's First Canto" *Harry Potter for Nerds: Essays for Fans, Academics, and Lit Geeks*. Ed. Travis Prinzi. [United States?]: Unlocking Press, 2011. Kindle e-book.

Singh, Ritika and Benjamin Wittes. "The Founding Fathers Vacillated on Government Snooping, Too." *New Republic*. 23 Oct. 2013. Web.

Steege, David K. "Harry Potter, Tom Brown, and the British School Story: Lost in Transit," *The Ivory Tower and Harry Potter*. Ed. Lana A. Whited. Columbia: University of Missouri Press, 2002: 140-156. Print.

Sturgis, Amy H. "When Harry Met Faërie," *Hog's Head Conversations*: Essays on Harry Potter. Ed. Travis Prinzi. Allentown, PA: Zossima Press, 2009: 81-101. Print.

Thomas, James W. *Repotting Harry Potter: A Professor's Book-by-Book Guide for the Serious Re-Reader*. Hamden, CT: Zossima Press, 2011. Kindle e-book.

U.S. Dept. of Homeland Security, National Operations Center. *Analyst's Desktop Binder 2011*. [Washington, D.C.]: DoHS, 2011. Rpt. on www.scribd.com/doc/82701103/Analyst-Desktop-Binder-RE-DACTED. n.d. Web.

Zamyatin, Yevgeny. *We*. Trans. Natasha Randall. New York: Modern Library, 2006. Nook e-book.

CHAPTER 10

Seeking Dumbledore's Mother:

Harry Potter in the Native American Context

Amy H. Sturgis

"Unlike any other creature on this planet, humans can learn and understand, without having experienced," J.K. Rowling said in her 2008 commencement address, "The Fringe Benefits of Failure, and the Importance of Imagination," at the Annual Meeting of the Harvard Alumni Association. "They can think themselves into other people's places."[1]

The Harry Potter series illustrates this clearly, as Rowling invites readers to empathize with wizards and half-giants, werewolves and goblins, merpeople and centaurs. The novels not only encourage such connections to fictional characters and their lives, but they also allow readers to use the metaphors and meanings behind the story of her magical world to "learn and understand" more about our own. If we can think ourselves "into other people's places," we can also see through different windows and read through different lenses. The rewards of seeking an American Indian context for the Harry Potter novels include greater insights into both Rowling's work and Native America itself.

---

[1] J.K. Rowling, "The Fringe Benefits of Failure, and the Importance of Imagination" *Harvard Magazine,* 5 June, 2008. <http://harvardmagazine.com/2008/06/the-fringe-benefits-failure-the-importance-imagination> Accessed 12 November, 2012.

Beginning with Navajo Eyes

Any discussion of the relationship between Harry Potter and Native America must begin with an early essay in Harry Potter studies, Hollie Anderson's foundational "Reading Harry Potter with Navajo Eyes," which appears in the 2002 collection *Harry Potter's World: Multidisciplinary Critical Perspectives*. At the time Anderson wrote, Rowling had yet to publish the final three books in her series. Despite the fact the Harry Potter saga was a work in progress, however, Anderson found she had plenty of material from which to draw some fascinating connections.

Anderson writes from the perspective of a Navajo woman who left her home reservation to pursue higher education and then returned to teach at a Navajo school. She explains that, without consciously intending to do so, J.K. Rowling has crafted stories that resonate especially deeply with Anderson's experience and heritage as a Native American.

Harry's acute awareness of his ignorance of Hogwarts and its traditions mirrors Anderson's own feelings upon leaving the Navajo Nation for Purdue University, for instance. She says, "I, like Harry, often questioned what people were talking about because I did not know some things that were everyday knowledge for someone from the local culture."[2] When, on the Hogwarts Express in *Harry Potter and the Philosopher's Stone*, Harry admits to Ron that he said Voldemort's name only because he didn't know it wasn't done, when he confesses no knowledge of Quidditch and its teams, Anderson sympathizes.

On his first fateful trip from Platform 9 ¾, Harry realizes that other students had known from infancy they would attend Hogwarts and had been raised with expectations and information about it, while he hadn't even known the place existed, much less that he would study there. Anderson notes how foreign college life and then graduate school appeared to her, how very far away both seemed—not halfway across the country, but literally worlds away—from her reservation, and how she found herself relying on helpful allies to serve as cultural translators (as Harry relies on Ron Weasley, Hermione Granger, and Albus Dumbledore,

---

[2] Hollie Anderson, "Reading Harry Potter with Navajo Eyes" in *Harry Potter's World: Multidisciplinary Critical Perspectives*. Elizabeth E. Heilman, ed. (New York: Routledge-Falmer, 2002): 97-107, 101.

among others), not only to explain the jokes she didn't get and the references she couldn't understand, but also to help her adjust to this different world and discover her rightful position in it. Her story of displacement and culture shock is not atypical for American Indians, especially those who have grown up on reservations, leaving their homes for colleges, universities, and/or urban settings.[3]

Due to her background "on the rez," Anderson finds that other aspects of the Harry Potter series resonate especially deeply with her, from the familiarity of the Weasleys' story—"although, they might not be as well off financially as the dominant culture might suggest is adequate, they emit the feeling that they are happy and thankful that they have their family"[4]—to the similarities between traditional Navajo beliefs in magic and shape-shifting witches who take on animal form and Rowling's depiction of the wizarding world and its animagi. Perhaps Anderson's most compelling insight, however, is her discussion of the parallel-in-reverse she observes in the metaphor of the boarding school that Rowling provides. This metaphor, Anderson explains, has given her a new window through which she can see and understand her families' and peoples' experience of "alienation and disconnection."[5]

Reconsidering the Boarding School

As Rowling's readers know and Anderson underscores in her essay, Harry's matriculation at Hogwarts becomes something of a homecoming for him. At last he is free to be himself in a setting that encourages his exploration of his identity as a wizard and facilitates his investigation of his own personal background and the larger culture of the magical world. Interludes such as the period during which he is ostracized by some of his classmates because they fear he is the Heir of Slytherin (in *Harry Potter and the Chamber of Secrets*) are the exceptions that prove the rule: Harry is accepted at Hogwarts and in Gryffindor House as a student, a friend, a team member, and even a leader. He is with his kind. He belongs.

---

[3] See, for example, the personal essays in the first two sections of *Genocide of the Mind: New Native American Writing*. MariJo Moore, ed. (New York: Thunder Mouth's Press/Nation Books, 2003).

[4] Anderson, 104.

[5] Anderson, 97.

In contrast, Harry's experience with the Dursleys is one of denial. For the first decade of his life, he is denied the knowledge of who he is as a wizard and as the son of James and Lily Potter, fighters against and victims of Lord Voldemort. What little his aunt and uncle tell him, namely that his good-for-nothing parents perished in a car crash, is patently false. Later, after he returns to Privet Drive from Hogwarts for the summer, he is denied the comfort of contacting his friends, continuing his studies openly, or even alluding to the idea of magic. He remains, for all practical purposes, a prisoner where he lives, as the bars on his window in *Harry Potter and the Chamber of Secrets* illustrate. At best, he receives neglect from the Dursleys, and at worst, open contempt.

Furthermore, Harry is forced to live a lie in Little Whinging. His aunt and uncle fabricate an alternate story to replace his own. In *Harry Potter and the Prisoner of Azkaban*, the Dursleys even insist that he accept it, pretending for Aunt Marge's benefit that he's a student—or is that inmate?—at St Brutus's Secure Centre for Incurably Criminal Boys. This falsehood is hardly flattering, but it orients him within the dominant Muggle culture as someone more acceptable and less threatening than who and what he actually is. He's not a Muggle and he never will be, but the lie lets him "pass" as one.

Anderson explains that this contrast between Harry's isolating experience at Privet Drive and the nurturing one at Hogwarts offers an inverse portrait of many Native Americans', including her own family members', experiences at home and at boarding school under the non-reservation Indian Boarding School and Indian Residential School programs that existed in both the United States and Canada for more than a century. Because few outside of Native America today are aware of the story behind the Indian Boarding Schools system, it is worth a brief introduction.

Residential schools for American Indians date back to the colonial period in North America; they were founded by individual missionaries, religious organizations, and local communities of Anglo-Americans or the Native nations themselves. Dartmouth College, in fact, began its life as one such institution. But a new era began in principle in 1869, with President Ulysses S. Grant's "Peace Policy," and in practice in 1879, when U.S. Army officer Richard Henry Pratt established the Carlisle Indian Industrial School at a former military installation in

Carlisle, Pennsylvania. The purpose of the school—and the many it would in-spire, including more than two dozen established by the Bureau of Indian Affairs and hundreds of others run by religious organizations across the United States—could be summed up in one word: assimilation. "A great general has said that the only good Indian is a dead one," Pratt said in 1892. "In a sense, I agree with the sentiment, but only in this: that all the Indian there is in the race should be dead. Kill the Indian in him, and save the man."[6] The Canadian government imported this system almost immediately.

"Killing the Indian" in both the United States and Canada meant separating Native American children from their families, stripping them of not only their clothes and hair but also their names, their languages, and their histories, and forcibly remaking them into individuals who could "pass" in the dominant white culture. After years in an often harsh boot-camp-like atmosphere, those children who survived—the death toll from disease, neglect, and abuse was appalling—would be outward practitioners (if not all true believers) of Christianity who could read and write in English and demonstrate all the skills necessary for en-tering the lower-class labor market in urban settings, as domestics, in the case of women, or manual workers, in the case of men.[7] Many could no longer, however, converse with their relatives in their native tongues or integrate into their na-tions' more rural economies, and none could reclaim years of lost life, accultura-tion, and nurture in their home communities and natural family environments.

Today, the efforts of survivors and their families to document what took place under this system have led to the creation of organizations such as the Boarding School Healing Project (http://boardingschoolhealingproject.org) and the production of documentary films such as *Our Spirits Don't Speak English: Indian Boarding Schools* (Rich-Heape Films, 2008) and *We Were Children* (Eagle Vi-sion/One Television/National Film Board of Canada, 2012), as well as dramatic

---

[6] Quoted in Charla Bear, "American Indian Boarding Schools Haunt Many," NPR.org. 18 May, 2008. Accessed on 12 December, 2012. <http://www.npr.org/ tem-plates/story/story.php?storyId=16516865>

[7] See Bear; Andrea Smith, "Soul Wound: The Legacy of Native American Schools," *Amnesty International Magazine*. 26 March, 2007. <http://www.amnestyusa.org/ node/87342> Accessed 30 November, 2012; and interviews with survivors in *Our Spirits Don't Speak English: Indian Boarding Schools* (Rich-Heape Films, 2008).

films inspired by actual events such as *Where the Spirit Lives* (Screen Door, 1989) and *Older Than America* (Tribal Alliance Productions, 2008). On June 11, 2008, Canadian Prime Minister Stephen Harper issued a formal Statement of Apology to former students of its Indian Residential Schools, saying,

> To the approximately 80,000 living former students, and all family members and communities, the Government of Canada now recognizes that it was wrong to forcibly remove children from their homes.... We now recognize that it was wrong to separate children from rich and vibrant cultures and traditions.... We now recognize that, far too often, these institutions gave rise to abuse or neglect and were inadequately controlled.... The Government of Canada sincerely apologizes and asks the forgiveness of the Aboriginal peoples of this country for failing them so profoundly.[8]

The Indian Boarding School system existed into the 1980s, well within living memory. In "Reading Harry Potter with Navajo Eyes," Anderson describes her mother's impressions from her years at the Fort Wingate Indian boarding school in New Mexico, which include memories of punishments for acting Navajo, for speaking the Navajo language even in a hushed voice to another student in the dormitory. Her mother longed to go home, "where she could freely express herself" and practice her culture, where she didn't have to live a lie, where being herself wasn't against the rules.[9] Anderson finds that taking Harry Potter's journey with him and feeling his emotions as he flourishes at Hogwarts and suffers at Privet Drive has given her new insights into her mother's and other Native Americans' experiences.

Anderson doesn't suggest Rowling intended to draw a comparison between Harry's forced assimilation among the Dursleys and American Indian students' forced assimilation in boarding schools, but she makes a convincing case for how seeing Harry Potter through this different lens may enhance our appreciation for the depth and subtlety of Rowling's work as well as the breadth of her novels' applicability. Furthermore, Anderson's essay suggests that sharing these insights

---

[8] Stephen Harper on behalf of the Government of Canada, "Statement of Apology to Former Students of Indian Residential Schools," 11 June, 2008. Official website of Aboriginal Affairs and Northern Development Canada. <http://www.aadnc-aandc.gc.ca/eng/1100100015644/1100100015649> Accessed on 26 November, 2012.

[9] Anderson, 99.

with students and fellow readers may open doors for fruitful discussions of sensitive topics that might otherwise be difficult to broach.

Rethinking Werewolves, Giants, and Goblins

In a July 7, 2000 *Entertainment Weekly* interview, J.K. Rowling admits, "bigotry is probably the thing I detest most. All forms of intolerance, the whole idea of 'that which is different from me is necessarily evil.'"[10] She explores the subject of prejudice and oppression in her books through a variety of metaphors. From some purebloods' disdain for the poor or non-pureblood magical folk, or the Dursleys' fear of anyone who doesn't fit their definition of "normal," to the centaurs' dislike of humans, or even the headless ghosts' marginalization of the nearly headless, Rowling provides a variety of examples of how bigotry may become entrenched in relationships and even government policy with tragic consequences.

Because she published her essay in 2003, Hollie Anderson lacked the benefit of drawing from material in all seven of the Harry Potter novels as readers may do today. If one rereads the complete saga with Native American issues in mind, other parallels suggest themselves. The wizarding community's positions toward werewolves, giants, and goblins, for example, invite comparisons with historical and contemporary Native America.

The plight of the werewolves in Rowling's series provides a case in point. Remus Lupin's tenuous legal standing as a werewolf—governed by a separate set of regulations from those that apply to his fellow "Marauders" or members of the Order of the Phoenix—is not unlike the still unique and problematic legal position of Native peoples in the United States. Lupin's actions, at least the strictly legal ones, are dictated by the Beast Division of the Department for the Regulation and Control of Magical Creatures, much as the options of Native Americans—despite repeated and numerous protests from Natives and non-Natives

---

[10] J.K. Rowling, Interview with *Entertainment Weekly,* September 7, 2000, as archived on *Mugglenet.com.* 19 August, 2003. <http://mugglenet.com/ewinterview1.shtml> Accessed 30 November, 2012.

alike[11]—are circumscribed by the Bureau of Indian Affairs of the U.S. Department of the Interior.

Just as the policies of the Werewolf Registry are altered when leadership changes hands in the magical world, so, too, have policies toward Native America proved fickle and changeable, from the recognition of private property under the Dawes Act in 1887 to the revocation of private property under the Indian Re-Organization Act in 1934, from the step away from sovereignty with the Termination Policy in the 1940s-1960s to the step toward sovereignty with the Self-Determination Policy in the 1970s-1980s. Rowling consistently portrays Lupin as holding an uncertain and thus subordinate status in the wizarding world due to his werewolf condition, one that is made possible because the mainstream views him as different and Other. His resulting vulnerability provides readers food for thought, especially when compared with contemporary "real-world" corollaries.

Readers familiar with Native American history may also find familiarity with what Harry learns about giants in *Harry Potter and the Order of the Phoenix*. As Hagrid explains, the giants once had been numerous—"there were loads once, musta bin a hundred diff'rent tribes from all over the world"[12]—but now only a fraction of their number survives. That remainder has been removed to remote regions, out of sight, mostly out of mind, and abandoned to the violent inter-tribal feuds caused by their forced close proximity to each other. Dumbledore, Hagrid notes, blames the wizarding community for the plight of the dispossessed giants and their current state: "it was the wizards who forced 'em to go an' made 'em live a good long way from us...."[13] Details like these evoke the rapid depopulation of Native America after the Columbian Encounter of 1492, the forced removal of Native nations through events like the Cherokee Trail of Tears and the Long Walk of the Navajo, and the resettlement of disparate and diverse tribes of

---

[11] For a brief discussion of protests against and calls for reform for the Bureau of Indian Affairs, see Amy H. Sturgis, "Tale of Tears," *Reason.* March 1999. <http://reason.com/archives/1999/03/01/tale-of-tears> Accessed 12 November, 2012.

[12] J.K. Rowling, *Harry Potter and the Order of the Phoenix.* Signature Edition. Originally published in 2003. (London: Bloomsbury, 2010), 377-378.

[13] *Order*, 378.

SEEKING DUMBLEDORE'S MOTHER ▪ 183

American Indians in places not of their choosing, such as so-called "Indian Territory," which later became the state of Oklahoma.

Furthermore, in the Harry Potter series readers watch both sides of the conflict in the magical world (the side of Voldemort and his Death Eaters and the side of Albus Dumbledore, the Order of the Phoenix, and Dumbledore's Army) seek an alliance with the giants. They might be a marginalized people, alternately ignored and hated, but when war approaches they take on new interest for both gathering forces. This brings to mind how the English and French sought Native nations as possible partners during the French and Indian War, how the English and Americans did likewise during the War of 1812, and how the Union and Confederacy followed suit during the U.S. Civil War.

Of all of the different magical creatures of Rowling's universe, the goblins offer a particularly compelling illustration of this phenomenon. Readers learn via Professor Binns's history classes at Hogwarts that a series of goblin rebellions took place in the past. According to Hermione's reading of *Sites of Historical Sorcery*, the one in 1612 was as close to the school as Hogsmeade, and the Three Broomsticks Inn was even used as the wizards' headquarters during the hostilities.[14] These wars and riots, "bloody and vicious,"[15] came about as the goblin population of the wizarding world revolted against discrimination and prejudice towards their kind.

According to the W.O.M.B.A.T., or the Wizards' Ordinary Magic and Basic Aptitude Test, specific rebellions may have occurred because of lack of goblin representation on the Wizengamot, attempts to enslave goblins as house-elves, stripping of wand privileges, wizard attempts to control Gringotts, or even brutal goblin slayings by Yardley Platt.[16] While taking his O.W.L. examination in his-

---

[14] J.K. Rowling, *Harry Potter and the Prisoner of Azkaban*. Signature Edition. Originally published in 1999. (London: Bloomsbury, 2010), 61.

[15] J.K. Rowling, *Harry Potter and the Goblet of Fire*. Signature Edition. Originally published in 2000. (London: Bloomsbury, 2010), 342.

[16] The W.O.M.B.A.T. appeared on J.K. Rowling's official website prior to its 2012 redesign. It is currently preserved via the Harry Potter Wiki under "Wizards' Ordinary Magic and Basic Aptitude Test." <http://harrypotter.wikia.com/wiki/Wizards%27_Ordinary_Magic_and_Basic_Aptitude_Test> Accessed 15 November, 2012.

tory, Harry recalls that when the International Confederation of Wizards con-
vened to unite the magical world across the planet, the goblins attempted to attend and represent their interests "and were ousted...."[17] Centuries later, Harry
discovers that the goblin Griphook remains bitter about wizards denying goblins
the knowledge of and right to use wands, effectively making them second-class
citizens in the wizarding world.[18]

Lack of representation, attempts at slavery, stripping of property rights, the
wresting of control of time-honored institutions, and a power imbalance due to
the technology of tools/weaponry: all of these ingredients evoke the so-called
Indian Wars of the 19th century, in which various Native nations asserted their
rights to self-determination and fought a U.S. government (in which they had no
say or representation) that sought to subordinate them.

For that matter, Griphook's anguish at seeing goblin-made treasures in the
hands and (often unrightful) possession of wizards is reminiscent of the outcry
that eventually led to the 1990 U.S. Native American Graves Protection and Repatriation Act, which requires both federal agencies and institutions that receive
federal funding to return Native American "cultural items" to lineal descendants
and culturally affiliated Indian tribes and Native Hawaiian organizations. Cultural items include human remains, funerary objects, sacred objects, and objects
of "cultural patrimony." The notion of objects of "cultural patrimony"[19] no doubt
would resonate with Griphook. After all, he recognizes the Sword of Gryffindor
by its older name: "That sword was Ragnuk the First's, taken from him by Godric
Gryffindor! It is a lost treasure, a masterpiece of goblinwork! It belongs with the
goblins!"[20]

---

[17] *Order*, 640.

[18] J.K. Rowling, *Harry Potter and the Deathly Hallows*. Signature Edition. Originally
published in 2007. (London: Bloomsbury, 2010), 394-395.

[19] "Native American Graves Protection and Repatriation Act," National Park Service,
U.S. Department of the Interior. 16 November, 1990. <http://www.nps.gov/ nagpraman-
dates/25usc3001etseq.htm> Accessed 30 November, 2012.

[20] *Hallows* (Bloomsbury), 409.

Seeking Dumbledore's Mother

Reading such parallels into Rowling's series offers a different and rewarding perspective on both Native America and Harry Potter. Rowling doesn't make readers do all of the work in building bridges between the two subjects, however. The Harry Potter saga includes subtle and not-so-subtle evidence that Rowling consciously wove Native America into the fabric of her magical world.

First, Rowling gives enough information from which we may extrapolate that Native America most certainly is part of her vision. Throughout the Harry Potter saga, Rowling places wizards and witches within world cultures that already have, in our reality, preexisting traditions of mythology, literature, and/or beliefs about magic, and she incorporates these traditions into her own history of the magical world. The wizards and witches who are honored on the chocolate frog cards that Harry and Ron share on the Hogwarts Express in *Harry Potter and the Philosopher's Stone* represent figures from Greek, Anglo-Saxon, Celtic, and Arthurian stories, among others, for example. The Weasley family's trip to Egypt, described in *Harry Potter and the Prisoner of Azkaban*, provides nods toward Egyptian mythology.

In her essay "Reading Harry Potter through Navajo Eyes," Anderson confirms that some Native peoples have traditions about magic, and in fact, many in her own Navajo culture (and she identifies herself among them) continue to embrace the idea of witchcraft and believe that its practitioners, like Rowling's witches and wizards, may be good or bad and may use their powers to pursue noble or wicked goals.

Rowling also builds on historical events related to witchcraft, including infamous witch trials. In *Harry Potter and the Goblet of Fire*, as Harry and Ron take in the campsite for spectators of the Quidditch World Cup, they see this: "a group of middle-aged witches sat gossiping happily beneath a spangled banner stretched between their tents which read: *The Salem Witches' Institute.*"[21] This is a reference to the hearings and prosecutions of women and men suspected of witchcraft in colonial Salem, Massachusetts in 1692 and 1693. The witches and wizards there, Rowling implies, were quite genuine, and the Muggles who tried to eradicate them failed.

---

[21] *Goblet*, 76.

It would follow from this pattern that, in the context of Harry Potter's world, other North American witch trials recorded in Muggle history likely also would point to the existence of real witches and wizards. It's worth noting, then, that witch trials existed within Native American communities as well as colonial American ones. One of the best known occurred in the first decade of the nineteenth century. As a response to the loss of their traditional lands and a terrible epidemic of disease, religious leaders among the Delawares and Shawnees claimed to have apocalyptic visions. The Delaware leader was a woman named Beata, and the Shawnee leader was a man named Lalawéthika, who took on the new name Tenskwatawa ("The Open Door") but became known best simply as The Prophet. (The Prophet was the brother of Tecumseh, the warrior-chief who would lead the largest pan-tribal alliance in history against U.S. encroachment on the continent before perishing in the War of 1812. Tecumseh distanced himself from and disapproved of his brother's involvement with witch-hunting.)

Both Beata and The Prophet said that their visions suggested that the White Menace from without (that is, Anglo-American encroachment and Westward expansion) was mirrored by an equally dire threat from within: witches working to undermine the Native nations, poisoning the villages from the inside out. In the end, both Beata and The Prophet tried to cleanse their people and lead them back to their traditional ways. Their efforts included witch hunts among the Delawares, Wyandots, and Senecas. Not unlike the stories of the earlier witch trials in Salem, some alleged witches were tortured for their confessions and others were executed. After a time, however, these witch trials inspired a backlash. Some claimed that young would-be leaders were exploiting the investigation of witches as a means of undermining the older, entrenched leadership elite, disguising political revolution as spiritual purgings.[22] This is exactly the kind of history Rowling has used to add depth, credibility, and richness to Harry's magical world.

Readers need not rely on extrapolations alone to make the connection. Rowling engages with Native America directly in the final book in her saga, *Harry*

---

[22] For a longer account of Beata, The Prophet, and this chapter in Native American history, see Amy H. Sturgis, *Tecumseh: A Biography* (Westport: Greenwood, 2008): 35–50.

Potter and the Deathly Hallows. While reading *The Daily Prophet,* Harry finds a picture of the Dumbledore family. The British edition from the Bloomsbury Signature series describes her thusly: "The mother, Kendra, had jet black hair pulled into a high bun. Her face had a carved quality about it. Despite the high-necked silk gown she wore, Harry thought of Native Americans as he studied her dark eyes, high cheekbones and straight nose."[23]

In the U.S. version of the text from Scholastic, the last line of the description differs slightly, adding that her expression appears "formally composed": "Harry thought of photos of Native Americans he'd seen as he studied her dark eyes, high cheekbones and straight nose, formally composed above a high-necked silk gown."[24] If the point had been simply to make Kendra Dumbledore exotic to Harry—that is, visibly non-Anglo-Saxon—Rowling had a globe's worth of backgrounds on which she could have drawn. Instead, she pointedly has Harry make the connection with Native America.

At the wedding of Fleur Delacour and Bill Weasley, Harry witnesses the following exchange between the Weasleys' Auntie Muriel and Elphias Doge:

> "Dumbledore's mother was a terrifying woman, simply terrifying. Muggle-born, though I heard she pretended otherwise—"
>
> "She never pretended anything of the sort! Kendra was a fine woman," whispered Doge miserably, but Auntie Muriel ignored him.
>
> "—proud and very domineering, the sort of witch who would have been mortified to produce a Squib—"
>
> "Ariana was not a Squib!" wheezed Doge.[25]

Was Kendra Dumbledore a "terrifying," "proud and very domineering" woman? When Harry uncovers the truth later in *Deathly Hallows,* readers are convinced otherwise. Like Harry, the reader discovers that Kendra's daughter Ariana, at the age of six, was violently assaulted by a group of Muggle boys, and became badly unstable after that, unable to control her use of magic. Kendra's husband, Percival

---

[23] *Hallows* (Bloomsbury), 178.

[24] *Hallows* (Scholastic), 216.

[25] *Hallows* (Bloomsbury), 129.

Dumbledore, was sent to Azkaban for hexing Ariana's attackers. Kendra was left alone to raise Albus, Aberforth, and Ariana, and she did so in seclusion at Godric's Hollow, in the effort to protect Ariana from certain institutionalization if her condition ever was discovered. Certainly, the idea that Kendra was proud and aloof plays into the "stoic Indian" stereotype, much as does the description of her as "formally composed," but it appears that Kendra Dumbledore was reserved because she was afraid of losing her daughter. This brings to mind Hollie Anderson's description of the "alienation and disconnection" of the contemporary Native American experience; Kendra Dumbledore had no allies or support, and she did the best she could alone to protect her family in a potentially hostile environment.

While it is true that Aberforth claims his brother learned the habit of "secrets and lies"[26] at their mother's knee, this sounds more like the complaint of a middle child, jealous of his gifted elder brother and a little sister who required most of their mother's attention, than a clear-minded analysis. But of course Kendra had kept secrets, and no doubt she had concealed these with lies; it seems Ariana's life and welfare had depended on these things. Kendra apparently made herself an outcast, a misunderstood and mysterious Other, because of this. And indeed Kendra ended up losing her life in her effort to protect her brutalized and unstable daughter.

Readers can imagine, though, that her self-possession—that formal composure Harry notes—and her own prodigious magical abilities, as well as her desire to protect those who could not protect themselves, are all qualities that are visible in the adult Albus Dumbledore. They are, surely, the qualities of a heroine, and the qualities that went into the making of a hero.

What might have Rowling hoped for, in claiming a Native American background for Kendra? Beyond isolating her from the English magical community and offering yet more reason for fellow witches and wizards to misjudge her and her motives during her life, perhaps Rowling hoped to offer a more lasting and positive lesson. Perhaps Kendra's heritage provides another example of how strength comes from diversity. In this case, the greatest wizard of his age might

---

[26] *Hallows* (Bloomsbury), 453.

be a product of not only the so-called "Old World," but also the "New World," as well.

Dumbledore's later life is marked by his respect for others, their cultures, and their homelands; after all, his funeral in *Harry Potter and the Half-Blood Prince* includes respects paid by the centaurs (whose claim to the Forbidden Forest Dumbledore honored) and the merpeople (whose language Dumbledore learned so he could speak with them on their own terms). It is not difficult to see the legacy of Native America and its history here, to imagine the lasting influence of Kendra Dumbledore.

Hollie Anderson challenges readers to find personal and lasting meaning in the Harry Potter series, to use the saga to open the doors of communication and the opportunities for learning, teaching, and connecting with the past as well as others today. Exploring Rowling's saga in a Native American context allows for such insights, reconsiderations, and bridge-building. One would like to believe that Kendra and her son Albus would approve.

Works Cited

Anderson, Hollie. "Reading Harry Potter with Navajo Eyes" in *Harry Potter's World: Multidisciplinary Critical Perspectives.* Elizabeth E. Heilman, ed. RoutledgeFalmer, 2002. 97-107.

Bear, Charla. "American Indian Boarding Schools Haunt Many." NPR.org. 18 May, 2008. <http://www.npr.org/templates/story/story.php?storyId=16516865> Accessed on 12 December, 2012.

Harper, Stephen. On behalf of the Government of Canada. "Statement of Apology to Former Students of Indian Residential Schools." 11 June, 2008. Official website of Aboriginal Affairs and Northern Development Canada. <http://www.aadnc-aandc.gc.ca/eng/1100100015644/1100100015649> Accessed on 26 November, 2012.

Moore, MariJo. *Genocide of the Mind: New Native American Writing.* New York: Thunder Mouth's Press/Nation Books, 2003.

"Native American Graves Protection and Repatriation Act." National Park Service, U.S. Department of the Interior. 16 November, 1990. <http://www.nps.gov/nagpra/mandates/25usc3001etseq.htm>

Accessed 30 November, 2012.

Our Spirits Don't Speak English: Indian Boarding Schools. Rich-Heape Films, 2008.

Rowling, J.K. "The Fringe Benefits of Failure, and the Importance of Imagination." *Harvard Magazine.* 5 June, 2008. <http://harvardmagazine.com/2008/06/the-fringe-benefits-failure-the-importance-imagination> Accessed 12 November, 2012.

___. *Harry Potter and the Deathly Hallows.* New York: Scholastic, 2007.

___. *Harry Potter and the Deathly Hallows.* Signature Edition. Originally published in 2007. London: Bloomsbury, 2010.

___. *Harry Potter and the Goblet of Fire.* Signature Edition. Originally published in 2000. London: Bloomsbury, 2010.

___. *Harry Potter and the Order of the Phoenix.* Signature Edition. Originally published in 2003. London: Bloomsbury, 2010.

___. *Harry Potter and the Prisoner of Azkaban.* Signature Edition. Originally published in 1999. London: Bloomsbury, 2010.

___. Interview with *Entertainment Weekly*, September 7, 2000, as archived on Mugglenet.com, 19 August 2003 <http://mugglenet.com/ewinterview1.shtml> Accessed 30 November, 2012.

___. "Wizards' Ordinary Magic and Basic Aptitude Test." Originally published on J.K. Rowling's Official Website.<http:// harrypotter.wikia.com/ wiki/Wizards%27_Ordinary_Magic_and_Basic_Aptitude_Test>Ac cessed 15 November, 2012.

Smith, Andrea. "Soul Wound: The Legacy of Native American Schools." *Amnes ty International Magazine.* 26 March, 2007. <http://www.amnestyusa. org/node/87342> Accessed 30 November, 2012.

Sturgis, Amy H. "Tale of Tears." *Reason.* March 1999. <http://reason.com/archives/1999/03/01/tale-of-tears> Accessed 12 November, 2012.

___. *Tecumseh: A Biography.* Westport: Greenwood, 2008.

CHAPTER 11

A Librarian's View of Madam Pince:

Promoting Stereotypes, Perpetually Absent, or Plot Device?

Alison R. Jones

J K. Rowling's *Harry Potter* series has furthered literacy and promoted reading perhaps more than any other recent work (Scholastic 48). They are beloved books of many librarians, whether school,
public, or academic. Yet, when librarians read the series, they do not see themselves reflected; rather, they find Madam Pince: the unlikeable, unhelpful, and
often conspicuously absent librarian. J.K. Rowling has apologized for Madam
Pince, stating "if they'd had a pleasant, helpful librarian, half my plots would be
gone. 'Cause the answer invariably is in a book but Hermione has to go and find
it. If they'd had a good librarian, that would have been that problem solved" ("An
Evening with Harry, Carrie and Garp"). But what do the books suggest? Is
Madam Pince simply a bad librarian, or does she represent an old stereotype of
librarians? Is she merely absent when Harry, Ron, and Hermione need her assistance most? Or is Madam Pince no more than a plot device because a library could
not be without a librarian? Rowling presents Pince as a stereotype, as absent, or
as merely a plot device at different times throughout the series, but based on
Rowling's description of Pince's character and duties, Pince is most often depicted
as a stereotypical librarian figure. Librarians—and indeed all those who believe
in the ideals of learning—should be concerned about this because librarian stereotypes keep library patrons from fully utilizing library services.

The question of Madam Pince's portrayal as a librarian was surprisingly untapped prior to 2011,[1] leaving a great gaping hole in the literature on this topic. Certainly, there were a few off-hand comments, blog posts, or mentions in short articles, but despite the fact that librarians seemed to be clearly displeased by Madam Pince, no one analyzed the subject in depth (Lianne; Politi; LisaQQQ; mary_j_59; Valenza). Jennifer Burek Pierce came the closest to addressing the issue in her article "What's Harry Potter Doing in the Library? Depictions of Young Adult Information Seeking Behavior in Contemporary Fantasy Fiction." However, her work focused on the information-seeking behavior of students in three works of young adult fantasy literature, rather than on librarians or libraries themselves. Interestingly enough, she gives Madam Pince a bit of a pass, stating, "These are among a number of descriptions in the Harry Potter stories which characterize libraries and their contents in ways that are other than welcoming....but interestingly, it is seldom the librarian who perpetuates such negative perceptions" (Pierce). Elizabeth A. Richardson and Sarah Wagner of Kent State University addressed similar issues in 2011, although their conference paper, "Restricted Section: The Library as Presented in Harry Potter," is less concerned with how such portrayals affect broader views of libraries and librarians.[2]

From the library profession's earliest days, stereotypes have been an obsession among librarians. As early as 1909, a librarian complained in the literature that "in fiction we are pictured either as the old fogy bookworm, or the ideal librarian ..." (Keller 297). Other authors writing on librarian stereotypes draw attention to this obsession on the part of the library profession (Arant and

---

[1] This paper was originally presented as "A Librarian's View of Madame Pince: Promoting Stereotypes, Perpetually Absent, or Plot Device?" at *Replacing Wands with Quills: A Harry Potter Symposium for Muggle Scholars* at James Madison University, Harrisonburg, VA, on November 10-12, 2011. It was later expanded into "The Mystery of Madam Pince: What We Know, What We Don't, and Why it Matters" at the East Tennessee Library Association (ETLA) meeting on April 12, 2012. This paper includes some of the additions from the later presentation, without the librarian-specific focus.

[2] Richardson and Wagner's paper was presented at the *Edinboro Potterfest Ravenclaw Conference* October 20-22, 2011. Like me, Richardson and Wagner started by reading the *Harry Potter* books and keeping statistics on mentions of the library, the librarian, library sources, etc. They chose to focus more on these statistics, while the statistics led me to try and address some of the questions these statistics raised.

Benefiel; Burns; McReynolds). Arant and Benefiel addressed it as such: "... there seems to be no profession as preoccupied with self-examination as that of librarianship ... the refrain heard over and over is startlingly similar to Dangerfield's 'I don't get no respect'" (1). They continue to point out that this is not limited to one type of library, "... from public librarians who (often rightly) complain of being treated like servants by the patrons they serve to academic librarians who are always trying to establish their 'faculty-ness' to the teaching professors" (Arant and Benefiel 1).

Although this may come across as paranoid or sensitive, librarians are not without cause for concern. Several authors connect librarian stereotypes with underutilization of library services because the public remains unaware of these services, as well as the skills and education of librarians (Kneale 3; Seale). Because of this ignorance, the public draws upon stereotypes to fill in what they do not know about librarians (Seale). Although librarians are generally described more positively in real life than they are portrayed in literature and media, the public still draws (whether consciously or unconsciously) upon stereotypes to fill in their ignorance about librarians. Far worse than adults relying on these stereotypes is the realization that children are exposed to them from an early age. Several authors specifically address the problem of librarian stereotypes in children's literature. Bargmann describes many "children's books that seem to have [one] thing in common: children hearing terrifying tales of a library and its librarian(s)." Yontz states, "Because adults strive to instill their most respected beliefs and values into children, the writers and publishers of juvenile materials reveal themselves through their choices of content" (86). Clearly, many children's authors subconsciously believe the library to be a foreboding place and are unconcerned with passing this view along to the next generation.

What exactly is known about Madam Pince and the Hogwarts library? Madam Pince is first described in *Harry Potter and the Chamber of Secrets* as "a thin irritable woman who looked like an underfed vulture" (163; ch. 10). This is echoed more than once, first when she is described in *Harry Potter and the Goblet of Fire*, and then again to an even greater extent in *Harry Potter and the Half-Blood Prince* where her "vulture like countenance" is expanded to disclose "her sunken cheeks, her skin like parchment, and her long hooked nose [...]" and her "clawlike hand" (*Harry Potter and the Goblet of Fire* [GF] 482; ch. 26; *Harry Potter and the Half-Blood Prince* [HBP] 307; ch. 15).

It is hard to distinguish Madam Pince's personality from her job duties. In many ways they appear to be one and the same. In *Chamber of Secrets*, Madam Pince is suspicious of the note Hermione brings from Lockhart, searching it carefully to make sure it is not a forgery (164; ch.10). In *Harry Potter and the Order of the Phoenix*, Madam Pince is portrayed as a suspicious woman who "prowled the aisles menacingly, breathing down the necks of those touching her precious books" (538; ch. 24). In *Quidditch Through the Ages* we learn that she does not want to hand over books willingly when Dumbledore wishes to have the book copied for charity (viii). In *Half-Blood Prince* she is upset at the defacement of any book, regardless of whether it is a library book or not (308; ch. 15).

The first question to be asked in regard to Madam Pince's job duties is whether she is actually a librarian. Madam Pince's title does not appear in the seven novels of the Harry Potter series. According to the first page of *Quidditch Through the Ages*, her title is "Hogwarts Librarian," but based on the novels' descriptions one wonders if she is really a librarian, or if the students are assuming that she is (1). She often comes across as a library clerk or a particularly strict study hall monitor. Most of her duties would not necessarily be typical of a librarian. One of Madam Pince's main duties, at least from the students' observations, is cleaning the library. In *Harry Potter and the Sorcerer's Stone* she appears waving a feather duster, and in *Chamber of Secrets* the students notice her polishing the cover of a book as well (*Harry Potter and the Sorcerer's Stone* [SS] 198; ch. 12; *Harry Potter and the Chamber of Secrets* [CS] 200; ch. 11). Madam Pince also takes care of fairly mundane circulation tasks: apparently checking out books by hand as observed from a distance in *Order of the Phoenix* and as evidenced by the list of borrowers and due dates in the front of *Quidditch Through the Ages* (*Harry Potter and the Order of the Phoenix* [OP] 655; ch. 29; *Quidditch* 1). She applies spells to the books that not only presumably keep books from being lost, but also keep patrons from defacing them or mistreating them and punish patrons if they do (*Quidditch* viii).

Though mentioned very rarely, the only clearly professional library duty in which Madam Pince is involved is the answering of reference questions. In *Sorcerer's Stone* Harry, Ron, and Hermione clearly realize that one can ask Madam

Pince a reference question about Nicolas Flamel. However, they decide not to ask her because "[t]hey were sure she'd be able to tell them, but they couldn't risk Snape hearing what they were up to" (198; ch. 12). The only other allusions to reference questions occur during the events of *Goblet of Fire*, when Harry asks Madam Pince for help finding information to succeed at the second task, but she is unable to help (482; ch. 26). It must be noted that although this might give Madam Pince a poor record in fielding reference questions based on these few descriptions in the novels, Hermione, who often finds the answers to the rest of the trio's questions in books,[3] was also unable to find an answer to Harry's question.

Little personal information is known about Madam Pince in general. In fact, the only time anyone sees Madam Pince outside the library is when she attends Dumbledore's funeral (HBP 640, ch. 30). *Half-Blood Prince* and *Quidditch Through the Ages* also contain the only proof that Madam Pince is not a squib. As mentioned previously, she casts spells on library books; however, in *Half-Blood Prince* she uses her wand to cause Harry's school items to chase Ginny and him from the library, hitting them over the head as they flee (*Quidditch* viii; HBP 656; ch. 29). This is especially significant given the only personal speculation about Madam Pince in the novels is the question of whether she and Filch, who is a squib, are in a relationship (HBP 308; ch. 15).

What, if anything, is known about the Hogwarts library must also be considered. Although the Hogwarts library is central to the *Harry Potter* series, there is relatively little known about it. First, the hours of the Hogwarts library appear to be quite extensive. In the novels, the library is open until eight or nine o'clock in the evening (GF 488; ch. 26; OP 608; ch. 27; HBP 307-308; ch. 15). It is also open on weekends (PA 152-153; ch. 8; 276-278; ch. 14). Unless Madam Pince works on a house-elf schedule of extremely long days with no days off, the information regarding library hours and staffing is clearly incomplete.

---

[3] The idea of Hermione as the real librarian in the *Harry Potter* series has only begun to be addressed. I presented "Hermione Granger, Librarian: Why Hermione is the True Librarian of Hogwarts" at the Potterwatch 2013 conference at the University of North Carolina at Charlotte on April 6, 2013. See also Freier, Mary P. "The Librarian in Rowling's Harry Potter Series," *GLCWeb: Comparative Literature and Culture* 16.3 (2014): n. pag. Web. 17 Jan. 2015.

The second fact learned about the Hogwarts library relates to its history regarding banned books. In *The Tales of Beedle the Bard* Dumbledore's footnotes reveal that Lucius Malfoy attempted to have "The Fountain of Fair Fortune" banned from the Hogwarts library, due to its promotion of the intermarriage of wizards and Muggles, but Dumbledore fought successfully against the request (39-42). It is also known that quite a lot of dangerous books are removed from immediate student access, both through the creation of the Restricted Section, where students must have a professor's permission to view specific books, and in Dumbledore's complete removal of books regarding Horcruxes (*Harry Potter and the Deathly Hallows* [DH] 101-102; ch. 6).

Beyond this, readers are given very little information about the Hogwarts library and its librarian. The full library hours or the composition of its staff (or whether there are magical ways of keeping the library open) is unknown. What kind of schooling, training, or certification does Madam Pince have? One would not even know that Madam Pince is, in fact, a librarian if not for the mention of her title in *Quidditch Through the Ages*. Further, only a bit of the circulation system is observed in *Quidditch Through the Ages* and a brief mention of checking out books in *Order of the Phoenix* (*Quidditch* 1; OP 655; ch. 29). It is unknown whether the system is fully manual or if there is a special quill or spell that writes out the names on the books (*Quidditch* 1). There is no information regarding whether there are magical spells that take the place of library catalogs and circulation systems. It is obvious there is an organizational scheme as Hermione, and even Ron and Harry, are able to find books as needed, but specifics are not given, and time and again, one often feels as if the trio relies on serendipity to lead them to the information they seek.

Nothing is fully known with regard to library policies, including policies and procedures for banned books. There is one example of Dumbledore defending a banned book and examples of him controlling access or even "banning," in effect, other books, but nothing is mentioned regarding the library or Madam Pince's role in the process. At one point, Professor Snape claims that "Library books are not to be taken outside the school," but Harry suspects that Professor Snape made up the rule, and it is not an official library policy (SS 182; ch. 11). However, there are many areas of education at Hogwarts for which the reader does not have full information, so perhaps we should not be surprised at the lack of information regarding the library.

What can the reader glean from the Harry Potter series regarding the importance of Madam Pince? First, there is the question of whether Madam Pince is simply a plot device. J.K. Rowling makes this claim as quoted earlier: "If they'd had a pleasant, helpful librarian, half my plots would be gone. 'Cause the answer invariably is in a book but Hermione has to go and find it. If they'd had a good librarian, that would have been that problem solved" ("An Evening with Harry, Carrie and Garp"). But is this entirely true, or is Rowling perhaps attempting to absolve herself with this answer? In five of the seven novels in the series, Hermione finds an answer in a book, unaided by Madam Pince. There are two exceptions, *Goblet of Fire* and *Order of the Phoenix*. In *Goblet of Fire*, one may suspect that Hermione discovers Rita Skeeter is an unregistered animagus as a result of extensive reading; in *Order of the Phoenix* one may convincingly argue Hermione used library books to help train Dumbledore's Army. But there is no evidence to this effect; it is pure speculation based on Hermione's personality and track record in the other novels.

However, even in the five novels where the students clearly utilize a book for a central purpose, their doing so does not necessarily affect the overall plot and is never sufficient to resolve the plot on its own. Arguably, finding out about Nicolas Flamel in *Sorcerer's Stone*, the basilisk in *Chamber of Secrets*, and the knowledge gained from *The Tales of Beedle the Bard* in *Deathly Hallows* had a noticeable effect on the overall plot (SS 219; ch. 13; CS 290; ch. 16; DH 406; ch. 21). However, none of these achievements on its own solved the plot. Even if Madam Pince helped them to find this information, the trio would still need to understand how to use it. Book use in the two other Harry Potter novels pertain to comparatively minor plot points: helping Hagrid with the defense of Buckbeak in *Prisoner of Azkaban* and discovering Eileen Prince in *Half-Blood Prince* are not pieces of information that would change the overall plot of either of the novels (*Harry Potter and the Prisoner of Azkaban* [PA] 274; ch. 14; HBP 538; ch. 25).

Additional evidence that Madam Pince is not simply a plot device can be found in the Harry Potter films. Madam Pince was only cast in *Chamber of Secrets* and is seen so rarely and without being identified that some viewers, upon seeing her seated next to Professor Snape at the leaving feast, assumed she was another one of the professors, such as Professor Sinistra (snapesmistress n.p.). The library itself appears in only four of the films: *Sorcerer's Stone*, *Chamber of Secrets*, *Goblet of Fire*, and *Half-Blood Prince*, and only once in each of those. The library's role in the novels as study space seems to be filled by the Great Hall in the films. If Madam Pince were integral to preventing the plot from being resolved too early, she would have been necessary in the films as well as the books. Even allowing for differences between mediums, however, it appears fairly obvious that the information found by Hermione and others in the books was important, but earlier knowledge of that information would not have resolved the plot sooner.

Thus, if Madam Pince is a plot device, she is not one of great importance. In fact, one might suggest that the entire argument against her functioning as a plot device lies in her rare appearances in the novels. Madam Pince seems to be absent from the library a good part of the time, and she is ignored or only seen at a distance the rest of the time. She is only seen during eight out of the fifteen directly mentioned library visits during library hours, not counting Harry's two visits under the invisibility cloak. This fact could be a function of the library's long hours, or it could imply that Madam Pince is not a very visible person in the Hogwarts library. Regardless, Madam Pince's absence clearly contributes to her minor role as a plot device.

During the scenes in which Madam Pince is present, there is much to suggest she represents a traditional librarian stereotype, whether or not it was J.K. Rowling's intention to do so. Madam Pince is not alone among the Hogwarts faculty in representing stereotypes. Professor Binns, for example, represents the stereotype of a boring history teacher. Megan Birch points out, "Most teachers at Hogwarts are stock caricatures. Their behaviors, their dress and appearance, the subjects they teach, and their instruction fit neatly into shallow and conventional stereotypes" (Birch 104). But for most of the other teachers, if they are viewed as poor teachers, the reader assumes it to be a function of their personality, rather than being a characteristic of their chosen career. This distinction is what sets Madam Pince apart from the others.

Much of what is known of Madam Pince fits several stereotypical portrayals of librarians in fiction and in media. Maura Seale lists fives stereotypes of librarians in her article "Old Maids, Policeman, and Social Rejects: Mass Media Representations and Public Perceptions of Librarians": the old maid librarian, the policeman librarian, the librarian as parody, the inept librarian, and the hero/ine librarian. Madam Pince fits three of Seale's stereotypes: the old maid, the policeman, and the inept. The "old maid" might be the most familiar librarian stereotype, but it is debatable whether this particular category applies to Madam Pince, as her marital status is unknown. One cannot automatically assume any of the Hogwarts professors are single, because most of them are never really described outside of the classroom setting. There is reason to suggest Madam Pince might be single, since students speculate about her relationship with Filch, but given how little the students appear to know about her, that may not be a reasonable assumption (HBP 308; ch.15). If she is single, then Madam Pince fits one of the oldest and most common stereotypes of librarians, often described with very negative connotations. Michael Engle suggests that the librarian stereotype may actually be a twisting of a deeper archetype: the Crone. He describes the Crone in phrases reminiscent of Madam Pince, "Free of the restrictions of fertility, she lives in the wilderness of forest or battle, related to no one, man or woman. She consumes the living and the dead. She is restrictive, possessive, and utterly without fear or scruple ..." (Engle).

The second librarian stereotype readily depicted in Madam Pince is the policeman librarian. Descriptions of this stereotype appear in several works by Radford and Radford, who suggest in their 2001 article that "fear is the fundamental organizing principle, or code, through which representations of libraries and librarians are manifest in modern popular cultural forms [....] Fear is the means by which the presence of the library setting, and the library characters within them, are to be understood" (300). Nearly every time that Madam Pince appears, there is at least a hint of this stereotype, as she seems to be completely concerned with enforcing the law of the library. She constantly reprimands students and stalks about the library hoping to catch someone mistreating her beloved books. There are even more examples of this stereotype in *Quidditch Through the Ages* when one reads about the library book curses and sees her warnings to patrons who mess up books. Seale summarizes the policeman librarian as such: "The main characteristics of the policeman librarian can thus be seen as the possession of authority and/or knowledge and the ability to act on it."

The third and final stereotype of librarians manifesting in Madam Pince is that of the "inept" librarian. This stereotype reflects both misconceptions about librarians' job duties and the intelligence necessary to perform them as well as the inappropriate attitudes of some librarians toward their patrons and responsibilities. Seale specifically acknowledges the typical member of the public's lack of knowledge in reference to the education of librarians and that librarians are generally seen as library clerks.[4] Many authors have written about this stereotype in fiction and media. Beth Postner perhaps best describes the inept librarian stereotype when she comments that people perceive librarians' jobs as requiring "little effort or intelligence" and that they "are shocked to discover that librarians are required to have a graduate degree (or two)...To them, a librarian's only ability and desire—other than to hide out in libraries and be left alone—is to check items in and out, assess overdue fines, and 'shush' library patrons" (113; 118).

Arnold Sable, in his article "The Sexuality of the Library Profession: the Male and Female Librarian," offers an assessment that seems to describe Madam Pince herself: "She exists to put a damper on all spontaneity, silencing the young with a harsh look or a hiss of air. Her only tasks seem to be the checking out of books and the collection of fines. Books to her are best left upon the library shelves where they do not become dirtied or worn" (748). Finally, Sharon Black, in her article "Checking Out the Librarian," also describes the inept librarian in a manner appropriate to describing Madam Pince: "She obstructs more than facilitates the learning and information seeking process in libraries with a range of behaviors towards patrons that run from less than helpful to downright hostile. If there was only one word to choose in describing her attitude toward the resources she presides over, it is proprietary" (58). Madam Pince is always described as irritable and as viewing the books themselves as being more important than students or student learning. The only time we see her fielding a reference question she fails; she appears to be more of a library clerk/study hall monitor[5] than a help to students. Therefore, one might argue that the latter category is the stereotype to which Madam Pince best conforms: unhelpful if not completely incompetent.

---

[4] Or rather more specifically, all library staff are seen as librarians, as Kitchen in "Librarian's Image in Children's Fiction" and Walker and Larson in "The Librarian Stereotype and the Movies" also address.

[5] Intriguingly, when presented at the East Tennessee Library Association meeting, several librarians jointly speculated that Madam Pince is not a librarian, that rather she had failed at teaching another subject, and Dumbledore thought he could safely stick her

Madam Pince ultimately reflects all of the above mentioned stereotypes, though J.K. Rowling may not have intended any malice. In the end, Madam Pince is a bit of a "throw-away" character. She is ultimately not of great importance to the series, perhaps not even as a plot device as Rowling has claimed. Madam Pince is a stereotypical librarian like many other librarians in literature, simply because it is easy to rely on stereotypes when creating minor characters. J.K. Rowling likely spent little time thinking about the character development of Madam Pince when writing the series and only realized how she had portrayed librarians when she was meeting with fans, many of whom were librarians.

Until the public perception of libraries and librarians is more aligned with the reality of the library profession, librarians should not be surprised to continue to see librarian characters portrayed in this manner. Librarian stereotypes do have consequences. Linda Abscher notes, "In the mind of the patron, the stereotype of the librarian as gate-keeper impedes access to services" (qtd. in Kneale 3).[6] Until this image changes, librarians will have to live with the fact that some of our favorite books, even some by brilliant writers, will continue to portray librarians as stereotypes, ignore them completely, or, at best, utilize them as a limited plot device. The Harry Potter series is just one of the best and most recent examples of this reality.

Works Cited

Arant, Wendi, and Candace R. Benefiel. "Introduction." *The Reference Librarian* 37.78 (2002): 1-4. Education Research Complete. Web. 8 Oct. 2011.

Bargmann, Monika, "Fearing the Library Dragon: Why Librarians Should Approach Users Instead of Waiting For Them." *GMS Medizin – Bibliothek – Information* 7.1 (2007). Web. 23 Sept. 2011.

Birch, Megan L. "Schooling Harry Potter: Teachers and Learning, Power and

---

in the library where it "wouldn't matter." Those in attendance agreed that this would be a "very Dumbledore" thing to have done.

[6] There was no citation in Kneale for this quotation beyond the author's name. The author quotes herself in her blog however: absherl [Linda Abscher]. "You Will Know Me by the Trail of Reserve Slips." *The Lipstick Librarian,* 16 Jan. 2004. Web. 22 Jan. 2015.

Knowledge." *Critical Perspectives on Harry Potter.* Ed. Elizabeth E. Heilman. New York: Routledge, 2009. 103-20. EBook Collection (EBSCOhost). Web. 6 Oct. 2011.

Black, Sharon. "Checking Out the Librarian." *Popular Culture in Libraries* 1.4 (1993): 35-62. Print.

Engle, Michael. "Remythologizing Work: The Role of Archetypal Images in the Humanization of Librarianship." *eCommons@Cornell.* Cornell University Library, 12 Feb 1998. Web. 4 Oct. 2011.

Harry Potter and the Chamber of Secrets. Dir. Chris Columbus. Warner Brothers, 2002. DVD.

Harry Potter and the Deathly Hallows: Part 1. Dir. David Yates. Warner Brothers, 2010. DVD.

Harry Potter and the Deathly Hallows: Part 2. Dir. David Yates. Warner Brothers, 2011. DVD.

Harry Potter and the Goblet of Fire. Dir. Mike Newell. Warner Brothers, 2005. DVD.

Harry Potter and the Half-Blood Prince. Dir. David Yates. Warner Brothers, 2009. DVD.

Harry Potter and the Order of the Phoenix. Dir. David Yates. Warner Brothers, 2007. DVD.

Harry Potter and the Prisoner of Azkaban. Dir. Alfonso Cuarón. Warner Brothers, 2004. DVD.

Harry Potter and the Sorcerer's Stone. Dir. Chris Columbus. Warner Brothers, 2001. DVD.

Keller, Helen Rex. "The Old-Fashioned Virtues Versus the Ideal Librarian." *Library Journal* 34.7 (1909): 295-98. Google Books. Web. 4 Oct. 2011.

Kitchen, Barbara. "Librarian's Image in Children's Fiction." MLIS thesis Kent State University, 2000. *ERIC.* Web. ED450801 25 Nov. 2009.

Kneale, Ruth. You Don't Look Like a Librarian: Shattering Stereotypes and Creating Positive New Images in the Internet Age. Medford, NJ: Information Today, Inc., 2009. Print.

Lianne. "Fictional Librarians." *The Silverfish Newsletter.* The Students of the Information School at the University of Washington, 26 Jan. 2009. Web. 24 Nov. 2009.

LisaQQQ. "What's Up With Madam Pince? Does Jo Need to Meet a Good Librarian?" *The Leaky Lounge: Librarians: The Shrieking Stacks.* The Leaky Cauldron, 9 Feb. 2005. Web. 24 Nov. 2009.

mary_j_59. Weblog comment. mary_j_59. n.p., 25 Nov. 2009. Web. 25 Nov. 2009.

McReynolds, Rosalee. "A Heritage Dismissed." *Library Journal* 110.18 (1985): 25-31. Education Research Complete. Web. 4 Oct. 2011. Pierce, Jennifer Burek. "What's Harry Potter Doing in the Library? Depictions of Young Adult Information Seeking Behavior in Contemporary Fantasy Fiction." *Iowa Research Online.* University of Iowa, June 2004. Web. 23 Sept. 2011.

Politi, Nicole. "The Library in Children's/YA Literature." *Dog Ear.* n.p., 5 May 2009. Web. 24 Nov. 2009.

Posner, Beth. "Know-It-All Librarians." *The Reference Librarian* 37.78 (2002): 111-29. Education Research Complete. Web. 8 Oct. 2011.

Radford, Gary P., and Marie L. Radford. "Libraries, Librarians, and the Discourse of Fear." *The Library Quarterly* 71.3 (2001): 299-329. Print.

Rosenberg, Robin S. "What Do Students Learn From Hogwarts Classes." *The Psychology of Harry Potter: an Unauthorized Examination of the Boy Who Lived.* Ed. Neil Mulholland. Dallas, TX: BenBella, 2006. 5-17. Ebrary. Web. 7 Oct. 2011.

Rowling, J.K. "An Evening with Harry, Carrie and Garp." Radio City Music Hall, New York. 2 Aug. 2006. Benefit Reading. *Accio Quote.* n.d. Web. 24 Nov. 2009.

Rowling, J.K. Fantastic Beasts & Where to Find Them. New York: Scholastic Press, 2001. Print.

Rowling, J.K. *Harry Potter and the Chamber of Secrets.* New York: Arthur A. LevIne Books, 1999. Print.

Rowling, J. K. *Harry Potter and the Deathly Hallows.* New York: Arthur A. Levine Books, 2007. Print.

Rowling, J.K. *Harry Potter and the Goblet of Fire.* New York: Arthur A. Levine Books, 2000. Print.

Rowling, J.K. *Harry Potter and the Half-Blood Prince.* New York: Arthur A. Levine Books, 2005. Print.

Rowling, J.K. *Harry Potter and the Order of the Phoenix*. New York: Arthur A. Levine Books, 2003. Print.

Rowling, J.K. *Harry Potter and the Prisoner of Azkaban*. New York: Arthur A. Levine Books, 1999. Print.

Rowling, J.K. *Harry Potter and the Sorcerer's Stone*. New York: Arthur A. Levine Books, 1998. Print.

Rowling, J.K. *Quidditch Through the Ages*. New York: Scholastic Press, 2001. Print.

Rowling, J.K. *The Tales of Beedle the Bard*. New York: Children's High Level Group, 2008. Print.

Sable, Arnold P. "The Sexuality of the Library Profession: the Male and Female Librarian." *Wilson Library Bulletin* 43.8 (1969): 748-51. Print.

Seale, Maura. "Old Maids, Policeman, and Social Rejects: Mass Media Representations and Public Perceptions of Librarians." *Electronic Journal of Academic and Special Librarianship* 9.1 (2008). Web. 8 Oct. 2011.

Scholastic. *2008 Kids & Family Reading Report: Reading in the 21ˢᵗ Century: Turning the Page with Technology. Scholastic.com*. Scholastic, 2008. Web. 24 Feb. 2012.

snapesmistress.Weblog entry.snapesmistress.tumblr.com. snapesmistress. 28 Sept. 2011. Web.

Valenza, Joyce Kasman. "On the Job: Librarian" *WorldAlmanacForKids.com*. WorldAlmanacForKids.com, n.d. Web. 25 Nov. 2009.

Yontz, Elaine. "Librarians in Children's Literature, 1909-200." *The Reference Librarian* 37.78 (2002): 85-96. Education Research Complete. Web. 8 Oct. 2011.

CHAPTER 12

Work in the Wizarding World

Madelyn V. Young

One of the most memorable economic quotes in the Harry Potter stories comes from Professor Dumbledore when he tells Harry, "It is our choices, Harry, that show what we truly are, far more than our abilities." (CS 18)[1] This comment is the quintessential definition of economics—the study of the allocation of scarce resources. Life is a series of choices, and thus trade-offs occur between all of the competing uses for time, money, and labor supply decisions. If scarcity did not exist, there would be no reason for any type of decision-making, and the economics profession would be reduced to the calculation of wealth and the summing-up of spending. But economists need not worry, for even in the magical world of Harry Potter there is scarcity, and because of it wizards and non-wizards alike must make decisions regarding the best use of their resources.

Alfred Marshall historically said that economics is an integral part of the "ordinary business of life." One important aspect of this "ordinary business," both in the human world and the Potterian one, is the world of work. Labor economics examines who works, what types of jobs are available and why people are paid what they are. The availability, financial compensation and psychological gratification of work are central to most of our lives, just as they are to the wizards and other creatures of the Potterian World. By including this aspect of the Potterian world in her stories, J.K. Rowling makes them even more relatable to the

---

[1] References for Harry Potter books refer to chapter numbers throughout.

non-magical, as readers, for the most part, can understand the need and desire to work.

With few exceptions, the majority of the wizards in the Potterian world work outside the home. They do this despite the fact that the wizards themselves can create many a needed commodity with the flick of their wands and a specific charm or spell ("hundreds of squashy purple sleeping bags" (PA 9)). If this type of commodity creation is possible, why do wizards work at all? For the same reasons the rest of us do: to earn money to buy the basic essentials of life; first and foremost, food. Wizards, like non-magical people, must "work to live"—to some degree. They face limitations on what they can and cannot do with their magic. The first thing they cannot do is create their own food. This is Exception #1 of *The Five Principal Exceptions to Gamp's Law of Elemental Transfiguration.* Hermione tells Ron this when he (erroneously) mentions how his mother "can make good food appear out of thin air." (DH 15) Ron then passes this information on to Neville after hearing that the Room of Requirement doesn't provide food to Dumbledore's Army. (DH 29)

Money is Exception #2, although this is not mentioned directly in the stories. Money, in the form of gold, silver and bronze, cannot be created out of thin air, and has to be mined. Wizards come to possess money, in the form of gold, silver or bronze coins, through labor, inheritance, luck, someone else's largess, or stealing. They cannot, however, obtain their money through magic. According to J.K. Rowling:

> There is legislation about what you can conjure and what you can't. Something that you conjure out of thin air will not last. This is a rule I set down for myself early on. . . . The five years I spent on HP and the Philosopher's Stone were spent constructing The Rules. I had to lay down all my parameters. The most important thing to decide when you're creating a fantasy world is what the characters CAN'T do. (South West News Service, 8 July 2000; http://www.accio-quote.org/articles/2000/0700-swns-alfie.htm)

Another reason for Exception #2 is put forth by Caius Marcius, who believes that "the restrictions on economics may reflect the fact that the wizards live in a capitalistic society. A great portion of the Wizarding world's populace make their living through commerce, and it would be destructive of their livelihood if other wizards could magically create the goods that they offer." ("The Limits of Magic" *by Caius Marcius,* http://www.hp-lexicon.org/essays/essay-limits-of-magic.html)

The wizarding world is more capitalistic than anything else, albeit with less competition. There are clearly defined property rights, no labor unions, no obvious collusion between firms, many small single proprietorships and partnerships (which are monopolistic in structure with a limited labor demand), one school (which selectively invites its students to attend but attendance is not mandatory), and a large bureaucratic government (The Ministry of Magic). Unless they are victims of a spell which prevents free will, adult wizards voluntarily sell their labor in the public or private sector, or work for themselves. They own the fruits of their own labor. Buyers of wizard labor include the largest one, The Ministry of Magic (MoM), slightly smaller ones such as Hogwarts, St. Mungo's, Gringotts, and much smaller ones represented by the wide variety of shops in Diagon Alley and Hogsmeade. Of course, some wizards work for themselves in various occupations, like providing musical entertainment, running pubs, or selling used cauldrons or robes.

The Potterian Labor Market Process

In the non-magical world, there are three forces that together determine who works where, the availability of jobs, and compensation. These are market forces, institutional forces and sociological forces. (Kaufman and Hotchkiss, 2006) In many ways these forces help determine the same outcomes in the wizarding world.

Market Forces refer to the supply of and demand for labor, which help determine wages and distribution of labor. Labor supply is made up of all individuals working or looking for work, and is derived from the individual's demand for income to purchase goods and services produced by businesses. Labor demand is made up of all of the business firms and nonprofits, such as the government, who compete for workers. Labor demand is also considered a derived demand, derived from the demand for the good or service being provided.

Labor theory suggests that firms want to maximize profits and individuals want to maximize well-being. Firms want to economize on labor and find workers who are likely to be the most productive and willing to work for the least amount of compensation. Individuals seek out the type of work that yields the highest return. These forces of supply and demand determine wages and ultimately cause individuals to move to employment which yields them their highest advantage.

Arthur Weasley is an example of someone willing to work and be productive for the least amount of compensation: "Arthur worked for years in the Misuse of Muggle Artifacts Office at the Ministry of Magic, a job that, though it doesn't pay well, he loves." (http://www.hp-lexicon.org/wizards/arthur.html) If Arthur has weighed the advantages and disadvantages of his job, countering the low pay with the psychological happiness he receives from working with Muggle objects, then he has, indeed, found a particular job that yields him the highest level of happiness, all other things constant. Unfortunately for the rest of the Weasleys, however, Arthur's working at his Muggle artifacts job and maximizing his individual utility does not afford them much beyond the bare necessities of life (such as bread), let alone any luxuries (roses). They are poor, although not destitute, as confirmed by a comment Ron makes to Harry in reference to owning a house-elf: "House-elves come with big old manors and castles and places like that; you wouldn't catch one in our house...." (CS 3) Another more pointed illustration of the well-known Weasley poverty is a comment from Lucius Malfoy to Arthur Weasley at the Quidditch Cup:

> "Good Lord Arthur," he said softly. "What did you have to sell to get seats in the Top Box? Surely your house wouldn't have fetched this much?"(GF 8)

Arthur's individual maximization of happiness with his choice of job comes at the expense of the family utility, at least with respect to income. Had he been acting according to the rules of the household model of labor supply, where the goal is to maximize the happiness of the family vs. that of the individual, Arthur may have supplied his labor in a better paying position within the MoM much sooner than he does. Of course, it could be that he tried to acquire another job and was not successful, or that he was prevented from rising in the MoM because of his Mugglephilia, which may have resulted in prejudice and discrimination against him.

The household model also analyzes the use of other family members' time, whether spent in market work, nonmarket or house-work, or leisure. As Molly does not work outside of the home, it can be inferred that her reservation wage (the wage needed to entice her to work one hour in the labor market) is greater than her market wage. Her reservation wage is determined by the opportunity cost of her time, the value of her next best alternative. Her market wage is determined by supply and demand, institutional, and sociological forces. Given that she and Arthur have seven children, with five still living in the home when they are not at Hogwarts, the opportunity cost of her time working at The Burrow is too high to be spent on work in the labor market. If the wages she could earn by working in the market were to become higher than her reservation wage, then possibly Molly could be enticed to supply her labor outside of The Burrow.

Lucius Malfoy is another example of one who always maximizes his well-being. Although he is a governor of the Hogwarts School of Witchcraft and Wizardry (CS 12), we do not know if this position generates his substantial income, or if he just lives off of inherited (or stolen) wealth. Regardless of how he acquired said wealth, his desire to increase his happiness through acquisition is shown by his home:

> "He always did himself well, Lucius. *Peacocks* . . . ." Yaxley thrust his wand back under his cloak with a snort. (DH 1)

There is plenty of evidence of the Malfoys' affluence, with an early example coming from Harry:

> Judging by the fact that Draco Malfoy usually had the best of everything, his family was rolling in wizard gold; he could just see Malfoy strutting around a large manor house. (CS 3)

This is also an example of a positive externality, or beneficial spillover. Draco has the best broom, robes, and the like as a direct result of Lucius's wealth and willingness to provide for his son. Although Draco is not involved in the generation or growth of his family's fortune, he definitely benefits from the depletion of it, with no monetary costs to himself.

Horace Slughorn also knows how to increase his happiness using all of the resources at his disposal. During his original tenure at Hogwarts and continuing after his initial retirement, Slughorn's students provide him a comfortable existence:

"Horace formed a kind of club of his favorites with himself at the center, making introductions, forging useful contacts between members, and always reaping some kind of benefit in return, whether a free box of his favorite crystalized pineapple or the chance to recommend the next junior member of the Goblin Liaison Office." (HBP4)

The second war forces him into hiding, but he eludes the Death Eaters by taking full advantage of unoccupied Muggle houses, each for a week at a time. The cost of having to move every week pales in comparison to the cost of being "recruited" by the Death Eaters. Dumbledore, however, "incentivizes" him to come out of retirement/hiding by showing him "what he has to gain by returning to Hogwarts" (HBP 4); i.e., the possibility of having "The Boy Who Lived" as a member of his soon-to-be-recreated "Slug Club." "The Chosen One" would be the jewel of his collection (HBP 4) and could help widen Professor Slughorn's network of "favorites," thus ensuring the continuation and possible magnification of his easy living at Hogwarts and beyond. Slughorn knows the positive externalities (spillover benefits) of collecting Harry Potter as a "Slug Club" member could be enormous and yield a long and fruitful return.

Wages and the distribution of labor change when demand and/or supply change. There are many factors that can change labor demand and labor supply. In the non-magical world the rise and fall of the economy over the business cycle will increase or decrease labor demand; in the wizarding world the demand for labor changes because of exogenous forces such as war, or endogenous ones like jinxes. Changes in population over time, the number of graduates of educational institutions, and other factors can increase or decrease labor supply in both worlds, but the wizarding world has the additional problem of supply-side jinxes to contend with as well.

The demand for and supply of a Defense Against the Dark Arts (DADA) professor provides an example of a specific labor market in the Potterian world which faces this supply-side jinx problem. There is a yearly demand for a DADA professor at Hogwarts. The turnover rate for this position is 100%. By his 6th year at Hogwarts, Harry has had a total of 6 different DADA professors (Quirinus Quirrell, Gilderoy Lockhart, Remus Lupin, Alastor Moody (really Barty Crouch, Jr. under the Polyjuice potion), Delores Umbridge and Severus Snape (with Horace Slughorn replacing Snape as the Potions professor)). In what would have been Harry's 7th year, Professor Snape is made headmaster and appoints the Death Eater Amycus Carrow to the position. In a "normal" labor market, one way to solve the problem of a high turnover rate would be to raise wages and/or non-monetary benefits. Slughorn makes this very request of Dumbledore when asked to teach Potions at Hogwarts (in order to free up Snape for the DADA position): "As they set off down the garden path, Slughorn's voice floated after them, 'I'll want a pay rise, Dumbledore!'" (HBP 4)

Increasing wages should induce a wizard to supply his or her labor in this position. However, wizards willing to teach the Defense Against the Dark Arts are almost nonexistent. This is most likely because many of the professors who have taken the job have either died or become temporarily or even permanently incapacitated. Clearly, there is something wrong with this position that a mere raise in pay will not fix: "You know what it's like, Hagrid told us, nobody wants the job, they say it's jinxed." (OP 13) Because wizards weigh the net advantages and disadvantages of the DADA position carefully, there is an annual vacancy for this position. The one exception to this is Remus Lupin, who would have gladly continued as the DADA professor had prejudice, fear, and risk aversion not driven him from it.

Other Hogwarts positions have very low turnover, suggesting that the professors who seek to maximize their net benefits have done so at Hogwarts. This is not to assume, however, that these professors have no other places to seek academic employment. After all, there is Beauxbatons Academy of Magic and Durmstrang Institute. In fact, according to HP-lexicon.org there are other wizarding schools that appear in the canon: a school in Brazil from which Bill Weasley had a pen-friend; The Salem Witches' Institute, U.S.A.; and Mahoutokoro in Japan. (http://www.hplexicon.org/wizworld/places/schools.html#Durmstrang)

The professors at Hogwarts are knowledgeable about these alternatives, as evidenced by Sybill Trelawney. After Delores Umbridge removes Trelawney as the Divination Professor, Dumbledore fills the position with the centaur Firenze. Upon Umbridge's departure, he splits the position between Firenze and Trelawney, something Professor Trelawney is not happy about: "If you will not banish the usurping nag, so be it....Perhaps I shall find a school where my talents

212 • HARRY POTTER FOR NERDS II

are better appreciated...." (HBP 20) She obviously believes her talents are in demand, although Dumbledore is highly skeptical.

Institutional Forces: Institutions such as the government, unions, and large corporations can also influence wages and labor distribution in the nonmagical world. Institutions can "balkanize" the labor market into a number of segmented submarkets. This segmentation is seen in the creation of internal labor markets through job ladders, which rely solely on hiring from a pool of workers who already work at the institution. Job ladders occur when workers who have been with the company retire or go to work elsewhere, creating vacancies. As the firm hires from within, workers move up the job ladder and vacancies appear at the entry level. The internal labor market intersects with the external labor market with these "port of entry" jobs. The Ministry of Magic (MoM) is one example of an institution that promotes from within. Percy Weasley graduates with the necessary OWLS/NEWTS to get a clerical job in the Department of International Magical Cooperation. He is soon promoted to personal assistant to his boss Barty Crouch, and then is promoted again to Junior Assistant to Minister Fudge. Arthur Weasley also works at the Ministry of Magic Misuse of Muggle Artifacts Office (with a warlock named Perkins) under Cornelius Fudge. Percy is eventually promoted to Head of the Office for the Detection and Confiscation of Counterfeit Defensive Spells and Protective Objects under Rufus Scrimgeour. Delores Umbridge also rose up in the ranks at the MoM: "At the age of 17, just after leaving Hogwarts, she started her political career as an intern in the Improper Use of Magic Office, and by the age of 30, she became the Head of the Office, due to her ruthless tactics and tyrannical leadership under her sweet attitude." (http://harrypotter.wikia.com/wiki/Dolores_Umbridge) Hogwarts also appears to use job ladders. Albus Dumbledore rises to the rank of Headmaster from Transfiguration professor, while Minerva McGonagall is promoted to the rank of Deputy Headmistress and Head of Gryffindor House. Horace Slughorn is promoted to the Head of Slytherin House when Severus Snape becomes Headmaster.

Institutions like the MoM and Hogwarts introduce rules and regulations that further define the dimensions of the labor market. These effectively delineate who can compete for specific jobs and who is most preferred. These rules are established in the form of personnel policies, union contracts and government legislation. Umbridge, in fact, "drafted a bit of anti-werewolf legislation two years ago that makes it almost impossible for him [Lupin] to get a job." (OP 14) Her bit of legislation could be considered a type of protective labor law that limits the ability of "half-breeds" to compete for certain types of work, effectively establishing a barrier to entry for that segment of the labor market.

A prime illustration of government legislation defining specific personnel policies is Gringotts Wizarding Bank:

> The bank was created by Gringott in 1474. The bank was then put in the hands of the Ministry of Magic. In 1865, the Ministry decided to put full control of Gringotts back in goblin hands. During Voldemort's control of the Ministry (1997 to 1998), the bank was put yet again under the Ministry. With the defeat of Voldemort and the end of the Second Wizarding War, Gringotts was presumably put back into Goblin management. (*Harry Potter and the Prisoner of Azkaban (video game)* - Gringott Wizard Card; harrypotter.wikia.com/wiki/The_Wizarding_World_of_Harry_Potter; Third question of the Third W.O.M.B.A.T. at J.K. Rowling's Official Site)

For reasons unknown, only goblins are allowed to work in certain jobs within Gringotts, as only they know how to adequately defend the bank against trespassers. In addition, goblins are very good metalsmiths and are responsible for minting the Galleons, Sickles, and Knuts used in the wizarding world; each coin is stamped with a serial number identifying the goblin who cast it. (OP19) This occupational licensing sanctioned by the MoM restricts the supply of goblin labor to these particular occupations, banking and metalwork. This supply restriction could increase wages in these jobs, provided that demand stays constant. Unfortunately, though, goblin occupational licensing also restricts the number of available jobs open to goblins, which could dampen wages. Correspondingly, wizards are forbidden to do the work that goblins do, but can work in other banking jobs, such as being a Curse Breaker, like Bill Weasley.

Sociological Forces are the third determinant of labor market outcomes. These represent the influence of social groups and norms on the determination of wages and the allocation of labor. Important factors, including family background, socioeconomic class, culture and discrimination, all have an important effect on a wizard's range of choice and mobility in the labor market.

One of the ways that family background and class can influence a wizard's choice of profession is through a stratification of the labor market due to "non-competing groups." J.E. Cairnes describes his theory of noncompeting groups in this way:

> No doubt various ranks and classes fade into each other by imperceptible gradations, and individuals from all classes are constantly passing up or down: but while this is so, it is nevertheless true that the average workman, from whatever rank he be taken, finds his power of competition limited for practical purposes to a certain range of occupations, so that, however high the rates of remuneration in those which lie beyond may rise, he is excluded from sharing them. We are thus compelled to recognize the existence of noncompeting industrial groups as a feature of our social economy. (J.E. Cairns, *Political Economy* (New York: Harper, 1974), 67 – 68)

Non-competing groups occur in the Potterian world between wizards themselves and between wizards and other magical beings, such as goblins. As previously mentioned, wizards do not compete with goblins in the labor market, most specifically the banking labor market. Gringotts Wizarding Bank does hire wizards, just not for the same jobs that goblins perform. This division between these two labor markets originates not only from government legislation but also because of differences in class and background as well as from differences in specific skills. Trolls only seem to be used for security jobs, and giants and centaurs are not employed in the Wizarding world at all, with the notable exceptions of Hagrid and Firenze.

Another way in which sociological factors affect labor market outcomes is through their influence on the supply of labor. A wizard's choice of occupation involves not only a consideration of market opportunities, of wages rates and employment prospects, but also the individual wizard's psychological feelings about which choice is valued more. The decision to enter a specific profession depends on ability, preferences and taste for each line of work. Not only is this shown by Arthur Weasley's desire to work in Misuse of Muggle Artifacts Office, it is also illustrated by the exchange below between Ron and Hermione regarding possible careers:

> "Well, I don't fancy Healing," said Ron on the last evening of the holidays. He was immersed in a leaflet that carried the crossed bone-and-wand emblem

of St. Mungo's on its front. "It says here you need at least 'E' at NEWT level in Potions, Herbology, Transfiguration, Charms and Defense Against the Dark Arts. I mean ... blimey ... don't want much, do they?"

"Well, it's a very responsible job, isn't it?" said Hermione absently. She was poring over a bright pink and orange leaflet, that was headed, SO YOU THINK YOU'D LIKE TO WORK IN MUGGLE RELATIONS?

"You don't seem to need many qualifications to liaise with Muggles; all they want is an OWL in Muggle Studies: *'Much more important is your enthusiasm, patience and a good sense of fun!'* ...

He was halfway through a pamphlet on wizard banking. "Listen to this: *'Are you seeking a challenging career involving travel, adventure and substantial, danger-related treasure bonuses? Then consider a position with Gringotts Wizarding Bank, who are currently recruiting Curse-Breakers for thrilling opportunities abroad...'* They want Arithmancy, though; you could do it, Hermione!"

"I don't much fancy banking," said Hermione vaguely, now immersed in: HAVE YOU GOT WHAT IT TAKES TO TRAIN SECURITY TROLLS? (OP 29)

In this conversation, both Ron and Hermione reveal their preferences regarding future professions. Hermione may be technically proficient at Arithmancy, a prerequisite for being a Curse-Breaker for Gringotts, but she doesn't "fancy banking" so she is not interested in supplying her labor to this market. Her behavior reinforces Dumbledore's economic comment to Harry on how choices, not abilities, reveal character. Hermione is being true to herself by disregarding an occupation she would not "fancy," despite her ability. Ron is not interested in Healing, preferring to become an Auror. The career of a Healer requires more and higher qualifications than one doing Muggle relations, as per the level of responsibility. This mirrors the idea that educational credentials are required for many types of "more responsible" careers in the non-magical world, either because the education increases productivity and ability directly, or it is used as a "screening device," giving potential employers a signal to the native intelligence and trainability of the applicant.

Discrimination is another sociological factor that can influence wage and labor distribution that is independent of labor market supply and demand: "Discrimination occurs whenever one person is treated preferentially over another even though both individuals are equal except for some characteristic such as gender, race, religion, or nationality." (Kaufman and Hotchkiss 2006) There is premarket discrimination that denies individuals an equal opportunity to develop their natural abilities and talents during their formative, pre-employment years, and there is market discrimination which occurs when people of equal abilities are given unequal job assignments, promotions, or rates of pay solely on the basis of some characteristic unrelated to their performance on the job.

There are many examples of market discrimination based on personal prejudice in the Potterian world. Umbridge has the opportunity to act on her prejudice against Muggle-born wizards once the MoM falls to the Death Eaters. She rules that Muggle-born wizards be sent to Azkaban, effectively decreasing their wages and mobility to zero. When she is Headmistress of Hogwarts she wants only pure or half-blood wizards to work at the school, as shown by her treatment of Hagrid and Firenze. (This is despite the fact that Hogwarts is the de-facto employer, and it is the Headmaster/Headmistress who makes the hiring/firing decisions.) By the time Harry returns to Hogwarts in *Deathly Hallows*, only pure or half-blood wizards are allowed to attend the school and, in fact, are now required to go. (DH 11) This rule restricts who can receive a Hogwarts education, causing jobs requiring OWLS and NEWTS to be consequently denied to Muggle-born wizards who cannot attain the necessary credentials for employment. (This is ultimately a moot point considering that by the time Harry returns, Muggle-born wizards are either in Azkaban or in hiding.) Although we readers do not know what Hogwarts professors are paid, either in wizard money or in "in-kind" goods and services, we do know that eventually Umbridge's employer prejudice against all non-pure blood wizards and other magical creatures causes poverty, hardship, and loss of freedom for those particular groups.

Discrimination also stems from prejudice by fellow workers and/or from consumers. Discrimination born from prejudiced workers may be even more powerful than employer prejudice. Prejudiced majority workers have disutility associated with working with minority workers. In theory, they demand to be paid a wage premium for working with people they are prejudiced against, resulting in increased costs to the firm (especially if the firm wants to keep an integrated work force). If consumers are prejudiced they will act as if the price of a good or service purchased from an offending worker is higher than the purchase price from a non-offending worker. Therefore, if the minority or offending worker comes into contact with prejudiced consumers, the worker must be paid less in order to allow the firm to lower its prices enough to induce these consumers to buy from them.

Remus Lupin suffers from the effects of both of these types of discrimination, as illustrated below:

> "... and Dumbledore's trust has meant everything to me. He let me into Hogwarts as a boy, and he gave me a job when I have been shunned all my adult life, unable to find paid work because of what I am." (PA 18)

> "You have only ever seen me amongst the Order, or under Dumbledore's protection at Hogwarts! You don't know how most of the wizarding world sees creatures like me! When they know of my affliction, they can barely talk to me!" (DH 11)

> "That was the final straw for Severus. I think the loss of the Order of Merlin hit him hard. So he—er—accidently let slip that I am a werewolf this morning at breakfast....This time tomorrow, the owls will start arriving from parents....They will not want a werewolf teaching their children, Harry." (PA 22)

It is painfully clear to Lupin that some of his colleagues at Hogwarts may not want to teach alongside a werewolf, for various reasons—employee prejudice being one of them—so he leaves before he can be discriminated against. In addition, he is quite aware of the fact that both the direct consumers (students) and indirect consumers (parents) of a Hogwarts education may not want a werewolf teaching them or their children, regardless of the fact that Lupin excels in teaching the DADA course and appears to be one of the few who can actually teach the students what they need to know. His teaching competency coupled with Dumbledore's trust is not enough, in his mind at least, to counteract the prejudice and resulting discrimination he fears from other professors, students and their parents; hence, his decision to leave. Had Lupin decided to stay at Hogwarts, however, his decision could have triggered an outcry for higher pay from the other professors (especially Snape), depending on their particular "taste for discrimination" and/or risk aversion to being in close proximity to a werewolf, regardless of the effectiveness of his safety precaution measures. In addition, some students and parents may have asked for some type of compensation for the psychic disutility of having to deal with a werewolf professor. This could not have come in the form of lower tuition, as Hogwarts is free, but in-kind benefits may have been offered, such as free books, cauldrons, brooms, etc., to entice students to stay and be taught by Professor Lupin.

Ultimately, however, it is Hogwarts's loss that he chooses to leave, opening up yet another vacancy in the DADA position, as he is clearly a talented DADA teacher and generally well regarded by students and his colleagues. Lupin's proficiency as a professor is evidenced by Professor McGonagall's comments to Professor Umbridge regarding Harry's ability to become an Auror:

> "I'm terribly sorry to have to contradict you, Minerva, but as you will see from my note, Harry has been achieving very poor results in his classes with me—"

> "I should have made my meaning plainer," said Professor McGonagall, turning at last to look Umbridge directly in the eyes. "He has achieved high marks in all Defense Against the Dark Arts tests set by a competent teacher." (OP 29)

McGonagall clearly does not hold Umbridge's DADA teaching, or anything else she does for that matter, in high esteem. Unfortunately for Lupin, however, it appears he never again holds a paying job, despite his eventual marriage and fatherhood.

Lastly, market discrimination can also be based on market power. When market power is the source of discrimination, the motivation is pecuniary gain, not personal prejudices. This power in the labor market is on the demand side, and enables the two largest institutions in the Potterian world, the MoM and Hogwarts, to have more control over wages and quantity of labor hired than they would have if they faced a more competitive market for wizard labor. Specifically, these two institutions can be considered to have some monopsonistic power. A monopsony is a labor market where there is one buyer of labor and both the MoM and Hogwarts employ many. Of course, there are employment alternatives for wizards at both institutions, but not for all. For example, Aurors have no choice but to work for the MoM as it is the only employer who hires them. This is also the case for professional Quidditch players, for if they want to play they must be hired by the International Association of Quidditch, which falls under the jurisdiction of the Department of Magical Games and Sports, part of the Ministry of Magic.

Although discrimination is practiced against many groups in the Potterian world, discrimination against house-elves is the most obvious. The wizarding world implicitly holds house-elves in inferior status and systematically denies them an equal opportunity to develop their potential capability, to use that capability in its most advantageous employment and to earn a wage that is equal to what others of the same capability are paid. House-elf discrimination can be likened to slavery in America. Although some slaves and house-elves were treated abysmally by their masters while others were genuinely loved and cared for, neither group was allowed to cultivate their own skills and venture forth freely into the labor market. This is clearly a case of pre-market discrimination. In current society the plight of the house-elf may be considered similar to what occurs with "hidden or invisible workers." These types of workers are often migrant domestic workers at risk of abuse and exploitation, who work behind closed doors, thus making it difficult for them to seek help or be seen by people on the outside. (Human Rights Watch 2014) According to the nonprofit group Free The Slaves:

> Forced labor is prevalent in five sectors of the U.S. economy: prostitution and sex services (46%), domestic service (27%), agriculture (10%), sweatshop/factory (5%), and restaurant and hotel work (4%)....Forced labor persists in these sectors because of low wages, lack of regulation and monitoring of working conditions, and a high demand for cheap labor. (Free The Slaves, Washington, D.C. and The Human Rights Center, University Of California, Berkeley, CA. 2004)

A more benign view of house-elves portrays them as unpaid domestic servants. Their lot in life is somewhat similar to the 1.5 million people employed as domestic servants in Britain in 1901. These servants also lived with their employers to attend to their every whim, whatever the time of day. The main difference, of course, is that the British domestics were paid for their work, which included being a butler, footman, governess, skilled cook, housekeeper, senior parlor-maid, head house-maid and lady's maid, kitchen-maid, scullery-maid, laundress, nursemaid, housemaid, stable-boy, etc. At the bottom of the ladder were the young girls who could enter service when they were 13, earning a few pounds a year. At the top was the butler, who was paid 10 times more. (Burnett

2001) House-elves, with the exception of Dobby, are not paid, nor do they want to be. If they were paid in the United States, their maid services would be valued between $7.68 and $14.19 per hour, with an average of $9.28 per hour. Their grounds maintenance services would be paid an average of $11.53 per hour, and their chef services would be valued at an average of $14.94 per hour, with the lowest 10% being paid $8.78 an hour and the top 10% being paid $21.69 an hour. (United States Department of Labor, Bureau of Labor Statistics: Occupational Handbook) Wizards wealthy enough to have house-elves definitely save money by not having to pay for their extensive service and loyalty.

The Theory of Human Capital

A discussion of labor economics as portrayed in the Potterian world would be remiss if it did not include the theory of human capital, originally accredited to Adam Smith. In modern human capital theory all human behavior is based on the economic self-interest of individuals operating within freely competitive markets. In this theory, investment in education and on-the-job training, whether it is general or specific, increases market skills, productivity and earnings.

In *The Wealth of Nations*, Smith discussed his theories related to the prosperity or "wealth" of a nation. "The main cause of prosperity," argued Smith "was increasing division of labor." Smith is widely regarded as the first to make a connection between the skill of the worker and higher wage levels. Later economists concentrated instead on investment in physical capital, but in the late 1950's, economists Jacob Mincer, Theodore Schultz and Gary Becker rediscovered Smith's ideas and used them to create the theory of human capital. Becker states that any activity that incurs a cost in the current time period and raises productivity in the future can be analyzed within the framework of investment theory. (Becker 1975) With respect to magical and non-magical individuals alike, education, training, migration, health care and job search are examples that fit this conception of an investment.

Education and training is the type of human capital investment that receives the most attention. While schooling at Hogwarts is partly a consumption good for some of the wizards who attend (think of Hermione, who appears to gain pleasure and satisfaction from the experience of learning), it is also treated by most as a clear investment in their future. All MoM jobs require NEWTS, as does being a professor at Hogwarts (with a few exceptions like Hagrid and Firenze).

Both Harry and Ron aspire to be Aurors after they leave Hogwarts. The education and training needed for this career is intense, as mentioned by Professor McGonagall:

> "Well, I thought of, maybe, being an Auror," Harry mumbled.
>
> "You'd need top grades for that," said Professor McGonagall, extracting a small, dark leaflet from under the mass on her desk and opening it. "They ask for a minimum of five NEWTs, and nothing under 'Exceeds Expectations' grade, I see. Then you would be required to undergo a stringent series of character and aptitude tests at the Auror office. It's a difficult career path, Potter, they only take the best. In fact, I don't think anybody has been taken on in the last three years. I would also advise Transfiguration, because Aurors frequently need to Transfigure or Untransfigure in their work. And I ought to tell you now, Potter, that I do not accept students into my NEWT classes unless they have achieved 'Exceeds Expectations' or higher at Ordinary Wizarding Level. I'd say you're averaging 'Acceptable' at the moment, so you'll need to put in some good hard work before the exams to stand a chance of continuing. Then you ought to do Charms, always useful, and Potions. Yes, Potter, Potions, she added, with the merest flicker of a smile. Potions and antidotes are essential study for Aurors. And I must tell you that Professor Snape absolutely refuses to take students who get anything other than 'Outstanding' in their OWLs, so—."(OP 29)

But getting ahead in the wizarding world doesn't necessarily mean getting an education. Another type of investment in human capital is on-the-job training (OJT). OJT can be general, much like some of the courses at Hogwarts are (Charms, DADA, Potions), or it can be specific, as in the Care of Magical Creatures course or Herbology. However, many wizards mentioned in the stories would have had to learn their trade through specific OJT, regardless of their formal schooling. Stan Shunpike and Ernie Prang of the Knight Bus, all of the specialty shop owners in Diagon Alley and Hogsmeade, the broom manufacturers, Ollivander the wand maker, Ludo Bagman when he was a professional Quidditch player, the dragon feeder at Gringotts, the food service witch on the Hogwarts Express tea trolley, Celestina Warbeck, the Weird Sisters, just to name a few, would have started as novices and gained their skills through hands-on experience.

Fred and George Weasley, after perfecting their owl-order business and doing the research and development of their products on their fellow Gryffindors, leave Hogwarts their final year to open Weasleys' Wizard Wheezes in Diagon Alley. This is a perfect example of relying on specific OJT, and not only formal education, to achieve success:

> He turned to his twin. "George," said Fred, "I think we've outgrown full-time education."
>
> "Yeah, I've been feeling that way myself," said George lightly.
>
> "Time to test our talents in the real world, d'you reckon?" asked Fred.
>
> "Definitely," said George. (OP 29)

Evidently Weasleys' Wizard Wheezes is still a successful business, as J.K. Rowling recently stated that Ron gave up his pursuit of being an Auror to help George run the business after the death of Fred. (http://www.pottermore. com/en-us/daily-prophet/qwc2014/2014-07-08/dumbledores-army-reunites)

To invest in one more year of education or training depends on the benefits and costs of doing so. Even though there is no direct tuition paid to Hogwarts, students must buy their books and magical supplies, own regular and dress robes, and have some type of animal (owl or cat or rat) in tow when at school. When they first enroll in school they must purchase their wands as well. There is also an indirect cost, or opportunity cost of attending. Presumably, he or she would alternatively be working and earning a living (unless there is family wealth to live on), or attending another school, or travelling. The total cost of investment in another year at Hogwarts is the direct + indirect cost of attending school the next year. The total benefits include the potential for increased earnings, more attractive employment opportunities and higher status and social prestige. Investment is a good idea whenever the increased benefits both pay back the initial costs and yield a rate of return at least as high as alternative investments of one's time and money. Harry, Hermione and Ron all decide to forgo their last year at Hogwarts because the opportunity cost of using their time to find the Horcruxes is too high. Even though their traditional in-seat education may suffer (although that is unlikely), they all gain valuable on-the-job training through completing Dumbledore's mission and fulfilling the prophecy.

Human Capital versus Screening

Some labor economists believe that the link between education and earnings is productivity. Additional schooling enhances an individual's innate intellectual ability with skills needed to be more productive at work. These skills include an increased facility for logical reasoning, conceptualization, and communication. Certain individuals earn more than others because they have the skills and tools that employers are willing to pay extra to get. Other labor economists, however, maintain that the primary reason education and earnings go hand in hand is because employers use education as a "screening device." To improve the probability that the best worker is hired, firms use "signals" such as years of education to sort or screen prospective workers into those most likely to be high or low productivity employees. Education and earnings are positively related not because the education itself increases productivity on the job, but because employers have found that the number of years of schooling is a reliable signal concerning native intelligence and trainability on the job. In Harry's case, he is able to become an Auror despite not finishing his last year at Hogwarts or passing the required number of NEWTS (minimum of five). He presumably is accepted into the post-Hogwarts program and passes the necessary tests which include demonstrating the ability to react well to pressure, perseverance, dedication, and great skill in practical defense. He would have also had to pass tests on Concealment and Disguise as well as Stealth and Tracking (OP 3). Given that he defeats the Dark Lord, Harry has definitely proven his ability to succeed in becoming an Auror to the new MoM, despite his apparent lack of a "diploma" from Hogwarts. Hermione also succeeds in the MoM without finishing her formal education, as reported by Rita Skeeter in the *Daily Prophet*, 8 July 2014: "After a meteoric rise to Deputy Head of the Department of Magical Law Enforcement, she is now tipped to go even higher with the Ministry. . . ." (http://www.pottermore.com/en-us/daily-prophet/qwc2014/2014-07-08/dumbledores-army-reunites).

The Theory of Compensating Wage Differentials

> The most detestable of all employments, that of public executioner, is, in proportion to the quantity of work done, better paid than any common trade whatever. (Adam Smith 1776)

Over 200 years ago Adam Smith realized that people choose an occupation based on a whole package of attributes, both positive and negative. Each worker compares the total of the advantages and disadvantages of each occupation and chooses the one yielding the highest level of net advantages. Because some occupations are more desirable than others, if the wage rates were equal, workers would crowd into the desirable ones and shun the undesirable ones. Wage rate differences among occupations represent compensating wage differentials because they equalize the net attractiveness of each occupation. Although wage differences between the professions are not discussed outright in the stories, the assumption is that an Auror earns more than a Healer does for a multitude of reasons, not the least of which is the danger an Auror faces. In addition, as becoming an Auror takes more time and training than becoming a Healer or a professional having to deal with Muggle relations, wage rates need to be higher to recoup the initial human capital investment cost.

With respect to compensating wage differentials and public executioners in the Wizarding world, it may be assumed that McNair, who works as an executioner of dangerous creatures for the Ministry of Magic, is paid more than some other MoM employees, given that his job is, in the words of Adam Smith, "the most detestable of all employments." (PA16, PA21, GF33)

Actual wages, although not mentioned in the stories, are mentioned in the Daily Prophet newsletters given out to the Official Harry Potter Fan Club (since disbanded) by Bloomsbury Press in England in 1998 and 1999. The first example mentioned is the occupation of Hit-Wizard/Witch for the Magical Law Enforcement Squad, which pays the most and requires the most education and training. It comes with benefits, too. A new hire's starting salary, together with a Ministry of Magic broomstick and one's own regular bed at St. Mungo's, is 700 Galleons per month. This converts to $6825 dollars/month, or a yearly salary of $81,900. This number is based on an exchange rate of $9.75 (which is the one mentioned by J.K. Rowling in a live chat with Comic Relief in March, 2001).

Given that being a Hit-Wizard/Witch is a dangerous, yet exciting and glamorous occupation, it appears to have a premium attached to it to compensate for the risk involved.

The second occupation mentioned in the newsletters pays less, as is fitting, given that it is the Assistant Manager at Flourish & Blotts Wizarding Bookstore. This salary is 42 Galleons/month, which converts to $409.50/month or $4914/year. This is obviously a much lower salary, with much less danger and risk connected to it, but not as low as the job of Dragon Feeder at Gringotts, the third salary mentioned, which pays 7 Galleons weekly, or $68.25 a week, $273/month or $3276 per year. It appears that the more education, training and danger involved, the higher the wages and benefits. Of course, it is not clear if these latter two wages are at or below poverty level, as the overall cost of living in the wizarding world is not mentioned, and we do know that poverty exists in the Potterian world.

Income Inequality, Poverty and Welfare in the Wizarding World

The Wizarding world does not appear to have any type of public or private welfare safety net, despite the clear evidence of poverty and income inequality. There is no system of income redistribution through taxation, no soup kitchens, food banks or places for the homeless, and no mechanism in place to help poor wizards get some financial or in-kind help to make ends meet. There seems to be no real explanation for the "rolling in it" wealth of the Malfoys or the ever-present poverty faced by the Weasleys. Why is this? According to Megan McArdle, the economy of the Potterian world just doesn't make any sense at all:

> Why are the Weasleys poor? Why would any wizard be? Anything they need, except scarce magical objects, can be obtained by ordering a house elf to do it, or casting a spell, or, in a pinch, making objects like dinner, or a house, assemble themselves. Yet the Weasleys are poor not just by wizard standards, but by ours: they lack things like new clothes and textbooks that should be easily obtainable with a few magic words. Why? The answer, as with so much of JK Rowling's work, seems to be "she didn't think it through."

J.K. Rowling explained why food and money cannot be created, and she has also laid down the rules concerning what her characters can and cannot do. In addition, she gives us the reasons for the grinding poverty of the Gaunt family, the last remaining descendants of Hogwarts co-founder Salazar Slytherin, who eventually died out. As Dumbledore tells Harry:

> "Lack of sense coupled with a great liking for grandeur meant that the family gold was squandered several generations before Marvolo was born. He, as you saw, was left in squalor and poverty with a very nasty temper, a fantastic amount of arrogance and pride, and a couple of family heirlooms. . . ." (HPB 10)

His nasty temper, arrogance and pride could very well have prevented Marvolo Gaunt from rising above his lot in life and earning some type of living for himself and his family. Instead, he wallows in his misery, treasuring his family heirlooms more than his own offspring. It appears he never made an effort to capitalize monetarily on his family name or use his magical capabilities to better himself in any way.

Rowling does not address governmental income and spending, any type of tax, inflation, unemployment, lending, interest rates, low population growth, or the lack of social mobility. Maybe she just didn't see the need in burdening the non-magical among us with these more mundane and ordinary aspects of real life. Or maybe she didn't want to make her stories any more complicated, perhaps thinking the addition of economics would bore her readers silly. Possibly, she just wanted her stories to be emancipating, more utopian, allowing the reader free rein of the imagination—without a thorough explanation of every economic detail—while exploring the co-existence of the magical world with the non-magical one. Or it could be that she was more interested in presenting class differences and discrimination, the social and cultural results of poverty, rather than exploring their root causes and the political and economic policies that may help alleviate it. Maybe, too, she is just letting the reader experience poverty in the vague way that children do: alternately ignoring it or just accepting it as a natural part of life.

Conclusion

J.K. Rowling intuitively employs the notion of scarcity and trade-offs, along with other supporting economic concepts, in her work. Her characters use cost-benefit analysis, make decisions at the margin, respond to incentives, experience unintended consequences, and are interested in not only maximizing their utility (happiness) but also their profits. They understand that opportunity cost is the true cost of any decision made, endure various types of discrimination, buy from sellers who possess market power over the price, suffer the consequences of protectionist trade policies, and, at the end, are at the mercy of dark forces which impact their daily economic lives. Above all, the majority of them work to earn a living to keep food on the table, clothes on their backs, and the ability to have a wand "at the ready." They work at all types of jobs; some rather pedestrian ones known to the reader, some exotic ones which are not known so much. They earn high wages and low wages, invest in their own wizard capital, get trained, and perfect their artisan skills. In some cases, they even devote their lives to their careers. Readers can relate to all of this (except possibly having a wand "at the ready"), even though the Harry Potter stories take place in a magical universe. This world is familiar and somewhat similar to their own economic life experience. They are knowledgeable enough about the details of Potterian society to be able to spend some time analyzing it from an economic point of view, yet distant enough from it to be able to do this dispassionately.

Works Cited

Accio Quote!, www.accio-quote.org/articles/2001/0301-comicreliefstaff.htm.

Becker, Gary S. (1975) *Human Capital Theory* 2nd ed. (New York: NBER).

Burnett, John (2001), "What Kind of Staff Would a Victorian Household Have?" http://www.victorianweb.org/history/work/burnett5.html.

Cairns, J.E. (1974) *Political Economy* (New York: Harper), 67 – 68, http://www.harrypotter.wikia.com.

Free The Slaves, Washington, D.C. and The Human Rights Center, University Of California, Berkeley, CA., (2004) "Hidden Slaves: Forced Labor in the United States," https://www.freetheslaves.net/ Document. Doc?id=17.

The Harry Potter Lexicon, http://www.hp-lexicon.org.

Human Rights Watch, (2014) "Hidden Away,"
    http://www.hrw.org/reports/2014/03/31/hidden-away-0.

Kaufman, Bruce and Hotchkiss, Julie (2006), *The Economics of Labor Markets*,
    7th edition (Thompson/Southwest), 28.

Marcius, Caius (2000), "The Limits of Magic,"
    http://www.hp-lexicon.org/essays/essay-limits-of-magic.html.

Marshall, Alfred (1890) *Principles of Economics* (London: Macmillian and Co.,
    Ltd.), Book I, Chapter I.

McArdle, Megan(2007) Harry Potter: the economics,
    (http://www.theguardian.com/commentisfree/2007/jul/20/harrypot-
    tertheeconomics).

Rowling, J.K. (1998), *Harry Potter and the Sorcerer's Stone* (SS), Book 1(London:
    Bloomsbury Publishing Plc.).

Rowling, J.K. (1999a), *Harry Potter and the Chamber of Secrets* (CS), Book 2
    (London: Bloomsbury Publishing Plc.).

Rowling, J.K. (1999b), *Harry Potter and the Prisoner of Azkaban* (PA), Book 3
    (London: Bloomsbury Publishing Plc.).

Rowling, J.K. (2000), *Harry Potter and the Goblet of Fire* (GF), Book 4 (London:
    Bloomsbury Publishing Plc.).

Rowling, J.K. (2003), *Harry Potter and the Order of the Phoenix* (OP), Book 5
    (London: Bloomsbury Publishing Plc.).

Rowling, J.K. (2005), *Harry Potter and the Half-Blood Prince* (HBP), Book 6
    (London: Bloomsbury Publishing Plc.).

Rowling, J.K. (2007), *Harry Potter and the Deathly Hallows* (DH), Book 7
    (London: Bloomsbury Publishing Plc.).

Smith, Adam (1975) *The Wealth of Nations* (Chicago: University of Chicago
    Press), 112 – 114.

South West News Service, 8 July 2000,
    http://www.accio-quote.org/articles/2000/0700-swns-alfie.htm).

Pottermore, http://www.pottermore.com/en-us/.

United States Department of Labor, Bureau of Labor Statistics: Occupational
    Handbook, http://www.bls.gov/ooh/home.htm.

CHAPTER 13

___

Un-Locke-ing *The Order of the Phoenix*

Carrie-Ann Biondi

The Political Turn in Harry's World

As Harry Potter's personal world expands, the reader who journeys through J.K. Rowling's *Harry Potter* saga is drawn into an increasingly complex fictional universe. We move with Harry from his cramped quarters in the cupboard under the stairs at Four Privet Drive to Hogwarts School for Witchcraft and Wizardry in *Sorcerer's Stone*.[1] Though the specter of Lord Voldemort always lurks in the background (and eventually forces its way into the foreground), repeatedly prompting Harry's concern with being a good person, Harry is mostly absorbed with friendship, family, and playing Quidditch throughout the first three novels. The boundary of his awareness expands significantly to the larger wizarding world in *Goblet of Fire*, where Harry realizes at the Quidditch World Cup that wizards exist outside of Great Britain: "It was only just dawning on Harry how many witches and wizards there must be in the world; he had never really thought much about those in other countries" (*GoF* p. 81).[2] Here, the narrative takes a much darker turn into the complexities of flawed legal and political structures that play into Voldemort's plans for destruction and domination.

___

[1] J.K. Rowling, *Harry Potter and the Sorcerer's Stone* (New York: Scholastic, 1997); hereafter, SS.

[2] J. K. Rowling, *Harry Potter and the Goblet of Fire* (New York: Scholastic, 2000); hereafter, GoF.

Goblet of Fire brings to the surface more prominently than do the first three novels most of the legal and political issues that drive the rest of the saga's plot: Muggle-wizard relations (e.g., p. 53), house-elf slavery (e.g., pp. 125, 224-25), corruption in the Ministry of Magic (e.g., pp. 101, 135-38), the return of Voldemort (pp. 638-43), and the resurrection of the resistance group the Order of the Phoenix (p. 713). Minister of Magic Cornelius Fudge, who thinks that Hogwarts Headmaster Albus Dumbledore wants to usurp his power, refuses to believe that Voldemort has returned (*GoF* pp. 702-10) and makes a series of ostrich-like choices that plunge the wizarding world simultaneously into authoritarianism and chaos during the following three novels. Not naturally drawn toward the wider legal and political concerns that consume his friend Hermione Granger, Harry can no longer avoid facing and participating in such issues. The most overtly political of the seven novels—*Order of the Phoenix*—opens with an attempt on the lives of Harry and his cousin Dudley Dursley.[3] The attackers are two dementors, who are supposed to guard the wizard prison of Azkaban. Harry's self-defensive use of a Patronus Charm sets into motion a chain of events that puts Harry in front of a corrupt court, allows him to return to a Hogwarts school that comes increasingly under Ministry control, and embroils him in a rebellion that he ends up leading. In addition to the explicitly Lockean political themes discussed below, we also see the students learning about political history in Professor Binns's class and getting tested on it on their O.W.L. exams—everything from the giant wars to goblin riots to the Formation of the International Confederation of Wizards (*OotP* pp. 229, 355, and 725-26). We also learn about nearly every administrative office in the Ministry of Magic while Harry and Arthur Weasley are riding the elevator up to Arthur's office and then down to the hearing (*OotP* pp. 129-30 and 134-35).

Although a good deal of ink has been spilled over Rowling's personal political views[4] and whether and to what extent the *Harry Potter* saga has libertarian or

---

[3] J.K. Rowling, *Harry Potter and the Order of the Phoenix* (New York: Scholastic Inc., 2003); hereafter, *OotP*.

[4] See, e.g., Jeff Jensen, "'Fire' Storm," *Entertainment Weekly*, September 7, 2000, accessed online at: http://www.accio-quote.org/articles/2000/0900-ew-jensen.htm; Lindsay Fraser, "Harry Potter—Harry and Me," *The Scotsman*, November 2002, accessed online at: http://www.accio-quote.org/articles/2002/1102-fraser-scotsman.html; and Ben

socialist strands,[5] surprisingly almost no one has noted what seems to be a manifest Lockean influence that leaps off the pages of *Order of the Phoenix*.[6] Seventeenth-century British philosopher John Locke (1632-1704) penned a number of influential works in the history of modern philosophy, but one was especially revolutionary: *Two Treatises of Government*, especially the *Second Treatise of Government* (1689).[7] Given Locke's place in British history as one of the grandfathers of the liberal political tradition, it would be unsurprising to find strands of his political thought woven into Rowling's saga. Whether such integration was intentional or not on Rowling's part, a close reading of *Order of the Phoenix* reveals that it shares—particularly through the character of Hermione—at least three striking thematic concerns with Locke's *Second Treatise of Government*: (1) all rational beings are morally equal, (2) rebellion against a corrupt government can sometimes be justified, and (3) consent of the governed is a necessary ingredient for political authority. I will argue not only that these parallels exist, but also that Harry and his friends in Dumbledore's Army and the Order of the Phoenix are

---

Leach, "Harry Potter Author J.K. Rowling Gives £1 Million to Labour," *The Telegraph*, September 20, 2008, accessed online at: http://www.telegraph.co.uk/news/ politics/labour/3021309/Harry-Potter-author-JK-Rowling-give-1-million-to-Labour.html.

[5] See, e.g., Travis Prinzi, *Harry Potter & Imagination: The Way between Two Worlds* (Allentown, PA: Zossima Press, 2009), esp. chap. 12; Benjamin Barton, "Harry Potter and the Half-Crazed Bureaucracy," *Michigan Law Review* 104 (May 2006), pp. 1523-38; and Beth Admiraal and Regan Lance Reitsma, "Dumbledore's Politics," in *The Ultimate Harry Potter and Philosophy: Hogwarts for Muggles*, ed. Gregory Bassham (Hoboken, NJ: John Wiley & Sons, 2010), pp. 113-27.

[6] The one exception I am aware of is a paper entitled "John Locke and the Problem of Civil Disobedience in *Order of the Phoenix*," delivered by Nathanial Warne on May 18, 2012 at the "A Brand of Fictional Magic: Reading Harry Potter as Literature" conference, held at University of St. Andrews, Scotland. I am grateful to him for bringing his paper to my attention while I was working on this project. Warne focuses on the issue of civil disobedience (which I address briefly below in Sections III.2 and III.3), while I explore broader Lockean political themes and emphasize the role played by reason and consent in political legitimacy.

[7] John Locke, *Second Treatise of Government*, ed. C.B. Macpherson (Indianapolis, IN: Hackett Publishing Company, Inc., 1980 [1689]); hereafter, *STG*. All in-text references to this work will identify the relevant numbered paragraph(s) in *Second Treatise of Government*.

neither "conservative," "paternalistic" Tories nor unruly "anarchists."[8] Instead, they represent the willingness of decent people to fight against corruption and oppression. They do this in order to restore a political order that offers the hope of becoming better than it has been at protecting the rights of all by recognizing more fully consent and moral agency.

II. Natural Law, Moral Equality, and Individual Rights

One of the hallmarks of Locke's political theory is his natural law approach, which provides pre-political moral standing that is the source of individual rights, a limited state (should a group of individuals choose to create one), and a moral justification for a right of rebellion. Even if a full Lockean analysis of rights is not completely paralleled in the *Harry Potter* saga, it is clear that its heroic protagonists believe in protecting all moral agents, and that they are justified in fighting for their right to self-protection.

1. State of nature and law of nature

Humans are naturally free and equal in a "state of nature" (*STG* secs. 4 and 6). While the state of nature is often considered to exist in the unusual circumstance where there is no political society, it more broadly is mankind's natural, pre-political moral condition, that is, the moral standing that all humans are born into in virtue of their nature. As such, the state of nature is a justificatory device that serves as a "supra-constitution"[9] by which all legitimate political societies

---

[8] For the charge of conservatism, see, e.g., Richard Adams, "Quidditch Quaintness," *The Guardian*, June 17, 2003, accessed online at: http://www.guardian.co.uk/books /2003/jun/18/harrypotter.jkjoannekathleenrowling, and Farah Mendlesohn, "Crowning the King: Harry Potter and the Construction of Authority," in *The Ivory Tower and Harry Potter: Perspectives on a Literary Phenomenon* (Columbia, MO: University of Missouri Press, 2002), pp.159-81. For the charge of unruliness and near-anarchism, see, e.g., James Morone, "Cultural Phenomena: Dumbledore's Message, *The American Prospect*, December 19, 2001, accessed online at: http://prospect.org/article/cultural-phenomena-dumble-dores-message.

[9] I thank Alexander Cohen for suggesting this phrase so as to clarify this point.

should be constrained. The strongest form of moral standing—and the one relevant for our purposes—is known as moral agency. Though Locke did not use the phrase "moral agency," he does seem to have something like it in mind. He regards the hallmark of freedom as possession of a rational faculty by which one can reason, deliberate, render moral judgments, etc. and in virtue of which one is thus held morally responsible for the actions over which one has control. The "principles of human nature" are inextricably tied to "the right rule of reason" and being a "free and intelligent agent" (*STG* secs. 10 and 57).

Locke claims that this "*state of nature* has a law of nature to govern it, which obliges every one: and reason, which is that law, teaches all mankind, who will but consult it, that being all *equal and independent*, no one ought to harm another in his life, health, liberty, or possessions" (*STG* sec. 6). This law of nature is promulgated, if you will, in the natures of things, and so can be "read" by those with the cognition to "see" it. Furthermore, Locke thinks that "it is certain there is such a law, and that too, as intelligible and plain to a rational creature, and a studier of that law, as the positive laws of common-wealths; nay, possibly plainer" (*STG* sec. 12). He continues to explain that the law of nature does not exist only for those who choose to remain outside of a formal political structure; it also constrains and provides the foundation for any proper "*municipal laws* of countries."

Natural law, then, is the source of individual rights to "life, health, liberty, [and] possessions." Locke refers to the protection of all of these (and, in addition, one's labor and land) in a shorthand way as protection of one's "property" (*STG* secs. 27, 85, 87, 95, and 123). This right to self-preservation, on Locke's view, emerges from an inalienable duty of self-preservation (and by extension the preservation of others) on account of our being God's property: individuals "will always have a right to preserve, what they have not a power to part with; and to rid themselves of those, who invade this fundamental, sacred, and unalterable law of *self-preservation*" (*STG* sec. 149).

Humans, however, are not born fully formed moral agents with the reasoning powers to discern the law of nature or the ability to protect themselves. Locke recognizes this fact:

> Children, I confess, are not born in this full state of equality, though they are born to it. Their parents have a sort of rule and jurisdiction over them, when

> they come into the world, and for some time after; but it is but a temporary one. The bonds of this subjection are like the swaddling clothes they are wrapt up in . . . age and reason as they grow up, loosen them, till at length they drop quite off, and leave a man at his own free disposal. (*STG* sect. 54)

Parents (or guardians, in case the parents die or default on their moral responsibility) do not have just "a sort of rule and jurisdiction over" children; they have a moral duty to protect and nurture the minors under their care "during the imperfect state of childhood. To inform the mind, and govern the actions of their yet ignorant nonage, till reason shall take its place, and ease them of that trouble, is what the children want and the parents are bound to" (*STG* sec. 58). In addition, while this "rule and jurisdiction" extends over guiding the actions and instruction of children, it never violates their lives or belongings; it "reaches not their life or their property: it is but a help to the weakness and imperfection of their nonage, a discipline necessary to their education" (*STG* sec. 65). Locke thus provides for some children's rights in his theory, which are to be exercised on children's behalf until they become moral agents. While Locke does permit particular political societies to determine an "age of majority," suggesting that twenty-one might be that age, he leaves open the possibility that the age of majority can be younger, depending on whether children have developed their rational faculties (*STG* sec. 59).

2. Lockean equality in a nutshell

a. *Equal moral standing.* Locke grounds *equal* moral standing in: (1) the possession/use of rational faculties and (2) the fact that such beings can recognize others who are like themselves in the relevant way:

> [F]or men being all the workmanship . . . of one sovereign master, . . . they are his property, whose workmanship they are, made to last during his, not one another's pleasure; and being furnished with like faculties, sharing all in one community of nature, there cannot be supposed any such *subordination* among us, that may authorize us to destroy one another, as if we were made for one another's uses, as the inferior ranks of creatures are for our's [sic]. (*STG* sec. 6)

By "inferior ranks of creatures," Locke means those beings without a rational faculty, which we can use for agricultural purposes, and can kill or consume for self-
preservation.

   b. *Equal rights of punishment.* From equal moral standing comes the right of
all people to punish transgressors of the law of nature who turn the state of nature into a "state of war" (at least until a group of people forms a political society
and transfers that right to specific agents vested with the right of enforcing the
law of nature). Locke explains that

> the *execution* of the law of nature is, in [the] state [of nature], put into every
> man's hands, whereby every one has a right to punish the transgressors of that
> law to such a degree, as may hinder its violation: for the *law of nature* would . .
> be in vain, if there were no body that in the state of nature had a *power to execute*
> that law, and thereby preserve the innocent and restrain offenders. (*STG* sec. 7)

From the assumption that the law of nature cannot be in vain, the duty of self-
preservation, and the equal moral standing of rational agents, Locke derives the
natural rights of law enforcement and punishment. These include self-defense,
protecting other innocent people from a threat, and taking punitive measures to
ensure that the offender does not harm again.

   It might be unclear how equal rights of punishment (including reparation,
restraint, and, at the outer limit, killing a threat to one's life) squares with equal
moral standing. Wouldn't the duty of self-preservation block such a strong right
to punish? Locke's response is that a transgressor of the law of nature is someone
who, by his violation of the Law of Nature, "declares himself to quit the principles
of human nature, and to be a noxious creature" and "renounce[s] reason, the
common rule and measure God hath given to mankind" (*STG* secs. 10 and 11).
Locke's views on punishment serve, then, to underscore how crucial is the role
of the rational faculty in equal moral standing. One need not be perfectly rational
in order to retain one's rights, but Locke regards it as rationally impossible to
reach the conclusion that one is permitted to engage in harmful conduct. Hence,
if one has caused harm, then one must have renounced reason and can be treated
as a non-rational threat to the harmed person's self-preservation.

3. *Moral equality threatened in* Order of the Phoenix

In the fifth book in the series, readers are introduced to a Wizarding World that is by no means free from inequality and prejudice—as evidenced by the institution of house-elf slavery and the Malfoy family's bias against non-pureblood wizards. There is, at least initially, equal protection of all wizards and a separate-but-(mostly)-equal legal stance toward Muggles (though most Muggles are unaware of it, and wizards' use of memory modification on Muggles is an attempt to keep things that way). A Lockean right of self-preservation is clearly recognized early in *Order of the Phoenix*. This can be seen in three facts surrounding the dementor attack on Harry and Dudley. First, Harry's natural impulse is to save his and Dudley's lives by performing a Patronus Charm to deflect the dementors, even though doing so violates the Decree for the Reasonable Restriction of Underage Sorcery (*OotP* pp. 18-27). Second, despite this decree, it has a clause that permits the "use of magic in life-threatening situations" (*OotP* p. 62). Third, no fewer than four different people (Hermione, Remus Lupin, Sirius Black, and Dumbledore) inform Harry of this self-defense exception, when justifying why they think that the Ministry of Magic will have to drop the charges and Harry will win his case at court (*OotP* pp. 62, 115, 123, and 148). These facts show that in the wizarding world the right of self-preservation is valued, is embodied in law, and is widely recognized.

Despite this backdrop of basic Lockean rights for wizards and Muggles, even they become trampled on in the course of *Order of the Phoenix*. One of the primary sub-plots of the saga concerns the destabilizing turmoil created by the increasingly unequal and unjust treatment of nearly all moral agents, be they pureblood, half-blood, or Muggle-born wizards; Muggles; centaurs; merpeople; goblins; elves; etc.[10] As the novels progress, the political turn in Harry's world hinges on recognizing and protecting moral standing, for it is the lack of this that leads

---

[10] For an excellent treatment of this sort of injustice, see Susan Peppers-Bates and Joshua Rust, "House-Elves, Hogwarts, and Friendship: Casting Away the Institutions which Made Voldemort's Rise Possible," *Reason Papers* 34, no.1 (June 2012), pp 109-24.

to the formation of extra-governmental self-defense and resistance groups in *Order of the Phoenix* and eventually to outright warfare in *Deathly Hallows.*[11]

While the equal rights of some beings who possess a rational faculty are either not recognized or are threatened throughout the entire *Harry Potter* saga—especially from *Goblet of Fire* onward—it's in *Order of the Phoenix* that we get to see close up (from Harry's perspective) and in a sustained way the ugly racism of characters like Dolores Umbridge and the portrait of Mrs. Black. Many other characters (Voldemort, the Malfoys, etc.) have always supported pureblood wizard supremacy, but here we experience vicious verbal abuse that gets crystallized in an avalanche of Ministry of Magic decrees. These decrees at first are intended to tighten the Ministry's power over Hogwarts so as to silence the voices of "undesirable elements" regardless of race or species, but then become explicit engines of racist persecution in *Half-Blood Prince* and *Deathly Hallows.*

The refusal to see all rational beings as morally equal is evident in the raving tirades of Mrs. Black's portrait at Twelve Grimmauld Place as she berates both various non-pureblood members of the Order of the Phoenix and those pureblood wizards who align themselves with the Order: *"Filth! Scum! By-products of dirt and vileness! Half-breeds, mutants, freaks, begone from this place! How dare you befoul the house of my fathers— . . . Blood traitor, abomination, shame of my flesh!"* (*OotP* p. 78). Such racism gains an official foothold in the person of Ministry-appointed Defense Against the Dark Arts teacher-turned Hogwarts High Inquisitor-turned Hogwarts Headmistress Umbridge. Alluding to former Defense Against the Dark Arts teacher Lupin (who is a werewolf), she says to her students: "'but you have been exposed to some very irresponsible wizards in this class, very irresponsible indeed—not to mention,' she gave a nasty little laugh, 'extremely dangerous half-breeds'" (*OotP* p. 243). She also screams at the centaurs: "Filthy half-breeds! . . . Beasts! Uncontrolled animals!" (*OotP* p. 755). It is under Umbridge's reign that Draco Malfoy—newly appointed member of her Inquisitorial Squad—gets to express his family's prejudice with impunity when he subtracts ten house points from Hermione simply for being "a Mudblood" (*OotP* p. 626).

---

[11] J.K. Rowling, *Harry Potter and the Deathly Hallows* (New York: Scholastic, 2007); hereafter, *DH.*

Since Locke did not venture into the realm of imaginary beings, we can only extrapolate his moral and political theory from his experience with humans and non-human animals onto the realm of the wizarding world. If any kind of being possesses and can use a rational faculty, then those beings have equal moral standing. In addition to the many places throughout the saga where Hermione and Dumbledore (the main voices of enlightened reason) defend the equal moral standing of various rational beings (such as elves, half-giants, and werewolves), we see some—most notably the centaurs—standing up for themselves in *Order of the Phoenix*. For example, when Dean Thomas poses an unintentionally offensive question to the new Divination teacher Firenze, who is a centaur—"Did Hagrid breed you, like the thestrals?"—Firenze quickly replies, "Centaurs are not the servants or playthings of humans" (*OotP* pp. 601-2). And when Umbridge insults the centaurs in the Forbidden Forest by calling them "half-breeds" with "near-human intelligence," a centaur named Magorian angrily replies, "Near-human intelligence? . . . We consider that a great insult, human! Our intelligence, thankfully, far outstrips your own—" (*OotP* p. 754). Since the wizarding community has not historically granted the centaurs equal rights, they have chosen to live as a community apart, as one centaur explains to Hermione: "We are an ancient people who will not stand wizard invasions and insults! We do not recognize your laws, we do not acknowledge your superiority" (*OotP* p. 757). In Lockean terms, the centaurs see that wizarding law is out of step with natural law, and proudly assert their moral agency.

III. Rebel with a Cause

Lockean pre-political moral standing becomes politically important for two reasons. It provides both the source of a limited state's purpose and the moral justification for a right to rebel against a state that oversteps its justified limits. This section focuses on Locke's discussion of why people often choose to form or join a state, the limits that the law of nature places on a state, and how these limits are flagrantly and repeatedly violated throughout *Order of the Phoenix*. Such violations begin to escalate at the end of *Goblet of Fire* with Minister of Magic Fudge authorizing extra-legal use of the Dementor's Kiss on Barty Crouch, Jr., rendering him "worse than dead" (*GoF* p. 703). The violations continue well after *Order of the Phoenix*, reaching a fever pitch in *Deathly Hallows* when Voldemort and his Death Eater followers officially take over the Ministry of Magic by murdering the next Minister of Magic Rufus Scrimgeour; Order member Kingsley Shacklebolt sends a Patronus to Bill Weasley and Fleur Delacour's wedding to warn them all that *"The Ministry has fallen. Scrimgeour is dead. They are coming"* (*DH* p. 159). Luckily, because self-defense organizations such as the Order of the Phoenix and Dumbledore's Army were (justifiably) formed in *Order of the Phoenix*, the saga's heroes are ready for war in *Deathly Hallows*.[12]

1. The purpose of the state

Locke leaves it open for individuals to remain in a pre-political state of nature where they are perfectly free and equal, but he realizes that there are certain "inconveniences of the state of nature" that lead many people to create or join a political society (*STG* sec. 90). The three main difficulties he identifies for life in the state of nature are: lack of "an *established*, settled, known *law* . . . to be the standard of right and wrong, and the common measure to decide all controversies"; lack of "a *known and indifferent judge*, with authority to determine all differences according to the established law"; and lack of "*power* to back and support the sentence when right, and to *give* it due *execution*" (*STG* secs. 124-126). While it is true that all people could use their reason to apprehend the law of nature and follow its principles, some choose not to engage in rational reflection and so do not have the natural law in mind to guide their actions. Even when people do use their reason to apprehend the law of nature, some might allow passion to bias them in judging others too harshly or in judging themselves too leniently—in either case causing injustice in execution of the law of nature. In addition, should

---

[12] I provide a basic summary in Sections III.2 and III.3 of Locke's right to rebellion and indicate some textual evidence from *Order of the Phoenix* for why the Order and the D.A. are justified in resisting the Ministry and Umbridge, but for an extensive analysis of both topics, see Warne, "John Locke and the Problem of Civil Disobedience in *Order of the Phoenix*." In addition, although he does not discuss this topic from a Lockean perspective, Barton also recounts the blatant Ministry corruption that exists through *Half-Blood Prince*; see Barton, "Harry Potter and the Half-Crazed Bureaucracy."

someone use his reason to render a perfectly just decision, it may be too danger-ous to enforce the judgment against a violent offender in the state of nature.

Outside of a political society, then, people's property "is very uncertain, and constantly exposed to the invasion of others," so they are "willing to join in soci-ety with others, who are already united, or have a mind to unite, for the mutual *preservation* of their lives, liberties and estates, . . . call[ed] by the general name, *property*" (*STG* sec. 123). The sole and proper purpose of a state is thus to protect people's natural rights to property (*STG* secs., e.g., 3, 87-90, 95, and 123-134). In order to achieve this purpose, a state's functions are promulgating a written legal code (that is informed by and does not conflict with natural law), authorizing impartial individuals to render judgments according to the law when it has been violated, and authorizing some individuals to enforce properly rendered legal judgments.

2. Lockean right of rebellion

Once a political society is set up, its legislature/ruler is not morally permitted to violate the trust placed in it to protect people's natural rights. So long as a government is upholding its fiduciary power to protect people's natural rights, then its power is supreme over (only) the specific functions that it is authorized to perform. However,

> there remains still *in the people a supreme power to remove or alter the legislative,* when they find the *legislative* act contrary to the trust reposed in them: for all *power given with trust* for the attaining an *end*, being limited by that end, when-ever that *end* is manifestly neglected, or opposed, the *trust* must necessarily be *forfeited*, and the power devolve into the hands of those that gave it . . . . And thus the *community* perpetually *retains a supreme power* of saving themselves from the attempts and designs of any body, even of their legislators. (*STG* sec. 149)

We might today refer to this as "popular sovereignty," though Locke did not use that phrase and he would not have meant by it what many people now associate with it. Today, many equate popular sovereignty with unlimited democratic rule, but Locke leaves it open for a government to take on a non-democratic form so long as it does not overstep its purpose.

The issue then becomes whether circumstances are such that the people's trust has been violated, in which case they are justified in rebelling against their government and replacing it with one that adheres to natural law. According to Locke, there are two types of corruption by which a government becomes "dissolved from within" (rather than a society's being conquered from without). (1) The dissolution of government occurs when "the legislative is altered" not in accordance with authorized procedures, such as when a ruler/prince substitutes his will for the rule of law, when the ruler/prince keeps the legislative from assembling or acting freely, when the method of election/electors are contrary to stated procedures, or when the ruler/prince hands over a people to a foreign power (*STG* secs. 212-220). (2) The dissolution of government occurs when "the legislative, or the prince, either of them, act contrary to their trust" by "invad[ing] the property of the subject" or by making themselves or others "arbitrary disposers of the lives, liberties, or fortunes of the people" (*STG* sec. 221). In either case, the people are absolved of obedience to the government, and the power then devolves to them to create a new legislative authority in keeping with the original purpose for which they created the society.

Lest anyone think that a right of rebellion will lead to frequent disruptions and anarchy, Locke assures us of two things. First, he points out that people have an aversion to significant institutional change; they tolerate a good many "wrong and inconvenient laws" and errors in governance caused by "the *slips* of human frailty," so they will not rebel at every injustice. It takes "a long train of abuses" where repeated and deliberate designs upon a people are manifest to rouse them justifiably to rebellion (*STG* sec. 225). Second, the people's right to throw off a government that violates its natural rights "is *the best fence against rebellion*," for the true rebels are those in the government who overstep their charge by employing force instead of exercising legal authority. The best "way to prevent the evil" of force is to make clear to "them the danger and injustice of it, who are under the greatest temptation to run into it" (*STG* sec. 226).

3. When a decent ministry goes bad

Many readers of *Order of the Phoenix* likely experienced a thrill of excitement when reading the following dialogue that takes place after a glorious batch of fireworks has been set off by Fred and George Weasley. They mischievously launch the disruptive pyrotechnics show when Umbridge installs herself as Headmistress of Hogwarts (by means of Educational Decree Number Twenty-Eight), after Dumbledore fights off Ministry officials and goes into hiding upon the discovery of the student resistance group Dumbledore's Army:

> Hermione returned to the table where Harry and Ron were sitting staring at their schoolbags as though hoping their homework might spring out of it and start doing itself.
>
> "Oh, why don't we have a night off?" said Hermione brightly, as a silver-tailed Weasley rocket zoomed past the window. . . .
>
> "Are you feeling all right?" Ron asked, staring at her in disbelief.
>
> "Now that you mention it," said Hermione happily, "d'you know . . . I think I'm feeling a bit . . . *rebellious*." (*OotP* p. 634)

Ron is stunned in this scene by Hermione's uncharacteristic dismissal of homework. However, when viewing Hermione's conduct from a Lockean perspective, she's just as in character here as she has ever been.

That these words come from Hermione, task-master of homework and follower of (most) rules, is especially telling—as is the fact that "*rebellious*" is italicized in the original text.[13] Hermione rebels not only here by encouraging them to slack off on homework for the night, but also by engaging in increasingly dangerous resistance measures. Such measures include helping Harry to break into Umbridge's office to see whether Sirius is home or is really being tortured by Voldemort at the Ministry (*OotP* chap. 32) and leading Umbridge into the Forbidden Forest to a supposedly secret weapon, where Umbridge instead gets carried off by angry centaurs (*OotP* chap. 33).

It takes a lot for Hermione/Reason to rebel. How does she get to the point where she feels "a bit . . . *rebellious*," and why is she justified in multiple acts of disobedience? Hermione—astute observer of politics and bastion of reason—saw

---

[13] In fact, words like "rebellion" and "resistance" are used five times in *Order of the Phoenix*, and all uses arise in the context of Umbridge's increasingly autocratic rule (*OotP* pp. 346, [twice on] 350, 397, and 634). Outright "revolution" is at last mentioned in *Deathly Hallows* at the brink of the Battle of Hogwarts (*DH* p. 581).

this trouble coming when Umbridge was first installed as the Defense Against the Dark Arts teacher at the beginning of the school year. After listening carefully to Umbridge's "welcome speech," Hermione translates the speech for Harry and Ron: "I'll tell you what it means," said Hermione ominously. "It means the Ministry's interfering at Hogwarts" (*OotP* p. 214).

Interference, indeed. There are numerous instances in *Order of the Phoenix* where the Ministry abuses its power, especially by violating the rights of Hogwarts students and teachers. I will here adduce a relatively brief summary of the "long train of abuses" that justifies Dumbledore's Army's Lockean rebellion against the Ministry-installed Umbridge.[14]

- Minister Fudge attempts to rig Harry's hearing by changing its time and location at the last minute, attempting to discredit or disregard witnesses for Harry's defense, and hurrying the proceedings so as to secure Harry's conviction and expulsion from Hogwarts. Fudge also fails to mention that there is a clause that allows Harry to break the law for purposes of self-defense (*OotP* pp. 134-51). It must be noted that the dementor attack Harry defends himself against is actually ordered extra-legally by Umbridge (*OotP* p. 747).[15]

- Umbridge inflicts malicious, painful punishment on those who say things that neither she nor the Ministry wants to hear, as when Harry "speaks truth to power" in Umbridge's class by contradicting Umbridge and announcing to the class that Voldemort has returned and murdered Cedric Diggory (*OotP* pp. 244-46, 265-68, and 272-75).

- Umbridge refuses to teach the students how to *use* defensive spells, insisting that they merely read about them "in a secure, risk-free way," nearly guaranteeing that the students would be killed in the event of a Dark wizard attack (*OotP* p. 242). She does this because

---

[14] These abuses also justify the Order of the Phoenix's resistance to the Ministry in *Order of the Phoenix*, and eventually everyone's rebellion against the Voldemort/Death Eater-controlled Ministry in *Deathly Hallows*.

[15] We also see a number of helpful articles exploring these legal and judicial issues collected in *The Law and Harry Potter*, ed. Jeffrey E. Thomas and Franklin G. Snyder (Durham, NC: Carolina Academic Press, 2010).

the Ministry is afraid that if the students know defensive magic, then Dumbledore will assemble them into an army and seize power from the Ministry (*OotP* p. 303).[16]

- By a series of arbitrary decrees, Umbridge uses Ministry power to usurp the authority of the other Hogwarts teachers and Headmaster Dumbledore himself and to set up her own personal reign at the school (*OotP* pp. 307, 351-52, 415-16, 551, 581, 624, and 628-29).

- Umbridge is willing to use one of the illegal Unforgivable Curses—the Cruciatus Curse—to torture Harry into telling her who he was trying to communicate with in her office (*OotP* pp. 746-47).

We can see from this summary of some of the Ministry's and Umbridge's most flagrant abuses of political power that the students' behavior at Hogwarts is no anarchic rabble-rousing. They are engaging in genuine, legitimate Lockean resistance to a corrupt and unjust government that has reached its tentacles into their school. It is the third item above that especially persuades Hermione that the time has come to take "matters into [their] own hands" (*OotP* p. 339). She knows the true purpose of a political society, noting several times that it is "about making sure we really can defend ourselves" (*OotP* p. 325; see also pp. 332 and 344). Unlike Umbridge, Hermione seeks to uphold the law of nature; her resistance to the "tyranny of Umbridge" (*OotP* p. 517) is a justified attempt to restore the legitimate order of right reason to Hogwarts (and the Ministry).[17] Locke would certainly agree with Hermione's conclusion that the students need to take "matters into [their] own hands," for their very lives depend on doing so.

IV. Political Legitimacy and Consent

An issue implicit in the previous section's discussion on the purpose of the state and the right of rebellion is that of consent of the governed. Recall that if a

---

[16] It is ironic that this very tactic leads to the formation of Dumbledore's Army.

[17] Hermione not only wants to restore legitimate rule to Hogwarts and the Ministry, but also to improve it. This can be seen in her almost single-handed crusade to eradicate house-elf slavery (and later in *Deathly Hallows* in her identification with the disparate treatment received by goblins; see *DH* pp. 488-89).

group of people finds the "inconveniences of the state of nature" too onerous, then in order to protect better their natural rights, they are free to consent to form a political society (or to join one that already legitimately exists) for the sole purpose of protecting and enforcing these rights. *Order of the Phoenix* shows signs in the formation of Dumbledore's Army of a Lockean (if not Locke's) approach to moving from a (quasi) state of nature to a (sort of) political society and to that move's being legitimately grounded in consent. The mostly underage witches and wizards (the age of majority in the wizarding world being seventeen) of Dumbledore's Army possess and use reasoning abilities, especially Hermione, who is the driving force behind Dumbledore's Army and embodies reason to the highest degree. The members of Dumbledore's Army count as moral agents, and so their consent can count as legitimate and morally binding. While Dumbledore's Army is not a political society, but rather a student-led defense organization, Lockean themes concerning consent and political legitimacy are present in this context. The Hogwarts students find themselves not only in an oppressive school, but in an increasingly Ministry-controlled school that is undermining the primary purpose of a political society. The students are as vulnerable (if not more so) to the same threats as the other citizens of the wizarding world, and so they are essentially thrust into a war-like condition where they are free to come together for self-protection.

1. The legitimizing role of consent

For those who choose to leave the state of nature and form a new political society, it is necessary, but not sufficient, that the political society's purpose and functions are in compliance with the law of nature. In order to make this move legitimately, they also need to give their consent at both stages of what is a two-stage move into political society. Consent is "the only way whereby any one divests himself of his natural liberty, and puts on the *bonds of civil society*" (*STG* sec. 95). This also applies to children of those who are already members of a political society. Once a minor has reached "the age of reason," he or she can choose to stay or leave, "for *every man's children* being by nature as *free* as himself, . . . may, whilst they are in that freedom, choose what society they will join themselves to" (*STG* sec. 73). This is Locke's famous "social contract" theory of political society.

The first stage in moving from the state of nature into a political society requires that each and every interested person joins together by unanimous and express consent to form a "society" (or "community," or "body politic") (*STG* secs. 95-97 and 119). Importantly, this leaves others free to remain in the state of nature, if they wish to brave its "inconveniences," since no one can decide the question for another (*STG* sec. 95).

The second stage involves creating by majority vote a government that then passes specific laws (whether by simple majority or more than a bare majority but less than unanimity). Locke provides several practical reasons why unanimous consent is unfeasible after the initial formation of a civil society: sometimes people are too ill to vote, some are involved in business and so are too busy to vote, and "the variety of opinions, and contrariety of interests" makes it nearly certain that not everyone will agree on any particular law (*STG* sec. 98). Requiring unanimous consent at the second stage would be tantamount to disbanding the society, since action for the sake of self-protection would be impossible and hence a violation of the law of nature that drove them together in the first place.

2. Consent and Dumbledore's Army

When we examine why and how Dumbledore's Army was formed as the brainchild of Hermione and under the tutelage of Harry, there are three strong parallels to Locke's two-stage account above. Dumbledore's Army meets the two criteria for a legitimate political society, because it aims at the proper purpose and follows Locke's two-stage model of consent.

First, as noted above, when Umbridge took over "teaching" Defense Against the Dark Arts, she de-fanged the class by teaching only theory and not practice. Because of this, the students were terrified that they would be defenseless against the return of Voldemort and the Death Eaters. Hence, the current social ordering left their right to life entirely vulnerable to plausible threats. Moving from their current state to a new, proper ordering would enable willing Hogwarts students to fulfill the self-defense requirements of the law of nature.

We can see this Lockean concern in Hermione's pitch to the other students about forming a secret student group:

"I had the idea—that it might be good if people who wanted to study Defense Against the Dark Arts—and I mean, really study it, you know, not the rubbish that Umbridge is doing with us . . . . I thought it would be good if we, well, took matters into our own hands. . . . And by that I mean learning how to defend ourselves properly, not just theory but the real spells." (*OotP* p. 339)

When pressed about her real motivation for forming such a group, Hermione explains that she is not merely interested in passing the Defense Against the Dark Arts component of her O.W.L. exams: "I want more than that, I want to be properly trained in Defense because . . . Because Lord Voldemort's back" (*OotP* p. 340).

Second, the initial formation of the emerging defense society is by unanimous and express consent after some heated discussion of the matter. Hermione suggests, "I—I think everybody should write their name down, just so we know who was here" (*OotP* p. 346). Then, "[w]hen the last person—Zacharias—had signed, Hermione took the parchment back and slipped it carefully into her bag. There was an odd feeling in the group now. It was as though they had just signed some kind of *contract*" (*OotP* p. 347, emphasis added). This satisfies the first stage of a legitimate move from a state of nature, and in a strikingly social-contract fashion.

Third, once everyone has consented to the formation of the society, they pass two measures—one concerning a "leader" and one concerning their name—that are voted on by majority rule. Unsurprisingly, Hermione insists on this voting procedure with respect to the first measure:

"I think we ought to elect a leader," said Hermione.

"Harry's leader," said Cho at once, looking at Hermione as though she were mad . . .

"Yes, but I think we ought to vote on it properly," said Hermione unperturbed. "It makes it formal and it gives him authority." (*OotP* p. 391)

Next, after several suggestions are made about a name for the group (the Anti-Umbridge League, the Ministry of Magic Are Morons Group, the Defense Association, and Dumbledore's Army), Hermione calls for a vote on the second measure: "All in favor of the D.A.? . . . That's a majority—motion passed!" (*OotP* p. 392).

We can look briefly beyond the formation of Dumbledore's Army to the more complicated case of house-elves to see the role that consent plays in political legitimacy and reform in the *Harry Potter* saga.[18] While this is a cursory look at the house-elf issue, it is instructive to take this glimpse so as to underscore the importance in *Order of the Phoenix* of securing the consent of moral agents—even those who are being oppressed and who would be the beneficiaries of greater freedom. Hermione's moral crusade to free house-elves and secure equal legal rights for them is met with various responses, ranging from sympathy to scorn on the part of other wizards and witches to fear and disgust on the part of house-elves themselves. When Hermione plants hidden clothing for the Hogwarts house-elves to pick up while cleaning (the taking of which would free them), even the normally indifferent Ron is angered by her surreptitious paternalism: "'That's not on,' said Ron angrily, 'You're trying to trick them into picking up the hats. You're setting them free when they might not want to be free.' . . . 'They should at least see what they're picking up'" (*OotP* p. 255). The need for consent is again emphasized by Dobby, the house-elf who *asked* to be freed and was then freed by Harry. Dobby tells Harry that the other Hogwarts house-elves refuse to clean Gryffindor Tower "with the hats and socks hidden everywhere" because "they finds them insulting" (*OotP* p. 385). Though Hermione is well-meaning, she needs to learn that she cannot force the house-elves to be free; they will choose freedom when they are ready, and they will do so voluntarily.

V. Conclusion

As can be seen from the foregoing analysis, Lockean themes abound in *Order of the Phoenix*. The way in which these Lockean themes play out in extensive and

---

[18] The complexities involved in freeing house-elves from slavery is explored insightfully and at much greater length by Prinzi, *Harry Potter & Imagination*, chap. 12; Travis Prinzi, "Don't Occupy Gringotts: *Harry Potter*, Social Upheaval, and the Moral Imagination," *Reason Papers* 34, no. 1 (June 2012), pp 15-24; and Alison McMorran Sulentic, "Harry Potter and the Image of God: How House-Elves Can Help Us to Understand the Dignity of the Person," in *The Law and Harry Potter*, ed. Thomas and Snyder, pp. 189-207. See also Kathryn N. McDaniel's "The 'Real House-Elves' of J.K. Rowling," Chapter 4 in this volume.

nuanced ways vindicates the power and influence of Locke's radical political philosophy on subsequent British political thought[19]—perhaps especially if Rowling did not have his work in mind as she wrote the saga. Rowling's vivid, realistic depiction of complex moral, legal, and political issues in *Order of the Phoenix* both shows how far ahead of his time Locke was and invites readers of all ages to grapple anew with the thorny issues that provoked Locke to pen his *Second Treatise of Government.*[20]

---

[19] Locke's political philosophy influenced far more than British political thought, though, with the writers of the U.S. Declaration of Independence and founders of the American republic being the most notable example.

[20] This project grew out of a series of blog posts I made at The Hog's Head (http://thehogshead.org) on November 29, 2011; March 5, 2012; and June 2, 2012. I would like to thank all the participants in those online discussions for their insightful comments and questions—especially Deborah Chan, Mary Ellen McCarthy, and Jenna St. Hilaire—and The Hog's Head founder Travis Prinzi for inviting me to develop those blog posts into an article. I am also deeply appreciative to Alexander Cohen, Marissa Coronado, Irfan Khawaja, Kathryn McDaniel, and Travis Prinzi for providing helpful feedback on an earlier draft of this article.

CHAPTER 14

Dumbledore's Army and the
White Rose Society:
Youth Justice Movements in the Wizarding World
and Nazi Germany

Kathryn N. McDaniel

"I also think we ought to have a name," [Hermione] said brightly, her hand still in the air. "It would promote a feeling of team spirit and unity, don't you think?"

"Can we be the Anti-Umbridge League?" said Angelina hopefully.

"Or the Ministry of Magic are Morons Group?" suggested Fred.

"I was thinking," said Hermione, frowning at Fred, "more of a name that didn't tell everyone what we were up to, so we can refer to it safely outside meetings."

"The Defense Association?" said Cho. "The D.A. for short, so nobody knows what we're talking about?"

"Yeah, the D.A.'s good," said Ginny. "Only let's make it stand for Dumbledore's Army because that's the Ministry's worst fear, isn't it?" (Order of the Phoenix, 392-393)

With Hogwarts under siege by a totalitarian regime—represented by the self-proclaimed Hogwarts "High Inquisitor," Delores Umbridge—a group of students form a rival organization to undermine her power in Book 5 of the Harry Potter Series, *The Order of the Phoenix*. Meeting initially outside of school grounds, at the Hog's Head pub in Hogsmeade, these Hogwarts students have two aims. First, they want to acknowledge and publicize the return of the dark wizard, Lord Voldemort, which the Ministry of Magic (represented by Umbridge) wishes to deny. Second, they intend to arm themselves against Voldemort and his followers, the Death Eaters, through self-instruction—or, rather, Harry's instruction—in defensive magic. Harry Potter scholars have confirmed that Book 5 and later Book 7, *The Deathly Hallows,* clearly describe the emergence of a totalitarian regime in the wizarding world, one pointing specifically to the Nazi regime of Adolf Hitler in 1930s Germany (Reagin). But through Dumbledore's Army, J.K. Rowling also invokes another connection to Nazi Germany: the student resistance movement of the White Rose Society. This parallel demonstrates Rowling's commitment to the practice of nonviolent resistance to oppression and the valuable role that young people have to play in toppling totalitarian dictatorships, not through military might but through the values of courage, independent thinking, love, and friendship.

Comparisons of the Death-Eater regime to that of the Nazis emphasize several common features. In both, narrow but politically and economically powerful segments of society promoted racial ideologies, enhancing their own status through exclusion and persecution of perceived enemies among the so-called racially "impure." Nazis targeted Jews, the Roma, Poles, and Slavs; the Death Eaters target Muggle-born wizards and "half-bloods," as well as other magical peoples like giants, centaurs, goblins, and so on. In both, parties initially perceived as illegal or even laughable in their extremism suddenly and effectively gained the reins of political and social power. In both, complicity within the bureaucratic systems managing the government and educational institutions enabled the persecution of individuals, as well as constraints on traditional liberties, and allowed oppressive policies to be accepted by the wider population. Both had compelling leaders (Hitler's counterpart in the Harry Potter series could be either Voldemort or Grindelwald), whose followers through over-weaning ambition sought collective salvation in the accumulation of raw power.

Although the tyranny of Lord Voldemort is analogous to that of Hitler, Nancy R. Reagin's work emphasizes that it does not provide a perfect parallel and that key differences emerge. I would like to suggest a similar relationship between Dumbledore's Army, a student resistance movement actively working against Voldemort's regime, and the White Rose Society, a student resistance movement that spoke out against Hitler's government during World War II and urged Germans toward passive resistance. Although they are not exact parallels, the two groups share the spirit of youth empowerment (developed particularly in the context of state-controlled educational institutions), resistance to oppression, vigilance against dictatorship, bold and open speech against totalitarian rule and, most importantly, the disarming of dictators through nonviolent means.

Amid the intensification of World War II in the summer of 1942, a small group of students at the University of Munich, under the particular leadership of medical student Hans Scholl, organized to protest Hitler and the war by distributing anti-Nazi fliers and graffiti. Several students made up the core membership: Alexander Schmorell, Christoph Probst, Willi Graf and eventually Hans's sister Sophie Scholl, among others. Their resistance also attracted a professor at the university, Kurt Huber, who scorned Hitler's rule and encouraged the students to think independently of Nazi propaganda about the war.

Hans and Sophie had both been members of Nazi youth groups earlier in their adolescence—Hans was a member of the Hitler Youth, Sophie of the League of German Girls—and both initially found something admirable in the nationalist rhetoric of the Nazis. As a squad leader in 1936, Hans went to a rally in Nuremberg. He had his squad carry its own flag decked out with "a mythic animal, colorful and rare," or "a glorious griffin" (Dumbach and Newborn, 34) instead of the appropriate Nazi banner. The boy carrying the banner was intimidated and threatened, and Hans intervened, socking the bullying Hitler Youth member in the face. Hans was stripped of his rank; this was the first of many acts of independence and defiance. His disillusionment with National Socialism grew rapidly over the next years, and he developed a nexus of like-minded young people around him, especially when he went to the University of Munich to study medicine at the beginning of the war.

By the Spring of 1942, he and his friends were determined to speak out openly, boldly, perhaps foolishly against the Nazi regime. Their plan was to write, duplicate, and distribute leaflets around Germany—sometimes left out strategically in public places; other times sent directly to people's homes by mail— to demonstrate that there was internal resistance and to wake up the German population to the corrosive and immoral nature of Hitler's ideology and government. The urgent, strident tone of the letters sought to stir Germans into action against Hitler. The first leaflet proclaimed,

> Nothing is so unworthy of a civilized nation as to allow itself to be "governed" without any opposition by an irresponsible clique that has yielded to its basest instincts. . . . If the German people are already so corrupted and spiritually crushed that they do not raise a hand, unquestioningly trusting in the dubious legitimacy of historical order; if they surrender man's highest principle, that which raises him above all God's creatures: his free will; . . . if they are so devoid of all individuality, have already gone so far along the road toward becoming a spiritless and cowardly mass—then, yes, they deserve their downfall. (Dumbach and Newborn, 186)

The second leaflet continued the theme in the particular context of genocide against Jews in Poland:

> Why are the German people so apathetic in the face of all these abominable crimes, crimes so unworthy of the human race? Hardly anyone thinks about that. It is accepted as fact and put out of mind. The German people slumber on in their dull, stupid sleep and thereby encourage these fascist criminals; they give them the opportunity to carry on their depredations; and of course they do so. (Dumbach and Newborn 191)

Stating boldly the failures at war, the crimes against humanity (as they would later be termed in the Nuremberg Trials), the irrationality and incompetence of Hitler and his cronies, the White Rose leaflets aimed to undermine totalitarianism by speaking the truth about it, openly, widely, and in no uncertain terms. Most of the fliers ended with a version of the statement, "Please make as many copies of this leaflet as possible and pass them on." The fourth, however, dramatically ended, "We will not be silent. We are your bad conscience. The White Rose will not leave you in peace!" (Dumbach and Newborn, 198).

The leaflets also emphasized a strategy through which ordinary Germans, the target audience for these papers, could bring about the defeat of the Nazi regime:

> Many, perhaps most, of the readers of these leaflets cannot see clearly how they can mount an effective opposition. . . . We have few choices as to these means. The only available one is passive resistance. . . . *Sabotage* armament industries, sabotage every assembly, rally, ceremony, and organization sponsored

by the National Socialist Party. . . . *Sabotage* in every scientific and intellectual field involved in continuing this war—whether it be universities, technical colleges, laboratories, research stations or technical agencies. . . . *Sabotage* all publications, all newspapers, that are in the pay of the "government" and that defend its ideology and help disseminate the brown lie. (Dumbach and Newborn 194)

In short, the White Rose promoted nonviolent resistance and the disarming of the German war machine. By the sixth leaflet (authored by Huber), the tone was even more forceful:

There is only one slogan for us: fight against the Party! Get out of all Party organizations, which are used to keep our mouths shut and hold us in political bondage! Get out of the lecture halls run by SS corporals and sergeants and Party sycophants! We want genuine learning and real freedom of expression. No threat can intimidate us, not even the closure of universities and colleges. (Dumbach and Newborn 202)

Indeed, the development of the White Rose is inseparable from the university in which it emerged. The Nazis certainly controlled the universities, including the University of Munich, which had never been particularly liberal. Though the Nazis did not, as threatened, close the universities, the state did replace key university personnel with Nazis. Annette Dumbach and Jud Newborn explain, "By 1942, when the White Rose had assembled there, the university was thoroughly integrated into the Nazi system. The students were imbued, to the point of boredom and apathy, with Nazi clichés from their days in the Hitler Youth, and all classroom and lecture halls were infested with spies from the National Socialist Student Association, zealously scribbling notes, their antennae groping for heresy while professors uneasily lectured" (82-83). Some professors whose views were in doubt disappeared (e.g., Professor Fritz-Joachim von Rintelen—whose absence did provoke protest from students), although others like Kurt Huber were able to maintain a tenuous position (84-85).

It was in this atmosphere of repression and ideological indoctrination that the White Rose developed its pamphlet strategy. Through a complex, onerous, and dangerous process, the students wrote, printed, and duplicated their letters in the thousands, and dispersed them throughout major German cities, intentionally giving the illusion of a wider membership than they really had. Meanwhile, Hans and his friends sought to link up with other resistance movements like the Red Orchestra. By January of 1943 the Gestapo considered the White Rose to be a major and infuriatingly slippery threat; officers were told to give the highest priority to the search for those responsible (Dumbach and Newborn, 126). On Thursday, February 18 Hans and Sophie Scholl brought a suitcase filled with a thousand or more leaflets to disperse throughout the university square so that students exiting their lectures would find them, and then on finding more in the suitcase, Hans and Sophie dropped them off the balcony. A custodian, Jakob Schmid, saw them and shouted, "You're under arrest!"[1] Hans and Sophie were taken to Gestapo headquarters, and the Gestapo started rounding up their friends and fellows in the White Rose.

Hans and Sophie, along with Christoph Probst, were tried the next Monday morning (February 22) in the so-called People's Court, tried by Judge Roland Freisler, who, Dumbach and Newborn note, "goes down in the unsavory history of the Third Reich as one of the most repellent figures in the constellation of power" (156). The students disdained to express regret or explanation and remained defiant before the court. Pronounced guilty of treason, they were sentenced to die immediately by guillotine. Sophie had written the word "Farheit" ("Freedom") on the back of her indictment. As the three awaited execution, Christoph said, "I didn't know that death could be so easy." When Hans left for the executioner's block, he shouted across the prison courtyard, "Long live freedom!" Other students of the White Rose were rounded up, tried, and executed, including Alex Schmorell who wrote to his parents, "I am going with the awareness that I followed my deepest convictions and the truth. This allows me to meet my hour of death with a conscience at peace" (Dumbach and Newborn 177). Having urged fellow Germans toward nonviolent resistance, these students stayed true to their aims and demonstrated fearlessness in the face of imminent death. Other German students would take up the charge and continue printing the six leaflets for distribution. Eventually, the United States would join in, reprinting tens of thousands of leaflets and dropping them over German cities.

---

[1] It makes for another fitting parallel that the students are foiled by a snooping collaborator in the form of a custodian. Argus Filch was certainly keen to nab Dumbledore's Army in similar style, though he failed to do so.

At this point, we can already see some clear parallels between Dumbledore's Army and the White Rose. At Hogwarts in Book 5 we have students with deep moral convictions, led by a particularly respected and maybe reckless student (Harry), experiencing repression in their school not unlike what the German students found at the University of Munich. Although the Dark Lord Voldemort has returned, the government denies the presence of this evil force and so becomes a collaborator with it, a promoter of untruths and passivity in the face of totalitarian encroachment. Those who speak the truth, like Harry, are considered enemies of the state. The Hogwarts High Inquisitor Delores Umbridge is a representative of the Ministry of Magic who serves as a spy for the government and as a controlling force to silence opposition and propagandize to young witches and wizards. Significantly, Umbridge is herself a racial ideologue who loathes "half-bloods" and other magic creatures, and she becomes a prominent bureaucrat in the Death-Eater regime of Book 7, creating a surveillance state to persecute those deemed "impure."

As young people, Harry, Ron, Hermione, and the rest of the D.A. have a unique ability to see the corruption at hand and, perhaps, the immaturity or naïveté to challenge it openly without regard to the potentially dire consequences. The Hogwarts students learned what passive-resistance theorist Gene Sharp calls "political defiance" at the hands of Mad-Eye Moody/Barty Crouch, Jr. in their fourth year. Especially relevant is Harry's instruction in how to overcome the Imperius curse. Professor Moody explains, "The Imperius curse can be fought, and I'll be showing you how, but it takes real strength of character, and not everyone's got it" (*The Goblet of Fire*, 213). In a later lesson he puts each student under the Imperius curse "to demonstrate its power and to see whether they could resist its effects" (230). After Harry watches "as, one by one, his classmates did the most extraordinary things under its influence," Harry's own turn comes. He describes experiencing the curse as "the most wonderful feeling . . . as every thought and worry in his head was wiped gently away, leaving nothing but a vague, untraceable happiness" (231). But then when Moody tells him to jump on the desk, a voice that "had awoken in the back of his brain," queries, "Why, though?" And, "Stupid thing to do, really," and then "No, I don't think I will thanks . . . no, I don't want to" (232). Then Harry stumbles into the desk and feels pain that increases as the "empty, echoing feeling in his head" fades. Moody congratulates Harry, saying, "They'll have trouble controlling *you!*"[2] Consider how important resistance to such control becomes in later novels: Gryffindor Quidditch teammate Katie Bell attempts to smuggle a deadly, cursed necklace to Dumbledore under the influence of Draco Malfoy's Imperius, and she nearly dies as a result.

Harry's experience with mind-control recalls the statements in the White Rose leaflets that the German people—"unquestionably trusting" and "so devoid of individuality"—had become "a spiritless and cowardly mass" who "slumber on in their dull, stupid sleep." Under the Nazi regime, they had relinquished their free will, the White Rose students said, urging Germans to wake up to the ways they were being controlled and used by "fascist criminals." The leaflets were intended to be that voice in the back of the brain that would say, "No, I don't think I will . . . no, I really don't want to . . . ." The fourth pamphlet, in fact, explicitly defined the White Rose as a voice in saying, "We will not be silent. We are your bad conscience." In order to protest the totalitarian system, the students had to be alert to that voice, to their consciences, despite the pain that might result. This required conscious effort and risk, but it also allowed the opportunity to raise that voice in the minds of others.

Resisting the Imperius curse is a lesson at which Harry excels. But Harry's inability in Book 5 to learn Occlumency—to close his mind to Voldemort—or to learn to cast spells without speaking perhaps references the loud, overt statements of defiance from the White Rose. Yet, surrounded by spies and repression, the D.A. faces the difficulty that the White Rose did: how to speak the truth, to be heard widely, without risking capture by those in power. Just as spies abounded at the University of Munich, at Hogwarts Umbridge is depicted interrupting the mail and other communication routes, observing teachers to ensure that they do not promote subversion or even, according to Educational Decree 26, talk with students about anything other than course content. She constantly reports back to the Ministry. Both the D.A. and the White Rose, therefore, had

---

[2] It's worth pondering the implications that this lesson is taught not by the real Mad-Eye Moody but by Barty Crouch, Jr. in disguise. The junior Barty was rebellious in his own time, in his own way, and seems to have specialized in this type of defiance, which can be used to promote positive or negative change.

to operate to some degree in secret, establishing forbidden societies that ran counter to the dominant, repressive system. Neither would be entirely successful in keeping their minds closed and their intentions hidden.

Despite the D.A. having established their group off-campus at the Hog's Head, Delores Umbridge gets wind of their new club through a well-disguised spy and issues, in classic Nazi bureaucratic fashion, Educational Decree 24, banning student organizations unless expressly approved by the High Inquisitor. This criminalizes the group's activities. The D.A. manages to find space for practices within Hogwarts in the Room of Requirement, where they learn practical defensive magic. They also find ways to broadcast the truth about Voldemort's return to the Wizarding World. Luna Lovegood, a member of the D.A., has a father who runs a tabloid newspaper called *The Quibbler.* Soliciting disgraced journalist Rita Skeeter to write the story, Harry and his friends tell the tale of Voldemort's return at the end of the previous school year. The resulting issue of *The Quibbler* is an unabashed hit, prompting another Educational Decree from Umbridge. But, as Hermione notes, that just makes the newspaper even more popular among students lured by the forbidden (*The Order of the Phoenix,* 582). This public truth-telling gains more support for Harry among his fellow students and the rest of the wizarding world and establishes a rival source of news with the *Daily Prophet,* which is Ministry-controlled.

The D.A.'s early efforts are not especially successful. They are discovered, caught, and punished by Slytherin students and Umbridge (not in this case by Filch, the collaborator-custodian who would dearly have loved to have uncovered their activities). But their practice of defensive magic becomes crucial for the students who use it to defend themselves against Death Eaters at the Ministry of Magic and, at the end of Book 6 *The Half-Blood Prince,* to defend themselves from Death Eaters who have invaded Hogwarts. In the final book, when Voldemort has indeed come to power, using an Imperiused puppet in the Ministry (Pius Thicknesse) to rule in his name, we can see the value of the D.A. in its foundation of rebellion and truth-telling. Members of the D.A. not only continue to speak truthfully in a time of repression, they also practice passive resistance strategies much like those advocated by the White Rose.

Under Neville Longbottom's leadership, D.A. members practice sabotage at Hogwarts. Neville refuses to perform the Cruciatus Curse when required to do so by a teacher and mouths off to his professors. He tells Harry, "The thing is, it helps when people stand up to them, it gives everyone hope" (*The Deathly Hallows*, 574). The D.A. at Hogwarts put graffiti on the walls, one of which proclaims, "*Dumbledore's Army, Still Recruiting*" (575). Michael Corner releases a first-year student who was chained up, but he is caught in the act and tortured. Neville— the boy who demonstrated as early as Book 1, *The Sorcerer's Stone*, his ability to stand up for what was right even at great risk to himself—and the D.A. turn the Room of Requirement into a resistance headquarters.

Outside of Hogwarts, Fred and George Weasley, whose pranks became big business in Weasleys' Wizard Wheezes joke shop, turn their pranks into effective weapons against the Death Eaters. D.A. member Lee Jordan hosts an anti-government radio show called *Potterwatch*: "the only [program] that tells the truth about what's going on!" says Ron (436). Through this program, Lee, Fred and George, and members of the Order of the Phoenix—which is Harry's parents' generation's version of Dumbledore's Army—offer support to Harry and promote passive resistance among others in the wizarding world. In an interview on the show, Remus Lupin notes that "'The Boy Who Lived' remains a symbol of everything for which we are fighting: the triumph of good, the power of innocence, the need to keep resisting" (441).

Nonviolent resistance is a strategy that many young people have used over the course of the 20th and 21st centuries to protest injustice and to topple dictatorial regimes. Indian anti-colonialist Mahatma Gandhi called it *satyagraha*, or soul force. Czechoslovakian dissident Vaçlav Havel called it "the power of the powerless." It was used as we have seen in Nazi Germany by the White Rose, in the American Civil Rights Movement and in the Vietnam War era; it was used to bring down the communist regimes in eastern Europe and the Soviet republics, and most recently in the Occupy movement and Arab Spring. Gene Sharp, who has written a widely influential handbook of nonviolent protest called *From Dictatorship to Democracy*, lists 198 forms of passive resistance that include rival newspapers, infiltration of government, pranks, and the formation of valid counterparts to replace the corrupt institutions created by dictatorship. Through the formation of this "parallel polis," as Havel called it, the oppressed create truly popular, free, and legitimate organizations that start underground but stand ready to emerge as the valid source of sovereignty when the totalitarian regime ultimately collapses.

Some people have confused the term "passive resistance" with "pacifism." Certainly, neither the students in Dumbledore's Army nor the members of the Order of the Phoenix should be considered pacifists. Gene Sharp insists that passive resistance is not pacifism; rather, it is war by nonviolent means, which can often be more powerful than violent ones, especially in the context of dictatorships. Moreover, note that passive resistance should not be equated with cowardice, unwillingness to contest oppressive power, or meek inaction. As Gandhi said, "Wherein is courage required—in blowing others to pieces from behind a cannon or with a smiling face to approach a cannon and be blown to pieces? Who is the true warrior—he who keeps death always as a bosom-friend, or he who controls the death of others?" (Gandhi, 114). Nor are those who pursue passive resistance always philosophically or morally opposed to violence; yet they recognize the fundamental power of it as a political strategy (Flintoff). In the wizarding world, the D.A. and the Order are both actively engaged in the Battle of Hogwarts, and not always nonviolently. Nevertheless, the successful chipping away of the Death-Eater regime at Hogwarts depends on their practice of sabotage, defiance both open and covert, truth-telling, and the establishment of parallel sources of authority, all of which are passive resistance strategies.

Nonviolent protest can indeed be successful against dictatorial regimes, even more so than violence, which is a language such regimes speak and can respond to in like manner. Passive resistance attacks the foundational supports of dictatorships—most importantly, popular support. It may seem strange to think that dictatorships require popular support in order to thrive, but this is what scholars like Sharp and Havel have argued. On this point, Sharp says that nonviolent action is based on the premise that political power of any kind requires consent: "that governments depend on people, that power is pluralistic, and that political power is fragile because it depends on many groups for reinforcement of its power sources" (Sharp, *The Politics of Nonviolent Action,* 8). Havel finds what he calls "post-totalitarian" dictatorships to be especially fragile because of their reliance on the daily contribution of all individuals in society to the "panorama of lies" created by modern dictatorial regimes. The least act of nonparticipation, illustrated by Havel's famous example of the greengrocer who declines to display a propagandistic poster in his shop window, can threaten the entire system by threatening to expose the lie of universal consent to totalitarian rule (Havel, 55-57).

For a political regime—perhaps especially an oppressive one—to stay in place, it requires the obedience of its population. Obedience can come from a number of human impulses, including habit, fear, ideology, self-interest, absence of self-confidence, and indifference (Sharp, *The Politics of Nonviolent Action*, 16-25). The White Rose leaflets seem to target especially the indifference ("apathy") of the German people under Hitler's regime, their ignorance or lack of self-confidence about how to resist Nazi rule (the leaflets provide the concrete advice to practice "sabotage"), and habitual deference to authority ("unquestioningly trusting"). Most often, ideology is given the blame for the lack of German opposition to Hitler's regime. Certainly, there were those in Nazi Germany who supported at least parts of the Nazi program to make Germany strong again, including in their childhood years Hans and Sophie Scholl. But many studies have demonstrated that fascist ideology was not close to being universally held, and indeed some of the greatest atrocities of the Holocaust were carried out by people who were not fascist ideologues but "ordinary men."[3]

Likewise, in the wizarding world, we can see that the Death Eaters, though they have some important supporters like the Malfoys, are a minority who gain control over the government and the consent of non-Death-Eaters to their regime in order to carry out their policies. Filch, our collaborator custodian at Hogwarts, is a good example of this phenomenon, as he gains power for himself through the Umbridge and then Death-Eater regimes, though there is no evidence that he himself espouses their ideology. Havel views this willingness to submit to totalitarian rule as a basic human tendency that we must confront within ourselves. In terms reminiscent of those in the White Rose leaflets, he says, "Therefore not only does the system alienate humanity, but at the same time alienated humanity supports this system as its own involuntary masterplan, as a

---

[3] Christopher Browning's book *Ordinary Men* is a good example of a historical study that identifies elements like peer pressure to be significantly more important than ideological indoctrination for gaining obedience to Nazi policies and participation in the Holocaust. His afterword provides a persuasive rebuttal to other works that attempt to argue otherwise.

degenerate image of its own degeneration, as a record of people's own failure as individuals" (54). But revoking that support, reclaiming oneself as an individual, "living in truth" instead of the panorama of lies can be relatively simple, if still very dangerous.

The naming of the D.A., not only a "Defense Association," but also "Dumbledore's Army," a rival force with a rival leader representing purity ("Albus," meaning pure or white) and legitimate authority, demonstrates its value as a parallel institution—like Havel's concept of the parallel polis—that greatly threatens the collaborationist regime merely by its existence: "that's the Ministry's worst fear," says Ginny. Only a fragile, oppressive regime would have anything to fear from a group of students forming their own club; this applies both to Umbridge's and the Ministry of Magic's response to the D.A. as well as to the Nazis' aggressive search for the White Rose students. By undermining the dictatorship's illusion of total control, exposing the "panorama of lies" for what it really is, and being disobedient, these groups were indeed quite dangerous to the regimes they resisted, without having to use violence.

It is incredibly significant that the D.A. practice defensive spells: the first spell they practice is Harry's favorite and the one with which he ultimately destroys Voldemort, Expelliarmus—the disarming spell.[4] His preference for this spell is seen with some exasperation by fellow students and by members of the Order of the Phoenix. Lupin believes Harry's use of it revealed which is the "real" Potter at the beginning of *The Deathly Hallows*, nearly getting him killed. Lupin chides him for his overuse of this spell, saying, "Harry, the time for Disarming is past!" Harry responds "defiantly" that even a Stunning spell could have killed Stan Shunpike as he flew through the air, and that Expelliarmus saved Harry from Voldemort two years before. Lupin notes, "it was a very unusual move then, under eminent threat of death. Repeating it tonight in front of Death Eaters who either witnessed it or heard about the first occasion was close to suicidal! . . . Expelliarmus is a useful spell, Harry, but the Death Eaters seem to think it is your signature move, and I urge you not to let it become so!" Once again feeling "a grain of defiance inside him," Harry replies, "I won't blast people out of my way

---

[4] Note also the emphasis on casting patronuses, which are purely defensive and often come in the shape of quite harmless animals.

just because they're there. . . . That's Voldemort's job." And that's the last word on that subject as "Lupin's retort was lost" when the action of the story continues (70-71). Disarming, instead of violent attack, is Harry's means of defense. Later at the Burrow, when Rufus Scrimgeour asks Harry to cooperate with the Ministry, Harry tells him, "I don't like your methods, Minister" (131), suggesting that the means of resistance are indeed important to him. In the final duel, J.K. Rowling is intentional about having Expelliarmus be the Dark Lord's downfall. At the exact moment Voldemort calls out *"Avada Kedavra!"*—the killing curse—Harry's *"Expelliarmus!"* disarms him. Not military strength, not wizardly skill, not raw power or talent kills Voldemort, but an elementary spell that merely knocks the wand out of one's rival's hand. In the final analysis, this is what matters: taking the power away from the dictator, not for one's own use, but to diffuse power in general.[5]

Disarming a totalitarian regime is dangerous. Members of the White Rose knew that death was a possible consequence of attempting to disarm the Nazi regime, and as we've seen, they were willing to sacrifice themselves for their cause. Likewise, Harry and the D.A. demonstrate that they will put their lives at risk—and indeed, some of them do perish. When Harry's quest for the Deathly Hallows takes him back to Hogwarts, he talks with Dumbledore's brother Aberforth, from whom he hears the voice of defeat and weariness. Aberforth urges Harry to leave the country, "Save yourself! . . . The Order of the Phoenix is finished. You-Know-Who's won, it's over, and anyone who pretends different is kidding themselves" (*The Deathly Hallows*, 561-562). In response, Harry says, "I'm going to keep going until I succeed—or I die. Don't think I don't know how this might end. I've known it for years" (568-569). In fact, Harry has seen a model for dying on one's own terms to serve a greater good in the supposed head of Dumbledore's Army, Dumbledore himself. He later says to Voldemort, "Yes, Dumbledore's dead . . . but you didn't have him killed. He chose his own method of dying, chose it months before he died, arranged the whole thing with the man

---

[5] We might also say that this is not only the final but the first lesson Harry learns about despotic power, since this is precisely how he gets hold of the Sorcerer's Stone to prevent Voldemort from gaining it in the first book (he wishes to find the source of power, "but not use it") (*The Sorcerer's Stone* 300).

you thought was your servant [Snape]" (740). Disarmed and weak, Dumbledore had ordered his own death as a way to serve a higher purpose.

Harry's decision to continue seeking the Horcruxes instead of pursuing the Elder Wand (or "Deathstick," as Ollivander calls it (*The Deathly Hallows*, 497)) demonstrates that his method of battling evil is not direct violent assault, but rather cutting off its supports at their source by eliminating the pieces of Voldemort's soul scattered through various objects and living beings, including Harry himself.[6] This decision weighs on Harry and forces him to confront the challenge of passive resistance: "The enormity of his decision not to race Voldemort to the wand still scared Harry. He could not remember, ever before, choosing not to act" (502). After the Battle of Hogwarts, Harry realizes he will have to present himself to Voldemort unarmed after a "cold-blooded walk to his own destruction"—quite a bold act, but deliberately a nonviolent one (692). While Harry uses the Resurrection Stone (to help him recognize death as a "bosom-friend") and the Invisibility Cloak (to help him move toward the point of his death), Voldemort waits with the Elder Wand, the violent and destructive one of the Deathly Hallows, the one that Harry chose not to seek. Harry tucks the cloak and his wand under his robes, thinking that he "did not want to be tempted to fight" (703).[7] And he feels that wand against his chest as Voldemort raises the "Deathstick" and delivers the fatal curse.

But Harry's (apparent) death is not the end. Even while they think he is dead, his fellows in the D.A. continue to resist. As Voldemort claims that Harry was killed "while trying to sneak out of the castle grounds" as a way to save himself, Neville Longbottom creates a "scuffle," and then when asked to join the Death-Eaters, he responds, "I'll join you when hell freezes over" and then shouts "Dumbledore's Army!"[8] Even as Voldemort responds, "Neville here is now going

---

[6] It is possible to interpret the Horcruxes as representing the plurality of power sources for totalitarian regimes. In that line, note that four of the Horcruxes (if we include Harry) symbolize Hogwarts founders, showing again the importance of education as a cornerstone for corrupt power.

[7] We might also note that this is not Harry's phoenix-feather wand at any rate, since Hermione accidentally broke it fighting off Bathilda Bagshot/Nagini in Godric's Hollow (*The Deathly Hallows* 349). Harry has in a sense been unarmed for more than half the novel.

[8] This may be a signal that cues the remainder of the Hogwarts residents to launch a new attack, since the Sorting Hat comes flying out of the window and "what sounded like

to demonstrate what happens to anyone foolish enough to continue to oppose me," he unknowingly gives Neville the opportunity to seize the sword of Gryffindor and eliminate the last remaining Horcrux (731-735). Contrary to Voldemort's intention, the lesson learned here is that opposition can be quite successful. Meanwhile, Harry disappears under his Invisibility Cloak and dispenses Shield Charms until he can track down Voldemort for their last duel in which he will disarm the source of the Dark Lord's violent power: *Expelliarmus!* Although there is violent resistance represented in the Battle of Hogwarts, it is important to note that Harry's role is mostly a nonviolent one. In facing death courageously, unarmed, he serves even in his absence as an icon of spirited resistance that inspires others—those who might otherwise have thought themselves powerless.

The White Rose students' deaths similarly did not mean their influence ended. Recall that in the later years of the war other German students took up the task of dispersing the leaflets, and that the United States military saw this as an effective strategy to promote internal resistance to Nazi rule as well. Unfortunately, in the immediate aftermath of the war the students of the White Rose were regarded with some hostility—demonstrating as they did (somewhat like Neville) that resistance was possible, that obedience to the repressive government could be revoked. They were scorned as foolish children who behaved recklessly, even traitorously (Dumbach and Newborn, xiii). Even today, some critics consider them to have been "self-centered" and "not careful enough" (McDonough, 156-157). But for most people now they stand as a powerful example of the possibility for resisting totalitarian oppression, celebrated as heroes who fought with compelling words and stirring ideas instead of guns and bombs.[9] Decades after their deaths, Hans and Sophie's sister Elisabeth explained

---

hundreds of people came swarming over the out-of-sight walls and pelted toward the castle" (*The Deathly Hallows* 732).

[9] My focus here has been the resistance of the students of the White Rose, but Sharp emphasizes the resistance of a group of Norwegian teachers under the Nazi puppet Vidkun Quisling's rule who successfully, and nonviolently, resisted his attempt to force the schools to teach fascist ideology. Quisling apparently claimed, "You teachers have destroyed everything for me!" (Sharp, *The Politics of Nonviolent Action*, 87-89). This underscores both the importance of educational institutions as a source of control for such regimes and the

their legacy: "Sophie tried to show another way to the German people—that they still had a choice. Sophie represents what the German people should have done. Young people in Germany can identify with her" (McDonough, 158).

The White Rose students are also celebrated for their deep friendship, and this, too, is one of Rowling's major themes in the Harry Potter books. Consider the original Order of the Phoenix, founded on the friendship bond represented by Moony, Wormtail, Padfoot, and Prongs—or Remus Lupin, Peter Pettigrew, Sirius Black, and Harry's father James Potter. The failures of their friendship broke their bond and prevented them from being entirely successful. Out of his own cowardly sense of self-preservation and personal ambition, Peter Pettigrew (the anti-Neville) betrayed their friendship, allowing for his friends' deaths, sowing the seeds of suspicion and bitterness among those remaining, and enabling the resurrection of Death-Eater totalitarianism in the next generation. Dictatorships rely on this kind of egoistic willingness to betray friendships. Alexis de Tocqueville, in his observations in *Democracy in America*, noted, "Despotism, which in its nature is fearful, sees the most certain guarantee of its own duration in the isolation of men, and it ordinarily puts all its care into isolating them. There is no vice of the human heart that agrees with it so much as selfishness: a despot readily pardons the governed for not loving him, provided that they do not love each other" (De Tocqueville, 485). That love for each other, so clearly reflected in both the White Rose and in the fictional Dumbledore's Army, creates a bond that foils the designs of totalitarian rule. It also most profoundly disarms violent power, as Rowling suggests when the most mysterious, locked door in the Department of Mysteries (which we assume to represent the force of love) melts the knife's blade used in an attempt to force it open, rendering the weapon "useless" (*The Order of the Phoenix*, 775-776).[10]

---

very real possibility for ordinary, unarmed civilians to disrupt and undermine violent power.

[10] Importantly, Harry uses Sirius's knife to attempt to open the door. Sirius is not a man drawn to nonviolent resistance—in fact, he will meet death in the Department of Mysteries precisely because of his inability to resist the opportunity to battle directly with the Death Eaters. But when Harry uses this knife on the mysterious door, the blade melts, perhaps foreshadowing Harry's quite different role in this new generation of Voldemort resisters. Note that Dumbledore always refers to Harry's capacity for love as a "power" (*HBP* 509), and indeed the one power that has the chance of defeating the Dark Lord.

In Dumbledore's Army, we see a successful movement to disrupt the repressive Death-Eater regime. But I think Rowling would not have us become complacent, thinking that this defeat of evil is final and complete. Her story tells us that evil reemerges in successive generations, and she exhorts her young readers to stand ready to defend what is right and good and just—not through violence but through passive resistance and the disarming of corrupt regimes through courage, independent thought, love, and most of all friendship.

Works Cited

At the Heart of the White Rose: Letters and Diaries of Hans and Sophie Scholl. Inge Jens ed. and J. Maxwell Brownjohn, trans. New York: Harper & Row Publishers. 1984.

Axelrod, Toby. *Hans and Sophie Scholl: German Resisters of the White Rose.* New York: The Rosen Publishing Group, Inc. 2001.

Browning, Christopher. *Ordinary Men: Reserve Police Battalion 101 and the Final Solution in Poland.* New York: HarperPerennial. 1998.

De Tocqueville, Alexis. *Democracy in America.* Harvey C. Mansfield and Delba Winthrop, trans. and ed. Chicago: University of Chicago Press. 2000.

Dumbach, Annette and Jud Newborn. *Sophie Scholl and the White Rose.* Oxford: Oneworld. 2006.

Flintoff, John-Paul. "Gene Sharp: The Machiavelli of Nonviolence." *New Statesman.* January 2013. www.newstatesman.com/politics/your-democracy/2013/01/gene-sharp-machiavelli-non-violence (accessed November 6, 2013).

Gandhi, Mohandas K. "Indian Home Rule." *The Gandhi Reader #1: A Source Book of His Life and Writings.* Homer A. Jack, ed. New York: Grove Press, Inc. 1956. 104-121.

Havel, Václav. "The Power of the Powerless." *Living in Truth.* Faber & Faber. 1990. 36-122.

McDonough, Frank. *Sophie Scholl: The Real Story of the Woman Who Defied Hitler.* Gloucestershire, England: The History Press. 2009.

Reagin, Nancy R. "Was Voldemort a Nazi? Death Eater Ideology and National

Socialism." *Harry Potter and History.* Nancy R. Reagin, ed. Hoboken, New Jersey: John Wiley & Sons, Inc. 2011. 127-152.

Rowling, J.K. *Harry Potter and the Deathly Hallows.* New York: Arthur A. Levine Books (Scholastic). 2007.

————. *Harry Potter and the Half-Blood Prince.* New York: Arthur A. Levine Books (Scholastic). 2005.

————. *Harry Potter and the Order of the Phoenix.* New York: Arthur A. Levine Books (Scholastic). 2003.

————. *Harry Potter and the Sorcerer's Stone.* New York: Arthur A. Levine Books (Scholastic). 1997.

Sharp, Gene. *From Dictatorship to Democracy.* East Boston, Massachusetts: The Albert Einstein Institution. 2010.

————. *The Politics of Nonviolent Action, Part I Power and Struggle.* Boston, Massachusetts: Extending Horizons Books, Porter Sargent Publishers, Inc. 2006.

Vargo, Marc. E. *Women of the Resistance: Eight Who Defied the Third Reich.* Jefferson, North Carolina: McFarland & Company, Inc. Publishers. 2012.

CHAPTER 15

Who Deserves the Truth?
A Look at Veracity and Mendacity in *Harry Potter*[1]

Laura Lee Smith

I t is a truth universally acknowledged that in Rowling's epic seven-volume tale of Good versus Evil, the young hero Harry Potter triumphs over Evil personified in the ruthless and creepy Voldemort. Yet ethicists and concerned parents may rightly ask: "Is Harry really all that good?" After all, Harry "blackmails his uncle, uses trickery and deception, and 'breaks a hundred rules' [...]. He frequently tells lies to get himself out of trouble and lets himself be provoked into revenge against his student enemies" (O'Brien n. pag.).

In the *Harry Potter* series, Rowling clearly subverts any simplistic view that equates truthfulness with virtue and lying with vice; but she also ultimately rejects the sophistry of a relativistic approach to truth. Instead, she sets out a challenging middle ground for her hero to grow into. For Harry, a mature approach to the truth requires embracing ambiguity and imperfections, as well as unwelcome revelations; in short, he must grow to appreciate, with Dumbledore, that truth is "a beautiful and terrible thing" (*PS*, 216), but still "generally preferable to lies" (*GoF*, ch. 37, at 957).

---

[1] I am grateful for helpful suggestions by Kathryn McDaniel and Kelly Orazi, who each kindly read and commented on a draft of this essay, as well as Amy Sturgis and Jessica O'Brien who first inspired me to take Harry seriously.

A Duty of Truthfulness

The philosopher Harry Frankfurt suggests that "most people" recognize and even readily acknowledge "that truth has considerable importance," but "few people are prepared to offer much real illumination of just what it is that makes truth so important" (6). Likewise, in her thoughtful examination of lying, the philosopher Sissela Bok suggests that similarly few have really considered the common assumptions about when it might or might not be permissible to lie.

Bok notes that some who have seriously considered the question, such as St. Augustine and Immanuel Kant, have taken the position that lying is never justified (33, 42-46). She attributes such rigid views to the influence of religious beliefs "stronger than intuition or common sense," which fundamentally "cannot be proved or disproved" (Bok 42-43, 45). As Bok sees it, the underlying perspective is "that God rules out all lies and that He will punish those who lie" (45). The core concept might equally well be expressed more positively, without reference to retribution: that "to a Christian, God is Truth" (West 7). Indeed, Kant argues in his essay "On a Supposed Right to Lie from Altruistic Motives" that it is not morally permissible to lie under any circumstances, even to a murderer who asks whether his intended victim has taken refuge in a particular building (Bok 38-39, 41; 267-72).[2] That is, assuming an answer cannot be avoided, Kant asserts it is better to facilitate a murder by telling the truth than to lie. This result is consistent with the theological perspective that "harm done to the immortal spirit is worse than harm done to merely mortal flesh" (West 7); indeed, West notes that Dante's *Inferno* is "quite orthodox" in treating liars more harshly than murderers (*id.*).

Although few would fully embrace Kant's absolutist position in real life—perhaps not even Kant himself[3]—even from a purely pragmatic and secular perspective, truthfulness is often recognized as essential in order for humans to live productively in community. It can be argued that "the fabric of society depends

---

[2] Bok includes excerpts from works by Augustine, Aquinas, Bacon, Grotius, Kant, Sidgwick, Harrod, Bonhoeffer, and Warnock in an appendix (Bok 250-88).

[3] The journalist Jeremy Campbell notes an instance where Kant, in his twilight years, purportedly "fudged the facts" in writing a reference for a long-time servant he had dismissed for cause (130).

on mutual trust, which large lies may harm badly, and which even small lies can erode" (West 7). Bok recognizes that "trust in some degree of veracity functions as a *foundation* of relations among human beings; when this trust shatters or wears away, institutions collapse" (31).

Frankfurt has further noted that healthy civilizations require "large quantities of *reliable factual information*" (34), essentially because "the relevant facts are what they are regardless of what we may happen to believe about them, and regardless of what we may wish them to be" (54). In other words, truth is necessary in order for humans to deal *at all* (whether badly or well) with reality. Thus, in the long term, societies simply "cannot afford" to be indifferent to "the distinction between true and false" (Frankfurt 33).

Those who argue for a high standard of truthfulness may also point to negative impacts *on the liar* from the act of lying. For example, Barbara Killinger, a clinical psychologist, lists "honesty" as the first of seven values required for integrity; and honesty, in turn, "requires truthfulness, freedom from deception and fraud, and fair and straightforward conduct" (29). Killinger further argues that even white lies may undermine one's ability to live with integrity, and thus concludes that, "no matter how well-meaning the intention, choosing to tell someone else a falsehood is wrong" (130). From a philosopher's perspective as well, one may recognize that a liar is "affected by his own lies" in significant ways (Bok 24). The liar "may regard the lie as an inroad on his integrity; he certainly looks at those he has lied to with a new caution," if only due to the risk of exposure which may jeopardize the liar's credibility (*id.*).[4] While Bok recognizes that it "may seem exaggerated" to suggest (as Kant does) that even one small lie "annihilates" the liar's "dignity as a man," she suggests that this position may nonetheless have merit "as a warning against *practices* of lying, against biased calculations of pros and cons, and against assuming the character of a liar" (46).

Although Bok rejects an absolutist position, she carefully builds an argument for her view that "lying requires explanation, whereas truth ordinarily does not" (30). Among other things, she posits that giving an "initial negative weight to lies" is necessary to provide "a counterbalance to the crude evaluation by liars of

---

[4] Successful liars may also grow increasingly reluctant to trust or believe others, once they have learned how easily they can deceive other people.

their own motives and of the consequences of their lies" (30). She argues that "in any situation where a lie is a possible choice, one must first seek truthful alternatives" (31). In Bok's view, every lie must meet the formal constraint of *publicity*, meaning that the moral principle offered to justify it "must be capable of public statement and defense," and the justification must be *directed to reasonable persons*, in order to counteract "the self-deception and bias inherent in the liar's perspective" (92).

Over the remaining chapters of her seminal work on lying, Bok systematically analyzes and refutes common assumptions about circumstances when lying might be automatically justified or excused. She permits no free pass merely because the liar believes he or she is telling "harmless" or "trivial" white lies; or when the lies are made in times of crisis; or when the lies are intended to protect peers or clients, or to promote the public good; or when the lies are addressed to "undeserving" audiences such as liars or enemies, "ignorant" audiences such as children or the mentally incompetent, or "fragile" audiences such as the sick and dying. Bok's position toward lying, though not technically "absolutist," is a severely uncompromising one.

Rowling has certainly created one character in the Harry Potter series who meets Bok's standard of uncompromising truthfulness: Luna Lovegood.[5] Luna has an affirmative knack for uncomfortable truths, always delivered mildly and without rancor. Within minutes of meeting the trio, she tells Ron that Padma Patil did not enjoy going to the ball with him because of the way he treated her (*OoP*, 189). She soon tells the trio and Ginny, with perfect truth, that Hagrid is not a good teacher, and sticks to this view even in the face of their fiercely loyal— but false—denial (*OoP*, 200). She informs Harry in front of his friends that he is "being rather rude" to them (*OoP*, 735) and responds to Harry's disclosure that Ron and Hermione have had a row by observing that Ron "can be a bit unkind. I noticed that last year" (*HBP*, 310).

---

[5] Neville may be a close second, as we never see him utter a direct falsehood, other than a mumbled excuse about "not wanting to disturb anyone" when it seems that Luna's "distinct dottiness" is his real reason for hesitating to take a seat in her compartment (*OotP*, 185). Tellingly, Neville is as gullible as only the naively honest can be in the face of Harry's ever-shifting lies when the two are stuck in the castle during their peers' excursion to Hogsmeade (*PoA*, ch. 14, at 241-42).

She is uncomfortably honest about herself as well. She notes, without resentment, that she is seen as odd, rather than cool, and is fully aware that some people call her "Loony" (*OotP*, 162; *HBP*, 139, 311). She has no illusions about her own popularity, explaining to Harry that she is "a bit lonely without the D.A." this term (*HBP*, 311) and that she misses the meetings because "it was like having friends" (*HBP*, 138). These are observations that many people might try to downplay, even to themselves; some researchers have gone so far as to suggest that a degree of self-deception may be necessary for mental health (Sullivan 179). Even those who are fully honest with themselves about their own social shortcomings and lack of popularity might hesitate to voice such thoughts to others, at the risk of having their worst fears confirmed, or even being shunned as a result. Harry's uneasiness with Luna's frank self-assessments is understandable; he cannot credibly deny these truths, and he cannot with any degree of courtesy or compassion agree with them. But Luna is not inclined to dissembling or concealment, even of her own weaknesses.

Indeed, Luna has a quiet but extraordinary integrity about her. For example, at Bill and Fleur's wedding, she tells Harry: "I told Daddy most people would probably wear dress robes, but he believes you ought to wear sun colors to a wedding, for luck, you know" (*DH*, 141). In other words, she is fully aware of the conventional and appropriate attire for a wedding, and advises her father of it; but thereafter calmly defers to and accepts his views and wears bright yellow robes to match his. Having made her decision about what to wear, she does not sulk or attempt to remain inconspicuous, but blithely heads out to the dance floor on her own where everyone will see her. Her conduct is dramatically different from Ron's when he attends the Yule Ball in his unfashionably feminine dress robes: Ron seeks to "hide behind Harry" when his crush passes by (*GoF*, ch. 23, at 359), and refuses to go out on the dance floor.[6] It is similarly a sign of Luna's

---

[6] Ron initially swears he will go naked rather than wear his formal robes, but he apparently lacks even the courage to decline to attend the Yule Ball. Instead, in last-minute desperation, he clumsily severs the lace trim. Of course, Ron's bad attitude at the ball itself is also motivated in part by his unexamined feelings for Hermione and his concomitant jealousy of Krum.

integrity that she is not deceived by the surface of things; at Bill and Fleur's wedding, she even recognizes Harry despite his "Barny Weasley" disguise, simply from his expression (*DH*, 140).

Indeed, the only deceptive words we hear Luna utter in the series—"Oooh, look, a Blibbering Humdinger!" (*DH*, 745)—do not appear to qualify as a lie, in the usual sense of the word.[7] Luna's only motivation is to distract everyone in the room momentarily so that an "exhausted and drained" Harry can slip under the Cloak and obtain peace and quiet after the final battle. Although Luna is briefly pretending to see a creature that is not present, there is no reason to imagine that Luna expects, or even hopes, to deceive anyone. Indeed, even accepting Bok's broad definition of a lie as "an intentionally deceptive message in the form of a statement" (15; italics deleted), Luna's conduct is an example of a justifiable lie under Bok's criteria, because the moral principle offered to justify it is "capable of public statement and defense" when directed to reasonable persons (92). More specifically, Luna's deception appears to be the rare "white lie" that Bok would expressly approve.[8] First, the lie is "truly harmless" (Bok 72) because Blibbering Humdingers are entirely mythical within the wizarding world; indeed, Luna has been publicly ridiculed for her belief in them (*OotP*, 262). It is highly unlikely that anyone who hears her will be deceived into believing they exist, and any flicker of doubt will immediately be resolved by looking where she is pointing. Second, the lie appears to be, at least from Luna's perspective, truly a "last resort" (Bok 72). While Luna herself believes in Blibbering Humdingers, she knows that her fellow witches and wizards are (at best) openly skeptical about their existence. Thus, her self-evidently false claim to be presently observing one will only further confirm others' unbelief and make them more resistant to what she believes is the truth. A reasonable person will readily conclude that Luna's statement is against her own interest. Moreover, a truthful statement (e.g., "Oooh, look, a

---

[7] By contrast, the statement "I am looking at a Blibbering Humdinger" would be directly and literally false and thus easily recognizable as a lie under virtually any definition.

[8] Bok does not automatically excuse the telling of "white lies," even though they are "the most common and the most trivial forms that duplicity can take" and are widely regarded as innocuous (57). Instead, she advises that "white lies should be kept at a minimum" and be used *only* "where truly harmless and a last resort" (72).

tree!") will not do; it simply will not draw the necessary attention to distract everyone's attention from Harry. She has chosen to say something that others will consider truly outlandish, something that will cause them to look at her with ready amusement or mockery. Critically, a more plausible false statement (e.g., "Fire!") would likewise attract attention but would not be harmless, because it could create unnecessary alarm in the room. Finally, the underlying motivation for her conduct is one that reasonable persons will surely approve. Luna perceives that Harry is emotionally drained and physically exhausted; he does not have the energy to make polite excuses and farewells to the throngs of friends and allies who stand between him and the exit. Her deception compassionately allows him to defer all such social interactions until he has had a chance to recuperate. Luna's one and only deceptive act passes the test of justification.

And yet, although Luna clearly has the virtues of truthfulness and integrity, Rowling does not hold her up for emulation. Rather, she is portrayed as unrelentingly eccentric and subject to ridicule—even from the trio initially, although less so as she fights Death Eaters at their side and they develop genuine affection for her. It is clear that Luna's uncompromising honesty (much like her radish earrings) is merely another manifestation of the eccentricity that flows from an utter lack of concern for public opinion. Even worse, Luna's credibility is ironically undermined by her own credulity, as she is prone to believing and defending her father's most fantastical and implausible theories about non-existent creatures. Given her glaring blind spots, Luna's commitment to *the truth as she sees it* does not inspire others to do the same. Indeed, her friends' affection for her is tempered by pity. As a result, even though Rowling has depicted a character whose personal commitment to honesty is consistent with the high value on truth favored by ethicists and theologians such as Bok, Kant, and Augustine, that character's presence in the story offers us no assurance that truth-telling is an important duty or virtue in Rowling's world.

Post-Modern Elements

In fact, when we look closely at the series, it may be surprising—or even shocking—to see how often, and how casually, Harry and his closest friends lie. It is easy to miss this at first because some of these falsehoods are ones that are commonly held to be excusable or harmless, such as social "white lies" intended to help others save face (Bok 57-59), or lies directed to hostile or evil characters (Bok 135-38).[9] Readers may also intuitively sympathize with lies or deceptions that may help counteract the discrepancies in power, knowledge, and experience between "a skinny, near-sighted, and abused orphan" (Prewitt 29) and his powerful, grown-up Death-Eater opponents. As the novelist Evelin Sullivan notes, the "trickster figure" of traditional folk tales and mythology is celebrated, not despised, for his successful trickery of the rich and powerful; there is a "sense that deception is justified to right an imbalance of power" (258).[10] All this is to say that Rowling has chosen to show Harry engaging in several kinds of lies that many people, especially those who have not considered the implications as carefully as Bok and Frankfurt, may be perfectly content to overlook.

But this hardly scratches the surface of Harry's lies. All three members of the trio lie to friends, allies, and neutral characters for self-interested reasons, and do so routinely in an effort to avoid the consequences of their own rule-breaking. Harry consistently lies to his friends and allies to avoid exposing his plans, or even his feelings, to the possible scrutiny or sage advice of others. Indeed, Rowling's narrator insists on Harry's mendacity, and frequently calls attention to it. For example, the simple and unambiguous phrase "Harry lied" (or its stylistic variation "lied Harry") appears in *every* book of the series: once in *Philosopher's Stone*, twice each in *Chamber of Secrets* and *Prisoner of Azkaban*, five times in *Goblet of Fire*, seven times in *Order of the Phoenix*, and three times each in *Half-Blood Prince* and *Deathly Hallows*.[11] It is clear that permanently inscribing "I must not tell lies" into his own flesh in his fifth year at Hogwarts does not cause Harry to

---

[9] Again, Bok disagrees with this view; she argues that these kinds of lies should be subjected to the test of public justification.

[10] Bok notes that "Injustice, exploitation, the disparity of power—these are held to excuse innumerable lies," but rejects this excuse as unduly subjective and thus "extraordinarily prone to misinterpretation and bias" (83). She concludes that the fact of an imbalance of power, by itself, does not justify dishonesty.

[11] The narrator flags many additional instances of Harry's untruths with varied wording that is harder to quantify through a simple search. Examples range from "he invented" (*PS*, 212) to "all three of them stated categorically and untruthfully" (*HBP*, 231).

desist from lying.[12] And, of course, in addition to the lie direct, the trio deceives others with Polyjuice Potion, and by telling half-truths or remaining silent when someone has a false impression of the facts.

The narrator also repeatedly emphasizes that lying is Harry's near-automatic or instinctive response. He lies reflexively and without premeditation to Stan Shunpike about his identity, "saying the first name that came into his head" (*PoA*, ch. 3, at 37).[13] To avoid trouble, Harry lies "quickly" to Filch about reading his Kwikspell promotional material (*CoS*, 128) and to Lupin about how he became familiar with the taste of butterbeer (*PoA*, ch. 12, at 215). To avoid questions and unwelcome interference, he lies "promptly" to Dumbledore that nothing has happened to him, even though he is shaking with rage after learning Snape's role in causing his parents' death (*HBP*, 547); he lies "defiantly" to Hermione that he is not worried about the Ministry hearing (*OotP*, 64); and he lies "easily" to Neville in denying that he plans to hand himself over to Voldemort (*DH*, 695). He "automatically" accuses Dudley of lying about overhearing Harry speaking in his sleep, even though he knows full well it must be true (*OotP*, 15).

By contrast, telling the truth is seldom automatic for Harry, except under the influence of Felix Felicis—he trusts the luck potion unquestioningly to guide his intuition about when to lie and when to stick to the truth in order to best manipulate Slughorn. Otherwise, truth-telling seems to be a matter of deliberate choice for him, whether speaking to Hagrid about his mistrust of Snape (*PS*, 141), or to Scrimgeour about his conversations with Dumbledore (*HBP*, 344). Tellingly, he lets slip to Ginny his true intention to "kill off Voldemort" only by accident after he uncharacteristically speaks "without thinking" (*DH*, 89). When she asks him about his comment, he immediately back-pedals and tries to pretend he was joking.

---

[12] Because Harry is being punished for *telling the truth*, the main effect of the experience is to make him hate Umbridge and the Ministry that placed her in a position of power.

[13] In a nice bit of foreshadowing, that name is Neville Longbottom, the only other boy who could have been the subject of Trelawney's prophecy. And in a charmingly playful and self-referential touch, the first name that pops into Ron's head when the Snatchers interrogate him is "Stan Shunpike" (*DH*, 382).

To be perfectly fair, in light of Harry's experience with the Dursleys, it is almost surprising that he has any regard for the truth at all. Although he does not initially suspect that his aunt and uncle have lied to him about his parents' deaths, he knows that they pretend to the world that their nephew does not exist. He has seen Dudley manipulate grown-ups with lies—such as pretend sobs—to get what he wants. And rather poignantly, when Harry promises to be on his best behavior at the zoo, the narrator says that "Uncle Vernon didn't believe him. No one ever did" (PS, 23). Harry, unaware of his own magical powers due to the Dursleys' lies, is perfectly sincere in disclaiming responsibility for the "strange things" that happen around him (PS, 23). Yet he is regularly punished for these incidents. The Dursleys have taught him, through their words and actions, that the truth is largely irrelevant. It would be very easy for Harry to take a cynical, postmodernist position on the existence of any objective truth.[14]

And indeed, Rowling depicts lying quite favorably at times. For example, a significant marker of Hermione's friendship with Harry and Ron is her newfound willingness to lie. She is initially a stickler for rules, and informs the boys that if they are caught after hours, "I'll tell [Filch] the truth, that I was trying to stop you, and you can back me up" (PS, 116). They are understandably indignant at her nerve and self-righteousness: she expects them to volunteer incriminating truths about themselves in order to save an officious intermeddler! But following the troll incident, Hermione tells "a downright lie to a teacher" to take the blame herself and spare the boys (PS, 131). Ron drops his wand in shock, and Harry is speechless at this unprecedented conduct: "Hermione was the last person to do anything against the rules, and here she was, pretending she had, to get them out of trouble. It was as if Snape had started handing out sweets" (PS, 131). It is worth emphasizing that Hermione's lie, although presented in a positive light, is a fairly dubious one. The truth was that Hermione had no idea that students had been ordered to return to their dormitories; the boys knew this and disobeyed the order only to warn her about the troll; and they inadvertently locked the troll

---

[14] Frankfurt's book *On Truth* is largely a response to this kind of cynicism. He writes, "These shameless antagonists of common sense—members of a certain emblematic subgroup of them call themselves 'postmodernists'—rebelliously and self-righteously deny that truth has any genuinely objective reality at all. They therefore go on to deny that truth is worthy of any obligatory deference or respect" (18-19).

in the bathroom with her but went in to help her once they realized she was inside. Had the truth been known, it is possible *no one* would have been punished. And yet Rowling chooses this point—when Hermione steps forward with an unnecessary and unjustifiable lie—as the moment when Hermione moves decisively from acquaintance to friend.

In a more somber mode, when Dumbledore and Harry go in quest of a Horcrux in the sixth book, Dumbledore makes Harry promise unconditionally to obey his orders, even if an order involves danger or is incompatible with Harry's notions of virtue and heroism (*HBP*, 550-51). Dumbledore's final order is "to make sure I keep drinking, even if you have to tip the potion into my protesting mouth," and he makes Harry reaffirm and renew his promise of obedience *after* hearing it (*HBP*, 569-70). Harry soon finds that he must lie to Dumbledore in order to keep his promise. The potion Dumbledore must consume is debilitating and excruciating, and despite his intention to recover and destroy the Horcrux, he can't help moaning, "Make it stop, make it stop" (*HBP*, 572). Harry lies, saying "Yes . . . yes, this'll make it stop," as he tips the contents of the goblet into Dumbledore's open mouth. Harry continues to refill the goblet and make Dumbledore drink it, overcoming Dumbledore's agonized pleas for mercy with false assurances that "Nothing's happening to you, you're safe, it isn't real, I swear it isn't real" and "you'll be all right" (*HBP*, 572-73). The cruel lies and false oath ("I swear it isn't real") are part of Harry's moral obligation to Dumbledore, a perverse and horrible sign of obedience and virtue.

It is worth noting that the lies in this scene, told to discharge an unconditional obligation imposed on the liar by the person lied to, actually appear to meet Bok's stringent criteria for a justifiable lie. In particular, Bok suggests that because deception and violence are both inherently coercive, lies may sometimes be permitted in circumstances when physical force is justified (103-04). She further suggests that deception may be justified where there is genuine consent, as when patients "give clear signals" of their wish to be spared bad news (Bok 238). As we see in this passage, Harry first tries reasoning with Dumbledore, reminding him, "You told me you had to keep drinking" (*HBP*, 571). Only when he sees that Dumbledore has lost command of himself and is no longer able to drink the potion voluntarily does Harry resort to the physical coercion that Dumbledore has expressly authorized, as well as the psychological coercion that appears to be an implied adjunct to Dumbledore's instructions.

And perhaps some of the most heroic and virtuous acts Rowling describes are the lies told to villains by people under torture. Indeed, these are truly redemptive lies on the part of hitherto unsympathetic characters such as Scrimgeour and Grindelwald. Arthur Weasley tells Harry that the Death Eaters are rumored to have "tried to torture your whereabouts out of Scrimgeour before they killed him; if it's true, he didn't give you away" (*DH*, 206). At King's Cross, the Dumbledore figure expresses hope that Grindelwald "showed remorse in later years" and speculates that Grindelwald's lie to Voldemort—i.e., pretending he never possessed the Elder Wand—may have been "his attempt to make amends" (*DH*, 456, 719). It must be admitted, of course, that efforts to "mislead one's torturers through every possible stratagem would clearly meet the test of public justification" (Bok 140-41), and would therefore be ethically permitted (if not actively celebrated) by all except the most rigid of moralists. Nonetheless, Rowling has chosen to include in her story the truly exceptional lies that are almost universally recognized as heroic and redemptive, alongside the far more ethically questionable lies which Harry routinely directs to his friends and allies.

A Desire for Truth

Despite Harry's unquestioned willingness to lie, and despite Rowling's often-sympathetic portrayal of lying, Harry nonetheless has, from the beginning of the series, an instinct that there are objective and important truths to be known, and a strong desire to learn them. This is a pattern set in Harry's very first debriefing with Dumbledore, when the boy immediately homes in on the one question Dumbledore is not ready to answer: "why would [Voldemort] want to kill me in the first place?" (*PS*, 216). The narrator characterizes Harry's attitude toward the truth in the first five or six books as an "excited, curious, burning to get to the bottom of a mystery" (*HBP*, 635).

In fact, Harry is so committed to these kinds of important truths that he is not just annoyed by or disapproving of efforts to obscure them; he is genuinely outraged, and his outrage fractures his self-control. He cannot restrain himself from denouncing the Ministry's willful blindness about Voldemort's return, even at the cost of detention with Umbridge, loss of his place on the Quidditch team, and the scorn of his fellow students. He is so goaded by Umbridge's self-promoting lie about "inheriting" the Horcrux locket she stole that he nearly jeopardizes both the success of his mission and the safety of Umbridge's latest victim. His voice "cracks with the strain" as he reflects on Dumbledore's woefully incomplete disclosures to him (*DH*, 362). Indeed, Harry takes as a personal betrayal "tantamount to a lie" Dumbledore's failure to tell him of their common connection to Godric's Hollow (*DH*, 159).

Thus, although Harry is certainly willing to lie, he is no relativist; he continues to believe there are objective truths to be discerned. As Westman has noted, our ability to see into Harry's mind "tempers our criticisms and maintains our sympathy," because we also see his "confusion and shame" (150)—as, for example, when he lies to his friends. When Harry is faced with rumors about Dumbledore's darker secrets, peddled by the mean-spirited Rita Skeeter and Aunt Muriel, he deeply resents the suggestion that he can "choose what to believe" about Dumbledore and his family; he wants to know the truth (*DH*, 185). There is a purity and intensity about Harry's desire for the truth.

There are, however, some uncomfortable parallels between the heroes and the villains when it comes to the desire for truth. Snape tells Harry at the outset of their lessons together that Voldemort is an accomplished Legilimens who knows when someone is lying to him (*OotP*, 530-31), surely a suitably creepy power for a villain. Nor does the power appear any more wholesome as Snape repeatedly uses it on Harry in the course of their lessons. Thus, we may well be taken aback by the revelation, after Sirius's death, that Dumbledore, too, has this power (*OotP*, 832). As Westman observes, these three skilled Legilimens "don't broadcast this talent" (159). Their secrecy about their ability to penetrate others' secrets suggests, among other things, that their power has an unsavory side. It is a power that may permit them to intrude, without permission, into recognized zones of privacy in another person's mind.

Moreover, Harry's enemies, like Harry himself, claim an *entitlement* to be told the truth. Indeed, they are willing to force the truth from others. We see this theme in at least three stages of Voldemort's life. As a boy on the cusp of admission to Hogwarts, Riddle is so accustomed to forcing the truth from others that he even tries his technique on Dumbledore:

> "I don't believe you," said Riddle. "She wants me looked at, doesn't she? Tell the truth!"
>
> He spoke the last three words with a ringing force that was almost shocking. It was a command, and it sounded as though he had given it many times before. (*HBP*, 269)

When Dumbledore remains entirely unperturbed, merely "smiling pleasantly" rather than complying with the order or visibly resisting it, Riddle becomes very wary indeed (*HBP*, 270). Clearly, Riddle is nonplussed at encountering someone whose powers are beyond his control, someone who can conceal his thoughts and feelings from him. Later, when Voldemort has been disembodied and is at his weakest, his "host" Quirrell peremptorily orders Harry to "come back" and "tell me the truth" about what he saw in the Mirror of Erised (*PS*, 212). Harry does not speak, but he finds himself rooted to the spot, and Voldemort seems to know (presumably through Legilimancy) the truth Harry had hoped to conceal. And finally, in the fullness of Voldemort's strength after his re-embodiment, we learn that Voldemort tortured Gregorovich for the truth about the Elder Wand, read his mind, and then killed him (*DH*, 279-82). In each instance, Voldemort clearly believes that he has the right to invade others' minds and search out the truth. As his power grows, so does his ruthless intrusion on the privacy of others; he will not in any way voluntarily restrain or condition his own power. That others might wish to keep secrets to protect themselves or others is of no concern to him.

Voldemort's attitudes are perfectly reflected, of course, in his devoted follower Bellatrix Lestrange, who backs up her demands for the truth with torture and death threats:

> From above came Bellatrix's voice.
>
> "You are lying, filthy Mudblood, and I know it! You have been inside my vault at Gringotts! Tell the truth, tell the truth!"
>
> Another terrible scream —
>
> "HERMIONE!"
>
> "What else did you take? What else have you got? Tell me the truth or, I swear, I shall run you through with this knife!" (*DH*, 465).

Bok notes that a torturer "has no claim to normally honest answers, having stooped to such methods in the first place" (141). Voldemort and his ilk will nonetheless use any means available to them—both the mental coercion of Legilimancy and the physical coercion of torture—as if they were fully justified in doing so; as if they were somehow entitled to the truth.

Although Umbridge is not a Death Eater, but merely an evil "fellow traveler" of sorts, she follows a similar pattern. She does not want Harry to tell the truth publicly about Voldemort's return, but she is more than willing to use Veritaserum or torture to force Harry to reveal various truths *to her* when it suits her needs.[15] Indeed, she does not really consider torture to be a method of last resort, though she pays lip service to this concept, uttering disjointed phrases such as "I am left with no alternative" and "You are forcing me, Potter. . . . I do not want to" (*OotP*, 746). But her true feelings are revealed by the "nasty, eager, excited look on her face" (*OotP*, 746)—she has been looking for an excuse to try the Cruciatus Curse on a human subject. Once again, a sense of *her own* personal entitlement to the truth (here accompanied by both sadism and hypocrisy) quickly translates into the use of power for this end.

But Rowling still introduces a degree of moral ambiguity here, because her heroes also use power to force the truth out of others, even if they stop short of torture. For example, in a move that uncomfortably foreshadows Umbridge's later (if less successful) efforts, Dumbledore tells Snape to "fetch me the strongest Truth Potion you possess," and then actually uses it to compel the truth from Barty Crouch, Jr. (*GoF*, ch. 35, at 587). Dumbledore makes no attempt to obtain Crouch's story, as police in the United States are expected to do, simply by asking him noncoercive questions which he is free to answer, or not, as he wishes. Nor does Dumbledore make any attempt to gain Crouch's consent to use of the Truth Potion. (It is at least possible that Crouch might, after some negotiations, agree to consume Veritaserum voluntarily, now that he has been caught and both his

---

[15] That Umbridge fails to carry out these particular schemes is due solely to the interference of others, rather than any crisis of conscience. A suspicious Harry does not drink the "tainted" tea she offers him, although as it turns out, Snape has only provided her with fake Veritaserum in any event (*OotP*, 833). Later, Snape pretends Umbridge has exhausted his supply of the potion (*OotP*, 744). After Snape leaves, Hermione heads off Umbridge's proposed torture session by pretending to confess (*OotP*, 746).

true identity and at least the broad outline of his scheme have been exposed.) Instead, while Crouch is unconscious, Dumbledore forces his mouth open and pours in three drops of the Truth Serum. Only after this procedure does Dumbledore revive him. Dumbledore then forces approximately 25 paragraphs of exposition from the magically drugged man. The incident should give readers pause. Dumbledore stops short of torture—he inflicts no bodily pain—and yet, he has violated an unconscious person's body in order to forcibly overcome that person's will.

In *Order of the Phoenix*, Dumbledore says, "I am a sufficiently accomplished Legilimens myself to know when I am being lied to and I—persuaded him [Kreacher]—to tell me the full story" (*OotP*, 832). Dumbledore is not Kreacher's master, and therefore he could not simply order him to tell the truth in reliance on the enchantments that bind house-elves. Moreover, Dumbledore's hesitation before selecting the word "persuaded" suggests that the persuasion was not accomplished by skillful rhetoric, but by less savory means that he would prefer not to specify. Indeed, this is not the only instance in which Dumbledore refers to his techniques for obtaining the truth from reluctant subjects as "persuasion." Westman notes that the memories Dumbledore has collected in his Pensieve raise ethical questions "since some of those memories have been retrieved through 'persuasion' and not freely given" (161; *see also HBP*, 198, 362). For example, Dumbledore tells Harry that while prospective informants were "too terrified" to tell him about their experience with Riddle in his pre-Voldemort days, he still managed to find some "who could be tricked into speaking" (*HBP*, 362). The term "persuasion" appears to be a euphemism for something more sinister, or at least more powerful, than mere honeyed words.

In *Deathly Hallows*, Harry similarly compels the truth from Kreacher. He has, by now, become Kreacher's master, and he takes full advantage of that fact: "'I've got a question for you,' said Harry, his heart beating rather fast as he looked down at the elf, 'and I order you to answer it truthfully...'" (*DH*, 191). He presses again for more information, knowing that the elf must obey: "Kreacher, I want the truth: How do you know Mundungus Fletcher stole the locket?" (*DH*, 192). And despite Kreacher's obvious discomfort in recounting and reliving his experience with Regulus Black and the locket, Harry also pursues this line of questioning "relentlessly, for he was determined to know the full story" (*DH*, 197). Only afterward does Harry make an effort to give the elf an order "kindly," even though "he could not pretend that it was not an order" (*DH*, 199).

Harry then compels the truth from Mundungus, apparently taking advantage of the latter's cowardice: "It felt wonderful to have something to do, someone of whom he could demand some small portion of truth. Harry's wand was now so close to the bridge of Mundungus's nose that Mundungus had gone cross-eyed trying to keep it in view" (*DH*, 220-21). Indeed, although Harry stops Kreacher from hitting Mundungus with a frying pan, he tells the elf: "We need him conscious, Kreacher, but if he needs *persuading* you can do the honors" (*DH*, 220-21; emphasis added). He is willing to threaten physical violence to extract the truth from Mundungus.

In other words, Rowling repeatedly places two of her most admirable characters, Dumbledore and Harry, along the same spectrum of *coercive* truth-seeking as some of her most despicable villains. The methods that Dumbledore and Harry use to compel the truth are less likely to cause physical harm than those used by Umbridge, Bellatrix, and Voldemort, but the possible psychic scars are left unexamined. Rowling has created a fictional world where even the desire for truth is presented as morally ambiguous.

Conclusion

As we have seen, Rowling resists any simplistic division of truth-telling and truth-seeking as virtuous and lying as evil; but she also resists the more subtle snares of denying the existence and importance of an objective, discernable truth. Indeed, when respected adult characters discuss truth and lies, they insist that truth has inherent value and meaning. In *Prisoner of Azkaban*, when Harry suggests that all his efforts were in vain because Pettigrew escaped punishment, Dumbledore says, "It made all the difference in the world, Harry. You helped uncover the truth" about the murder of Harry's parents, and then acted to save the innocent man who had been wrongly accused (*PoA*, ch. 22, at 367). Likewise, in *Deathly Hallows*, Amycus Carrow realizes that Voldemort will punish him for a false alarm, and hopes to shift the blame to innocent students, callously commenting, "Couple of kids more or less, what's the difference?" (*DH*, 593). McGonagall turns pale with anger, and retorts: "Only the difference between truth and lies, courage and cowardice; a difference, in short, which you and your sister seem unable to appreciate" (*DH*, 593). Dumbledore's and McGonagall's words suggest that they see the truth both as a worthwhile end in itself, and as an adjunct to justice. This is the crucial insight that distinguishes a virtuous desire for the truth from a villainous one: Voldemort and his followers demand the truth only as a means to an end—and that end is domination and control of others. Under Voldemort's regime, there would be no sphere of privacy and self-direction.

Harry slowly matures throughout the series, and his initial erroneous certainties about the truth frequently give way to deeper understanding. He is initially prone to see things in black-and-white: he idealizes his father and Sirius, and is all too quick to blame Draco or Snape for troubles at Hogwarts. Indeed, he resents any effort to provide him with a more nuanced view of the grays. It is not until *Deathly Hallows* that Harry gradually learns to accept that someone like Dumbledore can be a great and wise man, and also a fallible human being, while someone like Snape can be a mean-spirited and vindictive person, while courageously working to defeat Voldemort.

Dumbledore tells Harry early on that truth "is a beautiful and terrible thing, and should therefore be treated with great caution" (*PS*, 216). But Harry does not fully appreciate this sentiment until the final stages of his adventure. He experiences truth as a beautiful thing when he realizes that his Cloak is the third Hallow: he feels "as though great new vistas of truth were opening all around him" (*DH*, 430). Then, as he considers the implications of the actual physical existence of the Hallows, he realizes that Voldemort must be seeking them and experiences truth as a terrible thing: "All his excitement, all his hope and happiness were extinguished at a stroke, and he stood alone in the darkness, and the glorious spell was broken" (*DH*, 430). There is perhaps no finer testament to Harry's hard-earned maturity in his relationship with the truth than this simple statement after the final battle: "But first he owed an explanation to Ron and Hermione, who had stuck with him for so long, and who deserved the truth" (*DH*, 746). It appears that the time for concealment and deception is past, and Harry is ready to share the full story with his closest friends. Revealing the truth will, among other things, expose Harry's choices to possible questioning, criticism and judgment, as well as admiration, from those he trusts.

Which brings us back to our original question: "Is Harry really all that good?" The easy answer is that Harry is not a moral exemplar, and Rowling has not suggested that he is one. He has many very obvious weaknesses—beyond lying and rule-breaking, he makes many mistakes and spends a substantial portion of *Order of the Phoenix* alternately angry, sullen, and yelling at his friends— but he generally tries to do what is right, at least where he can understand the reasons for it, and he grows and matures tremendously over the course of the series. This is partly a question of genre; Rowling did not choose to write a thinly disguised book of moral instruction, in which the hero's struggles (if any) with temptations are unconvincing and clearly pre-determined. Nor did Rowling write a classical epic or romance featuring a fully mature archetypal hero in the model of Aragorn—one who may, in a modern tale, face complex situations with insufficient knowledge, but whose integrity and honor are "larger than life" and entirely beyond question (*cp.* Flieger 142). Rowling instead gave us a vulnerable, immature hero who will endure much, and learn much, over seven books. Would Harry be a more virtuous child if he obeyed those in authority without question, and obeyed every rule? Only if those placed in authority over him were *invariably* wise and good, and if the rules they promulgated were *invariably* fair and just. We need look no further than Umbridge and Fudge, and the entire power structure of the Ministry of Magic when headed by Voldemort's puppet, to find counterexamples. If children are to develop into independent moral agents, at some point it is no longer sufficient for them to say "I was following orders"—because not every order should be followed.

Harry indeed tells many lies, the vast majority of which cannot pass Bok's test for justification, and he does not always regret them. But surely it is significant that we repeatedly see Harry change his goals and plans when he learns important new truths about reality. This is particularly striking in his personal relationships: once he accepts the truths that are revealed to him about Sirius Black and Severus Snape, his relationships with these men are utterly transformed. He had, with good reason, thought them his enemies; on learning the truth, he quickly acts to save Sirius's life, and eventually names one of his sons after Snape. Harry is not at all indifferent to truth and lies, but shows ever-growing maturity in his understanding of them.

Most critically, we cannot ignore that Harry, as an underage wizard, consistently tells the truth about the single greatest threat to the wizarding world, i.e., Voldemort's return and rise to power. He does so despite vicious media attacks on him as an attention-seeker or a lunatic, despite ostracism from his peers, and despite sadistic punishments from a teacher who has carte blanche from the Ministry of Magic. The existence of a crisis does not excuse his lying on a myriad of other subjects, of course (cp. Bok 107-22), but it can help place things in perspective. Moreover, as soon as the crisis is over, he makes a point of telling his friends the full truth, recognizing that they deserve to know it.

Indeed, we are not left with any serious doubts in the end about which side fought with fairer tactics and which side ultimately embraced the truth. It was the victorious side, whose victory hinged on "Dumbledore's favorite solution, love" (DH, 739). It was the side led by a boy hero, who believed so deeply in the truths revealed to him that he was prepared to give himself up to suffering and death at the hands of his enemies in order to defeat Voldemort and save the lives of his friends. From this perspective, perhaps the danger Rowling faced, as a novelist, was that of creating a hero who might be too fanatically committed to the truth to be believable, given the extraordinary pressures he would face. She humanizes Harry and disguises his ultimately Christ-like nature by giving him many faults—including a propensity for lying on matters other than Voldemort's return—and allowing him to gradually find his way to that difficult middle ground, which we all perhaps must find, between truth and other countervailing virtues such as loyalty, courtesy, and compassion.

Works Cited

Bok, Sissela. 1979. *Lying: Moral Choice in Public and Private Life.* New York: Vintage Books, 1999. Print.

Campbell, Jeremy. *The Liar's Tale: A History of Falsehood.* New York and London: W.W. Norton & Company, 2001. Print.

Flieger, Verlyn. "Frodo and Aragorn: The Concept of the Hero." *Green Suns and Faërie.* Kent, Ohio: Kent State University Press, 2012. 141-58. Print.

Frankfurt, Harry G. *On Truth.* New York: Alfred A. Knopf, 2006. Print.

Killinger, Barbara. *Integrity: Doing the Right Thing for the Right Reason.* Montreal, Kingston, London, and Ithaca: McGill-Queen's University Press, 2007. Print.

O'Brien, Michael D. "Harry Potter and the Paganization of Children's Culture." *Catholic World Report,* April 2001. N. pag. *CatholicCulture.org.* 20 Sep. 2014 <www.catholicculture.org>.

Rowling, J.K. *Harry Potter and the Chamber of Secrets.* 1998. United States of America: Scholastic Inc., 2000. Print.

--. *Harry Potter and the Deathly Hallows.* United States of America: Arthur A. Levine Books, 2007. Print.

--. *Harry Potter and the Goblet of Fire.* 2000. Pottermore Limited, 2012. N. pag. EPUB file.

--. *Harry Potter and the Half-Blood Prince.* United States of America: Arthur A. Levine Books, 2005. Print.

--. *Harry Potter and the Order of the Phoenix.* United States of America: Arthur A. Levine Books, 2003. Print.

--. *Harry Potter and the Philosopher's Stone.* Great Britain: Bloomsbury Publishing Plc, 1997. Print.

--. *Harry Potter and the Prisoner of Azkaban.* 1999. Pottermore Limited, 2012. N. pag. EPUB file.

Sullivan, Evelin. *The Concise Book of Lying.* New York: Farrar, Straus and Giroux, 2001. Print.

West, Richard C. "'And She Named Her Own Name': Being True To One's Word in Tolkien's Middle-earth." *Tolkien Studies* 2 (2005): 1-10. *ProjectMuse.* 9 Mar. 2013 <http://muse.jhu.edu>.

Westman, Karin E. "Perspective, Memory, and Moral Authority: The Legacy of Jane Austen in J. K. Rowling's *Harry Potter.*" *Children's Literature* 35 (2007): 145-165. *Project Muse.* 24 May 2014 <http://muse.jhu.edu>.

CHAPTER 16

Watching the Defectives:
Identity, Invisibility, and What the Squib Saw

Robb A. McDaniel

> *"Why didn't you tell me you're a Squib?" Harry asked Mrs. Figg, panting with the effort to keep walking. "All those times I came round your house—why didn't you say anything?"*
>
> *"Dumbledore's orders. I was to keep an eye on you but not say anything, you were too young." (5:22)*

In a world of wizards, Squibs are easy to overlook. On the very first page of *The Order of the Phoenix*, we find Harry hiding in a flower bed, "behind a large hydrangea bush. . . quite invisible to passersby" (5:1). He's spying. His ears eavesdrop on his Aunt and Uncle as they listen to the Muggle news, while his eyes follow his neighbor:

> he watched Mrs. Figg, a batty, cat-loving old lady from nearby Wisteria Walk, amble slowly past. . . . Harry was very pleased that he was concealed behind the bush; Mrs. Figg had recently taken to asking him around for tea whenever she met him in the street. She had rounded the corner and vanished from view before Uncle Vernon's voice floated out of the window again. (5:2)

Harry watches Mrs. Figg, but not knowing she is a Squib, he doesn't really *see* her: She "vanished from view" in both a physical and a metaphorical sense. At the same time, Harry keeps listening to the news for "some small clue, not recognized for what it really was by the Muggles—an unexplained disappearance, perhaps," and marvels at how the Dursleys cannot see Dudley for who he truly is, thinking he might be getting tea with the neighbors when he is more assuredly engaged in acts of bullying and vandalism (5:3). For all his condescension toward the Dursleys and their myopia, Harry has been not-seeing people himself for a long time. Indeed, Harry has spent time with Mrs. Figg, staying over at her house, "every year" of his life, a fact we are told very early in the first book, *The Sorcerer's Stone*: "Harry hated it there. The whole house smelled of cabbage and Mrs. Figg made him look at photographs of all the cats she'd ever owned" (1:22).

Squibs occupy a strange borderland in the Harry Potter universe. Ron Weasley offers the first explanation of them in *The Chamber of Secrets* when he says, of Hogwarts caretaker Argus Filch, "A Squib is someone who was born into a wizarding family but hasn't got any magical powers. Kind of the opposite of Muggle-born wizards, but Squibs are quite unusual" (2:145). They may be "opposite," but they are not parallel. Whereas Muggle-borns like Hermione operate as full-fledged members of the wizarding world, Squibs seem to exist *between* the world of wizards and that of Muggles. Indeed, Filch and Figg, the two most prominent Squibs in the Harry Potter series, both "police" the boundaries. Filch does this quite literally, by supervising students as they come and go from Hogwarts, while Mrs. Figg surveils Harry on behalf of Dumbledore, helping to keep wizards and other magical creatures away from Little Whinging. She is Harry's summertime caretaker, all the more effective for her invisibility. If the Dursleys had suspected her connections to magic, they would never have given her access. Despite their relative invisibility, to both wizards and Muggles, the Squibs are a crucial component of J.K. Rowling's universe, precisely because they help to reveal the usually hidden boundary between her two competing worlds, and it is within that boundary that she explores the relationships between identity, perception, and power.

Ironically, Rowling wants us to see that, in the world of wizards, the extent of one's power matters less than the acuity of one's perception, something one learns not from the experience of strength but instead from moments of squibbish weakness. Like the Squibs, Harry often achieves the most when he is disarmed, disillusioned, and even invisible, hiding under a cloak that conceals both his celebrity and his scars. The Squibs, in other words, point beyond themselves to a more universal experience, one especially connected to adolescence: standing in an unstable boundary region, the teen sees a world of adult power but cannot yet act in it, lashes out but cannot exercise control. True power, we discover, comes from the ability to observe and transform, to forge an identity based on sympathetic witness rather than blind self-assertion.

Power of the Powerless, Vision of the Invisible

Mrs. Figg first reveals herself in the aftermath of the dementor attack against Harry and Dudley. She is disheveled after running to catch them ("her grizzled gray hair was escaping from its hairnet. . . and her feet were halfway out of her tartan carpet slippers") and immediately expresses her combination of powerlessness and frustration, raging at the absent Mundungus Fletcher, who "disapparated" when he should have been keeping watch on Harry (5:19). Barking at Harry to help get Dudley moving, she laments, "But come *on*—I'll be no help if they come back, I've never so much as transfigured a teabag" (5:21). J.K. Rowling signals this powerlessness in the names she gives her Squibs: "Arabella Figg" and "Argus Filch," with their identical initials; both begin in "Ar," the chemical symbol for argon (derived from the Greek, *argos*, meaning "inactive"), an inert, colorless gas. Ironically, the "F" in "Figg" and "Filch" corresponds to fluorine in the periodic table—a highly reactive gas—and yet this actually supports the hybrid nature of the Squibs perfectly, since those are their *family* (i.e., wizarding world) names, as opposed to their personal ones. Hence, the "Squibs" represent unrealizable potential energy: fireworks that do not actually go off.

No one in the Harry Potter series feels the frustrations of that powerlessness more acutely than Argus Filch, for good reason. Unlike most Squibs, whom Ron tells us are encouraged to assimilate into the Muggle world, Filch lives at Hogwarts all year round, surrounded by magic that he cannot perform and often cannot even see. It cannot be accidental that Harry often seems to encounter Filch while wandering the halls in his invisibility cloak. Harry discovers that Filch is a Squib in his second year, when the caretaker detains him for "dripping mud" inside the castle (2:125):

> Harry had never been inside Filch's office before; it was a place most students avoided. The room was dingy and windowless, lit by a single oil lamp dangling from the low ceiling. A faint smell of fried fish lingered about the place.

> Wooden filing cabinets stood around the walls; from their labels, Harry could
> see that they contained details of every pupil Filch had ever punished. Fred and
> George Weasley had an entire drawer to themselves. A highly polished collec-
> tion of chains and manacles hung on the wall behind Filch's desk. It was com-
> mon knowledge that he was always begging Dumbledore to let him suspend
> students by their ankles from the ceiling. (2:125)

Much like Harry, who once lived in a "cupboard under the stairs" (1:34) at the Dursleys', Filch's dank, windowless, dungeon-like office symbolizes his aliena-tion from the world in which he dwells. Filch compensates for his weakness in relation to his magical surroundings with obsessive vigilance and bureaucratic recordkeeping. His prime targets among the students are Fred and George, who get "an entire drawer to themselves," but his true nemesis is Peeves the Polter-geist, "a grinning, airborne menace who lived to cause havoc and distress" (2:126). Peeves taunts Filch by dropping his cat, Mrs. Norris, into suits of armor, a parody of Filch's own desire to shackle the magical mischief-makers around him in the well-polished manacles he keeps hanging in his office (cf. 1:248). After Harry has gotten to Filch's office, Peeves conveniently sets off an explosion (his fireworks, like Fred and George's, do not fizzle out), allowing Harry to read a letter on Filch's desk from "KWIKSPELL: A Correspondence Course in Beginners' Magic" (5:127). Upon returning, Filch suspects that Harry has seen the letter and, in his humiliation, lets Harry leave with a sputtered warning. Later Ron explains, with a "snigger," that Filch must be a Squib: "It would explain a lot. Like why he hates students so much. . . . He's bitter" (2:145). More specifically, Filch's position at Hogwarts makes him acutely aware of his own defectiveness, and he takes that frustration out on students, whose youth makes them defective too, but in a way that, unlike Filch, they can and will escape.

Like many of Rowling's characters—Harry, Snape, Lupin, Sirius, Wormtail, Voldemort—Filch lives "underground," in a way that reminds of Fyodor Dosto-evsky's *Notes From Underground*. Dostoevsky's nameless narrator paints a self-portrait of detached impotence: "I never even managed to become anything: nei-ther wicked nor good, neither a scoundrel nor an honest man, neither a hero nor an insect. And now I am living out my life in a corner, taunting myself with the spiteful and utterly futile consolation that. . . only fools become something" (1993, 5). Like the Underground Man, Filch dreams of power and control but resigns himself to a life of bitter observation, borrowing his character and identity (we might say "filched") from the stronger actors around him.

He can work interchangeably for Dumbledore, Umbridge, or McGonagall, although he seems to enjoy his role under Umbridge the most, maybe because she sees her job as preventing the students at Hogwarts from actually practicing magic. With her, he can transform them, if only temporarily, into Squibs like himself. Bureaucratic rule-making and institutional status-seeking—the only kinds of power Filch can exercise—take over only when natural gifts are constrained. As Dumbledore reminds students, Filch "has asked me, for what he tells me is the four hundred and sixty-second time, to remind you all that magic is not permitted in corridors between classes, nor are a number of other things, all of which can be checked on the extensive list now fastened to Mr. Filch's office door" (5:211). Of course, it is hard to imagine a less visible or effective place to post such rules than Filch's office door, a problem Dolores Umbridge rectifies upon becoming Hogwarts High Inquisitor when she and Filch start posting their "educational decrees" on all the student message boards. That said, Filch lacks the acute self-consciousness that defines the Underground Man's peculiar suffering. Filch clings too much to his borrowed legitimacy to question the wizarding world's hierarchies or sympathize with its students, and he always seems a step behind Peeves and the more mischievous young witches and wizards at Hogwarts.

Rowling does not envision the Squibs as an isolated phenomenon, however, since the combination of wizarding experience and powerlessness that defines the Squibs is a frequent occurrence in the Harry Potter series, particularly for Harry himself. Indeed, to some extent all Hogwarts students are Squibs for two months each year, during their summer vacations when wizard law prohibits them from practicing magic. Living with the Dursleys, where the presence of Muggles heightens the legal prohibitions on magic, Harry's daily humiliation is compounded by his inability to fight back against his mistreatment—thus, his need for "invisibility." Like Filch, Harry takes the opportunity to hone his powers of observation—as when he hides behind that hydrangea bush, spying on the Dursleys and Mrs. Figg simultaneously—even if he is not initially very good at it, unable to comprehend the telltale "*crack*" of Mundungus Fletcher disapparating in close proximity to him (5:4).

One of the most famous literary descriptions of the way invisibility shapes identity comes from Ralph Ellison's *Invisible Man*, a book inspired by Dostoevsky's *Notes From Underground*, and reimagining the latter's nameless narrator as an African-American struggling behind the veil of racial anonymity and marginality (1980, xix). In his opening lines Ellison writes:

> I am an invisible man. No, I am not a spook like those who haunted Edgar Allen Poe; nor am I one of your Hollywood-movie ectoplasms. I am a man of substance, of flesh and bone, fiber and liquids—and I might even be said to possess a mind. I am invisible, understand, simply because people refuse to see me. Like the bodiless heads you see sometimes in circus sideshows, it is as though I have been surrounded by mirrors of hard, distorting glass. When they approach me they see only my surroundings, themselves, or figments of their imagination—indeed, everything and anything except me. (1980, 3)

Wizards, like African Americans, are a feared "minority," and Squibs are a minority within that minority, thus offering some insight into how Rowling views issues of identity and marginality. Harry, of course, has deep experience with such invisibility, whether literal, as when he travels the corridors of Hogwarts under his invisibility cloak (almost getting caught once in Hogsmeade when his own "bodiless head" appears to Draco Malfoy (3:281)), or metaphorical, since his entire life at Privet Drive is hidden from both Muggles and wizards. In *Order of the Phoenix*, Harry can only leave Privet Drive once Mad-Eye Moody puts him under a "Disillusionment Charm": "Harry looked down at his body, or rather, what had been his body for it didn't look anything like his anymore. It was not invisible; it had simply taken on the exact color and texture of the kitchen unit behind him. He seemed to have become a human chameleon" (5:54). As in *Invisible Man*, Harry comes to find strength and escape in his ability to blend into his surroundings, but this also involves becoming "disillusioned" with the environs of his youth.

Although Ellison's invisible man describes himself as living in a "border area" and a "hole in the ground," he assures his reader that "it is incorrect to assume that, because I'm invisible and live in a hole, I'm dead" (1980, 5-6). At times, however, he and those he encounters might not be so sure:

> Or again, you often doubt if you really exist. You wonder whether you aren't simply a phantom in other people's minds. Say, a figure in a nightmare which

the sleeper tries with all his strength to destroy. It's when you feel like this that, out of resentment, you begin to bump people back. . . . You ache with the need to convince yourself that you do exist in the real world, that you're a part of all the sound and anguish, and you strike out with your fists, you curse and you swear to make them recognize you. And, alas, it's seldom successful. (1980, 4)

Like the Invisible Man, Harry spends most of *Order of the Phoenix* resentfully trying to prove that he does, in fact, exist, and not just as a "nightmare" he shares with Voldemort, the dark wizard the ministry wants to believe, against all evidence, is dead. Harry spends much of the book yelling and lashing out at his closest friends. But he is constantly met with confusion and disbelief, even when sharing his invisibility with the "secret society" that his elders have formed behind the carefully concealed walls at Number 12, Grimmauld Place (5:67). Part of his frustration lies in his being locked out of the Order's meetings—along with Ron, Hermione, Ginny, Fred, and George—thanks to their youth. Not surprisingly, Harry and his friends react to their exclusion through surveillance, using "Extendable Ears" (5:68).

Secrecy and its costs are core themes throughout the series. On the very first page of the first Harry Potter book we are told that the Dursleys see Harry as their "secret, and their greatest fear was that somebody would discover it" (1:1). Before Harry came to live with them, the Dursleys had pretended the Potters did not even exist, and after he is dropped upon their doorstep they hide him away, prohibiting him from talking with the neighbors (save Mrs. Figg), and routinely forgetting his birthday—hence his very existence. Looking at the loving pictures of Dudley on the Dursleys' mantle, Harry observes that "the room held no sign at all that another boy lived in the house, too" (1:18). Similarly, in *The Chamber of Secrets*, the Dursleys attempt to hide Harry, *on his birthday* (which they have again forgotten), from the Masons, dinner-party guests with whom Uncle Vernon wants to make a business deal: "No cards, no presents, and he would be spending the evening pretending not to exist. He gazed miserably into the hedge. He had never felt so lonely" (2:7). Notably, a "hedge" symbolizes boundary itself: it is a physical border that partly conceals one's home, hence one's identity, but in another sense "to hedge" is to play both sides at once, to exist in ambiguous duality.[1]

Rather than take Harry out in public on Dudley's birthday, the Dursleys routinely stow him with Mrs. Figg, who "made him look at photographs of all the cats she'd ever owned" (1:22). When Aunt Petunia hears that Mrs. Figg has broken her leg, she's horrified at the prospect of being seen with Harry and degrades him contemptuously: "The Dursleys often spoke about Harry like this, as though he wasn't there—or as though he was something very nasty that couldn't understand them, like a slug" (1:22). Although Harry is relieved that "it would be a whole year before he had to look at Tibbles, Snowy, Mr. Paws, and Tufty again," he does not really *see* those photographs any better than the Dursleys see him. As we discover in *Order of the Phoenix*, those cats have been keeping watch on Harry for years, a surveillance that bears fruit during the dementor attack; Mrs. Figg tells Harry that, "I'd stationed Mr. Tibbles under a car just in case, and Mr. Tibbles came and warned me" (5:20). Had he known Mrs. Figg was a Squib, Harry might have suspected something, since Argus Filch's cat, Mrs. Norris ("a scrawny, dust-colored creature with bulging lamplike eyes just like Filch's") performs the exact same role at Hogwarts: "She patrolled the corridors alone. Break a rule in front of her, put just one toe out of line, and she'd whisk off for Filch, who'd appear, wheezing, two seconds later" (1:132-133). Like Filch and Figg, Mrs. Norris is a solitary watcher, policing the boundaries of the magical youth with her "lamplike eyes." We might say that Mrs. Norris and Mr. Tibbles operate as "Extendable Eyes" for their masters. As a result, "Filch knew the passageways of the school better than anyone (except perhaps the Weasley twins) and could pop up as suddenly as any of the ghosts. The students all hated him, and it was the dearest ambition of many to give Mrs. Norris a good kick" (1:132-133). Harry's tunnel

---

[1] That sort of duality is Harry's core dilemma throughout *Order of the Phoenix*, a book where, having just witnessed fellow-student Cedric Diggory murdered, he has lost whatever innocence his youth may once have afforded him but has yet to "come of age" as a wizard; meanwhile, many of his classmates, misled by the *Daily Prophet*, which Harry too had once respected as an authority, suspect he is a liar and may be responsible for Cedric's death. Throughout his fifth year, Harry grapples with his relationship to Voldemort—expressed first in dreams where he acts as the snake, Nagini, and finally, in outright demonic possession (5:816)—hence with evil itself.

vision, like that of the Durselys, comes from underestimating creatures—cats, rats, "batty" old neighbors—he instinctively sees as beneath him.[2]

Harry does not remain invisible, of course. The real drama of *The Sorcerer's Stone* begins when Harry gets his letter from Hogwarts, addressed to "Mr. H. Potter, The Cupboard under the Stairs, 4 Privet Drive, Little Whinging, Surrey" (1:34). The Dursleys, having hidden Harry away so effectively for a decade, cannot initially fathom the situation. Flustered, Aunt Petunia asks, "how could they possibly know where he sleeps? You don't think they're watching the house?" To which Uncle Vernon responds, "Watching—spying—might be following us" (1:36). But who is watching? Harry doesn't know—Rowling titles the chapter "The Letters From No One"—but the mere prospect of being seen, even by someone invisible, is liberating (1:31). What Harry soon discovers is that he is famous ("the boy who lived"), although famous in an invisible world, or at least one in which ordinary perceptions are transformed, a reality carefully concealed from the Muggles.

W.E.B. DuBois once described the discovery of one's inherent difference as a peculiar awareness:

> [T]he Negro is a sort of seventh son, born with a veil, and gifted with second-sight in this American world—a world which yields him no true self-consciousness, but only lets him see himself through the revelation of the other world. It is a peculiar sensation, this double-consciousness, this sense of always looking at one's self through the eyes of others, of measuring one's soul by the tape of a world that looks on in amused contempt and pity. One ever feels his twoness. (1996, 5)

---

[2] Sirius Black will eventually die as a result of his own blindness, when he puts Kreacher the house-elf in position to betray him. As Dumbledore explains to Harry, "Sirius did not hate Kreacher ... He regarded him as a servant unworthy of much interest or notice. Indifference and neglect often do much more damage than outright dislike" (5:833-834). Harry comes to discover in *The Deathly Hallows* that this same failing—not seeing Kreacher—had led Voldemort into a critical error when, after using Kreacher to test the potion protecting his horcrux in the cave by the sea, he did not realize that Kreacher had the magical ability to escape the cave and reveal the scheme (7:195-198). Sadly, Sirius understood this in principle but was unable to live it out in practice. In *The Goblet of Fire*, while dissecting the ambitions of Barty Crouch, Sr., and his firing of his house-elf, Winky, Sirius commented to Harry, Ron, and Hermione that, "If you want to know what a man's like, take a good look at how he treats his inferiors, not his equals"(4:525).

DuBois emphasizes the advantages of such a "double-consciousness," even though it arises from an experience of alienation in "the revelation of the other world." Harry's "second sight" is different, since he discovers a physical/magical surplus rather than a perceived racial deficiency. Both, however, are experiences of boundary, difference, and altered perception. When those distinct worlds collide, the experience can be jarring, something Harry discovers after the dementor attack in *Order of the Phoenix*:

> The arrival of the dementors in Little Whinging seemed to have caused a breach in the great, invisible wall that divided the relentlessly non-magical world of Privet Drive and the world beyond. Harry's two lives had somehow become fused and everything had been turned upside down: the Dursleys were asking for details about the magical world and Mrs. Figg knew Albus Dumbledore; dementors were soaring around Little Whinging and he might never go back to Hogwarts. Harry's head throbbed more painfully. (5:37)

Harry finds himself in something of an identity crisis, one that will follow him through the remainder of his fifth year and alter his perception of himself and those around him. In the moment that follows the "breach in the great, invisible wall," Harry finally *sees*: "all of a sudden, for the first time in his life, Harry fully appreciated that Aunt Petunia was his mother's sister. . . . The furious pretense that Aunt Petunia had maintained all Harry's life—that there was no magic and no world other than the world she inhabited with Uncle Vernon—seemed to have fallen away" (5:38). From now on, Harry will see aspects of his world that had previously remained hidden—such as the Thestrals that pull the carriages into Hogwarts (5:196-197)—before finally wrestling with his own troubled duality in the Ministry's Department of Mysteries.

Identity and Transfiguration

Such boundary experiences are frequent occurrences in Rowling's work—Diagon Alley, Platform 9 ¾, the moving staircases and interactive paintings at Hogwarts, the Chamber of Secrets, Riddle's diary, the floo network, portkeys, 12 Grimmauld Place, and the Ministry of Magic being several of the key examples. The world of wizards is a place of change and "transfiguration." Indeed, transfiguration is the very first magic Rowling presents in the series: "he [Mr. Dursley] noticed the first sign of something peculiar—a cat reading a map" (1:2). As we soon discover, the cat is really Professor McGonagall, Hogwarts's transfiguration teacher and one of only a very few "Animagi," wizards who can transform into animals. This renders McGonagall (mostly) invisible to Vernon Dursley and enables her to surveil his house while awaiting Dumbledore, Hagrid, and the infant Harry Potter. Once again, the cat acts as an undercover observer, but in this case not as an extension of a Squib but, instead, the secret identity of a witch. That ability to transform, to cross seemingly unbridgeable boundaries, contributes much to Rowling's sense of virtue, as the Animagi demonstrate. Despite her stern demeanor, McGonagall is arguably both the wisest and most empathetic teacher at Hogwarts.

Years earlier, James Potter and Sirius Black had learned the art of animal transformation so that they could accompany their friend Remus Lupin when he underwent his involuntary transformations into a werewolf, helping him to tame his wildest instincts and giving him company in his moments of greatest isolation. As Lupin tells the story, his friends spent years learning to transform and would then sneak off together under James's invisibility cloak during the full moon.[3] Lupin, however, also relates that "the Animagus transformation can go horribly wrong—one reason the Ministry keeps a close watch on those attempting to do it" (3:354). We are never told exactly *how* such a transformation can go wrong, but we do have an example: Peter Pettigrew, the trusted friend turned betrayer of Harry's parents. When, in the Shrieking Shack, an abandoned haunt that had once been the friends' secret clubhouse, Lupin yells for Ron to "*give me that rat*," he is speaking in two senses (3:365). The proverbial "rat" is, literally, a rat. Returned to human form, Peter's "skin looked grubby, almost like Scabbers's fur, and something of the rat lingered around his pointed nose and his very small, watery eyes. . . . Even Pettigrew's voice was squeaky. . . his eyes darted to the

---

[3] This invisibility gives them the opportunity to chart Hogwarts and create the ultimate tool of both surveillance and its avoidance, the Marauders' Map. Appropriately, "Moony, Wormtail, Padfoot, and Prongs" will lose the map to Filch, who, lacking the ability to perform magic, cannot see it for what it is before it is recovered by Fred and George Weasley and then, finally, given to Harry and his own band of boundary-crossing "Marauders." Cartography also links the Marauders to McGonagall's feline map-reading in the opening pages of *The Sorcerer's Stone.*

door" (3:366-367). The metaphorical contrast with the enduringly loyal Sirius, who transforms into a dog, could not be sharper. In transforming, one assumes characteristics of the animal, and, for a relatively weak wizard like Pettigrew, it becomes difficult to fully regain one's humanity.

The ability to transform offers the possibilities of solace, hope, and community, but such virtue comes only with risk to one's identity, and not everyone will return. This is why, as Hermione reports, the Ministry puts all Animagi on a "register showing what animal they become, and their markings and things. . . . I went and looked Professor McGonagall up on the register, and there have only been seven Animagi this century, and Pettigrew's name wasn't on the list" (3:351). James, Sirius, and Peter needed their power to remain secret in order to save their friend Lupin, but that secrecy cuts in two directions—it both enables Sirius to escape Azkaban, avoiding detection by the dementors, and allows Pettigrew to remain concealed for twelve years as Scabbers, the Weasley family's pet rat and Voldemort's sleeper spy conspiring against Harry. Friendship, we might say, requires transfiguration. To understand one's friends involves crossing a boundary into their private world, leaving one's own solipsism behind in order to develop empathy. But as Aristotle observed, the friendships of youth typically depend more upon pleasure and utility than virtue, and so tend to be unstable. Virtuous friendships between "comrades" require a large measure of equality, and if friends are not genuine equals such relationships can breed resentment, as seems to happen with Peter Pettigrew (Aristotle 2000, 146-163).

Transformation figures most prominently in *Order of the Phoenix*, the book where Harry's own identity appears most at risk. Not surprisingly, this is also the book where Harry's behavior seems most characteristically adolescent—he's living on the border between youth and adulthood. Rowling highlights this state of transition when Sirius and Molly Weasley debate whether or not Harry should be told about the activities of the Order: "'He's not a child!' said Sirius impatiently. 'He's not an adult either!' said Mrs. Weasley, the color rising in her cheeks. 'He's not *James*, Sirius!'" (5:88-89) Not only does Sirius treat Harry as if he is already an adult but, as Mrs. Weasley points out, "'Sometimes, the way you talk about him, it's as though you think you've got your best friend back!' 'What's wrong with that?' said Harry. 'What's wrong, Harry, is that you are *not* your father, however much you might look like him!'" (5:89) Appearance suggests identity, but it may also be deceptive. In response to this challenge to his judgment, Sirius contends that it is Mrs. Weasley who suffers from mistaken identity: "'He's not your son,' said Sirius quietly. 'He's as good as,' said Mrs. Weasley fiercely" (5:90). There is a parallel confusion here, in that both Sirius and Mrs. Weasley see Harry through the central aspect of their own individual identities—friendship and motherhood, respectively—thus leading Sirius to conflate Harry with James and Molly to conflate Harry with Ron.

If similarity of appearance can create confused identity, alteration of one's appearance offers several related possibilities: escape, surveillance, and understanding. Like the Animagi, Metamorphmagi possess the ability to transform. Shortly after the dementor attack in Little Whinging, as Harry sits alone and isolated in his room pondering his imminent suspension from Hogwarts, he meets Nymphadora Tonks, part of an "advance guard" sent by Dumbledore to evacuate Harry from Privet Drive to Grimmauld Place. When Tonks accompanies Harry back to his room to pack up, she gives him a private tutorial on transformation, turning her hair "bubble-gum pink":

> "I'm a Metamorphmagus," she said, looking back at her reflection and turning her head so that she could see her hair from all directions. "It means I can change my appearance at will," she added, spotting Harry's puzzled expression in the mirror behind her. "I was born one. I got top marks in Concealment and Disguise during Auror training without any study at all, it was great."
>
> "You're an Auror?" said Harry, impressed. Being a Dark wizard catcher was the only career he'd ever considered after Hogwarts. . . .
>
> "Can you learn how to be a Metamorphmagus?" Harry asked her, straightening up, completely forgetting about packing.
>
> Tonks chuckled.
>
> "Bet you wouldn't mind hiding that scar sometimes, eh?"
>
> Her eyes found the lightning-shaped scar on Harry's forehead.
>
> "No, I wouldn't mind," Harry mumbled, turning away. He did not like people staring at his scar.

"Well, you'll have to learn the hard way, I'm afraid," said Tonks. "Meta-morphmagi are really rare, they're born, not made. Most wizards need to use a wand or potions to change their appearance." (5:52)

Harry both admires and envies Tonks here, as their eyes meet in the mirror. She is in many ways what he aspires to be: a confident adult who can easily transform, hide, and keep watch. Tonks, meanwhile, recognizes immediately that Harry's interest in her power is personal, that he desires to escape from his fame, which, for all its benefits, also isolates him, fixes his identity, and makes him into a ready target for Voldemort and his Death Eaters. Unfortunately for Harry, her power is not really teachable, meaning that he will need to deal with his scar "the hard way, I'm afraid."[4] He never actually loses the scar, although by finally defeating Voldemort he manages to erase the pain that goes along with it. In her very last lines, when Rowling tells us that, "The scar had not pained Harry for nineteen years. All was well" (7:759), she recalls Dumbledore's first sight of the famous scar, when Hagrid has arrived at Privet Drive with the infant Harry. "He'll have that scar forever," says Dumbledore. When McGonagall asks if he could just re-move it, he replies that, "Even if I could, I wouldn't. Scars can come in handy. I have one myself above my left knee that is a perfect map of the London Under-ground" (1:15).

There is a certain irony in the fact that Metamorphmagi are "born, not made." Although it is their nature to change, the Metamorphmagus's identity is none-theless largely fixed, determined by a magical surplus relative to other wizards who require artificial means, "a wand or potions to change their appearance." We might say, following Heraclitus or Nietzsche, that for her "being is becoming":

---

[4] As it happens, Harry can and does approximate Tonks's metamorphoses by way of "wand or potion." Along with Ron and Hermione, he uses the Polyjuice potion to spy on Draco during his second year and to infiltrate the Ministry of Magic in his seventh (2:216; 7:237). Hermione uses her wand to alter his appearance when they are caught by Snatchers later that same year (7:446). Such spells are merely temporary, however, and the attempt by wizards to harness such power more regularly proves both comic and tragic. In *Half-Blood Prince*, Mr. Weasley reports that "Some idiot's started selling Metamorph-Medals. Just sling them around your neck and you'll be able to change your appearance at will. A hundred thousand disguises, all for ten Galleons!' 'And what happens when you put them on?' 'Mostly you just turn a fairly unpleasant orange color, but a couple of people have also sprouted tentaclelike warts all over their bodies. As if St. Mungo's didn't have enough to do already!'" (6:87)

her malleability reflects her essence rather than the absence of one, like the river that one supposedly cannot step into twice (since its running waters make it always new), but which nevertheless remains itself. Rowling calls our attention to Tonks's continuity with her idiosyncratic but ever-present greeting, "Wotcher, Harry!" (5:47, 181; 6:82, 156). The words are playful, but also a pun. Tonks is a "watcher," sent to keep an eye on Harry and patrol the boundaries of his experience—much like Filch and Figg—both inside and outside Hogwarts. But unlike the Squibs she also represents a guide for his own development, his metamorphosis into adulthood, as he pursues his dream of becoming an Auror. In other words, Rowling seems to be saying, "Watch her, Harry." It is Tonks's ability to transform that ultimately makes her so capable of sympathy, and it is also the trait Harry will need to emulate so that he himself becomes "Watcher Harry," a sympathetic observer who can police his own boundaries.

Tonks has her own momentary identity crisis, however, in *The Half-Blood Prince*. At the Burrow with the Weasleys, Harry noticed that "she looked drawn, even ill, and there was something forced in her smile" (6:82). Later on the train Tonks finds Harry after he has been stupefied by Draco Malfoy and hidden under his own invisibility cloak, ironically imprisoned by his own secret means of escape and surveillance. Tonks, however, can see Harry even when he is concealed, not because she has special power, but because she is observant: "I noticed that you hadn't left the train and I knew you had that cloak. I thought you might be hiding for some reason. When I saw the blinds were drawn down on that compartment I thought I'd check" (6:158). Harry is beginning to see her, too, although his awareness remains dim through much of his sixth year. He notices that something is off about her as they leave the train; she lacks her usual good cheer and is "mousy-haired and miserable-looking" (6:157). Rowling reports that "Harry looked sideways at Tonks under his cloak" and that he then starts to speculate to himself on her discontent, wondering if she feels guilt over Sirius's death at the Ministry (6:158-159).

The reality is somewhat different, however. Unlike Harry—whose sympathy for Tonks merely projects his own guilt and anxiety—her worries come less from regret about Sirius than from her unrequited love for Lupin. Rather than lamenting the dead, she longs for the living. Although Lupin considers himself too old and too threatening for her, her ability to transform enables her to understand him in ways that few other wizards can. Notably, the wizard who manages to discern Tonks's affections during this incident is the decidedly unsympathetic Snape, whom we eventually discover suffers from his own unrequited love for Harry's mother. When Tonks brings Harry to the gates of Hogwarts, she sends her Patronus to alert Hagrid, only to have Snape intercept the message. After chiding Harry for lateness, Snape turns to Tonks:

> "I was interested to see your new Patronus."

> He shut the gates in her face with a loud clang and tapped the chains with his wand again, so that they slithered, clinking, back into place.

> "I think you were better off with the old one," said Snape, the malice in his voice unmistakable. "The new one looks weak."

> As Snape swung his lantern about, Harry saw, fleetingly, a look of shock and anger on Tonks's face. Then she was covered in darkness once more. (6:160)

Tonks's Patronus, we discover, has transformed into a wolf in a reflection of her passion for Lupin. Resenting her for her capacity to love the living, where he can only love the dead, Snape lashes out resentfully, literally slamming the gate shut in her face. He then reminds her of both Lupin's weakness and her own failure to get through to him. Once again in the dark about the adults around him, Harry does not recognize the extent to which Snape, as a double agent, has gone underground. Snape's bitterness derives from his knowledge that, even in transformation, he cannot find completion. His Patronus, much like Tonks's, has taken the shape of a doe in honor of his beloved, Lily Potter, but she can never receive the message.

What the Squib Saw

> Harry took off the Invisibility Cloak and looked down upon the man he hated, whose widening black eyes found Harry as he tried to speak. Harry bent over him, and Snape seized the front of his robes and pulled him close.

> A terrible rasping, gurgling noise issued from Snape's throat.

> "Take. . . it. . . . Take. . . it. . . ."

Something more than blood was leaking from Snape. Silvery blue, neither gas nor liquid, it gushed from his mouth and his ears and his eyes, and Harry knew what it was, but did not know what to do—

A flask, conjured from thin air, was thrust into his shaking hands by Hermione. Harry lifted the silvery substance into it with his wand. When the flask was full to the brim, and Snape looked as though there was no blood left in him, his grip on Harry's robes slackened.

"Look. . . at. . . me. . . ." he whispered. (7:657-658)

Toward the end of *The Deathly Hallows*, Harry steps out from under his cloak of invisibility to meet eyes with a dying Severus Snape. It is a powerful scene, maybe the most affecting in the entire Harry Potter series. Despite his hatred, Harry reaches out to a man he believes to be a traitor and relieves him of his final memories, memories to which Snape had long and desperately clung. If the Animagi and Metamorphmagi symbolize the moral dimension of transfiguration, Slytherin House reflects the opposite instinct: the closed door, the inability to accept those from another world or the "mudbloods" whose identity is drawn from the borderlands between the magical and the Muggle.[5] Insofar as we identify Snape with Slytherin, we cannot help but hold him under suspicion, just as Harry does. Of all the adults whom Harry has failed to "see" in his seven years at Hogwarts, no one has escaped him more completely than Snape. But that evasion ends in this moment of unexpected vulnerability and unmerited compassion.

What Harry discovers from those memories is that Snape had wanted desperately to be known: "Look. . . at. . . me. . . ." Indeed, Snape reveals himself first as a hidden watcher, silently observing Lily and Petunia Evans as the former practiced her pre-Hogwarts magic on a playground in front of her disapproving elder sister. Snape cannot keep himself concealed, however, leaping out from behind a bush to announce the magical connection he shares with Lily, provoking only scorn and derision:

---

[5] The Dursleys represent the same phenomenon from the other side: the Muggles whose willful denial of the world of magic would blot it out of existence. From Snape's memory we get Lily's conflict with her sister: "'It *is* real, isn't it? It's not a joke? Petunia says there isn't a Hogwarts. It *is* real, isn't it?' 'It is real for us,' said Snape. 'Not for her'" (7:666).

"You *are* a witch. I've been watching you for a while. But there's nothing wrong with that. My mum's one, and I'm a wizard."

Petunia's laugh was like cold water.

"Wizard!" she shrieked, her courage returned now that she had recovered from the shock of his unexpected appearance. "*I* know who *you* are. You're that Snape boy! They live down Spinner's End by the river," she told Lily, and it was evident from her tone that she considered the address a poor recommendation. "Why have you been spying on us?"

"Haven't been spying," said Snape, hot and uncomfortable and dirty-haired in the bright sunlight. "Wouldn't spy on you, anyway," he added spitefully, "*you're* a Muggle." (7:665)

Snape offers his generosity in the form of identification, an attempt to help Lily understand her basic difference, but Petunia rebukes him by marking that identity as fantasy and abnormality. His response, to call Petunia a "Muggle" unworthy of observation, only confirms his oddity, revealing his concealment to be a form of dishonesty and even bigotry. A natural Slytherin, he can only sympathize with those like himself, although he does have moments of nobility, as when he later reassures Lily that her family origins will not affect her wizarding status: "'Does it make any difference being Muggle-born?' Snape hesitated. His black eyes, eager in the greenish gloom, moved over the pale face, the dark red hair. 'No,' he said. 'It doesn't make any difference'" (7:666). Snape is lying again. Although he and Lily become close friends, Snape continues to harbor secret resentments, and, years later, when Lily intervenes as James and Sirius humiliate him, he pridefully brands her a "mudblood," creating a lasting breach with the woman he loved (7:675).

Snape, however, has reserves of strength and decency that set him above his Slytherin peers, most of whom become loyal Death Eaters for Voldemort. At first, he pleads with Dumbledore to save Lily—not by direct confrontation with Voldemort, but instead through concealing her whereabouts. When that plan fails and the Potters are killed, Dumbledore prevails upon Snape to help protect her child, even though Snape cannot bear Harry's resemblance to his nemesis

James. Dumbledore's appeal is telling. As he peruses, aptly, a copy of *Transfiguration Today*, he says: "Her son lives. He has her eyes, precisely her eyes. You remember the shape and color of Lily Evans's eyes, I am sure?" (7:678)[6]

Of course, what matters about Lily's eyes is less how they look than *how they see*. No one else sees Snape for who he might become rather than simply "that Snape boy. . . separated from normal people," although Dumbledore does come to value their friendship. Still, Snape has trouble seeing Harry as anything more than "mediocre, arrogant as his father, a determined rule-breaker," and begrudges Dumbledore's having confided things to Harry he continues to hide from Snape (7:679 ff.). Dumbledore's final secret—that Harry must sacrifice his life to take that of Voldemort—remains hidden until the end nears. When he finally discloses it to Snape, the former potions master reveals, in his outraged reaction, how much he has come to care for Harry: "'I have spied for you and lied for you, put myself in mortal danger for you. . . to keep Lily Potter's son safe. Now you tell me that you have been raising him like a pig for slaughter'" (7:687). Snape has changed. By going underground, living a life of secret devotion to a lost love while publicly playing the villain, Snape has transformed into the ultimate sympathetic observer. In his dying moment, Snape needs nothing more than to know that "Lily Evans's eyes" finally see him, that her cause has become his, and that his sacrifice has not been in vain.

Snape is not the only character who steps out of the shadows at the end of *The Deathly Hallows* looking for understanding. As Harry will discover, Dumbledore too has been struggling with guilt and loss, although Harry does not yet know it. After reliving Snape's memories in the Pensieve, Harry once again dons his invisibility cloak to make what he expects to be his final journey. He goes

---

[6] Rita Skeeter reported in her unauthorized biography of Dumbledore that "Bathilda Bagshot, the celebrated magical historian" had reached out to the young Albus at Hogwarts "having been favorably impressed by his paper on trans-species transformation in *Transfiguration Today*. This initial contact led to acquaintance with the entire Dumbledore family" (7:354-355). Transfiguration and Animagi were, for Dumbledore, lifelong interests. Indeed, although not an Animagus himself, Dumbledore undergoes his own radical "transfiguration" from callow striver to empathetic mentor. Once again, empathy comes from going underground, becoming effectively invisible: "Why had Dumbledore taken James's Invisibility Cloak? Harry distinctly remembered his headmaster telling him years before, 'I don't need a cloak to become invisible'" (7:181).

into the woods to encounter Voldemort and sacrifice his life so that the part of Voldemort's soul that has been hidden in his scar for the last seventeen years can be destroyed. Before walking unarmed toward his execution, however, he remembers that he is carrying the Golden Snitch, left to him by Dumbledore in his will and bearing the words, "I open at the close." Sensing this refers to crossing the final boundary, into death, Harry "pressed the golden metal to his lips and whispered, 'I am about to die.' The metal shell broke open. He lowered his shaking hand, raised Draco's wand beneath the Cloak, and murmured, 'Lumos'" (7:698). The Snitch—a spy that reveals hidden truths—offers Harry a genuine epiphany (i.e., an invisible illumination), the Resurrection Stone, and with it, the embodied forms of his parents, along with his now-dead mentors Sirius and Lupin. Reassuring Harry, they tell him that sacrifice is worth its price and that they will stay with him, "'Until the very end,' said James. . . . 'We are part of you,' said Sirius. 'Invisible to anyone else'" (7:700). Harry, the invisible man, no longer afraid of death, no longer lashing out at the world to prove he exists, wielding only the memories of his loved ones, can now walk confidently toward the abyss.

The cloak allows Harry to appear before Voldemort on his own terms, stalking his own death rather than let it capture and torment him. That moment comes quickly. Finally revealing himself to the Death Eaters, Harry pockets his wand, hides the invisibility cloak that had so often hidden him, and allows Voldemort to strike him down. In this, his bravest moment, Harry is less a wizard than he is a Squib, defined not by his power but by his seeming powerlessness—his active choice to relinquish his magic, to not strike at those who will surely strike at him.[7]

Rather than simply dying, however, Harry finds himself in another one of those invisible boundaries that have defined so much of his life: "He lay facedown, listening to the silence. He was perfectly alone. Nobody was watching. Nobody else was there. He was not perfectly sure that he was there himself. A long time later, or maybe no time at all, it came to him that he must exist, must be more than disembodied thought" (7:705). Harry soon realizes that he is in a cloudy,

---

[7] Rowling foreshadows this moment when, earlier, Harry realizes that Voldemort must have stolen the Elder Wand from Dumbledore's grave: "The enormity of his decision not to race Voldemort to the wand still scared Harry. He could not remember, ever before, choosing *not* to act" (7:502).

unformed chamber, much like the King's Cross train station where he once waited to board the express to Hogwarts, and he is not really alone. Appearing as a purgatorial guide, Dumbledore helps Harry sort out events and reveals his own regrets, both for his mistakes of judgment in the battle against Voldemort and for a youthful alliance with the dark wizard, Grindelwald, which cost Dumbledore his sister Ariana. In this moment, the relationship between Harry and Dumbledore flips upside-down: "For the first time since Harry had met Dumbledore, he looked less than an old man, much less. He looked fleetingly like a small boy caught in wrongdoing. 'Can you forgive me?' he said. . . . 'I crave your pardon, Harry. I have known, for some time now, that you are the better man'" (7:712-713). Dumbledore reveals that, unlike the selfless Harry, he had once selfishly sought power by uniting the legendary Deathly Hallows—the Elder Wand, the Invisibility Cloak, and the Resurrection Stone—in an effort to become "master of Death" (7:713).[8] That quest resulted in Dumbledore's first battle with Grindelwald, which the former won, but at the expense of Ariana who was struck down in the crossfire.

Ariana Dumbledore, in death, became the pivotal figure in her brother's life, the ghost that haunted him (7:567-568). She had been largely invisible to Dumbledore in life. As Aberforth angrily tells Harry, "*I* was her favorite. . . . Not Albus, he was always up in his bedroom when he was home, reading his books and counting his prizes. . . . *He* didn't want to be bothered with her" (7:565). Ariana's story is the mystery at the heart of *The Deathly Hallows.* When we first see Harry in the final book, he has awoken from another murderous nightmare only to cut himself on a broken mirror. Rowling's imagery slyly signals the psychological implication of Harry's torturous introspection, that which would eventually

---

[8] It is an interesting question whether this is *really* Dumbledore, or just Harry's projection of him, an issue that Dumbledore gracefully eludes when he says, in departure, "Of course it is happening inside your head, Harry, but why on earth should that mean it is not real?" (7:723). We cannot know if these are his actual regrets or, instead, Harry's sympathetic imagination of them as he makes final peace with the mentor by whom he had recently felt betrayed. Either way, however, it is not true that Harry was immune to the lure of the Hallows. Indeed, upon discovering the legend he began obsessing over them, much as Dumbledore had (7:435). So this may be Harry's way of dealing with his own guilt for (briefly) craving power—imputing that sin to Dumbledore, allowing the great man to absolve him, and then asking for Harry's own absolution, thus enabling forgiveness.

find remedy in the purgatorial King's Cross: "He had never learned how to repair wounds, and now he came to think of it. . . this seemed a serious flaw in his magical education" (7:13-14). At breakfast Harry reads two competing memorials for Dumbledore, a glassy-eyed tribute from Elphias Doge and a gossipy expose by Rita Skeeter, both of which recount aspects of Dumbledore's family history about which Harry had been thoroughly ignorant. Later, at Bill and Fleur's wedding, Ron's Aunt Muriel confronts Doge over the Dumbledore family secret: "I daresay you'll still think he was a saint even if it does turn out he did away with his Squib sister!" (7:154)

In the Wizard world, there are few disgraces worse than having a Squib in the family:

> "Ariana was not a Squib!" wheezed Doge.
>
> "So you say, Elphias, but explain, then, why she never attended Hogwarts!" said Auntie Muriel. She turned back to Harry. "In our day, Squibs were often hushed up, though to take it to the extreme of actually imprisoning a little girl in the house and pretending she didn't exist—" . . .
>
> "Squibs were usually shipped off to Muggle schools and encouraged to integrate into the Muggle community. . . much kinder than trying to find them a place in the Wizarding world, where they must always be second class; but naturally Kendra Dumbledore wouldn't have dreamed of letting her daughter go to a Muggle school—"
>
> "Ariana was delicate!" said Doge desperately. "Her health was always too poor to permit her—"
>
> "—to permit her to leave the house?" cackled Muriel. "And yet she was never taken to St. Mungo's and no Healer was ever summoned to see her!" (7:155-156)

Although the Dumbledores had tried to render Ariana invisible ("pretending she didn't exist"), she nonetheless reappears as a rumor and a scandal. Muriel even suggests, to Doge's horror, that Ariana killed her mother in rebellion and that Albus had in turn killed her, provoking a "coffin-side brawl" with Aberforth (7:157). Shocked, Harry can only recall his own youth: "Numbly Harry thought of how the Dursleys had once shut him up, locked him away, kept him out of sight, all for the crime of being a wizard. Had Dumbledore's sister suffered the same fate in reverse: imprisoned for her lack of magic? And had Dumbledore truly left her to her fate while he went off to Hogwarts, to prove himself brilliant and talented?" (7:156) Harry's own invisibility now makes it possible for him to see the invisible forces that shape others, the stories they keep hidden, although the initial effect of this is profoundly disillusioning.

In her tell-all book, Rita Skeeter speculates salaciously about Ariana's death, connecting the incident to Grindelwald's scheme to overturn the Wizards' "Statute of Secrecy," thus erasing the boundary between the two worlds in order to "establish Wizard rule over Muggles" (7:357). Skeeter asks, "Was she the inadvertent victim of some dark rite? Did she stumble across something she ought not to have done, as the two young men sat practicing for their attempt at glory and domination? Is it possible that Ariana Dumbledore was the first person to die 'for the greater good'?" (7:359) Of course, Skeeter has things all wrong, and the truth is more complicated. Secretly, Rita Skeeter is herself an Animagus, capable of transforming into a beetle, which is what enables her both to invisibly observe and also to bear false witness (5:727). Like Peter Pettigrew, Skeeter represents transfiguration gone wrong. She internalizes the qualities of her "insect" alter ego, reflected in the name "Skeeter." Rita is a parasite whose self-interested observations peddle the illusion of empathy while pandering to the powerful.

As Harry, Ron, and Hermione discover once they have dispelled Skeeter's poisoned pen account, Ariana was not a Squib, at least not in the most technical sense. Aberforth, still bitter decades later, reveals that Ariana had been born with magical power but was brutally attacked by three neighborhood Muggle boys, after which she chose not to use her magic again:

> "They'd seen her doing magic, spying through the back garden hedge. . . . They forced their way through the hedge, and when she couldn't show them the trick, they got a bit carried away trying to stop the little freak doing it. . . . It destroyed her, what they did: She was never right again. She wouldn't use her magic, but she couldn't get rid of it; it turned inward and drove her mad, it exploded out of her when she couldn't control it, and at times she was strange and dangerous. But mostly she was sweet and scared and harmless." (7:564)

Ariana had been concealed for her own protection, both from the Muggles who feared her and the wizards who would have confined her to a St. Mungo's psych ward. Now, in death, her portrait guards a different kind of hedge, the last hidden entrance to Hogwarts; she is the link between her brother Aberforth's humble pub on one side and her brother Albus's storied legacy on the other. Like Argus Filch and Arabella Figg, Ariana Dumbledore (another "Ar")—Squib by choice and traumatic circumstance rather than birth—stands watch and polices the border.

Once Harry and his friends convince Aberforth to help them, the latter looks at Ariana and says, "You know what to do." After turning and walking back into the portrait's background until she is "swallowed by the darkness," Ariana returns with a second person at her side: "the whole thing swung forward on the wall like a little door, and the entrance to a real tunnel was revealed. And out of it, his hair overgrown, his face cut, his robes ripped, clambered the real Neville Long-bottom" (7:569-570). Neville, the awkward boy whose family had feared he was a Squib, the lackluster student who never seemed capable of casting a spell properly, strides from the shadows to reveal that, in Harry's absence, he has been leading the Hogwarts resistance movement against the oppressive administration of Voldemort's Death Eaters: "We used to sneak out at night and put graffiti on the walls: *Dumbledore's Army, Still Recruiting*" (7:575).[9] Along with Luna and Ginny, Neville has converted another invisible space, the Room of Requirement, into headquarters for the fight against wizarding supremacists who would erase the boundaries between worlds, asserting the dominance of the pure-blooded. It is also Neville to whom Harry trusts a final mission: the killing of Nagini, Volde-mort's snake, the final Horcrux keeping the Dark Lord alive. As Harry walks to-ward the Forbidden Forest to face his death, he removes his Invisibility Cloak only once, to reveal himself to Neville and tell him what only he, Ron, and Her-mione knew about the snake's importance (7:695). Rising to the occasion, Neville kills the snake and in the process provides a powerful counterpart to Harry. Whereas the powerful Harry must learn how not to act, the squibbish Neville must take action (7:731-733). Especially important, even after everyone thinks Harry to be dead, Neville stands before Voldemort and bears ongoing witness to

---

[9] In their second year, fearing an attack by the basilisk, Neville comments that, "everyone knows I'm almost a Squib" (2:185). At their very first Hogwarts banquet, after getting sorted into Gryffindor, Neville tells his new friends that, "the family thought I was all-Muggle for ages. My Great Uncle Algie kept trying to catch me off my guard and force some magic out of me ... but nothing happened until I was eight" (1:125).

the resistance: "'I'll join you when hell freezes over,' said Neville. 'Dumbledore's Army!' he shouted, and there was an answering cheer from the crowd" (7:731).

What the Squib Said

Harry learned from Dumbledore how to see the strength in those weaker than himself and share responsibility. Although Rita Skeeter had speculated that the attack on Ariana, coupled with Dumbledore's youthful friendship with Grindelwald, had turned him into a closet Muggle-hater, the reality was the reverse. Instead of seeking revenge, as had his father, Dumbledore came to respect those whose abilities fell short of his own, making him well-suited to serving as Headmaster of Hogwarts. At Hogwarts Dumbledore admits the squibbish Neville and celebrates his courage, permits the teaching of Muggle Studies, keeps Hagrid on as gamekeeper and then teacher even though he had once been expelled (and so is not a full-fledged wizard), employs a werewolf to teach Defense Against the Dark Arts, and hires Dobby the house-elf as a paid employee. He also stands before the school after Voldemort's return and bears witness against evil when the Ministry is most desperate to conceal the truth: "It is my belief, however, that the truth is generally preferable to lies, and that any attempt to pretend that Cedric died as the result of an accident, or some sort of blunder of his own, is an insult to his memory. . . . Remember Cedric Diggory" (4:722-724). When Dumbledore reforms the Order of the Phoenix in response, he even includes a Squib, Mrs. Figg (4:713).

Mrs. Figg's membership proves crucial, as Harry learns in the aftermath of the dementor attack in Little Whinging. Not only does she appear when needed to evacuate Harry and Dudley, she is also essential to Harry's defense against the Ministry's charge that, in warding off the dementors, he illegally used magic in the presence of a Muggle. Mr. Weasley escorts Harry to the Ministry for his hearing, but insists on using Muggle transport, saying, "it's best we arrive in a thoroughly non-magical fashion. . . makes a better impression, given what you're being disciplined for" (5:124).[10] Fittingly, they take the London Underground.

---

[10] Arthur Weasley is the fourth notable character whose name starts with "Ar," although as a pure-blood wizard he might appear not to fit the same Squib mold. Mr. Weasley, however, is the wizard most obsessed with Muggle culture, working at the Misuse of

318 • HARRY POTTER FOR NERDS II

Rowling emphasizes this underground position repeatedly. Upon arriving at the Ministry's guest entrance, an old phone booth, they feel the floor shake and then "were sinking slowly into the ground" (5:126); seeing sunlight out the windows, a perplexed Harry asks, "aren't we underground?" (5:131); discovering their venue has been moved, they travel even further down subterranean steps ("Down here, down here. . . . The lift doesn't even come down this far") to Courtroom 10 (5:135). Accused of improper boundary crossing, Harry has himself been converted, ironically, if only temporarily, into a Squib; he is deprived of his defining power, at the seat of magical authority, when he is forced to relinquish his wand at the gate (5:128).[11]

Harry's trial before the full Wizengamot—originally announced as a simple hearing—reflects the depth of his disempowerment. Staring up at the assembled judges, "about fifty of them," Harry sits alone and below, in the center of the room, in a chair "covered in chains" which "clinked rather threateningly but did not bind him" (5:137-8). He is the object of juridical gaze, isolated and measured like Josef K in Kafka's *The Trial* or the prisoners in Jeremy Bentham's famous Panopticon (see Kafka 1956; Foucault 1977, 195 ff.). Luckily for Harry, Dumbledore quickly arrives to redress the imbalance of power as "Witness for the defense," although Harry is disconcerted that the Headmaster refuses to look at him: "He wanted to catch Dumbledore's eye, but Dumbledore was not looking his way" (5:139). During the trial, Dumbledore again averts his gaze, "oblivious to Harry's attempt to catch his eye" (5:150). He does this a third time once the trial is over:

Muggle Artifacts Office while secretly tinkering with magical adaptations of Muggle objects, like the flying car in *Chamber of Secrets* (2:38-39). He consistently defends Muggle interests even when it hinders his career (2:57-64; 4:102).

[11] There's a lot of talk in book 5 about proper wand management. The adolescent Harry is battling to control his own potency. When Mrs. Figg arrives to help Harry and Dudley following the dementor attack, "Harry made to stow his wand hurriedly out of sight, but—'Don't put it away, idiot boy!' she shrieked. 'What if there are more of them around?'" (5:10); and shortly later Mrs. Figg repeats, "'Don't put your wand away boy, don't I keep telling you I'm no use?' It was not easy to hold a wand steady and carry Dudley along at the same time" (5:46); the wand theme continues for several pages, even as Harry finally pockets his: "'Don't put your wand there, boy!' roared Moody. 'What if it ignited? Better wizards than you have lost buttocks, you know! ... Elementary wand safety, nobody bothers about it anymore'" (5:48). Maturity, for Rowling, appears to involve knowing when, and *when not*, to use one's powers.

"without looking once at Harry, he swept from the dungeon" (5:151). Throughout his fifth year, Harry's frustration is heightened by his seeming invisibility to a man he has come to see as a father-figure—the man whose admission letter from Hogwarts had for the first time rendered Harry visible—to the point where Dumbledore finally apologizes to Harry at the book's close (5: 828).

Leading the interrogation at trial, Cornelius Fudge, the Minister of Magic, frames his questions to solicit an admission of guilt while not allowing Harry any explanation as to why he had conjured a Patronus in Dudley's presence. Fudge then sharply rejects Harry's insistence that dementors had provoked the incident. Dumbledore responds by summoning Mrs. Figg to testify on Harry's behalf:

> She looked scared and more batty than ever. Harry wished she had thought to change out of her carpet slippers. . . .
>
> "And who exactly are you?" said Fudge, in a bored and lofty voice.
>
> "I'm a resident of Little Whinging, close to where Harry Potter lives," said Mrs. Figg.
>
> "We have no record of any witch or wizard living in Little Whinging other than Harry Potter," said Madam Bones at once. "That situation has always been closely monitored, given. . . given past events."
>
> "I'm a Squib,' said Mrs. Figg. "So you wouldn't have me registered, would you?"
>
> "A Squib, eh?" said Fudge, eyeing her closely. "We'll be checking that. You'll leave details of your parentage with my assistant, [Percy] Weasley. Incidentally, can Squibs see dementors?" he added, looking left and right along the bench where he sat.
>
> "Yes, we can!" said Mrs. Figg indignantly. (5:143)

The invisible Mrs. Figg, whose identity has remained concealed from both Muggles and the wizard establishment, steps forward to bear witness in Harry's defense. Where he cannot act, she can. Her eyes and her voice become the power of the powerless, despite Fudge's skepticism that she actually exists or that she could possibly have seen anything. After she describes the dementor attack in great detail, Fudge looks at her dismissively and asks, "That's what you saw, is it?"

to which Mrs. Figg cleverly replies, "That was what happened," eluding the question of whether she had, in fact, been able to see dementors (5:145). We should not underestimate the dramatic importance of this moment. By taking the stand as witness, Mrs. Figg has bravely transformed her seemingly passive surveillance into a model of justice in action.

In some ways Mrs. Figg's testimony anticipates Harry's own mission. As Sirius tells Harry when he is preparing for his hearing, "you survived to bear witness" (5:92). On his way down through the Ministry before his trial, Harry noticed a fountain depicting a wizard and a witch surrounded by a house-elf, goblin, and centaur. Harry promises himself that if he prevails in his hearing he will throw ten galleons into the fountain, the proceeds of which go to "St. Mungo's Hospital for Magical Maladies and Injuries" (5:127). But on the way back up from underground, having been saved by Mrs. Figg's testimony, he realizes that he had not actually seen the Fountain of Magical Brethren properly:

> He looked up into the handsome wizard's face, but up close, Harry thought he looked rather weak and foolish. The witch was wearing a vapid smile like a beauty contestant, and from what Harry knew of goblins and centaurs, they were most unlikely to be caught staring this soppily at humans of any description. Only the house-elf's attitude of creeping servility looked convincing. With a grin at the thought of what Hermione would say if she could see the statue of the elf, Harry turned his money bag upside down and emptied not just ten galleons, but the whole contents into the pool at the statues' feet. (5:156)

Having been stripped of his wand, exposed, accused, and finally freed, thanks to the word of a Squib to whose true identity he had long remained oblivious, Harry comes away with a "second sight." He no longer sees the world as the powerful want to depict it, but recognizes the evasions at the root of the wizarding world's reigning ideology; he donates his entire purse to the cause of healing magical injuries. Of course, as fraudulent as the statues' images are, they at least acknowledge the existence of goblins, centaurs, and elves. The Squibs, however, remain invisible, existing completely outside the official registries of the magical community and its claims of fraternal solidarity.

Those statues return, dramatically, in the climactic battle that closes *Order of the Phoenix*. Back at the Ministry, this time accompanied by his closest friends from Dumbledore's Army, Harry once again takes the lift from the underground floors into the Atrium, now in pursuit of Voldemort's lieutenant and Sirius's murderer, Bellatrix Lestrange. When she takes aim, he hides behind the statues, only to see Bellatrix blast the head off the golden wizard and the arm from the centaur. Harry finds himself on the defensive, "crouching behind the centaur's legs, his head level with the house-elf's," while Bellatrix taunts him with her greater power: "I know spells of such power that you, pathetic little boy, can never hope to compete" (5:811). Then Voldemort himself arrives. He "appeared in the middle of the hall, his wand pointing at Harry who stood frozen, quite unable to move" (5:812). Raising his wand, Voldemort casts the killing curse at a defenseless Harry whose "mind was blank, his wand pointing uselessly at the floor." Only the curse failed: "the headless golden statue of the wizard in the fountain had sprung alive. . . and landed on the floor with a crash between Harry and Voldemort" (5: 813). Returning at the decisive moment, Dumbledore deployed the various statues to protect Harry, remove him from battle, and charge his attackers. The fountain where he had once given all his gold to heal magical injuries had, poetically, come to life to shield him against destruction.

Watching the Defectives

While it may not be actual centaurs, goblins, and elves that save Harry here, Rowling uses this moment symbolically to reveal a larger feature of her narrative. Harry never achieves his victories on his own, he is often caught weak and defenseless in critical moments, and it is often the seemingly weak who ride to the rescue: Neville, Luna, Dobby, Kreacher, the goblin Griphook who gets them into the Gringotts vault, the centaurs who fight off first Quirrell and then Umbridge, and of course Mrs. Figg and her cats. It is just such an "extraordinary assortment of people" who come together at Dumbledore's funeral, "shabby and smart, old and young" (6:641). Serenaded by the merpeople and given an archer's salute by the centaurs, Dumbledore, the man with the scar above his left knee "that is a perfect map of the London Underground," receives a fitting requiem (1:15). Mirroring that moment, in the Battle of Hogwarts, old and young, wizards, elves, and centaurs will make common cause in the fight against evil. Rather than simply taking up arms, they bear witness to the fallen. Unlike Voldemort, Harry takes notice of all those weaker than himself and reaches out to them in brother-hood—not the sham unity of the fountain, where the lesser creatures stare up at the golden wizard in glassy-eyed admiration, but rather in a bond of reciprocity, service, and respect. By going underground, transfiguring himself into a crosser of boundaries, and by learning from his invisibility the powers of observation and witness, he gains a sympathy and understanding that would always escape Voldemort's gaze. Harry is watching the defectives and they, in turn, are watching out for him.

Works Cited

Aristotle. 2000. *Nicomachean Ethics.* Ed. Roger Crisp. New York: Cambridge University Press.

Dostoevsky, Fyodor. 1993. *Notes From Underground.* Trans. Richard Pevear and Larissa Volokhonsky. New York: Vintage.

DuBois, W. E. B. 1996. *The Souls of Black Folk.* New York: Modern Library.

Ellison, Ralph. 1980. *Invisible Man.* New York: Vintage.

Foucault, Michel. 1977. *Discipline and Punish: the Birth of the Prison.* Trans. Alan Sheridan. New York: Pantheon.

Kafka, Franz. 1956. *The Trial.* Trans. Willa Muir and Edwin Muir. New York: Schocken.

Rowling, J. K. 1997-2007. *Harry Potter.* Vol. 1-7. New York: Scholastic.

Meet the Nerds

Kathryn N. McDaniel is McCoy Professor of History and chair of the Department of History, Philosophy, and Religion at Marietta College in Marietta, Ohio. She holds a B.A. from Davidson College, and an M.A. and a Ph.D. from Vanderbilt University. Although her specialty is early modern British history, she also teaches and studies modern European history with a particular interest in cultural concepts of gender, race, and power. Having published and presented on British travel literature and also pedagogy, she is delighted to have added Harry Potter scholarship to her résumé in recent years, including participation in a Mugglenet Academia podcast about the house-elves. She can't wait to introduce her three young children to the wizarding world (and fervently but vainly hopes they'll read the books *before* they see the movies).

Travis Prinzi holds graduate degrees in education and theology from the University of Rochester and Northeastern Seminary. He has been publishing on the Harry Potter books as well as other fantasy fiction since 2008 and has been a featured speaker at 5 Harry Potter conferences in the US and Canada. He lives in Western New York with his daughter Sophia, son Jack, and their dog Moses.

Deborah M. Chan, a freelance writer, bibliophile, synesthete, and baker of gluten-free goodness, is a newspaper columnist for the *Spokesman-Review* in Spokane, Washington, where she lives with her husband Richard and cat Casey Rose. First as Arabella Figg and now under her own name, Deborah has been writing on Harry Potter for over a decade and enjoys exploring the characters' inner lives. She considers the funny hat she wears on the Blogengamot at The Hog's Head to be the coolest ever.

Katherine Sas works as an academic coordinator at the University of Pennsylvania in Philadelphia, Pennsylvania. She received her B.A. in English from Messiah College and is currently pursuing a master's degree in English with the Mythgard Institute at Signum University. In addition to *Harry Potter*, her areas of scholarly interest include the Inklings, *Doctor Who*, and the imaginative tradition in literature, television, and film. She writes a blog called Raving Sanity and co-hosts "Kat and Curt's TV Review," a weekly podcast on *Doctor Who* and *Buffy the Vampire Slayer*. Kat first read *Harry Potter* between the publication of books five and six and has been advocating for a Marauders era prequel ever since.

Carol Eshleman is a Hufflepuff, and she's been loyal to the Potter fandom since 2001. She received her Bachelor's degree in Drama and Speech from Loyola University of New Orleans, and holds a Master's degree in British Literature and Modern Rhetoric with a reading ability in Latin from the University of New Orleans. Together with her husband, Mrs. Eshleman was the owner and operator of True Brew Theatre in New Orleans before Hurricane Katrina. She gives credit especially to J.K. Rowling whose stories helped pull her through that time. Mrs. Eshleman has spoken at numerous conferences, including Ascendio, LeakyCon, and Potter conferences at the University of North Carolina in Charlotte and the University of St. Andrews in Scotland. She has also spoken at the University of North Carolina in Chapel Hill and the University of North Alabama. Carol is the theatre director and teaches Fine Arts and Speech and Debate at Archbishop Rummel High School in Metairie, Louisiana. She and her husband Roch have two incredible kids, Vito and Lizzie, who both know the most important rule in her house, "Don't play with Mommy's good wands!"

Kelly Orazi is a graduate student of medieval and fantasy literature at the Mythgard Institute. Her scholarly work on fantasy has been presented at Mythcon 43, Mythmoot III and one of 2013's largest *Harry Potter* conferences, LeakyCon Portland. Her work on *The Hobbit* is published in issue 5 of *Silver Leaves*, a journal devoted to Tolkien studies. As a dedicated Ravenclaw, she currently contributes to the Harry Potter website MuggleNet.com, the Tolkien and fantasy website

LegendariumMedia.com and writes regularly on *Harry Potter* and other fantasy works on her own literary blog, themiddlepage.net. When not writing about or reading *Harry Potter*, she can be found at home drinking too much coffee and hanging out with her exceptionally energetic dog, Lupin.

Rochelle Deans, who read the first Harry Potter book when she was 12, and the last when she was 19, is a bona fide member of the Harry Potter generation. She works as a freelance editor from her home in Portland, Oregon. You can find her on Twitter @RochelleDeans or writing about (mostly) writing on her blog: http://www.rochelledeans.com.

Emily Strand is author of the book *Mass 101: Liturgy and Life* (Liguori, 2013), Master Catechist for the Roman Catholic Diocese of Columbus, Ohio, and teaches Comparative Religions at Mount Carmel College of Nursing. Her interest in the Harry Potter series stems, in part, from her more fundamental interest in the Christian mystery, its celebration in worship and its implications for Christian living. Emily is a part-time Master's student at the Mythgard Institute. She was particularly suited to conduct her study of the symbolic function of Quidditch by her total lack of interest in sports on their own terms, which is related to her embarrassing lack of talent for activities involving gross-motor coordination. Strand is also a musician and amateur potioneer who, when ingredients like boomslang skin and bezoars are hard to find, makes do with Muggle spirits.

Michael Burson is currently earning his Master's in Clinical Mental Health Counseling from the University of North Carolina at Charlotte. He has a B.A. in Psychology and Anthropology, also from UNCC, where he founded *Potter Watch*, a club for *Harry Potter* fans to come together and share in their love of the books and films. A proud Ravenclaw, Michael has been a *Harry Potter* geek since getting *Sorcerer's Stone* from his grandparents in 1998. **Hayley Burson** works as a teen services specialist for Charlotte Mecklenburg Libraries and is a Master's student in Library and Information Studies at the University of North Carolina at Greensboro. She earned her Bachelor of Arts in English from UNC Charlotte in

2011 and was the secretary of *Potter Watch*, the *Harry Potter* club of UNC Charlotte, for two years. She enjoys developing *Harry Potter* and other YA programming for libraries and is passionate about youth outreach. She has always seen herself as a hard working Hufflepuff. Hayley and Michael live in Charlotte, North Carolina, with their pets Bilbo and Luna.

Kris Swank is Library Director at Pima Community College—Northwest Campus in Tucson, Arizona. She can't seem to leave school and get a real job. So far, she's managed to complete a B.A.—Humanities and English, Dana College; an M.L.S.—Library Science, University of Arizona; an M.B.A.—International Management, Thunderbird School of Global Management; and most recently, an M.A. in Tolkien Studies, Mythgard Institute. Her essays on fantasy literature have appeared in *Tolkien Studies, Mythlore,* TheHogsHead.org, and two forthcoming essay collections. She has also written for *Library Journal, American Libraries,* and other library publications. Surprising no one, Kris was sorted into Ravenclaw.

Amy H. Sturgis earned her Ph.D. in intellectual history at Vanderbilt University, and, if Harry Potter fan sites are to be believed, she then became the first instructor in the world to dedicate a college-level course to the Harry Potter series. She now teaches Harry Potter at both the undergraduate and graduate level, as well as other subjects in her fields of Science Fiction/Fantasy and Native American studies, at both Lenoir-Rhyne University and Mythgard Institute at Signum University. The author of four books and the editor of six others, Sturgis has published more than forty essays and articles and is a regular speaker at universities and genre conventions across North America and Europe. In 2006, she received the Imperishable Flame Award for Tolkien/Inklings Scholarship. She also contributes regular "Looking Back on Genre History" segments as well as dramatic readings for StarShipSofa, which in 2010 became the first podcast in history to win the Hugo Award. Her official website is amyhsturgis.com.

Alison R. Jones is Electronic Resources and Instruction Librarian and Assistant Professor of Library Science at Carson-Newman University in Jefferson City, Tennessee, where she attempts to avoid stereotypes, be an actively present and engaging librarian, and generally do the opposite of whatever Madam Pince would do. She has a B.M. in Voice Performance from Montreat College, and a M.L.I.S. from the University of North Carolina at Greensboro. In her spare time, Alison can be found performing in community theatre and music groups, reading everything from YA literature to weighty theology tomes, and watching entirely too much British television. Her Harry Potter claim to fame is that if the series were real, she would have been Luna Lovegood's roommate in Ravenclaw tower.

Madelyn V. Young (Dr. Mad.) is an Associate Professor of Economics at Converse College. She has presented the "Economics of Harry Potter" at several economics teaching conferences, and has twice taught the economics portion of "The Economics and Psychology of Harry Potter" January-Term course. Her research interests are in the areas of economics pedagogy and labor economics. She has published in economics journals, leadership journals, popular culture conference proceedings and the proceedings from annual dismal science teaching conferences. She has also conducted study/travel programs to 15 countries and taught in Iceland and Japan. She holds a Ph.D. in Economics from Georgia State University, an M.A. in Economics from the University of Notre Dame, and a B.A. in Economics and English/Writing from Indiana University/South Bend. She is the current president of the National Economic Teaching Association (NETA). Dr. Mad is the crew chief of a championship winning race team, likes to scuba dive, and lives in the upstate of South Carolina with her husband, four cats, and her red Porsche 911 Carrera, which flies as fast as a Firebolt Supreme.

Carrie-Ann Biondi is an Associate Professor of Philosophy and Chair of the Department of Philosophy and Religious Studies at Marymount Manhattan College, New York City. She holds a B.A. and M.A. in American Studies and an M.A. and Ph.D. in Philosophy. Her research interests include citizenship theory, consent theory and political obligation, patriotism, Aristotelian virtue ethics, children's rights, and Socratic pedagogy. She has over fifteen years of experience in professional editing (of books and academic journals), and is Co-Editor-in-Chief (with Irfan Khawaja) of *Reason Papers*.

Laura Lee Smith received her J.D. *magna cum laude* from Boston University School of Law in 1999. She lives and works in New York City, and is also enrolled part-time at Signum University/Mythgard Institute, an online center for graduate-level scholarship in fantasy literature. She has presented papers at the 48th International Congress on Medieval Studies, Mythcon 43 and 44, the Celebrating The Hobbit Conference, and Mythmoot III: Ever On.

Robb A. McDaniel earned his B.A. from Davidson College and his Ph.D. from Vanderbilt University. He teaches political theory at Middle Tennessee State University where he won the Outstanding Teacher Award in 2008. He is a former President of the Tennessee Political Science Association and has published essays on the writings of John Locke, John Lilburne, Leo Strauss, and Emmanuel Levinas. He is also researching the English Levellers and the political fiction of the novelist Philip Roth.

Made in the USA
Lexington, KY
27 October 2015